MW01292500

Roman Aquileia

The impenetrable city-fortress, a sentry of the Alps

Natale Barca

OXBOW | books

Oxford & Philadelphia

Published in the United Kingdom in 2022 by
OXBOW BOOKS
The Old Music Hall, 106–108 Cowley Road, Oxford, OX4 1JE

and in the United States by
OXBOW BOOKS
1950 Lawrence Road, Havertown, PA 19083

© Oxbow Books and the author 2022

Paperback Edition: ISBN 978-1-78925-774-8
Digital Edition: ISBN 978-1-78925-775-5

A CIP record for this book is available from the British Library

Library of Congress Control Number: 2021950254

All rights reserved. No part of this book may be reproduced or transmitted in any form or by any means, electronic or mechanical including photocopying, recording or by any information storage and retrieval system, without permission from the publisher in writing.

Printed in the United Kingdom by Short Run Press

Typeset in India by Lapiz Digital Services, Chennai.

For a complete list of Oxbow titles, please contact:

UNITED KINGDOM
Oxbow Books
Telephone (01865) 241249
Email: oxbow@oxbowbooks.com
www.oxbowbooks.com

UNITED STATES OF AMERICA
Oxbow Books
Telephone (610) 853-9131, Fax (610) 853-9146
Email: queries@casemateacademic.com
www.casemateacademic.com/oxbow

Oxbow Books is part of the Casemate Group

Front cover: IKON, 'A digital farm of Staranzano, Italy'

Contents

Map 1. Localization of Aquileia, Italy

Abbreviations

Ambr.	Ambrose, *Epistolae*
Amm. Marc., *Res Gestae*	Ammianus Marcellinus, *Rerum Gestarum*
App. *Ill.*	Appian, *Helleniké*
App. *Mac.*	Appian, *Macedoniké*
Auson.	Ausonius, *Ordo urbium nobilium*
Athanasius	Athanasius, *Apologia ad Constantium*
Cato	*Cato, Oratio de re Histriae militari*
Caes.	Caesar, *Bellum Gallicum*
Cic.	Cicero, *Brutus* or *De Claribus Oratoribus*
Claud.	Claudianus, *De Consulatu Honorii*
Claud., *In Ruf.*	Claudianus, *In Rufinum*
CI	*Codex Iustinianus*
CTh	*Codex Theodosianus*
Dio Cass.	Dio Cassius, *Historia romana*
Epit. de Caes.	*Epitome de Caesaribus* (in Teubner Aur. Vic. Caes. ed. F. Pichlmayer 1911, pp. 133–76)
Eutrop.	Eutropius, Flavius, *Breviarum ab urbe condita*
FastTr	*Fasti Triumphales*
FastCons.	*Fasti Consulares*
Flor.	Florus, *Epitomae de Tito Livio Bellorum omnium annorum DCC*
Frontin.	Frontinus, *Stratagemata*
Herodian.	Herodianus, *Historia Augusta*
Hyd.	Hydatius, *Chronicon*
Hieron.	Jerome, *De viris illustribus* (in von Gerbhart 1896)
InscrIt	*Inscriptiones Italicae* (Rome, 1931-)
Inscr. Aq.	*Inscriptiones Aquileiae*
Iul.	Iulianus, *Orationes*
Isid.	Isidorus, *Origines*
Jord.	Jordanes, *Getica*
Joseph	Joseph, *Bellum Iudaicum*
Lib.	Libanius, *Oratio*
Liv.	Livy, *Ab Urbe Condita*
Liv. *Epit.*	Livy, *Epitome*
Liv. *Per.*	Livy, *Periochae*
Not. Dign. (Occ.)	*Notitia Dignitatum in partibus Occidentis*

Oros.	Orosius, Paulus, *Historiarum adversum paganos libri VII*
Pan. Lat.	*XII Panegyrici Latini*
Paulus Diaconus	Paulus Diaconus, *Historia romana*
Paus.	Pausanias, Ἑλλάδος περιήγησις (*Helládos Periēghēsis*)
Philostorgius	Philostorgius, *Historia eccelsiastica*
Plin.	Pliny (the Elder), *Naturalis Historia*
Plut. *Mar.*	Plutarch *Vit. Marius*
Polyb.	Polybius, *Historiai*
Proc. *Goth.*	Procopius, *De bello Gothico*
Proc. *De Bellis*	Procopius, Ὑπέρ των πολέμων (*Hypèr tōn Polémon Lógoi*)
Sen.	Seneca, *Thyestes*
Socr.	Socrates Scolasticus, *Historia Ecclesiastica.*
Sozom.	Sozomen, *Historia Ecclesiastica.*
Strab.	Strabo, *Geographica.*
Suet.	Suetonius, *Vita of Divus Iulius*
Val. Max.	Valerius Maximus, *Factorum et dictorum memorabilium libri IX*
Vell. Pat.	Velleius Patercolus, *Historiae Romanae*
Zonar.	Zonaras, *Epitome Historiarum* (*Historiae Romanorum Excerpta VIII*)
Zos.	Zosimus, *Historia ecclesiastica*
Zos. *Hist.*	Zosimus, *Historia Nova*

Preface

Located in the extreme northeast of Italy, precisely in Lower Friuli, just behind the Adriatic coast, about 10 km from the seaside resort of Grado, Aquileia is a small agricultural and tourist center, extending for about a kilometer around an impressive medieval basilica, decorated with wonderful mosaics. However, this is not the only touristic attraction of the place. The modern town overlaps a larger area of archaeological interest, which has returned an abundant quantity of ancient remains dating back to various eras and hides many others. The finds indicate that the site was initially occupied by prehistoric settlements, then by a city that has evolved in three main phases: the Roman, the Medieval, and finally, the Patriarchal. The Patriarchal phase of the history of Aquileia refers to the homonymous Patriarchate. From 1027 onward, Aquileia was the home of the Prince of the Patria del Friuli, understood as the territory where the Patriarch of Aquileia exercised temporal power.

The place of which we are talking is one of the most interesting and evocative in northern Italy. In cultural importance, it is equal to Ravenna and Brescia. Evocation of its memory, mainly of the Roman city, raises an emotional wave that spreads to the surface and depth. This, not only in Italy but also further north, in the heart of Europe. From the Natisone River to Lake Balaton, from the Carnic and Julian Alps to the Dinaric Alps, and between the Inn and Danube rivers, in fact, it makes sounds and images, analogies and memories resurface, meanings and dreams, in a movement that affects experience and memory, fantasy and the unconscious. This is due to the fact that Aquileia is not only the name of a city but also the symbol of identification of a transnational cultural *koiné*, which has its roots in Roman antiquity.

The most important historical phase of the city, in fact, is the first. The Medieval and Patriarchal cities never managed to equal the Roman in terms of size, political, economic, and strategic importance, magnificence, or prestige. The Roman phase begins in 181 BC when Aquileia is founded by the will of the Senate of Rome as the urban center of the homonym colony. The city was built in the typical Roman style in the same place as an emporium of an indigenous population, the Veneti, mainly widespread in nearby Veneto. Since its beginnings, it was a fortress and a military base, but also a center of agriculture, commerce, and handicraft production, a large market, and the most important import–export center in northeastern Italy. Mainly, it was a city-fortress, the northernmost of the Roman strongholds, in contact with the Gauls of the Noricum (southern Austria and western Slovenia), the Gauls of Carnia—a mountainous region of northeastern Italy, just south of today's Austrian border—and hostile Illyrian populations. Starting from the interventions to reinforce the northeastern border of Italy carried out by Julius Caesar in the 1st century BC,

Aquileia was the fulcrum of the defensive system of the Eastern Alps. In particular, it was the most solid bulwark against invasions from across the Julian Alps. It also was an important springboard for war operations in the Western Balkans and the Danube area. Roman legions used to leave Aquileia and return there at the end of the campaigning season to pass the winter there, waiting to return to the attack the following spring.

In the Early Roman Empire, Aquileia was the most important city in the Augustan subdivision known as *Regio X Venetia et Histria* and a stronghold of Orthodox religious thought, of Nicene Christianity, that intertwined relations with the Church of Alexandria in Egypt and pushed its missionary activity as far as the Danube and southeastern Europe. In the Middle Roman Empire, it had to face great sieges, first by the Germanic Quadi and Marcomanni, then by the usurper Maximinus Thrax (AD 235–238). After the Crisis of the Third Century (AD 235–284), Aquileia was besieged again, this time by the army of Iovianus, a general of the emperor Julian (AD 361–363). In the Late Roman Empire, Aquileia was a great metropolis, famous for its walls and port. In dimensions, population, and political and economic importance, it was the fourth city of Italy, after Rome, Mediolanum, and Capua, and the ninth of the Empire. It was the residence of emperors and theatre of important historical events, relevant to the fate of the entire Empire.

The hitherto splendid life path of Aquileia underwent a sharp decline about three centuries and a half after the foundation. On 18 July 452, a horde of Huns, led by Attila, took the Virgin Fortress after a siege, then plundered and devastated it, with horrible slaughter. A mass of refugees, under the direction of their bishop, reached the nearby Grado, the seaport of Aquileia and a fortified place, where they would start a new life. Possibly, some of them found refuge further south, in the Venetian Lagoon; if so, it is possible that they contributed to the founding of Venice. It is worth noting, in this regard, that one of the most prominent craft productions of the Roman city of Aquileia was that of glass objects and that this activity has been practiced in Venice since its origins, which should be searched in the Late Antiquity. Even today, the islet of Murano, in the Venetian Lagoon, is a famous center for glass manufacture.

Aquileia survived as a market center until 568 when the city fell into the hands of the Lombards, who had invaded Friuli through the Julian Alps, descending from the Vipacco Valley, and were the first to occupy Forum Iulii (present-day Cividale del Friuli, about 37 km north of Aquileia as the crow flies); shortly thereafter the Lombards continued their advance and occupied large parts of Italy. That tragic event marked the true end of Roman Aquileia.

In 616, the Bishopric of Aquileia was split (one bishop in Grado, under the authority of Byzantium, and one in Aquileia, under the authority of the Lombards). In the 7th century, there were some Benedictine monastic foundations in the territory of Aquileia, very sparsely populated, and malarial. In the 8th century, the seat of the Lombard Patriarchate was transferred to Forum Iulii. In the 10th century, the raids of the Hungars caused serious damage to Aquileia as well as to all the extreme northeast of Italy.

Aquileia regained vitality and prestige under the guidance of Bishop Poppo (1019–1042). On 6 April 1027, Poppo obtained the patriarchal dignity by Pope John XIX, which took him precedence over all Italian bishops. From then on, Aquileia was the spiritual "capital" of the homonymous Patriarchate. As we noted earlier, however, Patriarchal Aquileia was a center of moderate vitality, not comparable to the previous Roman city in terms of wealth, splendor, and role, so much so that the prelates were preferring to reside and exercise a political role in other localities, such as the present-day Cormons, Cividale del Friuli, Udine, or Sacile. The temporal power of the Patriarch of Aquileia ceased in 1420 when the city passed under the dominion of the Serenissima Repubblica of Venice while remaining the patriarchal seat.

* * *

Roman Aquileia shows how what started as a military colony became a large, impressive, and prosperous city, legendary for its walls and port, able to play a basic role in the great strategy of ancient Rome between the Po and the Danube, spanning the centuries from its foundation (181 BC) to the fateful days of blood and violence of its fall (AD 452). Based on a study of ancient sources, contemporary literature, and the latest archaeological research, and written in a fast-paced and accessible style, this book provides a portrait of Aquileia in a diachronic key, under various aspects; sets this city in the complex societal and political system of the time; gives a thorough account of the great events of which it was a protagonist or victim; and offers detailed portraits of key figures, whether famous or less well-known, and analyses of epic battles. Combining academic scholarship with storytelling, biographies of important personalities, and stories of political intrigue, assassinations, and full-scale warfare which narrate the evocative epic of the rise, decline, and disappearance of ancient cities, *Roman Aquileia* highlights a significant topic in Roman political, social, economic, religious, and military history, but one which has been inexplicably neglected in the Anglo-Saxon world until now.

The subject is developed in an Introduction, 10 chapters, and an appendix. A chronology, a list of abbreviations, the chapter notes, a list of the works cited in the chapters, and a list for further reading accompany the text. The abbreviations are those of the *Oxford Classical Dictionary*'s 4th edition (primary sources) and those of the *Année Bibliographique* (scientific journals). The Bibliography list the works of contemporary authors mentioned in the book. The personal names shown in the text are those resulting from the commonly accepted English translation of their Latin or Greek correspondents. The places are indicated by the ancient name—usually Greek or Latin—and the modern correspondent is reported in brackets next to each ancient. The places indicated in brackets that are not accompanied by the specification of the national state in which they are located are understood to be located in Italy. The exceptions here are the best-known cities (*e.g.* Athens, Alexandria in Egypt, etc.), the places that have always been called the same (*e.g.* Rome, Parma, Verona, etc.), and those that have disappeared into the archaeological record. The years before Christ are accompanied by the initials BC. For those after Christ the abbreviation AD is omitted, except for those of the 1st century, which are thus distinguished from the corresponding BC.

The historical narrative contained in the book is a chronologically ordered *continuum.* The aim is not that of providing an exhaustive report, but to compose a broad and evolving picture in which, in their consequentiality, the facts and their connections find their place. I refer to the facts as they are reported in the primary sources, or are deducible from the stories of ancient historians, and so are not necessarily the truth of the facts.

It should be emphasized that some of the topics covered in the book, especially the historical events of the Late Republic and the Roman Empire in which Aquileia had no part or a completely marginal part, lend themselves to interminable insights. In this book, they are barely hinted at, as a summary overview of the general context, for the sake of brevity.

The book introduces and explains, and if necessary repeats, in order to be read, and even to excite. "In communicating history, in fact, it is not possible to obtain by being read if one fails to combine the scientific solidity of the research with the possibility of reconstructing events in the form of an exciting story. It is not necessary to write a historical novel to tell history because history is itself a novel, but the narrative must be compelling."[1] This approach mirrors that of my previous books, which deal with different aspects of the political and military history of Rome, between the age of the Gracchi and the death of Sulla (133–78 BC). I refer to the following:

- *Roma dopo Silla. Una storia in quindici vite* (2021)
- *Roma contro i Germani. La Guerra Cimbrica (113-101 a.C.)* (2020)
- *Rome's Sicilian Slave Wars* (2020)
- *I Gracchi. Quando la politica finisce in tragedia* (2019)
- *Gaio Mario. Alle origini della crisi di Roma* (2017)
- *Sangue chiama sangue. Terrore e atrocità nella Roma di Mario e Silla* (2015)

One of the common features of these works is the use of the "historical present" to represent events and construct the text. The historical present, I recall, is a form that refers to events that belong to the past, but presents them as contemporary or close to the moment of enunciation, thus obtaining the effect of a perspective approach and an actualization of the same.

Roman Aquileia is the result of my own research project, but it was made possible by the support and assistance of a number of people whom I would like to thank. First of all I should like to thank Julie Gardiner, Felicity Goldsack and Jessica Hawxwell for the initial vote of confidence and giving full support, as well as all the staff of Oxbow Books for being supportive in the making of this volume. I am deeply indebted to

Anthony Wright for his kind assistance, attention, helpful comments and suggestions in the linguistic editing and proofreading of the text. Of course, where inconsistencies or errors remain they are of my own making. I owe a debt of gratitude to Cristiano Tiussi (Fondazione Aquileia) for illuminating the urbanistic development of Roman Aquileia. I would also like to thank Enrico Degrassi (Ikon Srl, Digital Farm). A grateful thought also to Paul Richgruber for his encouragement. Now on with the book.

Natale Barca
Trieste, 27 August 2021

Note

1 A. Schiavone, quoted in A. Carioti, "Storici in cerca di lettori", *Corriere della Sera,* 21 April 2013, p. 10.

Introduction: The background

An emporium on the banks of the Natissa River

In 186 BC, Lower Friuli is a lowland rich in woods, springs, waterways, wetlands, and deciduous. The harsh winters, the dense vegetation cover, and the flooding of the rivers make it an area not particularly good for human settlements. However, its coastal area, between the Bocche del Timavo up to the lagoon island of Grado, is the maritime terminal of the Amber Road and the Iron Road, two commercial itineraries coming from Northern and Central-Eastern Europe through the Eastern Alps. This has always been a powerful motif of attraction and explains why, throughout time, numerous village communities, belonging to different peoples and cultures, and inserted in a wide net of exterior contacts, have lived there. See, for example, those who succeeded on the banks of the Natissa, about 10 km from the mouth, from about 1600 to 1200 BC, between the 14th and 12th centuries BC, and between the end of the 10th century BC and the beginning of the 8th century BC. The Natissa is a navigable river, therefore it allows the ships to go upstream. It originates from the confluence of the Natisone and the Torre rivers, receives water from tributaries of Isonzo River, and flows into the Adriatic Sea at the height of Grado. Their banks continued to be a place of convergence of merchant traffic in the 5th to 3rd centuries BC. At that time, the local trade took place under the protection of Belenus, a divinity of Celtic origin but is also part of the pantheon of the Ligurians and of that of the Hispanics. So, the cult of Belenus is also widespread north of the Eastern Alps (Dobesch 1993: 16), Cisalpine Gaul, Transalpine Gaul, and even in the British Isles. Belenus is a divinity linked to health and the revelation of the future. Also, he is a solar god, the god of light. In this respect, the Romans have identified him with Apollo, who is also (among other things) a god of light. The myth of Belenus tells of a dead man—probably drowned—and risen. In Belenus' sanctuary in Lower Friuli, in the Iron Age, the liturgies were officiated and sacrifices were offered, all linked to the solstices and, therefore, to the solar cycles of the year. These involved the use of black-painted ceramic jars, perhaps of Umbrian, Etrusco-Latial, or Adriatic manufacture. The devotees of the place, to strengthen their prayer or testify to the grace received, sometimes dedicated a bronze statuette to Belenus depicting a warrior, an offerer, or Hercules, as appropriate (Càssola Guida 1989).

At the beginning of the 2nd century BC, Lower Friuli is still sparsely populated, and the site 10 km from the mouth of the Natissa is still occupied by a commercial structure. We refer to an emporium of the Veneti of the Adriatic, which is also frequented by buyers coming from Noricum, Upper and Middle Friuli, and Istria. The Veneti of the Adriatic belong to a native population—the Veneti—more widespread in nearby Veneto. The Veneti are friends and allies of the Romans. They are always on the side of the Romans, they help them whenever they can, both because they have understood their strength and because they are in some way similar to them. In fact, they pride themselves on having in common with the Romans the fact that they are descended from a Trojan refugee: Antenor. The Romans, in fact, trace their ancestors back to the Trojan Aeneas, prince of the Dardani and hero of the Trojan War, who fled the burning city of Troy[1] along with a group of other refugees, set sail in search of land, and finally landed in Lazio, in Italy, and settled down there. In the case of the Veneti, it is not a question of Aeneas, but of Antenor. During the journey, Antenor, Aquilius, and Clodius are said to have dissociated themselves from Aeneas and guided some of the refugees to the Venetian Lagoon, where they founded Patavium (Padova), Aquileia, and Clodia.

Aeneas is the focal point of the intertwining of the Trojan myth and the legend of the origins of Rome.[2] The same can be said for his son Ascanius, or Iulus, founder and first ruler of the city of Alba Longa and founder of the dynasty of Alban kings. A few centuries after the founding of Alba Longa, a member of the royal family of that city named Romulus founded Rome and became its first king.

The *transgressio in Venetiam*

In 186 BC, a multitude of Transalpine Gauls,[3] coming from the Noricum, probably Taurisci,[4] penetrate into Lower Friuli through the gorges of a previously unknown pass of the Julian Alps, perhaps that of *ad Pirum* (Hrusica).[5] They travel on foot, on horseback, and in wagons, bringing with them livestock, removable tents, and household items. Estimates regarding the consistency and quality of the moving mass diverge, nor is it clear to which people they belong and for what purpose they came to Italy. They perhaps number 36,000 to 48,000 men, women, the elderly, and children (Bandelli 2003: 51–52), looking for land to cultivate, wherever it may be, having had to abandon their own, possibly due to reasons of overpopulation. In any case, it seems to be possible to rule out that the foreigners in question are an army dedicated to plunder and conquest. They are definitely migrants, not invaders.

The migrants cross Lower Friuli until they meet the Natissa. They choose to settle permanently on those banks, about 17.5 km from the emporium of the Veneti of the Adriatic.[6] The newcomers have just begun to build a fortified village when the managers of the nearby emporium protest. In short, the tension reaches a climax, and the latter invoke the intervention of the Romans.[7] The Senate of Rome, after a discussion, resolves to subordinate any decision that may involve the use of force to a preliminary ascertainment of the truth of the facts and to the possible failure of an attempt at a peaceful settlement of the dispute. Therefore, it sends an embassy to Noricum to contest that the Gauls entered the area without permission and occupied territory without having the right to do so and to ask that the illegal immigrants be recalled to their homeland. The Romans use the name *regnum Noricum* to refer to an alliance of Gaulish peoples living beyond the Eastern Alps (Lower Austria, western Slovenia), hegemonized by the Taurisci, whose capital is the fortified village of Noreia in Carinthia (Lower Austria). However, the leaders of the Norici declare to the Roman messengers that the Gauls to which the Roman ambassadors referred left without their authorization and that they do not know what they are doing in Italy.

Since the attempt to resolve the issue in a painless way has failed, Rome changes the register, though not for another three years.[8] In 183 BC, the consul Marcus Claudius Marcellus, who militarily presides over Cisalpine Gaul (northern Italy), and the proconsul Lucius Porcius Licinius agree that the latter will lead the legions under his command up to the site occupied by the Gauls on the banks of the Natissa. Licinius is an expert magistrate. He was a praetor in 193 BC in Sardinia and a consul in 184 BC. Afterward, he collaborated with Publius Claudius Pulcher in the war against the Ligurians. Upon his arrival on the Natissa, he lines up his troops and orders the Gauls to surrender, hand over their weapons together with any other possessions they have (believed to be the result of looting perpetrated in the surrounding countryside), and to leave; failing that, he will attack them. The Gauls do not resist but ask and obtain the power to make a plea to the Senate of Rome.

The Gallic legates are introduced to the Senate by the praetor Caius Valerius. They argue in a subdued tone that their group was pushed into Italy by the excess population in its former lands, the scarcity of arable land, and poverty. They point out that they have peacefully occupied uncultivated and uninhabited lands without causing damage to either the countryside or any city. They beg the Senate of Rome and the Roman people not to rage on them more than on their enemies.

The Senate deplores that the Gauls came to Italy and occupied land without permission but adds that it does not like to strip those who surrender of their possessions; therefore, on the one hand, it confirms the eviction order but, on the other, it recommends that Licinius return to the Gauls everything that was seized from them on the condition that they undertake to return home. He also sends a delegation to Noreia, in Carinthia (southern Austria), to make the Norici understand that the Alps are an insuperable border for them.

The Gauls obey, obtain the restitution of their belongings, and leave Italy, returning to the places they came from.[9] The legates to the leaders of the Norici are Lucius Manlius Purpureus, Quintus Minucius, and Lucius Manlius Acidinus. They accomplish their mission, after which they return to Rome and report to the Senate that the Norici had commented that the Romans had treated the Gauls with indulgence whereas it should have punished them, partly to prevent others from following their bad example.[10]

The Second Istrian War (191–181 BC)

In 183 BC, two Roman colonies—Mutina (Modena) and Parma—are founded in the Po valley, with the settlement of a total of two thousand men. Also, other minor centers—*fora*—are founded, where markets will be held and justice will be administered. In the same year, the Galli Carni of Tergeste (Trieste) ask Rome to free them once and for all from the nightmare of the pirates of Istria. The Istri, in fact, had not been completely defeated by the Romans in 221–220 BC (First Istrian War). They have rebuilt their castles and their maritime potential, they have outfitted and armed new ships, and, after the death of King Epulon and the accession to the throne of his son Epulus (191 BC), they have resumed raids for the purpose of robbing Roman ports, the colonies of Latin law, and the Italic communities of the western Adriatic coast, especially Brundisium (Brindisi) and Tarentum (Taranto). Consul Marcus Claudius Marcellus crosses the river Ospo (Istrian border) and enters Istria with his legions. The enterprise ends in a stalemate, however. In fact, shortly after, Marcellus has to stop, go back and dissolve the army due to having to return to Rome to preside over the election for the renewal of the consulate.[11]

In 181 BC, the Senate of Rome expresses a favorable opinion on the passage to a vote of the Roman people gathered in the assembly of a bill aiming at the foundation of a colony in Lower Friuli, in the same place as the emporium of the Veneti of the Adriatic, in agreement with the latter. This assumes that northeastern Italy, from the river Adige to the Middle Friuli and to the Adriatic Sea, is Roman territory and is necessary to take control of the passes of the Carnic and Julian Alps as well as the Karst. The primary purposes of the new settlement are those of controlling the recently acquired territory of which we have just told and defend it from invasions comping through the "eastern door of Italy", guaranteeing logistical support in the fight against Istrian piracy, and being a launchpad for the military enterprises of Rome in the Western Balkans, aimed at subduing new territories and amassing rich spoils of war. A further, not secondary, purpose of the projected foundation is to develop trade in an area that from time immemorial has been traversed by the merchant traffic of agricultural products, whether processed or semi-finished and precious raw materials. The urban center of the colony, in fact, will be built in the same place as an emporium of the Veneti of the Adriatic, with the aim of transforming the latter into a pole of convergence of traffic in a vast area on both sides of the Eastern Alps (Rossi 1973: 51–52), so that this becomes the new center of attraction for the trade of the entire border area between Cisalpine Gaul and Istria, in competition with the traditional center of Val Rosandra (near Trieste), which thrives on trade with the Istri, the Iapodes, and the Dalmatians. The colony involved in the project will be a colony under Latin law.[12]

Notes

1   Troy was a city-state in Asia Minor. It is commonly believed that it was located on the Asian coast of the Dardanelles (Turkey), in a place now called Truva.

2   The myth of Aeneas, in the Augustan Age (27 BC–AD 14), became the subject of the *Aeneid*, an epic poem by Virgil, though it had already existed for many centuries before, during which it underwent numerous changes and additions, which had in common the fact that, uniquely

among the great heroes of the Trojan War, Aeneas had had a future. Therefore, the *Aeneid* is only a variant of that myth, albeit the most authoritative. The fundamental difference between the Virgilian variant and the others is that Aeneas is not seen as the one who founds a new city of Troy on the ruins of the old one but as the descendant of Dardanus, son of Coritus, king of the homonymous city-state of maritime Etruria, and as the origin of the process that will lead to the foundation of a city in the area of origin of the Troadic lineage, that is, central Tyrrhenia, destined to be the fulcrum of a millenary empire. See Publio Virgilio Marone 2012; Bettini and Lentano 2013 (with its extensive bibliography).

3   According to Zaccaria (1992: 76), Sartori (1960: 12–16) and Càssola Guida (1972: 28), the *Galli transgressi* were Taurisci. According to Egger (1954–1957: 386–387), they were Taurisci coming from Czech Republic and Slovakia. Dobesch (1993: 14–80) says that they could have been a conglomerate of different tribes of Gauls settled in the geographical space now corresponding to Carinthia, who had separated from the rest of their people after coming into conflict with the *seniores* and had emigrated without the authorization of their leaders. Brizzi (1992: 111–123) argues the *Galli transgressi* should be identified with the Scordisci originating from Noricum. It cannot be ruled out that they were Ambisontes, a Taruiscian tribe living beyond the Julian Alps—in particular, along the mid-upper part of the Isonzo/Soča (138 km), a river that flows for the most part in western Slovenia and for the remaining part in northeastern Italy—and dominating the trade between the Sava valley, the Ljubljanica, and Tergeste (Trieste in Italy) through Nauportum (Šašel Kos 1997: 23–25). In this case, the purpose of the *Galli transgressi* could have been to establish an emporium in the Lower Friuli plain to compete with the nearby emporium located on the shores of the Natissa river, managed by the Veneti of the Adriatic and frequented also by the Galli Carni.

4   Among the Gallic and Illyrian-Gallic tribes that migrated from Bavaria to Switzerland, Austria, Slovenia, and northeastern Croatia, there were the Alauni, the Ambilici, the Ambisonti, the Ambitravi, the Laianci, the Taurisci, the Sevati, and the Uberaci. It is worthwhile to dwell on the Taurisci. The Taurisci live in southern Austria (Carinthia, Styria), central and eastern Slovenia, and northwestern Croatia. Their lands border those of the Pannoni (along the Sava) and of the Scordisci (along the Danube) to the east and with those of the Iapodes (Linka and valley of the river Una) to the south. Their main center is Noreia, a fortified village located in southern Austria, larger than a simple village but not as large as a city and not as complex, as it serves as a reference point for the villages of a large district. The Romans call this type of settlement an *oppidum* (pl. *oppida*). As they live immediately north of the Carnic Alps, the Taurisci are neighbors of the Galli Carni living in Italy. In the second half of the 2nd century BC, the Galli Carni, the Taurisci, the Alauni, the Ambilici, the Ambisonti, the Ambitravi, the Laianci, the Sevati, and the Uberaci federated among themselves, recognizing the pre-eminent authority of the tribal ruler of the Taurisci, living in Noreia. The Romans call the political organization described above *regnum Noricum*, and its members Norici. They also use the word *regulus* to refer to the chief of the chiefs of the Norici.The Norici are sometimes called Taurisci, as if these ethnonyms were synonymous. In reality, the Taurisci are only one of the tribes of the *regnum Noricum*, the one that holds political primacy within this realm.

5   The identification of the route followed by migrants to access the Friulian plain is a matter of discussion. Cecovini (2013: 182–183) excludes that the pass in question can be the Passo di Monte Croce Carnico, the Passo di Pramollo, the Sella di Camporosso, or the Valico del Predil because the transit would have been difficult and, in any case, they were well-known routes. He excludes the Sella di Camporosso also due to the presence of the Fella, a forceful stream, in the valley and due to the proneness of the slopes to landslides. He also excludes the Isonzo/Soča valley, both because it does not cross the Alps but remains within the Alps, because its medium-high part should not have been overpopulated to the point of forcing tens of thousands

of people to emigrate, and, finally, because it is not clear how the mass of migrants, in order to reach the Lower Friulian plain, had to pass through the Judrio valley instead of the wider and more comfortable Natisone valley; the latter, however, was not an unknown route. Instead, he leans toward the pass of *ad Pirum* (modern Hrusica, in Slovenia), between the Vipava valley and the Sava basin. He also claims that the migrants came down to the Vipava valley. See also Maniacco 1985: 21–22. Alfoldy (1984: 31) indicates, as an alternative to the Tagliamento valley, the road passing through Hrusica/Birnbaumer Wald. Dobesch (1993: 14–80) excludes a passage through the Julian Alps, because the word *saltus* ("throat"), used by Livy, evokes a tormented orography, and this is not the case in the Julian Alps; in addition, he excludes the Pass of the Okra, located in the Selva del Pero, between the Vipava valley and the Ljubljanica basin. Instead, he leans toward the Pass of Monte Croce Carnico or the Sella di Camporosso near Tarvisio, albeit while admitting that it would have been very difficult for a large mass of migrants to travel through them due to the roughness of the soil. Maniacco (1996: 13) assumes the Monte Croce Carnico Pass. Considering that Livy writes that it was a previously unknown pass, any route through the Eastern Alps has been excluded because all of them have been well-known since prehistoric times. Due to the nature of the terrain, the Canal del Ferro and the Monte Croce Carnico Pass did not allow the transit of a large mass of migrants (see Marchetti 1958: 7–9). Egger (1954–1957: 386–387) assumes it was one of the Karavanke passes. Sartori (1960: 12–16) leans toward a route across the Karst unknown to the Transalpinians but well-known to the inhabitants of the Friulian plain. Càssola Guida (1972: 28) opts for a branch of the Amber Route that passed through the Karst, or a route through the Carnic Alps or the Julian Alps, including the Isonzo/Soča valley, which, through the hills of Rocinj and Kambresko, leads to the valley of Judrio.

6　Pliny the Elder identifies this locality 12 Roman miles from Aquileia (1 Roman mile = 1,480 m), taking this data from a fragment by Lucius Calpurnius Piso Frugi, consul in 133 BC, author of *The Annales,* a universal story in seven books: it could therefore be the hilly town of Medea. It should be noted that in the municipality of San Giorgio di Nogaro there is today a locality of the Gauls, which has always been called this way, perhaps in memory of an ancient episode of Gallic occupation, which could be the *transgressio in Venetiam* narrated by Livy.

7　This is a mere guess. Livy (39.22) does not say. On the other hand, the Senate of Rome could not know what was happening in the Lower Friuli plain. Who else, if not Natissa's Galli Carni and Veneti, who were directly interested in what was happening, could have informed it? And what interest would Rome have had in interfering in a question that arose within the territory of the Galli Carni if not that of responding to an explicit request for intervention not only on their part but also on the part of the Veneti, all equally friends and allies of the Roman people?

8　According to Cecovini (2013: 187), "*Il ritardo potrebbe essere giustificato dalla presa di coscienza nel tempo della vera natura del sito: una testa di ponte sul suolo italico dei Galli Taurisci e dei loro interessi commerciali*" ["The delay could be justified by the gradual realization of the true nature of the site: a bridgehead on Italian soil for the Taurisci Gauls and their commercial interests"].

9　Liv. 39.22: *Eodem anno Galli Transalpini transgressi in Venetiam sine populatione aut bello haud procul inde, ubi nunc Aquileia est, locum oppido condendo ceperunt. Legatis Romanis de ea re trans Alpes missis responsum est neque profectos ex auctoritate gentis eos, nec quid in Italia facerent sese scire;* Liv. 39.45: *Galli Transalpini per saltus ignotae antea uiae, ut ante dictum est, in Italiam transgressi oppidum in agro, qui nunc est Aquileiensis, aedificabant. id eos ut prohiberet, quod eius sine bello posset, praetori mandatum est. si armis prohibendi essent, consules certiores faceret: ex his placere alterum aduersus Gallos ducere legiones;* Cass. Dio 19; Zonar. 9.6.

10　Liv. 39.55: *Legatis Romanis Transalpini populi benigne responderunt. seniores eorum nimiam lenitatem populi Romani castigarunt, quod eos homines, qui gentis iniussu profecti occupare agrum imperii Romani et in alieno solo aedificare oppidum conati sint, impunitos dimiserint: debuisse grauem temeritatis mercedem statui. quod uero etiam sua reddiderint, uereri ne tanta indulgentia plures ad talia audenda impellantur. et exceperunt et prosecuti cum donis legatos sunt.*

11 Liv. 39.56: *Ex Histria revocatus M. Marcellus exercitu dimisso Romam comitiorum causa rediit.*

12 For the settlements founded by the will of the Senate of Rome and called *coloniae* by the Romans, and for the juridical difference between the Roman colony and the Latin law colony, see the Appendix.

Chapter 1

The northernmost stronghold

The foundation of Aquileia

In 181 BC, 12,000–15,000 war veterans, and their families, camp on the banks of the Natissa, next to the emporium of the Veneti of the Adriatic, to found the urban center of a colony of Latin law together with numerous Veneti, among which there are also some magistrates and entrepreneurs, who belong to prestigious families. The war veterans, in particular, are 3,000 infantry, 300 knights, and 60 centurions. They come from central Italy, partly from Lazio, Umbria, and Samnium, partly from the coastal strip of the Marche. All the settlers are led by Publius Cornelius Scipio Nasica, Caius Flaminius, and Lucius Manlius Acidinus Fulvianus (Liv. 40.34). The *triumviri deducendae coloniae* just mentioned are all former senior civic magistrates, military commanders, and ambassadors, and are therefore men of the institutions, well-known and respected people. Scipio Nasica is a cousin of Publius Cornelius Scipio Africanus, the winner of the Battle of Zama, the episode that ended the Second Roman-Punic War (218–202 BC). In 191 BC, he was consul and fought victoriously against the Lusitani and the Galli Boi in Hispania.[1] He enjoys great esteem among his fellow citizens as one of the most virtuous Romans. For this reason, in 204 BC, he was commissioned by the Senate of Rome to welcome a venerated object of worship that arrived in the port of Ostia from the sanctuary of Cybele in Pessinus, Phrygia (Ballıhisar, Turkey). Caius Flaminius was consul in 187 BC and promoted the construction of the Via Flaminia Minor, the road that now connects Bononia (Bologna) to Arretium (Arezzo), urban centers of colonies of Latin law founded in 189 BC and 268 BC, respectively.[2] Acidinus Fulvianus was praetor in 188 BC. In 182 BC, he was part of an embassy sent by the Senate of Rome to the tribal leaders of Noricum in relation to the *transgressio in Venetiam*, together with Lucius Furius Purpureus and Quintus Minucius. We refer here to the episode of a large group of transalpine Gauls' clandestine immigration into Lower Friuli that we recounted in the Introduction.

The territory assigned to the colony corresponds to the extreme northeastern part of Italy (present-day Friuli, Carnia and the Tarvisiano area; Venezia Giulia, bordered to the east by the ridge of the Julian Alps; the Karst).[3] It extends, in particular, from the Livenza river in the south to the Middle Friuli in the north, and from the right bank of the Tagliamento river in the west to the shores of the Gulf of Trieste, up to the Bocche del Timavo, in the east. It is crossed by numerous waterways that, over time, have formed higher areas, lowlands, and marshes nearer the sea and is covered with thick vegetation, except for some clearings.

Within this territory, the land surveyors parcel out the arable areas in proportion to the number of settlers. Finally, a plot of fertile land is assigned to each family of settlers. The area of the single lot differs according to the military status of the single householder: 50 *iugera* if he is an infantryman, 100 *iugera* if he is a centurion, and 140 iugera if he is an *eques*, "knight" (the *iugerum*, pl. *iugera*, is a Roman measure of area; it is equivalent to ¼ ha, or 2,500 square m). Each infantryman, therefore, receives 12.5 ha of arable land; each centurion, 25.5 ha; and each *eques*, 35 ha.[4] The lots are unusually large in order to reward participation in the enterprise, but they also have an economic significance linked to the commercial function that will be carried out by the city alongside the military one.

The urban center of the colony is located between the Torre river and the Natissa river on one side and a swamp to the south on the other. The remediation of the latter will be carried out through the construction of hydraulic works. The Torre and the Natissa limit the city to the west and east, respectively. The first is a tributary of the second and reaches the southwest of the city. The port and the warehouses will be built along the Natissa. One of the main founding ceremonies is that which consists of the opening of the *sulcus primigenius* (*pomerium*).[5] The scene is animated by a man in a toga, the traditional garb of the Roman citizen, holding a plowshare that is pulled by a pair of oxen, and he is inciting the oxen with his rod while another man pulls the oxen by the reins; four magistrates, who follow the first two, comment on the event (Scrinari 1975: 193, n. 600). During the ceremony just described, an eagle appeared in the sky, and the name of the colony, Aquileia, thus derived from this episode. The first part of this story could be true, the second part probably not. In fact, it seems that the toponym Aquileia derives from the Venetic name of the river that laps the sides of the city: Akilis, or Akilia, whose root means "dark place" or "watery". The primitive city has a rectangular plan, with streets crossing at right angles and districts placed as on a chessboard, like at the Roman military camps (Latin *castrum*, pl. *castra*).

The new colony is exposed to the dangers of enemy attack more than any other colony of Rome in northern Italy. In fact, it is located about 300 km away from the closest Roman strongholds, which are Bononia (Bologna) and Ariminum (Rimini). The problem does not arise with regard to the Veneti of the Adriatic, who are friends and allies of the Romans, nor to the Galli Carni, whose threat has now disappeared, if it ever actually emerged, but to the Istri, with which Rome has been at war for 10 years (Second Istrian War, 191–181 BC).

The war is still ongoing. In 181 BC, praetor Quintus Fabius Buteo, who has obtained Gallia Cisalpina as his province, is fighting in Istria, but with poor results.[6] In 180 BC, peace will be restored, but it is fragile, and the common opinion is that it will not last long.

In 179 BC, 3,000 Galli Carni, led by a tribal chief named Catmelus, descend from Carnia to Lower Friuli and ask consul suffectus Quintus Fulvius Flaccus, brother of Lucius Manlius Acidinus Fulvianus, that land be assigned to them to graze their flocks. Flaccus rejects the request but nevertheless offers a job to the applicants, hiring them as mercenary soldiers.

The Third Istrian War (178–177 BC)

In 178 BC, the fighting between the Romans and the Istri resumes. Consul Aulus Manlius Vulso leads his army from Aquileia toward Istria. Under his command are two legions of Roman citizens (the First and the Third), two *manipula* of the Second Legion, and a cohort of auxiliaries, made available to him by the Roman colony of Placentia (Piacenza in the Po Valley). At the end of the day, the Romans camp in a hilly area on the border with Istria, 3 km from Mugla (Muggia, near Trieste), crossed by the Rosandra river. The area, easily reachable by sea, is inhabited by the Istri and is frequented by the Veneti of the Adriatic for commercial reasons.

The First Legion occupies the main camp, located at the top of a hill, close to a water source. The Placentine cohort is placed on guard on the side facing Istria. The *manipula* of the Second Legion are deployed between the sea and the main camp to protect the drinking water supply lines. The Third Legion, with the military tribunes, is established on the road to Aquileia to protect the supply lines for wood and hay. Meanwhile, 10 warships and other merchant ships, all commanded by Caius Furius, drop anchor in the Timavo-Locavaz river basin (the mouth of the Timavo river, called Bocche del Timavo, near the modern city of Monfalcone), an excellent port, protected from the sea, thanks to the natural "dam" formed by the two islets of Sant'Antonio and della Punta, as well as from the winds, and with an easily defensible entrance.

Furius is one of the duumvirs who command the warships that are stationed in Ankon (Ancona in the Marche) and have the task of both keeping this city under control and protecting the Adriatic coast from attacks by Illyrian pirates. He protects the stretch of the western Adriatic coast between Aquileia and the mouth of the Timavo with 10 ships. Vulso's colleague, Lucius Cornelius, protects the stretch of the western Adriatic coast between Ankon and Aquileia with 10 other ships.

Vulso orders Furius to move to Mugla, one of the most protected natural ports in the Upper Adriatic, 3 km away from the main camp. The Istri observe the movements of the Romans from afar. They consider the Romans' defenses to be weak, deduce from this that the enemy is disorganized, and attack the Placentine cohort and the *manipula* on the road between the camp and the sea. The cohort is intent on building and supplying the camp. Its members do not know how to accurately assess the extent of the attack, they panic, and, shouting "To the ships! To the ships!", they flee toward the sea, unnecessarily detained by the consul and officers. In short, most of the First and Third Legions follow the fugitives. Only 600 soldiers remain in the camp.

The Istri burst into the camp through the wide open and no longer manned gates, overwhelm the defenders, and sack and devastate the camp. When they find a lot of food and wine, they feast, forgetting everything. This gives the Romans time to regroup. They have time to take stock. It is clear that the entire army would have fallen prey to the enemy "if only this one had remembered to keep fighting" (Liv. 61.1–5). All that remains for Vulso is to withdraw, so he returns to Aquileia, where the army will spend the winter.

The Romans take fierce revenge in 177 BC. Four legions under the orders of the consul Caius Claudius Pulcher and the proconsuls Aulus Manlius Vulso and Marcus Iunius Brutus, supported by the Galli Carni of Catmelus, move from Aquileia, heading for Istria. After entering Istria, they carry out indiscriminate looting and destruction and defeat an improvised enemy army in the Mirna river area (near Buzet and Pula, Croatia). The Istri lose between 4,000 and 8,000 men in the fight. The survivors take refuge in Vizače (Ližnjan in Croatia), a fortified center of Istria of pre-Roman foundation.[7]

Vizače is located on the rocky southeastern coast of Istria, overlooking the Kvarner bay, a couple of kilometers as the crow flies from the Adriatic Sea, in a dominant position on the protected natural bay of Budava, an ancient seaport of the locality. It is a commercial center and a haunt for pirates. The Romans siege Vizače and, to break the resistance of its defenders, deviate the river that goes to it. The defenders interpret this event as the fact that the gods have abandoned them. Epulo, king of the Istri, so as to avoid falling prisoner and ornating the triumph of the winner, commits suicide, stabbing himself. Also, his soldiers and their wives and children prefer to kill each other, or throw themselves from the walls, rather than let themselves be made slaves. The Romans take Vizače and destroy it. According to the Roman sources, over 8,000 Istri and about 200 Roman soldiers were killed in this campaign.[8]

Afterward, the praetor Quintus Fabius Buteo conquers and razes the fortified villages of Mutila and Faveria to the ground. The Istri surrender, but the Romans, in revenge, kill all their leaders and enslave over 5,000. Thus, the Senate of Rome suppresses the Kingdom of the Istri. From now on, Istria will be garrisoned by Roman soldiers. Vizače is refounded with the name of Nesactium and becomes a fully fledged Roman city. Nesactium, in 54 BC, will become a *municipium*, and it will continue to be an important center in Istria until the times of Emperor Augustus (27 BC–AD 14).

A fortification system is established on the Istrian border near Mugla (Muggia). It consists of a large central camp (San Rocco) and two minor forts (Grociana Piccola and Montedoro). The fort of San Rocco occupies an area of 13 ha (equivalent to 13 football fields) and is defended by large bastions.[9] The minor encampments are outposts for the control of the south and north. Montedoro serves as a lookout point for the fleet. The Grociana Piccola, as an advanced fort with a view, serves to look out for further incursions and as a sighting center to prevent any threats. These structures are the first of their kind in the Eastern Alps.

The Galli Carni of Catmelus and some Latin support troops form the first nucleus of the garrison (from now on, we will call the Galli Carni in question "southeastern Galli Carni"). Likely, the fort of San Rocco is so extensive because it incorporates the local market frequented by the Veneti of the Adriatic. Therefore, the latter becomes a fortified village, garrisoned by the southeastern Galli Carni (see Strabo 7.5.2: *Tergheste komès Karnikès*).

The fortification system we are talking about strengthens the military defense system of the far northeast of Italy, previously consisting of Aquileia alone. It is destined to support Aquileia from now on as a link between maritime traffic and terrestrial transalpine roads.[10] It will maintain a strategic role over time, though perhaps not continuously, at least until the foundation of Tergeste on Colle di San Giusto in the middle of the 1st century BC.[11]

The Third Macedonian War (171–168 BC)

Pleuratus II (*c.* 260–250 BC), king of the Illyrians, ensured valid support for Rome in the Second Macedonian War (200–197 BC). In 172 BC, Gentius (180–168 BC), son and successor of Pleuratus II, begins to behave in an ambiguous way. The Greek city of Issa, a Roman protectorate, openly accuses him of wanting to go to war alongside Macedonia against Rome. In the meantime, relations between Rome and Perseus, son and successor of Philip V (221–179 BC), king of Macedon, have deteriorated, and the outbreak of the Third Macedonian War seems imminent.

Rome sends an embassy to Gentius to complain that the pirate raids along the Adriatic coast are damaging its interests and those of its allies but also, and above all, to ascertain his intentions.

The Third Macedonian War breaks out in 171 BC. Consul Caius Cassius Longinus, who has Cisalpine Gaul as his province, leads his army toward Macedonia through Illyria but is stopped by the Senate of Rome. On the way back, he allows his soldiers to loot and kill, set fires, and enslave entire populations in the lands of the Iapodes, Istri, and southeastern Galli Carni. All those peoples had previously collaborated with him, showing him the way to Macedonia. Longinus' soldiers also sack some villages of Alpine populations (Taurisci?) and, even here, enslave thousands of people.

Longinus does not justify his hostile behavior. The episode damages both the good relations between the Romans and the southeastern Galli Carni as well as the economic interests of the Romans and Italics in the extreme northeast of Italy. Some of the exports from Aquileia are in fact transported by wagon to Nauportum (Vrhnika in Slovenia)—a center of the Taurisci—and on board boats along the Ljubljanica and Sava rivers to Segestica in Pannonia (near Sisak in Serbia), from where they continue to the Danube and the neighboring region.

The problem is solved through diplomatic channels. In 170 BC, an embassy of Taurisci, Iapodes, Istri, and southeastern Galli Carni, led by the brother of the ruler of the Norics, Cincibilus, goes to Rome and protests before the Senate over the damage and injustice suffered. The Senate grants a certain satisfaction to the offended: it recalls Longinus to Rome from Macedonia, where he was in command of a legion of the army of consul Aulus Hostilius Mancinus, sends ambassadors with gifts to the tribal leaders of the Taurisci to restore good relations, and exceptionally grants the ambassadors of the injured parties permission to buy up to a maximum of 10 horses each from the Veneti and to take them to Noricum (Liv. 43.5.1–10).

The strengthening of the colony (171 BC)

The Roman expansion in the extreme northeast of Italy does not take place through military conquest but through diplomatic actions, with the consequence that Rome does not exercise direct control over the region. The territory continues to be the scene of peaceful and mutually beneficial interactions between the Aquileians, the Veneti of the Adriatic, the Galli Carni, the Istri, and the Iapodes, but only because the agreements between the *regnum Noricum* and its allies hold sway. If the peace is broken, the trade will cease, and Aquileia will be exposed to enemy attacks.

If attacked, Aquileia will not be able to defend itself effectively because its surrounding walls are not only incomplete but also quite narrow, and its population has been considerably reduced because of the abandonment of many settlers due to the difficulties and risks of the settlement.

The outbreak of the Third Macedonian War feeds residents' fears. The thought of these negative possibilities that might happen causes the *duumviri* of Aquileia to draw the attention of the Senate of Rome to the precarious conditions of the city (Liv. 43.1.5–6).[12]

The *duumviri*, we recall, are two elected magistrates who carry out administrative duties in the colony. In 171 BC, those of Aquileia exhort the Senate of Rome to finance the completion of the walls of their city and to send new people to reinforce the population of Aquileia. The reinforcement contingent arrives on the spot in 169 BC. It is made up of 1,500 families, counting Italics and Veneti, and headed by five quaestors (Liv. 43.17.1).[13]

In order to allow the newcomers to settle in the city, the *duumviri* make a very significant variation to the urban planning instrument that regulates the building activity within the colony. From now on, the urban area will expand northward, partly conditioned by the Natissa river, which borders it to the east. This implies a considerable expansion to the walls. Due to this expansion, the city will eventually get three times larger than the primitive one.

The walls of the Republican age of Aquileia are 3 km long and enclose an area of 42 ha. They consist of a double brick curtain with a high-sand dry core. The cladding curtains are brick faces of conspicuous and anomalous dimensions and are 2.4 m thick.

There are five doors, at least one of which is made of large square stone blocks, with a rather small atrium (quadrangular courtyard) and two foreparts. The enclosure we are talking about was built between 181 BC and the middle of the 2nd century BC. It will not undergo changes before 90 BC, when Aquileia will obtain full Roman citizenship, in the application of the *lex Iulia municipalis*.

The Third Illyrian War (169 BC)

At the beginning of the spring of 169 BC, two legionary armies leave Aquileia at the same time. One is commanded by consul Lucius Aemilius Paullus and is headed for Macedonia. The other is commanded by praetor Lucius Anicius Gallus and is headed for Illyria. The latter consists of 20,400 infantry and 1,400 horsemen.

On reaching its first destination, the army is supplemented by a contingent of auxiliary, made available by the Partini, an Illyrian tribe, based in the islands of southern Illyria (modern Albania) and the Shkumbin valley controlling the Via Egnatia, the important route built by the Romans between the Adriatic Sea and Macedonia. Then it continues to the Genzasus river (Shkumbi), on whose banks are camped the small army of Appius Claudius Cento, which also includes the auxiliaries made available to him by the communities of Apollonia (near Pojani in Albania) and Dyrrachium (Durrës in Albania), as well as the Bullini, an Illyrian Epirote tribe, that occupies the territory between Apollonia and Oricum (a city located at the south end of the Bay of Vlorë in Albania). Gallus also aggregates Claudius Cento's men to his army so that it is further strengthened, reaching 30,000 men. The warships that transport the ground troops, before they move toward Bassania—a Roman-friendly city, located in the area of Scodra (Shkodër in northwestern Albania)[14]—put some Illyrian ships to flight.

Gentius, as the Romans approach, breaks off the siege of Bassania and retires to Scodra. Gallus occupies Lissus (Lezhë) and marches on Scodra. Gentius, rather than resisting a long siege, attempts a sortie but is defeated and surrenders, invoking clemency. Thus ends the Third Illyrian War. The conflict lasted just 30 days.

The Illyrians partly submit to Rome and partly go into hiding and become a constant danger for both Dalmatians and Roman and Italic merchants. Gallus places military garrisons in Scodra, in the nearby port of Olcinium (Ulcinj in Montenegro), and/or in Risinium (Rizhon in Montenegro), further north, at the bottom of Bay of Kotor. Then he leads the army to Epirus. The Epirotes surrender en masse without a fight. Only their leader Cephalus and a few others resist and die fighting.

In 169 BC, the Rhodians send ambassadors to Rome to attempt mediation between Rome and Perseus. In 168 BC, the fourth year of the war, the successes of the Romans alarm Perseus, who, in order to earn the military help of Gentius (who continues to take no position, despite Rome and Perseus each sending him an embassy one after the other), agrees to pay him 300 talents. A treaty is signed and confirmed by oaths and the exchange of hostages. Gentius gathers his forces in Lissus, on the southern border, besieges Bassania, and sends Caravantius, the half-brother of Gentius, to fight against the cities of the Cavî tribe (Durnium and Caravandis) with 1,000 infantry and 500 cavalry. Then he finally positions himself against Rome, having two Roman ambassadors arrested and attempting to occupy the cities of Apollonia and Dyrrachium. Just then, Perseus withdraws his ambassadors from the king of the Illyrians and does not pay the agreed sum. Although defrauded by his ally, Gentius does not ask for peace.

The Third Macedonian War ends in 168 BC with the victory of the Romans at the Battle of Pydna. Perseus takes refuge in the Sanctuary of the Great Gods on Samothrace, an island in the northern Aegean, where he then surrenders to admiral Cnaeus Octavius Rufus. Aemilius Paullus celebrates with a triumph in Rome, exhibiting very considerable riches and booty from the war, which also includes Perseus' library,[15] and receives the honorary appellation of Macedonicus from the Senate.

One of the consequences of the defeat of the Macedonians is the dissolution of the Kingdom of Macedon and the dismemberment of its territory into four independent parts, controlled by the Romans. In 168 BC, the Roman province of Illyria is also created after the defeat of Gentius and the dissolution of the *regnum Illyricum*. Gentius and his family are deported to Italy and adorn the triumph of Gallus (167); later, they are incarcerated in Umbria, first in Spoletium (Spoleto) and then in Igiturvium (Gubbio). As for the Daorsi, southern neighbors of the Dalmatians, they are rewarded with an exemption from the obligation to pay taxes.

The Achaean League, a political-military alliance of Greek city-states, fought alongside Perseus against Rome and was overwhelmed along with Macedon. Its pro-Roman party hands over 1,000 hostages to Aemilius Paullus Macedonicus as a guarantee of its observance of the peace treaty. One of the hostages is the historian Polybius.

Born in Megalopolis (still today called Megalopolis), a city located in Arcadia in the Peloponnese, Polybius is the son of Lycortas, a former commander-in-chief of the army of the Achaean League. He himself commanded the cavalry of the League. He arrives in Rome at the age of 33. Having vast cultural knowledge, he is chosen by Aemilius Macedonicus to be the tutor of his sons Publius and Quintus. Polybius will become a scholar of the history and civilization of the Romans, and he will "convert" to their cause, though not without an inner struggle. He will be convinced that the reasons for the success and greatness of Rome are to be found in the superiority and solidity of its legal systems, mainly in its form of government, which summarizes in itself, by tempering them, monarchy, oligarchy, and democracy, and allows it, therefore, to avoid having to choose between one form and the others and risking the chosen model degrading into tyranny, oligarchy, or demagogy.

Polybius is a rational and pragmatic man. He believes that religions are a form of superstition but that they are useful for political life. He is convinced that Rome created its *imperium* because it was in the plans of Fortune that this would happen, that is, because Rome was destined from birth to govern other peoples. In 150 BC, he returns to his family and homeland, but he leaves a few years later to accompany Publius Cornelius Scipio Aemilianus, son of Aemilius Macedonicus, on his African campaign. Perhaps, in 147 BC, he has already begun to write his *Historiai* (Histories).[16] This work is the most important of Polybius' literary production. It narrates the historical events of the East and the West. In the end, it will be composed of 40 books.[17] The research activity of Polybius aims to highlight the causes of the events and to expose them objectively. His narrative style is simple and flat, without rhetorical artifices. At the siege of Carthage (149–146 BC), Polybius has the task of keeping a chronicle of the events up to date.

The First Dalmatian War (157–156 BC)

In 158 BC, the Greek city of Issa complains to the Romans about the problems created by the Dalmatians in its settlements of Tragurium (Trogir in Croatia) and Epetium (Stobrec in Croatia) on the mainland (the Dalmatians have attacked the Daorsi, their southern neighbors, and those Greek cities). Similar complaints are communicated to Rome by the Daorsi, who, at the time of the establishment of the Roman protectorate over southern Illyria (167 BC), were rewarded with a tax exemption. They fear for the safety of Narona (3 km away from present-day Vid in Croatia), an emporium and river port, located in the Naro valley (Narente, today's Neretva, a river which flows into the Adriatic at Ploče, Croatia), on the right bank of the river, at the southern end of Illyria.

The Senate of Rome instructs its own delegation to investigate the situation in Illyria, with particular reference to the activity of the Dalmatians. The head of the delegation is Caius Fannius Strabo. He was consul in 161 BC together with Marcus Valerius Messalla. During his consulate, all foreign rhetoricians were expelled from Rome, and Fannius himself promoted and brought to approval a *lex sumptuaria* (a Roman law that prohibits the purchase and/or use of luxury goods with the aim of limiting expenditure on food, with particular reference to electoral banquets and, therefore, to obstruct electoral corruption).

The envoys accomplish their mission in Delminium (Zupaniac in Bosnia-Herzegovina), the capital of the Dalmatians, and report that the chieftain not only refused to give them an audience but did not arrange to house them either and even attacked them. They added that some of them had been killed, and their horses, which had been borrowed for the journey, had been stolen. The behavior of the Dalmatians fills the Senate with indignation, which creates a pretext for it to unleash war. But nothing happens, at least for the moment. However, two years later, in 156 BC, the Dalmatians attack some other settlements in Illyria, including some Roman ones, and then ignore the protests and the claims for damages; indeed, they imprison and kill some non-Roman ambassadors. This time, the Senate of Rome decides to intervene.

In 155 BC, proconsul Caius Marcius Figulus and consul Publius Cornelius Scipio Nasica Corculum leave Aquileia at the head of two separate armies. The first reaches

Illyria by sea, sailing probably from Rabenna (Ravenna), and the second by land. Figulus probably lands at the mouth of the Neretva. He then reaches Narona without encountering resistance, but while his men are busy setting up the camp, the Dalmatians attack them in force. Taken by surprise, they are forced to retreat. Scipio Nasica is also defeated in Segestica in Pannonia and has to return to base.

The double reverse of the Romans entices many Illyrian tribes to launch attacks against them. The Iapodes, in particular, attack the Roman positions on the border of Istria (App. *Ill.* 11; Dio Cass. 20.25; Strab. 7.5). After some time, Figulus manages to fight back and push himself as far as Delminium (now Raša, in eastern Istria); almost inaccessible and impregnable, it is a city-fortress of 5,000 inhabitants, surrounded by a ring of smaller fortresses. He passes through the Trebizat valley but fails to surprise the enemy, and, despite conquering some minor fortresses before winter begins, he can only organize the siege of Delminium. Eventually, he conquers and burns Delminium and demolishes its fortifications, "turning it into a sheep pasture" (Strab. 7.5). Corculum, in turn, conquers some cities and takes numerous prisoners, whom he will sell as slaves (Dio Cass. 20.25); he forces the entire coastal area between the Arsia and Naro-Narente rivers (in modern Raša) into submission. Then Figulus and Corculum come back to Rome and celebrate their triumph. It could have been following these events that the province of Illyricum was born.

Pannonia and the Pannoni

Pannonia is an Illyrian toponym. It identifies the physical region between the Danube and Sava rivers, which is home to large forests, crossed by these great rivers, the largest of which is the Danube (corresponding to its part in Slovenia and Hungary), and means "swamp" or "marsh" in reference to the marshy areas of the plain between these rivers. The region in question encompasses the western part of Hungary, part of Austria up to Vienna (Burgenland), northern Croatia, and part of Slovenia. The Romans collectively call the inhabitants of Pannonia—Celtic and Illyrian populations—*Pannoni* and describe them as bold, warlike, cruel, and deceptive individuals.

The Pannoni are mostly shepherds, living in fortified villages and open settlements. They do not live in cities but are scattered in the countryside and in villages, where they aggregate on the basis of family ties. They do not come together to make common decisions, and there are no people among them whose authority is recognized by all, except for the forgetful. In times of war, they manage to field even a hundred thousand men, but having no central power, they never join forces (App. *Ill.* 22). Among the Pannoni are some Norici, the Amatini, who live north of the Scordisci, the Dardani, who live to the south of the Scordisci, as well as the Breuci, the Andiseti, the Ditioni, the Peirusti, the Mazei, the Dasitati, etc. (Strab. 7.5.3).

The Scordisci, in particular, are people born from the physical mixing and cultural osmosis of groups of Thracians and Illyrians. Since the 4th century BC, they have settled in the heart of the Balkan Peninsula, together with other less important Celtic tribes. Their lands are bordered to the north and east by the Danube, to the west by Noricum and the extreme northeast of Italy, to the southwest by Dalmatia, and to the southeast by Bulgaria and Romania, including northern Serbia,[18] between the lower courses of the Morava and Drava rivers. Perhaps the Scordisci moved to that territory from the area of the Scordus mountains, located in Albania and western Macedonia. They are organized in a tribal kingdom and exert hegemony over the whole area, but also beyond, toward Illyria and the eastern Balkans, where they receive tribute from the Triballi,[19] the Autariati,[20] the Dardani, and the Moesi.

In the 2nd century BC, this kingdom is the most important political organization in the western Balkans. It was founded by some veterans of the Great Expedition carried out in Greece from 280 to 278 BC by Celtic-Danubian hordes, who, on their way back to their points of departure, stopped in Serbia, then settled there permanently. Its capital is Segestica (Siscia, modern Sisak in Croatia), a hillfort, the largest of its kind in the upper Sava valley, located in an extremely favorable position at the confluence of the Kupa and the Odra rivers in a region inhabited by Celtic and Illyrian tribes (App. *Ill.* 11). The Sava is the longest right tributary of the Danube, second overall behind the Tisza.[21]

An expedition against the Scordisci (141 BC)

The Romans made their first true thrust into Pannonia, along the Sava's route, in 156 BC, moving out from Aquileia (in the past, the Roman army had limited itself to maintaining control of the pass between the Okra and Nauportus). The campaign is led by consul Lucius Cornelius Lentulus Lupus, a patrician criticized by some for his decadent and corrupt lifestyle, who has already been or will be accused of extortion (Val. Max. 5.9.10).

Lentulus Lupus is a *decemvir sacris faciundis.* In other words, he is a member of the college of 10 members—five patricians and five plebeians—who are responsible for consulting the Sybilline books, organizing and managing the games in honor of the god Apollo (*ludi Apollinares*), and also exercising other functions of a religious nature.

The *decemviri sacris faciundis* were established in 367 BC in place of the *duumviri*, two men, both patricians, who had the same tasks. They are also called *decemviri sacrorum.* They are co-opted by members already in office and remain in office for life.

Lentulus Lupus participated in the Battle of Pydna in 168 BC. In 162 BC, he was elected consul for the first time with Caius Marcius Figulus. In 159 BC, he was censor together with his colleague Marcus Popilius Laenas and built the first water clock in Rome, which was placed in the Basilica Aemilia. In 156 BC, he was elected consul for 155 BC with Marcus Claudius Marcellus. That of 155 BC was, therefore, his second consulate.

In 141 BC, a legionary army, which started out from Aquileia, invades the lands of the Scordisci again to punish them for having attacked Macedonia the year before

(Macedonia was established as a Roman province a few years before). It goes as far as Segestica, without knowing it is about to face a disastrous defeat. The episode is yet more proof that the Romans do not win all their battles, nor all their wars. Among the precedents, consider the successes of the Carthaginians in the Second Punic War (218–202 BC), which Rome was only able to survive thanks to the rapid replenishment of the voids that opened in its ranks by its allies, subjugated peoples, and the Roman colonies and colonies of Latin law.

The Second Dalmatian War (135 BC)

A further military expedition originates in Aquileia in 135 BC under the leadership of consul Sergius Fulvius Flaccus, an enriched plebeian,[22] a man of letters, and an eloquent man (Cic. *Brutus* 21.32). It is directed to the lands that extend from the left bank of the Neretva, opposite the one where Narona, an emporium and river port, stands.

The Neretva river is the southern border of the territory claimed by the Romans along the eastern Adriatic coast. South of this river, along the coast of Montenegro, at the level of the island of Hvar, are the lands of the Ardiaei and the neighboring Pleriei. The Ardiaei and Pleriei have plundered a couple of Roman settlements in Illyria and continued to attack the settlements in the area despite the demand of the Roman authorities to suspend these attacks. Having no other options, the Senate of Rome sent consul Sergius Fulvius Flaccus to face those tribes. Flaccus leaves Aquileia together with two legions and two *alae* (formations of cavalry)—10,000 infantrymen and 600 horsemen—and penetrates the lands of the enemy. Upon the news of the arrival of a regular army, the Ardiaei and Pleriei surrender and beg Rome's pardon (for Flaccus' expedition against the Ardiaei: App. *Mac.* 10).

New military operations in Illyria (129 BC)

In 129 BC, the Roman army returns to operate in Istria, Dalmatia, and Albania, generally along the coast. The aim is to convince the inhabitants of the Adriatic and the eastern Alpine hinterland —the Istri, the Taurisci, the Iapodes, and perhaps also the southeastern Gauls and the Liburnians—to refrain from harassing the Romans, friends of the Romans, and their activities, with particular reference to commercial interests that focus on Nauportus. The enterprise of consul Caius Sempronius Tuditanus should be placed in this context. Tuditanus is an annalist historian, a scholar of public and intellectual law, and a philhellene. He fought in Greece under the command of Lucius Mummius, the destroyer of Corinth (146 BC). He is an *optimas,* therefore he was a political opponent of Tiberius Sempronius Gracchus, the tribune of the plebeians assassinated in 133 BC.

He starts out from Aquileia at the head of 3,000 auxiliaries, made available by the *regnum Noricum* (App. *Ill.* 10; Liv. *Epit.* 59), goes into the Istrian hinterland up to the Titius river (Kerka), emerges victorious from clashes with bands of Iapodes, Taurisci, and Istri, and takes control of the mountain pass of the Okra and Nauportus area, thanks also to the collaboration with his legate, Decimus Iunius Brutus Callaicus (App. *Ill.* 10; Liv. *Epit.* 59). Brutus Callaicus is the former governor of the Roman province of Hispania Ulterior. In that position, he crushed the revolt of the Lusitanians, led by Tantalus, the successor of Viriatus, who had been killed by treason in 139 BC. Later, he founded the city of Valentia Edetanorum (Valencia) in the Roman province of Hispania Citerior, to which he transferred the ex-combatants of Viriatus.

Tuditanus, to remind posterity of his victory, rearranges the area of the ancient sanctuary at the Bocche del Timavo into a Roman form, also placing an honorary monument to himself there. Later, he had a triumphal panel with a dedication to the god Timavus (*InscrIt* 10.4.137; Alfoldy 1984: 87, nr. 43) posted on the podium or on a jamb of the cell of a temple located in the suburban area of Aquileia. The honorary monument bears a coroplastic decoration—an Amazonomachy—and a dedication in Saturn verse, which expresses the dedicatory intent of the work. The reorganization of the Timavo sanctuary is the official act that marks the Romanization of the local river cult. In that context, Tuditanus confirms the prerogatives and privileges, even economic ones, of the sanctuary.

The cult of the god Timavus will persist until the beginning of the Augustan Age and will also spread to places distant from its area of origin (see the donations offered in the second half of the 2nd century BC by private, neo-Romanized north Adriatic individuals, both in the area of the sanctuary and in a locality of Val Cellina where the waters gushing from the rock are worshipped).

Tuditanus then returns to Rome to celebrate his triumph (*FastCons.* I.I.XIII, fasc. I, ad an. DCXXIV). In the future, he will return to conduct military operations in the far northeast of Italy, particularly in the Trieste Karst. The citizens of Aquileia, to remember his deeds, will dedicate a statue to him with an inscription in Saturn verse.[23] The epic poet Hostius will also immortalize him in the hexam of his epic *Bellum Histricum.*[24]

The Third Dalmatian War (119–117 BC)

In 124 BC, consul Caius Cassius Longinus embarks on a military expedition to inner Istria, starting from Aquileia, but he meets unsurpassable resistance and is forced to return. The Senate of Rome deplores his initiative, accusing him of jeopardizing the security of the northeastern border of Italy. In 119 BC, consul Lucius Aurelius Cotta, starting from Aquileia, unleashes the Third Dalmatian War. The purpose of the operation is the same as always: to discourage the inhabitants of the Adriatic and eastern Alpine hinterland from harassing the Romans, their friends, and their business. In 117 BC, Aquileia is the meeting place of the army of consul Lucius Caecilius Metellus, about to set out toward an inland area of Dalmatia on the border between the lands of the Dalmatians and the lands of the Illyrians of Pannonia.[25] Preparations for their departure are well underway. Everyone knows what to do and collaborates so that everything is ready within the established time frame. The reason that justifies Metellus' campaign is the same as previous, similar operations. No war has been declared, so the Dalmatians are not at fault; it is strongly suspected that they are the intended victims of a cynical operation that aims to procure another triumph for the Metelli. The enterprise, if it can be called that, takes place without bloodshed: the Dalmatians surrender without a fight, either because they have been suddenly attacked and are faced with the impossibility of reacting effectively or because they have given up opposing (App. *Ill.* 7), and so they welcome Metellus as a friend. The latter will spend the winter among them in Salona, a maritime city that became the new capital of the Dalmatians after the destruction of Delminium. Metellus' enterprise ends the same year with the fall of Segestica. This success opens up new perspectives in Rome for its merchant traffic and introduces progressive conquest and organization to the province of the territories between the Alps and the Danube and the Illyrian territories south of the Danube, as well as the creation of military settlements along the Danube.

The Senate of Rome authorizes the victorious commander to celebrate a triumph and gives him the honorary title of Delmaticus. To obtain this result, to which he aspired with all his strength, he had attacked the Iapodes in the absence of any provocation (App. *Ill.* 11 and 33; Liv. *Per.* 62; Eutropius 4.23.2). On the occasion of his sumptuous ceremony, Metellus Dalmaticus announces the reconstruction of the Temple of the Dioscuri in Rome at his own expense.[26]

Such a temple is located in the southeastern corner of the Roman Forum, near the Spring of Juturna. It was dedicated in 484 BC by the son of the dictator Aulus Postumius Albus Regillensis, who had promised it in 499 or 496 BC after the Battle of Lake Regillus and after the Dioscuri had appeared to him in a dream in the act of watering their horses at a spring. Postumius' son was appointed *duovir* precisely to oversee its construction. From 160 BC, the temple in question is one of the venues where the Senate meets and is the seat of an important court.

The official weights and measures are kept inside it, and some rooms are used as "banks" or deposit rooms. Some legislative rallies are held in the square in front, and it is from here that the traditional parade of the *equites* starts. We refer to the parade that was established in 304 BC by Quintus Maximus Rullianus and is held every year on 15 July, the anniversary of the Battle of Lake Regillus. The Temple of the Dioscuri is therefore related to the *equites*, the social group to which Metellus Dalmaticus belongs.

Marcus Aemilius Scaurus' blitzkrieg (115 BC)

Between 147 and 132 BC, fairly pure gold has been discovered in the lands of the Taurisci. The Taurisci exploit that resource together with Italics for two months;

when the price of gold falls by a third, they remove the Italics to ensure a monopoly over sales. The expulsion of the Italics ruined the relations between the Galli Carni and the Romans. This will not remain without consequences.

In 116 BC, the local government of Aquileia makes a representation in Rome of the gravity of the threat looming over the city caused by a change in the attitude of the Galli Carni toward the Romans (northern Gauls of Friuli, living in Carnia?). Consul Marcus Aemilius Scaurus, in agreement with the Senate of Rome, decides to intervene. The campaign begins in Aquileia and is a blitzkrieg: it lasts less than three weeks (from 15 November to 8 December 115). Scaurus cut the Galli Carni to pieces, forcing the survivors to retreat. Moreover, he accumulates rich spoils of war, which also includes numerous prisoners who will be sold as slaves. Scaurus' success is very significant: it allows Rome to extend its sovereignty in the northeastern corner of Italy, up to the Carnic and Julian Alps, and its influence to the regnum Noricum and even extending behind these mountains. Even the *regnum Noricum* recognizes the hegemony of Rome and agrees to bind itself to it with a *foedus* and, therefore, to pay tribute to Rome and to provide the Roman army with military aid upon request. In short, it has become a friend and an ally state of Rome, in practice a client-state or satellite-state. The value of Scaurus' success is not only military and political but also economic. In fact, the agreement with the regnum Noricum also concerns trade. In order to stimulate local production, to better organize traffic, to control trade routes, and to introduce the way of life of the Romans to the Norici, an emporium is established in Noreia for the exchange of semi-finished and finished products (glass, terracotta, metal ingots, animals, wool, resin, wax, honey, and others), open to Latin and Italic merchants.

While celebrating his triumph (*FastCons.* I.I.XIII, fasc. I, p. 85), Scaurus announces that he will allocate his part of the war booty to finance the reconstruction of a temple on the Capitoline, that of the Fides Publica, a divinity whose cult began in Rome under the reign of Numa Pompilius, the first successor of Romulus, with the construction of a chapel, which was later replaced by a temple. Scaurus thus becomes one of the protagonists of the development process of the urban decoration of Rome, in imitation of the patrons of similar works who preceded him, including his grandfather-in-law, Quintus Caecilius Metellus Macedonicus (210–116 BC), who had been praetor in Macedonia in 148 BC, who had won the Fourth Macedonian War (149–148 BC), and who, on the occasion of the celebration of his triumph, had announced the construction of the Porticus Metelli, a monumental portico that encloses a square, with two temples in the middle, to be located on the Campus Martius.

The reconstruction work on the Temple of Fides Publica will be completed in 109 BC. The new building will have a rectangular plan, which will be 30–35 m long and 20 m wide. It will have a six-column portico on the facade (it will not have external columns on the remaining sides) and a much more developed cella than the space between the cella and the columns, used as an atrium or vestibule. The cella will be decorated with prominent columns and niches.

A rebellion in Dalmatia (78 BC)

The Dalmatians have fought and been beaten by the Romans several times: in 156–155, in 129, and in 117 BC, when they were defeated by Lucius Caecilius Metellus, who for this reason was called Delmaticus. However, they never gave up and remained refractory to the dominion of Rome. The peace would last for 40 years. In 78 BC, the year of the consuls Marcus Aemilius Lepidus and Quintus Lutatius Catulus, the Dalmatians rebel. The repression of the revolt ends in 76 BC when proconsul Caius Cosconius takes Salona (Solin), an emporium of the Greek city of Tragurion (Trogir in Dalmatia, Croatia). In those same years, Rome also fights against the Iapodes and

Map 2. The urbanistic layout of Aquileia in the Late Roman Republic

penetrates deeper and deeper into the Balkan region. Furthermore, in 76 BC, Caius Scribonius Curio, proconsul of Macedonia, begins a campaign against the Scordisci. Macedonia, we recall, has been a Roman province since 148 BC. This is largely the result of the annexation of the territory of the four republics which had been established in place of the Kingdom of Macedon, dissolved in 167 BC after the Battle of Pydna (168 BC), which marked the definitive defeat of King Perseus in the Third Macedonian War. It also includes part of Albania and the Stobi area and extends east to Thrace and south to Mount Olympus, encompassing Epirus and Thessaly. Furthermore, in 146 BC, the territories of central and southern Greece were added to Macedonia, and, in 126 BC, the territories of Chersonesus Thracicus (Gallipoli Peninsula) and the island of Aegina were added too. The Macedonian province is governed by a proconsul based in Thessalonica (Thessaloniki).

Scribonius Curio was a tribune of the plebeians in 90 BC. He participated in the First Mithridatic War (89–85 BC), playing a decisive role in taking Athens. Returning to Italy in 83 BC, he benefited from his friendship with Sulla. In 76 BC, he is consul, and then he was appointed to govern Macedonia. He fights for three years against the Scordisci, who, we recall, live in northern Serbia, therefore between the Noricum and the Danube and between the lower courses of the Morava and the Sava. In 73 BC, he and his legion are the first Roman soldiers to come within sight of the Danube. In 72 BC, Curio fights against the Dardani, who occupy Moesia (Kosovo and central-southern Serbia), together with the Moesi and the Triballi. Returning to Rome, he celebrates a triumph. All the operations we have mentioned started from Aquileia.

Notes

1   The ancient Greeks called the Gauls who were living in Europe *Keltòi* ("Celts") and their settlement area *Keltiké* ("Celtic"), while they called the Celts of Anatolia *Galatai* and their area of settlement *Galatia*. *Galli* is instead the collective name that the Romans used for both the *Keltòi* and the *Galatai.*

2   Not to be confused with the Via Flaminia, built in 220 BC by Caius Flaminius Nepos, father of our Flaminius, to connect Rome with Ariminum (Rimini).

3   In 7 BC, the year in which Augustus introduced his administrative reform of Italy, the eastern border of *Regio X Venetia et Histria* was set at the Arsa river. In the 2nd century, it was moved forward, up to the Eneo river. At that point, *Regio X* included Friuli, including Carnia and the Tarvisiano area; Venezia Giulia (bordered to the east by the ridge of the Julian Alps); the Karst; Istria; Trentino and a part of Alto Adige; Veneto; and also the territories of Cremona, Brescia, and Mantua.

4   Liv. 40.34 (*Aquileia colonia Latina eodem anno in agrum Gallorum est deducta. tria milia peditum quinquagena iugera, centuriones centena, centena quadragena equites acceperunt*); Zonar. 8.20.10; Bandelli 1981; 1999: 285–301. The criteria that presided over the assignment of the plots to the Venetian settlers are unknown. Unless you think that they were ex-soldiers too, already framed in auxiliary units, organized in the same way as the Roman army.

5   The scene is depicted in a beautiful bas-relief found by chance in 1931 in Aquileia, which was recomposed from two large fragments and splinters.

6   Liv. 60.18 (*Comitia consulibus rogandis fuere: creati P. Cornelius Lentulus M. Baebius Tamphilus. praetores inde facti duo Q. Fabii, Maximus et Buteo, Ti. Claudius Nero Q. Petilius Spurinus M. Pinarius Rusca*

L. Duronius. his inito magistratu prouinciae ita sorte euenerunt: Ligures consulibus, praetoribus Q. Petilio urbana, Q. Fabio Maximo peregrina, Q. Fabio Buteoni Gallia); Liv. 40.36 (*Q. Fabio Buteoni prorogatum in Gallia imperium est*).

7 We refer to the ancient settlement located in southern Istria, Croatia, between the villages of Muntić and Valtura. The original Istrian name of this place is unknown.

8 Liv. 41.8: "The elections were then held, in which Caius Claudius Pulcher and Tiberius Sempronius Gracchus were chosen consuls. Next day the following persons were elected praetors, Publius Aelius Tubero, a second time, Caius Quintus Flamininus, Caius Numisius, Lucius Mummius, Cneius Cornelius Scipio, and Publius Valerius Levinus. Claudius obtains Istria. Claudius assumed the administration, a cursory mention only was made of the provinces of Sardinia and of Istria, (...) that were involved in war." A reference to the war in Istria is found in Polyb. 25.4.

9 Possibly, this is the *phrourion* ("fortress") mentioned by Strabo (5.1.9, 215c): "After the Timavo there is the coast of the Istri up to Pula, which belongs to Italy. In the middle is the fortress of Tergeste, which is 180 stadiums from Aquileia." Strabo (60 BC–AD 21/24), in attributing Istria to Italy, implicitly refers to the fact that Istria was included by Augustus in the *Regio X Venetia et Histria*.

10 Until recently, no significant archaeological materials dating back to before the 1st century BC had been found on the hill of San Giusto in the urban area of Trieste. For this reason, some scholars had hypothesized that the primitive settlement of Tergeste, the predecessor of the Roman colony planted on that hill in the middle of the 1st century BC, was to be found elsewhere, namely in the relatively fertile and water-rich area between the Rosandra and the Ospo (San Rocco), where material and structures attributable to the 2nd century BC and to the oldest Roman fortifications in the far northeast of Italy were found, imposing structures strategically placed a short distance from a water source—the Rosandra—and in the most protected part of the bay of Muggia. Lastly, evidence of the existence of a prehistoric settlement has been found on that hill. Indications of pre-Roman settlements have also emerged in the peripheral areas of Trieste and on Monte Grisa, a locality located on the Karst edge, near Trieste. In Piazza della Cattedrale (Colle di San Giusto), an arrangement of stones of different shapes and sizes and with a north–south trend emerged during excavations for the reconstruction of the gas, water, and electricity networks in connection with a circular area, burned by fire and partly covered by an accumulation of ash. This would turn out to be the remains of a hut built with the use of perishable materials, with a hearth in the center. A second-floor level, located north of the first, could indicate more levels of use of the structure. The material associated with the structures consists of fragments of pottery from the 9th to the 6th century BC. Therefore, the Colle di San Giusto must have been occupied by man at the latest by the end of the Bronze Age or the beginning of the Iron Age. A pillar 1.2 m high and attributable to a more recent era, executed with great care and covered with white plaster on three of its four sides, was also found in the site's area. This could testify to the existence of an important public building in the period prior to the colony of the 1st century BC, perhaps a portico or a sanctuary overlooking the northern edge of the plateau.

11 A fenced area of rectangular shape, oriented north–south, of 165 × 134 m, with a smaller perimeter inside (100 × 43 m) of different orientation, was found on Mount Grociana Piccola, in the Triestine Karst, in the area of the Castelliere of Slivia, 5–7 km beyond the Bocche del Timavo and 7 km from the ancient port of Stramare, one of the first landing points in the Istrian region. The structure could be the *castrum* described by Titus Livius since, in addition to dry limestone walls, some fragments of amphorae of the Lamboglia 2 type, which belong to a type produced between the end of the 2nd century BC and the beginning of the 1st century BC, were also collected on the site, as well as some hobnails from *caligae*, typical Roman military shoes. The structure, therefore, dates back to the end of the 2nd century, but it could be

older. A large central military camp and a smaller fort, located immediately south of the main camp, were found in San Rocco and Montedoro, both of which are located in the Muggia area, near Trieste. Among the ceramic fragments found in San Rocco, some belong to Greek-Italic amphorae of the first half of the 1st century BC, imported from Lazio and Campania. However, the camp already existed in the second half of the 2nd century. The archaeological evidence we are talking about, all from the Late Republican Age, refers to the oldest military structures documented in Europe so far.

12 Liv. 43.1.5–6: *querentes coloniam suam novam et infirmam necdum satis inter infestas nationes Histrorum et Illyriorum esse.*

13 Liv. 43.17.1: *Eo anno postulantibus Aquileiensium legatis, ut numerus colonorum augeretur, mille et quingentae familiae ex senatus consulto scriptae triumuirique, qui eas deducerent, missi sunt T. Annius Luscus, P. Decius Subulo, M. Cornelius Cethegus.*

14 Located 5 miles south of Lezhë in Albania, perhaps adjacent to the site of Pezana, near the Mati.

15 Isidorus, *Orig.* 6.5.1: *Romae primus librorum copiam advexit Aemilius Paulus, Perse Macedonum rege devicto.*

16 Polybius probably expanded the *Historiai*'s master plan in the course of its construction, which at first might have been limited to the period 220–168 BC, considered in the preface as "the 53 years that changed the world". The problem is relevant in order to establish when the author started writing the work, whether after 160 BC or after 144 BC.

17 The *Historiai* narrate the historical events of the East and the West from the beginning of the Punic Wars (264 BC) to the destruction of the foundations of Carthage and Corinth (146 BC). Of his 40 books, only the first five have come down to us in full; all the others are known through excerpts (in particular, through the following: books 1–16 and 18 in the Vaticanus Urbinas code and books 18–39 in the *Excerpta historica* edited by Emperor Constantine VII Porphyrogenitus, 10th century AD). The structure of the *Historiai* is as follows. Books 1–2: after a preface, in which the principles of the Polybian historiographic method are exposed, the facts from 264 BC (outbreak of the Punic Wars) to 220 BC (prodrome of the second) are briefly narrated. Books 3–5 give a detailed exposition of the facts up to 216 BC (Battle of Cannae). Book 6 is an excursus on the theory of constitutions. Books 7–11 provide the facts after Cannae, arranged according to an annalistic method. Book 12 is a polemical excursus on previous historians, in particular on Timaeus of Tauromenium. Books 13–39 provide the historical facts up to 144 BC, these too according to an annalistic method, except to reserve more space for more recent facts (books 30–39). Book 34 is a geographical excursus. Book 40 is a chronological review. Cicero also mentions a Polybian monograph on the theme of the Numantine War, which ended in 133 BC.

18 Serbia is a territory located east of the Dinaric Alps between the Danube and the Balkan Peninsula. It borders Hungary, Romania, Bulgaria, North Macedonia, Kosovo (which separates it from Albania), Montenegro, Bosnia-Herzegovina, and Croatia.

19 The Triballi were a tribe of Thracians, wild and warlike. They were based in the lowlands that stretch between Serbia and Bulgaria.

20 In the beginning, the Autariati were the largest and most powerful Illyrian tribe. Later, they Celtized and mixed with the Scordisci.

21 The Tisza originates from different springs in the Eastern Carpathians in Ukraine and Romania, crosses the Hungarian plain, receiving tributaries from left and right, and joins the Danube, on its left side, in Vojvodina (Serbia).

22 The *gens Fulvia* was a family clan of plebeian origin. It included the Bambalio, Centumalusm Curvus, Flaccus, Gillo, Nacca, Nobilior, Paetinus, Veratius or Neratius families.

23 [FAVSTEIS] SIGNEIS CONSI[LIEIS PRAECIPV]OS TVDITANVS / [ITA ROMA]E EGIT TRVMPV[M, AEDEMQVE] DEDIT TIMAVO / [SACRA PAT]RIA EI RESTITV[IT, ATQVE MAGIST]REIS TRADIT. On this subject: Bandelli 1989: 111; Braccesi 1972; Strazzulla 1987. Two inscriptions attest to

the presence of Tuditanus in Aquileia: the titulus attributable to the tradition of the *tabulae triumphales,* of urban origin, which on two mutilated blocks recalls the dedication placed by Tuditanus to the deified Temavus (hereinafter a triumphal inscription) and the less mentioned fragment of a large base, found reused in the Castle of Duino (Trieste) that probably came from the nearby sanctuary of Fons Timavi (agro Aquileia), where his name and position can be read. See Chiabà 2013: 107–125 with its extensive bibliography. Among the titles mentioned in that article, the following should be noted: Bandelli 1984: 97, n. 2; 1989: 111–131; Brusin 1968: 15–28; Fontana 1997: 178–179, n. 4, 361, fig. 1; Lettich 2003: 40, n. 32; Strazzulla 1990: 297. In the latter, the traditional definition of the elogium of the Aquileian inscription (predominant after the 1907 work of A. von Premerstein) is challenged and a classification of the text as a *tabula triumphalis* is proposed (an idea already suggested by H. Dessau). This latter interpretation is commonly accepted in later literature.

24   A work in seven books, of which only a few fragments are preserved. These are collected in Buhrens 1884 and Weichert 1830.

25   It seems that Caecilius Metellus' consular colleague, Lucius Aurelius Cotta, also participated in this campaign. Smith 1867: I, 867. Broughton 1951: I, 525.

26   The Temple of the Dioscuri was made of cappellaccio masonry (square work), was of the Italic type, with three cellas and a deep pronaos, and had an architectural decoration in terracotta. In 160 BC, it underwent a transformation, linked to the institution of the court mentioned in the main text: the pronaos was made shallower and the front part of the podium was lowered and covered with peperino slabs so that it could be used as a court. The temple was surrounded by columns on three sides (the side without columns was the one at the back). The cella floor was in white mosaic. When the building was rebuilt, the podium consisted of three concrete structures, respectively for the cella, the pronaos, and the court in front, with the outermost walls of the oldest podium used as foundations for the side columns. A tribune would take his place on the podium, which could be used to deliver political speeches and as a presiding forum during legislative rallies. The new building had the same orientation as the previous one, compared to which it was slightly larger, however. It had eight columns on the front and a row of columns on each side except at the back. Between the intercolumns on the eastern side were a few bankers' shops. The columns and the entablature were in travertine covered with stucco. The cella had walls in Aniene tuff blocks, interior walls decorated with three columns each, and a mosaic floor, with a border decorated with a polychrome meander seen in perspective.

Chapter 2

Caesar's seat for Illyrian affairs

A situation of tension is created in Transalpine Gaul

Consul Caius Iulius Caesar has taken possession of his office in 59 BC with great plans and ambitions, curious to know what his fate will bring. To reach his goal of being elected by the people gathered in the assembly he made many debts and he is now in search of a military success that allows him to accumulate a substantial spoil of war and grow in power and prestige (his aim is to equal Pompey and Crassus). Currently, he watches over the Gallia Cisalpina and Illyricum, which form a Roman province, being understood as a geographical area under the responsibility of a Roman magistrate. Gallia Cisalpina encompasses the whole of northern Italy, while the Illyricum corresponds to the Roman territories along the eastern Adriatic coast. Caesar's term is expiring, but the *Lex Vatinia de provinciis Caesaris*, just approved in Rome, has already appointed him proconsul as well as for Gallia Cisalpina and Illyricum, also for Gallia Narbonensis, for five years.

The Roman province of Gallia Narbonensis stretches from the Alps to the Pyrenees, and from the Mediterranean coast to the northern edge of Massif Central (Auvergne). Its capital is Narbo Martius (Narbona, present-day Narbonne in southwestern France). The double charge of Caesar implies the command of four legions, of which three, for the most part, are headquartered in Aquileia, the most important military base north of Rome. Therefore, Caesar must be concerned as much with the affairs of the Roman Gauls (Cisalpina, Norbonensis), as with the affairs concerning the Illyricum. For this purpose, he uses to spend the winter in Gallia Cisalpina, preferably in Aquileia, from where he can also take care of Illyrian affairs, and the rest of the year in Gallia Narbonensis.

In 58, Proconsul Caesar is in Gallia Narbonensis when the Aedui call for help from the Romans, appealing to the treaty of friendship and alliance with Rome in force, because they are menaced by the Germans of Alsace. The Edui have always been and are currently friends and allies of the Romans, of whom they consider themselves brothers and relatives.

In the past, the Edui and their allies were one of the blocks that, in the Celtic universe of Gallia Narbonensis, competed for primacy. The other block was made up of the Arverni and their allies, the Sequani. The Aedui live in the Nivernese and Burgundy areas, between the Loire and Saone rivers. The Arverni, in turn, live in Auvergne. The Sequani, in the upper basin of the Saone (Franche-Comté and part of Burgundy).

The blocks mentioned confronted each other for many years, then the Aedui were finally defeated and had to hold their noblest citizens hostage to the victors and pledge not to ask the Romans for help. The Aedui harbored revenge and prepared the war. In 61–60, the Arverni and the Sequani, in view of the resumption of the fight against the Aedui, hired 15,000 mercenaries, led by Ariovistus, a prince of the Cherusci, who served in the Roman army as commander of an auxiliary formation, a Cheruscan cohort. The Cherusci are a tribe of the German people of the Suebi, very warlike.

Ariovistus and his warriors crossed the Rhine and defeated the Aedui. After that, they settled in Alsace. Over time, they have been joined by many other Germans, so much so that the number of Germans in Alsace has grown to 120,000. Lastly, 24,000 Arudi arrived. To house them, Ariovistus ordered the Sequani to cede a third of their land. At that point, the Sequani understood that Ariovistus had become their master, they made peace with the Aedui, and, together with them, they faced the Germans of Alsace. On 15 March 60, a great battle took place at the Gallic fortress of Admagetobriga, with the final defeat of the Aedui and Sequani.[1]

In the same period in which the Edui and the Sequani call for help from the Romans to be defended by the Germans of Alsace, some peoples of different discent, culture and origin, all together, undertake a mass migration in order to reach the lands of the Santoni, in the southwest of Transalpine Gaul, north of Burdigala (Bordeaux, southwestern France).[2] They are the Celtic Aurici, Boi, and Latovici, the Helvetian Tigurini, and the German Tulingi, Latobrogi, and Rauraci. In all, 368,000, they are between men, women, and children, of which about 90,000 are able to handle a weapon.[3] From now on, we will collectively call all these peoples Helvetians, unless otherwise specified.

The migrants set fire to their inhabited centers to make them unusable by anyone else and start a slow westward movement. When they arrive on the shores of Lake Geneva, they are undecided as to which path to take. They can choose between three different itineraries: crossing Narbonne Gaul, taking a route immediately further north, between the Rhone and the Jura massif, or passing even further north. The first option would be the best, were it not for the fact that it involves crossing the Roman province. The second itinerary is longer and the route is narrow and difficult. The third is the worst alternative because it brings them straight into the mouth of the Germans. Their chieftains decide to go through Narbonne Gaul, and, to find out how the Romans will react, they send an embassy to Caesar.

Caesar intervenes

Caesar was aiming for a war of conquest in the Western Balkans, but the call for help of the Edui and the Sequani, and the threat implied in the mass migration of the Helvetians causes him to revise his plans. He decides to intervene for two main reasons, he says: 1) the transit of migrants will cause large-scale destruction and looting, and will push the Allobroges to break the alliance with Rome; 2) if the lands in the Swiss plateau that have been vacated by migrants are occupied by the Germans, the Romans will have very warlike and ferocious neighbors, and this could pose a danger to them.

First of all, he strengthens the army. To this end, he returns to Gallia Cisalpina, where he will enlist two legions—the XI and the XII—bypassing the Senate of Rome, which is the constitutional organ legally entitled to ban the draft. Then he goes to Aquileia, from where it will restart shortly after, at the head of three other legions—the VII, VIII, and IX—and the relative support troops, made available by the allies (in Latin, *auxilia*) (Caes. I.10.3.). Finally, he sets off again to return to Gallia Narbonensis with five legions, reinforced by the auxilia.

When they arrive in northwestern Italy, Caesar's army undertakes the Via Domitia, the road about 480 km long, built by Cnaeus Domitius Henobarbus between 120 and 118 to connect Italy to Spain through France, and elevated by Pompey the Great to the rank of the military road. The Via Domitia is the easiest way to cross the Western Alps. It starts from Augusta Taurinorum (Turin) and connects the Val Susa and the Durance and Rhone valleys, crossing the Cottian Alps—the stretch of the Alpine chain that goes from Monviso to Moncenisio—at the Pass of Mons Matrona (present-day Montgenèvre, 1854 m).

The passes of the Western Alps are under the control of local populations. Every crossing implies the payment of a toll, every provision of services must be paid, and the agreements concluded by the Romans with these tribes are not often respected.[4] The passes of the Cottian Alps, in particular, are in the hands of the Celtic-Ligurians, very primitive people, who are traditionally hostile to the Romans and practice banditry at the expense of travelers. We refer to the Ceutroni, living in the upper Isère valley; the Graioceli of the Moncenisio Pass, and the Caturigi of the Montgenèvre Pass.

The crossing of the Cottian Alps by Caesar's army begins in Ocelum (near Avigliana, west of Turin in the Susa valley). The column is about to cross the Passo of the Mons Matrona when the Ceutroni, stationed on the heights, try to block his way, despite its very considerable size. But the Romans repel the attackers in a series of clashes and continue the march (Caes. I.10). The crossing of the Alps lasts six days. On the sixth day, Caesar and his army reach the territory of the Voconzi, in Transalpine Gaul (Caes. VII.34). From there, Caesar passes into the lands of the Allobrogi and then into those of the Segusiavi, beyond the Rhine. Meanwhile, he assumed command of legio X "Equestris", or "Veneria", which was headquartered for the winter in Narbonne.

In all, Caesar disposes of six legions, for a total of 24,200 combatants, of which 19,200 are legionaries, 3,000 are Cretan archers and 2,000 are Balearic slingers, specialized troops, necessary to integrate the main military action. In addition, he has a number of support troops. In particular, Numidian light infantry, probably javelin throwers; local infantry, recruited from the faithful tribes (10,000 Aedui) (Caes. VIII, 10), and even German infantry. He has no legionary cavalry, made up of Roman citizens, except for a few trusted gatekeepers, but of 2,000 knights between Numidians and Hispanics, divided into four *alae* (allied cavalry formations, deployed on the battlefield at either end of the legion lineup). Since the reform of the army and the draft introduced by Caius Marius in the last years of the 2nd century BC, the legions of Roman citizens are formed only by heavy infantry.

For some time, he has been thinking of going to war against Ariovistus to push him back beyond the Rhine. Before moving in this direction, however, he wants to verify if it is possible to avoid conflict. He uselessly asks Ariovistus for a meeting to negotiate an agreement. Despite the silence of his counterpart, he warns him not to bring other Germans to the Gallic bank of the Rhine, to return the hostages, and not to cause any other offense to the Aedui and their allies, threatening him with the consequences. Ariovistus replies scornfully.

Caesar is tempted to lash out at him with his legions, but prudence suggests he strengthen himself preliminarily to be more sure of winning. Furthermore, his most pressing problem at the moment is that of preventing the passage of migrants through the Roman territory. First, he strengthens the static defenses of the border. Among other things, he has a 5 m high wall erected, which runs for 28 km along the border, parallel to a moat. Then, he leaves Gallia Narbonensis temporarily to gather other troops. He delegates the command to his lieutenant Titus Labienus and orders him to prevent illegal immigrants from gaining access to the province, resorting to force if necessary. He then rapidly returns to Italy.

During the winter of 59–58 BC, Caesar recruits soldiers in Gallia Cisalpina, bypassing the Senate of Rome, the constitutional body that is exclusively responsible for banning military drafts. He manages to enlist as many recruits as needed to form two legions and, at the beginning of the spring of 58, he sets off again for Gallia Narbonensis at the head of three legions and auxiliary troops (the third legion is one of those stationed in Aquileia).[5] Along the way, he clashes with the Celtic-Ligurians who control the passes of the Western Alps.

The Gallic War breaks out

On 2 April 58, Caesar receives the migrant ambassadors, headed by Nammeius and Verucletius, who inform him of the orientation of their leaders to pass through Narbonne Gaul. He pretends that he is willing to consent but postpones any decision until 13 April. His intention is quite different. As soon as the legates have left, he orders to destroy the bridge over the Rhone near Geneva, to fortify in record time the left bank of the river, from Lake Geneva to the Jura massif, and to prepare to repel any attempt to force the wall. A 5 m high embankment, 28 km long, is thus built, interspersed with towers and forts, and preceded by a moat, thanks to the discipline, organization, and expertise of the legionaries, who are fighters, but also, if necessary, engineers, commanded by engineers and architects.

On 13 April, the ambassadors return to Caesar and learn that their request is rejected and that migrants are warned against entering the Roman territory. During the subsequent weeks, the Helvetians try in vain to overcome the barrier, on boats, rafts, or simply by swimming. Eventually, they give up and change their itinerary, choosing to go further north, through the lands of the Sequani and the Aedui, between the Rhone river and the Jura massif. The Sequani allow them to pass on conditions that hostages are handed over to them. The Helvetians then enter the lands of the Aedui. The dreaded devastation takes place there. The Aedui resist, but ask Caesar for help, making available 2,000 soldiers on horseback. Caesar leaves some cohorts to guard the fortified stretch of the state border, commanded by Titus Labienus, and leads four legions—20,000 legionaries and 4,000 knights—to the lands of the Aedui, where he will supply himself with food. His cavalry is formed, for the most part, by Aedui. The first is commanded by Lucius Aelius, the latter by Publius Licinius Crassus, the youngest son of the triumvir Crassus.

On 6 June 58, three legions attack the Tigurini as they cross the Saone river (at the confluence of this river with the Rhone), at night, loaded with luggage, and behind all the other migrants. It is carnage. The survivors hide in the thick vegetation that forms the riparian belt, the interface between the land and the watercourse. Thus begins—with the extermination of a people on the way, who did not show hostility and were treacherously attacked in a difficult situation—the conquest of Gaul, even if, at the moment, no one realizes it, because no one can foresee the future. But it is only the first of the many massacres that will punctuate the course of that enterprise. In the end, it will be possible to speak of a genocide committed against the Helvetians in Gaul and a part of the Transalpine Gauls.

Caesar's account of his campaigns beyond the Alps

At the end of the fighting, the balance of the Gallic War (58–51) will be the extension of the sovereignty of Rome to the center and north of Transalpine Gaul, paid for by the vanquished with 1,200,000 dead and 1,000,000 prisoners of war, made slaves.[6] There will be those who, among the most warned Romans, will bluntly consider that undertaking as an outrage to mankind.

Caesar will narrate the development of his military campaigns beyond the Alps in a commentary, both to recount his military exploits, and the many curiosities about the habits and customs of the Gauls and Germans, with the addition of elements of propaganda and defense of their work. To this end, it will set up within its staff an office for the written elaboration of the reports of the war operations, so that the latter will serve as a basis for the drafting of the reports intended for public opinion, but first of all for the Senate of Rome, so that it is convinced of the need to support it.

A commentary is, in this case, a writing of personal memories, or a historical tale, mostly with a strong apologetic tone, but without a particular stylistic elaboration, of which the author is also the protagonist or one of the protagonists. In any case, it is based on a sketch of notes on disparate topics taken graded by the author and referring to his entire life or to a period of it; therefore, it is an author's diary, intended as a chronicle, or a collection of daily annotations in which significant facts, political, social, economic events, scientific observations, etc., are described.

Caesar loved to write and publish his writings. He had already published some prayers and other compositions, including a tragedy (Oedipus), a poem (The praises of Hercules),[7] and a collection of maxims. To write his commentary, he will draw inspiration from the Anabasis of Xenophon, and from the Ephemerides of Alexander the Great, a chronicle of the exploits of Macedonian, which was compiled day-by-day by a team coordinated by Eumenes of Cardia and personally controlled by Alexander himself. He will finish the work only in 52, then he will publish it between 51 and 50 with the title *C. Iulii Caesaris commentarii rerum gestarum*, or more simply *De bello gallico*, "The Gallic War", and it will go down in history as one of the major works of Latin literature. The work will consist of seven books.[8] Later, Caesar will also write another commentary, on the civil war against Pompey (49–48), in three books. But we will talk about this later.

Caesar's commentaries are works similar to the memoirs of Publius Rutilius Rufus, Quintus Lutatius Catulus Caesar, Marcus Aemilius Scaurus, and Lucius Cornelius Sulla, all typologically referable to the so-called memorialist vein of Latin literature, which was added at the end of the 2nd century to the traditional annalistic and monographic strands, and currently represents the beginnings of autobiography.

The destruction of the Helvetians (Caes. I.24–28)

After having destroyed the Tigurini, Caesar instructs his engineers to build a bridge over the Saône in a single day and leads his men to the opposite bank of the river, despite the fact that Roman law forbids the governors to leave the province with an army of their competence and to unleash a war without the authorization of the Senate and the consuls. He then negotiates with the Helvetians, without reaching an agreement that avoids confrontation. Therefore, he chases the imposing column of the migrant-invaders. Four-thousand soldiers on horseback, under the command of Lucius Aemilius, control it from a distance while it winds its way along the road to Bibracte, remaining between 7.5 and 9 km away. Every now and then they come closer and tease the rear.

Bibracte is the political, economic, and religious capital of the Aedui and one of the main hillforts of Gaul (the Romans will call it Augustodunum). It is located at the top of Mont Beuvray (821 m) and dominates the confluence of the Saone, Yonne,

Seine, and Loire river basins, where various trans-European itineraries intertwine. Mont Beuvray is part of the Morvan massif (present-day in the commune of Saint-Léger-sous-Beuvray, near Autun in Burgundy-Franche-Comté). It is a lump of volcanic rocks, cloaked in the woods. The area is rich in mineral resources.

Caesar is short of supplies and wants to reach Bibracte, to ensure the necessary supplies, before facing the migrants. His six legions (25,000 men in all, all Roman citizens), their support troops (4,000–5,000, mostly Aedui), and their non-combat personnel (10,000), are now about 25 km south of Bibracte and 3 km from the Helvetians. They are the Tenth, which Caesar sent from Spain, the Seventh, the Eighth, and the Ninth, which he himself led from Aquileia to Gaul, as well as the Eleventh and Twelfth, which he recruited in haste in Gallia Cisalpina. The combatants wear a feathered helmet and breastplate, loricata or segmented; they are equipped with a rectangular shield and are armed with two javelins and a short, sharp-tipped sword.

The Romans and their allies are marching towards Bibracte when the fighting forces of the migrants—60,000 Helvetians and 15,000 between Boi and Tulingi— attack the 4,000 mounted soldiers who are tailing the column. Caesar responds by having a hill occupied and the legions deployed in several rows. The deployment takes place amidst trumpet blasts, waving banners and clouds of dust, raised by the studded sandals of the soldiers and the hooves of the pack animals and by the wagons carrying the complex of food, wagons, ammunition, and baggage. The Seventh, Eighth and Ninth, as well as the auxiliaries, create three lines of defense halfway up the hill. The baggage stores are gathered higher up, inside ditches dug in haste.

The Helvetians overwhelm the cavalry of Lucius Aemilius, which is dispersed; then they move forward to the base of the hill. They are armed with a helmet adorned with horsehair, a small breastplate, a round shield, and a long spear. The Helvetians arrange themselves to form phalanxes, then gather the phalanxes into a single cluster of spearmen. At the start of the battle—a mournful sound of the horn—they climb up the hill and are greeted by the Romans, with a dense throw of javelins, which opens countless gaps in their ranks and prevents the survivors from using the shield because the javelins stick into it and cannot be drawn easily. Immediately afterwards the Romans attack, throwing themselves down the hill, with the gladius unsheathed.

The Helvetians resist the impact as long as they can, then split up: one part remains on the hill, faced by the Tenth, the rest folds, and retreats for over a kilometer, towards the circle of wagons. They are pursued by the Seventh, the Eighth, the Ninth, who advance at a marching pace and in battle formation (the Eleventh and Twelfth remain on the hill, guarding the baggage). Fifteen-thousand between Boi and Tulingi attack the Romans on the right flank. Some of the Romans faced the attack, the remainder continued the pursuit.

Finally, the Helvetians reach the circle of wagons and barricade themselves inside. Meanwhile, 132,000 women, the elderly, and children have evacuated the place and set off on their way to the Vosges. We fight until the evening on the hill and until late at night around the wagons, with the immense massacre. The Helvetians hold out, but are eventually overwhelmed. Most of them fall in combat. A few thousand flees, but they are chased, pursued, hunted down, and hit relentlessly. The survivors surrender. Among others, there are many non-combatants and some young people from noble families. Counting the victims is impossible: there are too many—hundreds of thousands—for the most part Helvetians. Their bodies will remain unburied. All the goods of the vanquished become the war spoils of the victors and are divided between officers and soldiers.

The women, the elderly and the children, and 6,000 defeated warriors, fleeing towards the Vosges, are pursued. They all surrender, except the warriors, who are rounded up and killed by the Celtic allies of the Romans. Prisoners are treated with leniency. They are returned to the Swiss plateau—with the exception of 20,000 Boi, who will remain in the area as "customers" of the Aedui—but not before they have been forced to work for the Aedui, to repair the damage caused by migration. Thus, the migration of the Helvetians to Transalpine Gaul ends with the return of the surviving migrants to their areas of origin. Just then Ariovistus reappears.

The Germans are defeated and put to flight

Sixteen-thousand Arudi, Marcomanni, Nemeti, Sedusi, Suebi, Triboci, and Vangioni, all headed by Ariovistus, are about to invade the lands of the Aedui and the Sequani when Caesar rushes to the aid of the latter. The legions reach Vesontio in forced marches (Besançon in Burgundy-Franche-Comté), a fortified village among the most important in Transalpine Gaul, the capital of the Sequani. Vesontio is located in a bend of the River Doubs, surrounded by hills, at the point where the Jura massif meets the vast arable plains of Franche-Comté. The Romans occupy the post and take wheat and weapons from the warehouses. When the locals describe the Germans to them as giants of incredible courage and skill in the use of weapons, they are frightened just by looking at them, the awareness of their inferiority disheartens them. Caesar stings them with pride and heartens them.

In early August 58, Caesar leaves a garrison in Vesontio, crosses the Belfort pass (on the border between France and Switzerland), intercepts the enemy, superior in number, at the foot of the Vosges, in the plain between Mulhouse and Cernay, and plants the field about 35 km away from this lowland.

Caesar and Ariovistus, each escorted by numerous soldiers on horseback, meet in a location halfway between their camps, to try to reach an agreement that avoids confrontation. The interview takes place at the foot of a hill, on the edge of the extensive plain. Caesar orders Ariovistus to stop harassing the Aedui and their allies, to return the hostages, and to not allow other Germans to cross the Rhine. Ariovistus explains that he did not come to Gaul at the request of the Sequani, who had promised him strong rewards; that the lands he occupied in Gaul were not extorted from him, but were granted to him; that the hostages were handed over to him spontaneously; and that he receives taxes, according to the law of war, those that the victors are accustomed to imposing on the vanquished. It was not he who attacked the Gauls, but it was the Gauls who attacked him. All the Gauls had taken the field against him, he repulsed and defeated them in a single battle. All this happened before Caesar and his army came out of Narbonne Gaul and pretended to be his friends when instead they aimed to overwhelm him. If Caesar withdraws, says Ariovistus, addressed to his interlocutor, he will continue to be considered a friend, he will be adequately rewarded and he will be allowed to make war on whoever he wants. Otherwise, he will be considered an enemy and killed, and this will be pleasing to many Roman citizens and will be worth their friendship to Ariovistus (Caes. I.44).

Ariovistus is still speaking when his escort, made up of impetuous young men, lashes out at Caesar's, throwing stones and other bullets. Due to that incident, Caesar withdraws from the negotiation. Then he is strengthened and remains on the defensive.

Ariovistus moves the camp closer to that of the Romans (before it was 35–36 km away, now it is 9). The next day, he gets even closer, up to 3 km away. His goal is to prevent the Aedui and Sequani from supplying the Romans with provisions. In the following days, there are continuous clashes, to engage Ariovistus using 6,000 knights and as many infantry, fast in the race (Caes. I, 48, 4–7). Caesar moves the troops closer to the enemy (the distance between the two sides is reduced to 600 paces), then sets them up so that the first two rows defend the third while it is intent on setting up the camp.

Ariovistus attacks with 16,000 men but is rejected. Caesar leaves two legions and part of the support troops to garrison the camp and leads the other four legions into a larger camp. In the meantime, he has put five legions and a quaestor at the head of his legions, pointing out how this happened occasionally and at his discretion (Caes. I.52). Furthermore, since he did not trust the Gallic auxiliary cavalry, he had the infantrymen of the X legion mounted on horseback to escort him (Caes. I.52).

The next day Ariovistus throws his entire army against the second camp of the Romans. It is fought from noon to evening, without either side being able to prevail. The decisive battle takes place the next day. Caesar goes on the offensive, making all six legions advance towards Ariovistus's camp, arranged in three ranks.

Ariovistus arranges his men outside the camp, sorting them by tribe: first the Arudi, then the Marcomanni, the Triboci, the Vangioni, the Nemeti, the Sedusi, finally the Suebi. Each tribe is perched inside a circle of wagons. Above the vehicles, the women, to incite the combatants to battle, implore them not to abandon them to the mercy of the Romans. Caesar takes the lead of the right-wing and leads the attack. The legionaries throw themselves at the enemy, who, in turn, rushes towards them, throwing javelins. At the moment of impact—very hard—hand-to-hand combat starts. The Romans put the left-wing of the enemy to flight. But the right-wing press on them and they face it with difficulty. The sending of reinforcements by the young Publius Crassus, commander of the cavalry, decides the fate of the battle. The Germans flee. The Roman cavalry pursues them as far as the Rhine, a few kilometers away, catches them while they try by any means to cross the river, and exterminates them for the most part (Caes. I.52–53). Ariovistus is saved thanks to his lucky star: at the moment of maximum danger he finds a boat tied to the shore (Caes. I, 53). When the battle is over, the plain is littered with corpses and remains. The casualties are counted. For the Germans, the loss account is terrifying: 80,000 have fallen (Appian, *Galliké*, fragment 4.22). From now on, Ariovistus will no longer disturb the sleep of the Romans, the Rhine will be the northern border of the Roman world in Western Europe for 400–500 years, and Celtic Gaul, saved by Caesar from Germanic danger, will remain subject to Rome.

Caesar's provisions for Illyricum

Caesar annexes the lands of the Sequani to Gallia Narbonensis and quarters the legions there for the winter of 58–57 BC. When spring arrives, he marches beyond Durocortorum (Reims in northern Fance). He accepts a proposal for an alliance with the Remi, inflicts severe blows on the Suessiones, Ambiani, and Nervii, and captures 50,000 prisoners, whom he will sell as slaves. He also fights victoriously on a stretch of coast between Brittany and Normandy against the Veneti and their allies. The defeated leaders are killed, and survivors are enslaved and sold. Eventually, Caesar comes back to Italy. He spends the next winters in Aquileia (57–56 and 56–55 BC).

During the winter of 57–56 BC, Caesar deals with some issues concerning Illyricum and the territory of Aquileia, toward Istria. Among other things, he strengthens Roman control over Dalmatia. He re-founds Salona, an emporium of Tragurion (Trogir in Croatia). Located on the northern side of the mouth of the Jadro river, in an ideal position for trading with the inland, Salona controls one of the few flat and fertile areas in the area. By the will of Caesar, Salona becomes a colony destined for war veterans and their families and the capital of Illyricum, the object of a major urban development program. From now on it will be called Colonia Martia Julia Salonae. Caesar also founds in Dalmatia the military colonies of Narona, at the mouth of the Neretva, and Iader.

Notes

1 The location of this site is uncertain. It is likely that it was in Alsace, near Sélestat, or on the hill of Mont Ardoux, in Pontailler-sur-Saône/Heuilley-sur-Saône.
2 The Santoni lived specifically in the area of the modern city of Saintes, which would later be built in the province and called Mediolanum Santonum. For the most part, the area (known as Saintonge) is now included in the Charente-Maritime department in France.
3 The figure of 368,000 results from some tablets inscribed in Greek characters, found by the Romans in the circle of enemy chariots. Later Caesar ordered the count of the survivors. Caes. 1.29.
4 Ralf-Peter 2018: 64.
5 Caes. 1.10: *tris quae circum Aquileiam hiemabant ex hibernis educit.*

6 Appian, *Galliké*, fragment 2, he claims that Caesar fought more than 4,000,000 individuals of 400 tribes, captured 1,000,000, killed more than 1,000,000, and subdued more than 800 cities. *Vell. Pat.*, II, 60.5, speaks instead of 400,000 dead and a greater number of prisoners.

7 The early works of Caesar have not been survived and nothing more is known about them than the respective title. It is known, however, that Octavian, after 28 BC—the year of the establishment of the large bilingual library on the Palatine Hill—forbade the superintendent of this library, Pompey Macro, to circulate them (Suet., 56). The reason for that prohibition should not be sought in the fact that, probably, they were not masterpieces, but, more likely, in the field of politics or morality. Canfora 2008: 33.

8 An additional book, the eighth, written by Aulus Irtius, narrates the collateral and subsequent events to this conflict, in particular, the expeditions to extinguish the latest outbreaks. Irtius was a legion commander in Caesar's army during the Gallic War from 54 BC onwards. During the Civil War, he sided with Caesar and fought in Spain and Asia Minor. In 46 BC, he became praetor. In 45 BC, he became proconsul for Transalpine Gaul. In 44 BC, he was consul. He fell in the Battle of Modena on 21 April of that year.

Chapter 3

The capital of the *Regio X-Venetia et Histria*

The Iapodes attack Tergeste

The Iapodes are an Illyrian people, whose culture has been strongly influenced by the Celts. They live in the interior of the eastern Adriatic region, north of the Liburnian lands and east of Istria, between the Colapis (Kupa) and Oineo (Una) rivers and the Mons Baebius (Alpi Bebie, central Croatian hinterland and valley of the Una river in Bosnia-Herzegovina). In particular, they live on the slopes of the Albii mountains, which extend from the borders of Istria to the Una basin and meet the sea at the Bocche del Carnaro. They are divided into various tribes, each of which is centered on a main fortified village. Their major centers are Vendone, Arupio, Monezio, and Metulo. The Iapodes are devoted to Bindo, a divinity equivalent to the Greek god Poseidon and the Roman god Neptune, whose center of the cult is a sanctuary near a spring not far from the course of the Una.

The Romans know them as individuals of robust constitution, a ferocious disposition, unfair behavior, and poor living conditions who live off raids against their neighbors. In 171, the consul Gaius Cassius Longinus, on his return from Macedonia, plundered the territory of the Iapodes. In 129, the consul Gaius Sempronius Tuditanus triumphed over the Iapodes, but his victory seems to have had a lasting effect only with regard to the tribes of the coast. Gaius Cosconius, proconsul for Illyricum, fought against the Iapodes in 78–77. In 56, the Iapodes joined Rome with a *foedus*, thus becoming friends and allies, obliged as such to pay the *tributum*. In 52, they rebel. Together with the Taurisci (the Norican tribe living in southern Austria and in Slovenia, of which we have told earlier), they swarm along the Isonzo river and through the Friuli, but they are stopped and repelled in Aquileia (App. *Ill.* 18). Unlike the Taurisci, who return to their lands, the Iapodes leave the territory of Aquileia, and lash out against Tergeste. Tergeste is devastated and plundered (Caes. 8.24).

It is necessary to specify that the Tergeste of which we are talking is a different settlement from the one located between the Rosandra valley and the Ospo, and became a "Carnic village" around 177 BC, being therefore more ancient. It is located about 35 km from Aquileia, between the Karst plateau and the shores of the Gulf of

Trieste, on the seaward side of an easily defensible hill (today's Colle San Giusto) protected from the bora, a chill wind coming from the northeast. Therefore, it occupies a somewhat secluded position with respect to the Vipava valley, the main northeastern access route to Italy, which leads to the Isonzo river and the great Friulian plain, where Aquileia is located. The local population lives mainly on commerce. This activity is practiced by land and also by sea, through the port. The sea trade of the merchants of Trieste takes place mainly with Istria, Dalmatia, the Eastern Mediterranean,[1] and the Iberian Peninsula. The port of Tergeste is an alternative to that of Aquileia for products of the eastern Adriatic coastline and a privileged port of call for the transport of timber, stone materials (limestone and sandstone), and products from Istria, especially oil, but also the wool obtained from the sheep and mountain goats in the senatorial properties and the territories of the Karst communities. For exemple, the *Tullii Crispini,* a Tergestine family, play an active part in the export of oil and olives from northern Istria to the markets of Noricum and the Drava valley and military camps in the Danube region. In 90 BC, or at the latest in 89 BC, Tergeste became a *municipium*[2] under the recent laws on citizenship *(lex Iulia de civitate latinis et sociis danda, Lex Plautia Papiria de civitate sociis danda,* and the *lex Plautia ex Pompeia de Transpadanis).* On that occasion, the city received citizenship under Latin law, a form of Roman citizenship with reduced rights.

Caesar calls in the Fifteenth Legion in order to secure the Roman citizens living in northeastern Italy from the attacks carried out through the Julian Alps. The Fifteenth is one of the legions that were enlisted in 53 in Gallia Cisalpina. It participated in the final stages of the Gallic War, in particular the sieges of Avaricum and Alesia.

The Fifteenth chase them to their territory and take Metulus after a siege. The success of that enterprise opens the way to Hungary for the Romans, and in due course the legions will walk through it, victorious, up to the Danube.

The Fifteenth is posted to Transalpine Gaul (in the winter of 52–51, it will winter among the Sequani in Vesontio, together with the Seventh Legion and the cavalry of Titus Labienus), while Caesar has the damage done to Tergeste repaired and changes its status to a Roman colony thus establishing the first Roman colony in Illyricum, assimilated in fact to the colonies of Roman citizens of northeastern Italy (Fraschetti 1975: 319–335). As part of the attribution of the status of *colonia,* Tergeste becomes a Roman administrative center with control over its own territory (Zaccaria 2001b: 95–118). It receives not only the territory and surrounding population of Castelliere di Elleri in Mugla (Muggia)—which is not yet Romanized—but perhaps also the whole of Istria. It should be remembered that, in this phase, Tergeste remains in Illyricum, therefore it is not yet part of Gallia Cisalpina, which has been a province since 1989, or since 81, and, toward the northeast, extends until the eastern limit of the Aquileian territory, the Bocche del Timavo. With this, the Roman presence in Illyricum increases, already established south of the Timavo (or rather in Istria, north of Rižana in Slovenia), from the municipium of Agida, which is mentioned in a republican inscription from Elleri/Jelarji.

Caesar strengthens the northeastern border of Italy

Caesar also takes other measures, which will mark a fundamental stage in the colonization, defensive organization, and Romanization processes of Eastern Transpadana Gaul. In this context, a formerly Venetic and Celtic settlement, which since prehistoric times has connected the Alpine and Transalpine territories to the Friulian Plain, is raised to the legal status of *forum* (pl. *fora*). The *fora* are small communities of Roman citizens established on roads of strategic and commercial interest, for economic, administrative, and military purposes, by a magistrate whose name they bear.

The settlement in question is *Forum Iulii Transpadanorum* (Cividale del Friuli), a place of considerable commercial importance, significant also from a strategic-military point of view (it is located at one of the access points that most exposes Italy to an invasion from the northeast), served by efficient and busy road links. It is primarily connected with Aquileia, about 37 km away as the crow flies, but also with Pannonia and Istria.

The roads to Pannonia and Istria both originate in Aquileia. The first heads north and toward Forum Iulii, bends decidedly toward the east, crosses the Isonzo river at Mainizza, continues toward the valley of the Frigidus river (Vipava), crosses the Julian Alps, finally enters Pannonia. The second crosses in a straight line across the plain east of Aquileia, crosses the final stretch of the Isonzo, marked by various branches of the main river, and from there continues towards Lacus Timavi (Bocche del Timavo), Tergeste, and Istria.

Caesar further reinforces the northeastern border of Italy through the strengthening of a military fort in the plain of the Middle Friuli and the establishment of another fort, in the Upper Friuli.

The first fort is that of *Ad Tricesimum* (Tricesimo), so-called because it is located about 30 Roman miles north of Aquileia. The second is that of *Iulium Carnicum* (Zuglio). This is the northernmost stronghold of northeastern Italy. In fact, it is located in the Carnic Alps—a vast mountainous territory that extends to the Alpine watershed and is traditionally occupied by the Galli Carni—specifically on the hill of San Pietro, which dominates the upper valley of the But, a tributary of the Tagliamento. This is the first place you encounter after crossing the Alpine watershed at the Passo di Monte Croce Carnico (Mainardis 2008).

The garrisons of these forts have the tasks of protecting the northeastern border of Italy from raids for the purpose of robbery and from armed invasions from the adjacent transalpine regions, and to tame any revolts that break out in the Aquileian territory (which, we recall, goes from the Livenza river to the Adriatic Sea and from the Carnic and Julian Alps to the Timavo river). That of Ad Tricesimum will guarantee the safety of extra-urban roads that go from Aquileia to the Alpine passes, while that of Iulium Carnicum will monitor entries into Italy from Noricum (in particular, from the present-day Carinthia).

Although there are some differences, all Roman forts have the same general structure and maintain a bond with the locals. They have a playing card-shaped plan, external moats, walls, four gates to the cardinal points, and, inside, barracks, officers' quarters, and workshops. Normally, the largest host between 5,000–6,000 men; the smallest, between 50 and 1,000 men. Their garrisons are made up of legionaries or auxiliaries. Generally, those who oversee the security of the political borders of the Roman state are largely auxiliaries and, therefore are not Roman citizens but troops made available by allies to reinforce the Roman army. Those who interact with the locals are therefore soldiers from other areas of the Roman world and even from outside its borders. Usually, near a fort, a settlement (*vicus*, pl. *vici*) soon develops to take advantage of the garrison's economic needs. It might be a new settlement or a settlement that develops from a pre-Roman settlement that was previously built on the same site. The *vicus* is made up of rectangular buildings of wood or stone, which serve as houses, workshops, and shops at the same time, as well as some public buildings, such as a bath and an inn. Its inhabitants provide a range of goods and services to the fort as a whole and to individual soldiers, obtaining cash in payment. The local artisans produce both traditional artifacts and other goods requested by clients: for example, traditional ceramics, characteristic Roman-style objects made on a lathe, metal artifacts, tanned leather, leather artifacts, fabrics, and clothing items. The vicissitudes associated with Roman forts allow the soldiers to have relations with local women, albeit with their observance of the limitations deriving from the prohibition for the Roman military to marry during their service (this interdiction will persist until the reign of Septimius Severus, AD 193–211). Such relationships often end up creating stable unions with children, and they are places where an exchange of cultural information takes place.

With the passage of time, each of the forts of Ad Tricesimum and Iulium Carnicum will expand, welcome families and merchants, and develops a *vicus,* that will be a civic, non-military center, with its own administrative autonomy (therefore with its own magistrates) within the colony of Aquileia. In the case of Forum Iulii, this will occur in continuity with the pre-existing structure of the area inhabited by the Galli Carni.

In 45 BC, the Partini destroy the army of Aulus Gabinus at the Battle of Sinotium (Sinji, Croatia), after which, also in 45 BC, they are attacked by a subordinate of Julius Caesar, Publius Vatinius, who fights some battles against them, though without ever being able to defeat them permanently. Later, however, the Partini apologize to Caesar for what they had done, declare their friendship to him, and offer to fight alongside him in the wars he was preparing, one in Thrace against the Getae and the other against the Parthians. An agreement is reached, on the basis of which the Partini agree to deliver hostages and pay an annual tribute. Caesar sends three legions under the command of Vatinius to enforce the conditions and receive the hostages and tribute.

Caesar dies in 44 BC, the victim of a conspiracy of senators, and, upon opening his will, it is learned that he had adopted his great-nephew Caius Octavius Thurinus, the son of Atia, who is the daughter of Julia, who in turn is the sister of Caesar. To better illustrate the family relationship, it is necessary to consider it as follows. From the marriage of Caius Julius Caesar and Aurelia Cotta, three children were born: Julia Maior, Julia Minor, and Caius (Julius Caesar). Julia Maior and Julia Minor should not be confused with the paternal aunts of the same name, one of whom, the eldest, married Caius Marius. Julia Maior was married twice—first to Lucius Pinarius and then to Quintus Pedius—and had a child in each marriage. Julia Minor married Marcus Atius Balbus,[3] a member of a senatorial family of plebeian origin, originally from Aricia,[4] a town in the Alban Hills. Atius Balbus is a relative of Cnaeus Pompeius Magnus (Pompey the Great) on his mother's side. From his marriage with Julia, two daughters were born, both named Atia. The eldest of the Atia sisters married Caius Octavius Thurinus, an *eques* from Nola in Campania, and gave birth to two children: Octavius and Octavia.

Octavianus accepts the adoption and the related, immense inheritance and, in accordance with the rules of Roman onomastics, changes his personal identity to Caius Julius Caesar Octavianus. His path takes him through the Second Triumvirate (the agreement between Octavianus, Marcus Antonius, and Marcus Aemilius Lepidus), a war against Caesars' assassins, then the Third Civil War (44–31 BC) against Antonius that will intertwine with an exterior war against Cleopatra VII's Egypt. In 41 BC, he is elected to the consulate for 40 BC. When, in 27 BC, he is acclaimed *princeps* and *augustus*, the form of government of the Roman state will change, passing from *res publica* to Principate.

Octavianus opens the way of the Central-Eastern Europe

In 44 BC, after the assassination of Caesar, the Partini denounce the agreement they had made with him and attack Vatinius. They kill about 2,500 Roman soldiers and their commander, a member of the senatorial order named Bebius, in battle. Vatinius is withdrawn with the rest of the troops at Epidamnus/Dyrrachium (Durrës in Albani), while the Partini carry out raids throughout Macedonia and take possession of Salona.

As usual, the Senate of Rome reacts very calmly (revenge is a dish best served cold...). In 39 BC, Caius Asinius Pollio is appointed by the Senate of Rome as proconsul of Macedonia, with the priority task being regaining control of Salona. Asinius Pollio fought under the banner of Julius Caesar in the battles of Pharsalus, Thapsus, and Munda. After the assassination of Caesar, he fought against Sextus Pompey in Spain. After the Battle of Modena, he gave help to Marcus Antonius in Transalpine Gaul and was with him and Marcus Aemilius Lepidus when they made the triumvirate pact with Octavianus. He is known more, however, for his poetic and oratorical skills than for his military ones. He sets off from Aquileia with 11 legions and fights victoriously against the Partini, from whom he confiscates weapons, livestock, and lands (Frontin. 2.15), so much so that he will celebrate his triumph in Rome in the same year and receive the honorific appellative of Delmaticus. On that occasion, he announces that he will use his share of the spoils of war to finance the construction of the first public library in Rome.

Octavianus is in competition with Antonius: every time the latter obtains anything, he tries to outdo him. This explains why, in 36 BC, after having to defeat Sextus Pompey permanently, he prepares his own expedition in Illyricum in order to conquer not only Dalmatia but all the Western Balkans, from the Adriatic Sea to the Danube. The year after, he launches his attack from Aquileia and defeats eight Illyrian tribes. Furthermore, he forces six other Illyrian tribes to pay their annual tribute, which they have not paid for a long time. Two Illyrian tribes spontaneously surrender to him, driven by fear, after he has taken the islands of Melite (Mljet) and Corcyra (Corfu), slaughtered all their adult inhabitants and sold all the others as slaves, and destroyed the fleet of the Liburnians. A third Illyrian tribe flees as they approach, abandoning all their settlements and then surrendering shortly thereafter.

Afterward, Octavianus comes back to the Balkans, crosses the Sava river, and invades Pannonia, a land of great forests. He defeats the Iapodes in battle at Promona, chases them to their lands between the Selva di Piro and the Colapis river (Kupa, Slovenia), and conquers Segestica, the capital of the Iapodes, after a month-long siege. Then he builds a fortress on the left bank of the Colapis, a mile before the confluence of this river into the Sava, opposite Segestica, in a convenient position for a war against the Dacians. This fortress is destined to be the nucleus of what will become Siscia,[5] the future capital of the Roman province of Pannonia Savia. The success of Octavianus and his generals leads in particular to the establishment of two new provinces: Illyricum Superius (future Dalmatia) and Illyricum Inferius (future Pannonia). However, he is unable to subdue the Pannonians, so it cannot be said that they will no longer be a worry or that their lands have been annexed to the Roman state. The Dalmatians and the Iapodes will not cease to represent a problem for Rome. Illyricum will, in fact, be the scene of new uprisings in 16 BC and AD 11. Only when Emperor Tiberius manages to reconquer the Illyrian territories bordering Pannonia in AD 9 can it be said that Dalmatia has been completely and definitively conquered.

After the victory in Illyricum, Octavianus remains in the extreme northeast of Italy for some time. While in Aquileia, he founds the colony of Iulia Concordia (near today's Portogruaro, in eastern Veneto), has some roads built for Noricum, and, in 33/32 BC, rebuilds the walls of Tergeste and provides the city with an aqueduct. Meanwhile, Tergeste has recovered from the sacking and devastation suffered due to the attack of the Iapodes, which occurred in 52 BC. From now on, Tergeste will grow and develop from its land trade, while its sea trade will mainly take place with Istria and Dalmatia, the Roman East, and the Iberian Peninsula.

With the passage of time, the city assumes a characteristic triangle shape in plan, the apex of which is the top of Colle di San Giusto and the two catheti are the walls that descend toward the sea.

On the top of the hill, protected by the walls of the acropolis, is where the main public buildings are grouped: the forum, which is the center of public life; the Curia, seat of the local Senate; the civil basilica; and the Temple of Jupiter Capitolinus, with a double row of columns on the facade.[6]

Lower down, on sloping terraces, rise the houses. Lower still are the theater and the port, with perhaps even a trading forum at the port. The theater is located on the seashore, near two small ports and at the arrival point of an aqueduct, which comes from Monte Spaccato. Also by the sea, but outside the city walls, is a necropolis, while further on is the Campus Martius, a large parade ground used for popular assemblies and for military exercises.

Villages, hamlets, and farmhouses are distributed in no particular order outside the walls, in the surrounding area, on the Karst plateau, along the coast up to the Timavo, and in the opposite direction toward Istria.

The institution of *Regio X-Venetia et Histria*

In 27 BC, Octavianus is acclaimed as *princeps*, the *augustus*, and this marks the transformation of the form of government of the Roman state, which has persisted for 500 years, and now passes from the *res publica* to the *principatus*.

Augustus, in practice, is the first Emperor of Rome. He introduces numerous reforms. In AD 7, he divides Italy into 11 regions and the territory of the city of Rome into 14 zones. One of the Augustan regions is that which occupies northeastern Italy and is called *Regio X-Venetia et Histria*. To the west, it borders the *Regio XI-Transpadana*, from which it is separated by the rivers Oglio, Serio, and Adda; to the south, *Regio VIII-Aemilia*, from which it is separated by the Po; to the north, the provinces of Raetia and Noricum, from which it is separated by the Karawanks and the Eastern Alps; and to the east, the province of Illyricum (the provincial boundary goes from the Troyan pass to the Arsia river).

As the name implies, Regio X is made up of two distinct parts: Venetia and Histria. The first is geographically between the rivers Adige and Timavo. The second is between the Timavo, the Rižana, and the Ras. In this region, there are 26 colonies and municipalities, and there are both mixed groups of Italics and Latins and groups of other ethnicities: Cenomani, Euganei, Reti, Galli Carni, Istri, and Taurisci. They are assigned as tributaries of the most important Roman cities of the region. Respectively, the Cenomani of Brixia (Brescia) and Cremona; the Euganei, of Brixia, Cremona, and Verona; the Veneti, of Ateste (Este) and Aquileia; the Reti, of Tridentum (Trento) and Verona; the Galli Carni, of Tergeste; the tribes of the Julian Alps, of Pula (Pola) and Tergeste; the Istri, of Pula and other Roman centers of Istria; and the Taurisci, of Iulia Aemona (Ljubljana).

The capital of Venetia et Histria is Aquileia. Augustus takes great care of this city and stays there repeatedly,[7] in a residence decorated with frescoes and probably with mosaic floors,[8] and carries out government activities: he signs edicts, grants hearings, etc.

He also stays in Aquileia in 10 BC with his wife Livia, other family members, and the court. In AD 12, Herod the Great (about 43–4 BC), king of Judaea, is received by Augustus there, together with his sons Alexander and Aristobulus.[9]

In AD 14, all of Illyricum that extends north of the Colapis river (Kulpa) becomes a province in its own right known as Pannonia. Two legions are established in the remaining part of Illyricum, located south of the Colapis. In the future, this territory will develop only along the coast, and urban centers such as Iader (Zara) and Salonae (Solin) will rise there.

Pannonia, since it borders the lands of very warlike Germans such as the Quadi and the Marcomanni, must be heavily garrisoned and fortified; in consideration of this, it will have three legions assigned to it. In the future, this province will develop a very flourishing urban life in centers such as Carnuntum, Aquincum, and Sirmium, each of which evolved from a Roman fortified camp thanks to their involvement in commercial traffic between the cities of Venetia et Histria, the coastal centers of Illyricum, and the Danube area, gaining impetus especially from the activities of the merchants of Aquileia and Tergeste.

Notes

1   The term "Eastern Mediterranean" is used in this book to mean the whole of Asia Minor, the Balkan Peninsula, Greece, Cyprus, the southern Levant, and the city and territory of ancient Cyrene in Libya.

2   All the cities included in the territories conquered by Rome were classified by the Capitoline government bodies as a *municipium* (pl. *municipia*). More accurately, the *municipia* were conquered cities that had not been destroyed in order to be assimilated and that had been able to preserve their respective institutions (a change occurred in this regard at the end of the Social War in 91 BC). In the *municipia*, a community of Roman citizens supported the indigenous community. Different from the *municipia* were the Roman foundations abroad called *coloniae* (sing. *colonia*).

3   He became praetor and governor of the province of Sardinia et Corsica in 60 BC.

4   A town located about 26 km from Rome on the Via Appia between Albano and Genzano.

5   Siscia was a fortified city of 40,000 inhabitants with a forum, basilicas, temples, a theater, and two river ports. It was the capital of the province of Pannonia Savia.

6   Some columns of the ancient temple are now visible inside the Cathedral of San Giusto.

7   This is evident, among other things, from the not few inscriptions by praetorians found in Aquileia dating back to the beginning of the Principate.

8   A literary source speaks of a fresco that was in a palatium in Aquileia which portrayed Fausta Augusta in the act of giving a golden helmet to her consort, Constantine I. It should be emphasized that the palatium we are talking about would have existed in an age following the Augustan one, namely that of Constantine I the Great and his dynasty (4th century AD).

9   The Jewish historian Josephus (37–after AD 93) talks about this visit in his work *The Jewish War*. Herod owes his reign to the Roman triumvirs. In fact, in 37 BC, a Roman contingent stormed Jerusalem—the ancient capital of King David, founder of the Kingdom of Israel—to further his interests, thus ensuring the basis of his power. Herod rules Judaea according to the model of the Hellenistic kingdoms, that is, building and embellishing the city with great works and

ensuring peace and prosperity. Among other things, he enlarges the walls, builds palaces and public facilities, including a theater and an amphitheater, and expands the Temple of Solomon, the most important seat of worship in the Jewish religion. Herod's palace is the Herodion, a complex of buildings built on top of a hill in Jerusalem, masked by an artificial embankment that runs all around it and was fed by an aqueduct. It is accessed by a staircase of 200 stone steps that passes through an opening carved into the rock, dominated by the main tower. In 14 BC, the Herodion hosts Marcus Vipsanius Agrippa, faithful collaborator and brother-in-law of Augustus, creator of many of Octavianus's military successes, such as the victory in the naval battle of Actium against the forces of Marcus Antonius and Cleopatra (31 BC), and builder of the Pantheon, "the temple of all the gods", in Rome. Herod enjoys the trust of Augustus, but he is an arrogant and cruel tyrant and will end up losing the support of the Romans due to his misdeeds. The Jews also hate him because he is a foreigner.

Chapter 4

A portrait of a Roman city in the Early Empire

The urban area

Aquileia, the capital of the *Regio X-Venetia et Histria*, is in the Early Empire one of the two most important cities in northern Italy, the other being Mediolanum (Milan), which is the capital of the *Regio XI-Gallia Transpadana*. It is a typical Roman city, with a grid of internal streets obtained from the intersection of *decumani* and *cardi* and an orderly arrangement of blocks packed with houses, buildings and public facilities, headquarters of corporations, etc. There are also institutional headquarters, administrative offices, temples, a basilica, warehouses, etc. The public facilities include a theater, an amphitheater, some gyms, *thermae*, latrines, a market, etc. The city is served by an aqueduct, a sewer system, and a drinking water distribution network with fountains at intersections and connections to buildings. A sewer branch passes under the *decumanus maximus* (main internal street), crosses the *cardo maximus* at the Forum, and leads from the Forum to the market and the river port, both located in the eastern sector of the urban area.

The walls

A brick wall with walkways, monumental gates, and jutting towers with a square base surrounds the urban area. It was built around the middle of the 2nd century BC to protect the city from enemy attacks and allow it to be an obstacle to military invasions of the Italian Peninsula coming from the east. In 52 BC, after the assault on Tergeste by the Iapodes, it was rebuilt. Later, it was partially demolished in several sectors to allow the expansion of the city, given that there was no more danger of wars in which the citizens would have to defend themselves since Rome had now firmly affirmed its dominion in the Danube region and in the Balkans (originally, the urban area extended for 42 ha within the republican fortifications; with passage of time, it expanded well beyond this wall, with the constitution of a suburb, which is mainly to the west of the walled city). The demolitions occurred in the port area and the northern part of the circuit. Currently, on the western side of the defensive perimeter, the brick masonry rests on an ashlar base and, for a stretch, runs parallel to the port-canal,

at a distance of about 25 m from the pier. There are five city gates. One, located in
the southeastern corner of the circuit, is of the type with a quadrangular internal
courtyard. It dates back to an earlier date than 131 BC, possibly 171 BC and the first
few years thereafter. The tower's structure is 2.4 m thick, and the thickness at the
corners and doors is doubled. The street that crosses the door is inserted obliquely
in a pre-established system of doors and streets.[1]

Housing architecture

The dwelling houses are all low; at most, they have a mezzanine floor.[2] Every
building type intended for residential use is present, including the *domus* (pl. *domia*),
that reflects the high social status and the prosperous economic condition of the
family that lives there, and therefore it denotes the belonging of the latter to the
ruling class. The *domus,* intended as a building type, has a rectangular plan and is
enclosed by very high walls without windows that make it a sort of small fort, and
is characterized by the presence of an impressive entrance hall (*atrium*), one or
more dining rooms (*triclinium*), a study (*tablinum*), several bedrooms (*cubiculum*),
a kitchen to the north, and an internal garden, located at the back of the house
and surrounded by a colonnaded portico (*peristilium*). The atrium has a high
sloping ceiling on four sides, supported by four columns, and a central basin for
collecting rainwater, which is connected to a cistern. Among the domestic rooms,
some are enriched with fine furnishings and decoration: mosaics, wall paintings,
columns with worked capitals, small sculptures in bronze or marble, etc. The wall
paintings depict familiar scenes, fantastic views, still lifes, literary subjects, or
subjects related to love, and are set against red or yellow backgrounds or, more
rarely, black, green and blue. The columns of the portico are made of brick and
covered with stucco. Part of the house might be occupied by shops or taverns,
which open onto the street.

Usually, the floors of the houses in Aquileia are in cocciopesto. They are often
adorned with mosaics made of black and white *tesserae* and sometimes also with wall
paintings.[3] A house located not far from the Forum has a floor with a mosaic border
and the central part in marble inlay, consisting of an infinite variety of colored marbles,
some of which have been imported from Africa. A mosaic depicts two knotted vine
shoots with a bow in the center. In another house, the floor of a (supposed) bedroom
includes a polychrome mosaic depicting Europa on the bull. A *triclinium* is adorned
with a polychrome mosaic depicting an unswept floor. Another house, located in the
same area, has—perhaps in the kitchen—a mosaic with a motif of stars made up of
rhombuses, with a two-handled vase in the center.

Another mosaic, coming from the northern part of the urban area, repeats the
so-called "clypeus" or "shield" motif, which consists of triangles with white and
black curvilinear sides that gradually narrow as they approach the center, while the
border alternates squares, lozenges, and rectangles. A further mosaic dating back to
the end of the 1st century BC–beginning of the 1st century AD adorns the floor of

a large room. It is white, surrounded at the edge by two decorative bands in black, one with vegetable motifs and one with Greek motifs, and has a polychrome square, perhaps imported, with a fish in the center.

Another large mosaic floor, belonging to a *triclinium* and datable to the very beginning of the 1st century AD, in the area of Monastero, is in the shape of a T.

A *domus* from the Augustan Age, with mosaic floors, is accessible from the port area, which is about 45 m away.

The *peristilium* of a house located in the area where the amphitheater will rise in the future and inhabited in the first half of the 1st century AD is 10 m long and 7.5 m wide; it is supported by brick columns covered with stucco and has a floor in cocciopesto with flakes of limestone. The floors of this house rest on a crawl space of overturned amphorae, deprived of their necks, and are decorated with mosaics. The building contains a *cubiculum*, a *triclinium*, which is accessed from the porch, a room used for weaving, and a kitchen. The *cubiculum* floor is embellished with a mosaic depicting a deer and that of the *triclinium* by a mosaic of white tiles surrounded by a simple black frame, interspersed with white tiles. In addition to the mosaic floor, the *triclinium* is also decorated with a wall painting that can be framed in the sumptuous IV Pompeian style (*c*. AD 60–79), the final evolutionary stage of the great Pompeian painting style, that makes the walls a collection of framed paintings, or panels, depicting scenes from mythology, landscapes, floral designs, and still lifes in intense colors and delightfully shaded.

A majestic house, one of the largest in the city, is the home of a wealthy citizen, Titus Macro. The building extends 77 m in length and its maximum width is 25 m, covering an area of 1,700 m². It is located between two parallel paved streets, which run in a north–south direction, in one of the southern blocks of the city (area of the Cossar Fund), where there is also a mosaic of the rape of Europa, a beautiful pavement with a vine branch with a bow, the "unswept floor" that we have already mentioned, as well as the mosaic of the Good Shepherd from the 4th century, which we will deal with later. Built in the first century BC, it is still in use in the mid-1st century AD.[4] It has a wooden roof, covered with tiles, and develops according to the classic scheme of a house with an atrium. The domestic environments are decorated with floor mosaics, using geometric patterns, with black and white tiles or polychrome inserts. It has 320 m² of mosaic floors dated to the end of the 1st century BC and the middle of the 1st century AD.

The house is accessed from its west side through an atrium supported by four columns and equipped with a central basin for collecting water and a well. In line with the entrance, there is a *tablinum* with a rich mosaic floor. The back garden is surrounded by a mosaic corridor and is equipped with a fountain. A large *triclinium* opens onto it, from the south, flanked by living rooms and a *cubiculum*. The *triclinium* is adorned with a large peach mosaic. The kitchen, with a masonry counter, is located to the north, while in the eastern part of the house there are four shops, one of which encloses a bakery oven.

The Forum

Within the urban area, the *decumani* proceed in a northwest–southeast direction. The *decumanus maximus* is located in the Forum area, about one-third of the way into it, where it crosses the *cardo maximus*. The Forum is that which has begun to form in the 2nd century BC. In the first half of the 1st century AD, it took on its final appearance.[5] It consists of a square 141 m long and 55 m wide, entirely paved with Aurisina limestone slabs, free from road crossings and surrounded by a colonnaded portico. The paving slabs have a constant width and variable length. In some cases, they have been replaced with reused materials, which may bear inscriptions.

On the east and west sides of the square, the portico is accessible by three steps. The western side was built around AD 50; the eastern side will be rebuilt in the Antonine Age (Antoninus Pius, AD 138–161; Marcus Aurelius, AD 161–180). Under its vaults, on the ground floor of the building, there are some shops. Here the columns are *rudentatae* (with grooves filled up to a third of the height with sticks called *rudenti*), have composite-style capitals, and support a raised floor. Above the lintel runs a balustrade consisting of parallelepiped blocks corresponding to the columns and slabs in the space between them. The slabs are carved in relief with festoons supported by cupids or eagles and bear inscriptions in the upper part, one of which mentions Lucius Manlius Acidinus, one of the founders of the colony in 181 BC. The blocks are decorated in relief with large heads of Medusa or with the head of Jupiter Ammon. These subjects were chosen to remind and reaffirm to everyone the extent of the dominion of Rome: the whole known world, from the west (Medusa) to the east (Jupiter Ammon).[6]

In the southeast corner of the portico, the rhythm of the columns is interrupted by a system of arches, which denotes the presence of an independent building overlooking the square.

On the northern side of the Forum, two reduced-height steps—at the base of which runs a channel for the drainage of rainwater—lead into a space occupied by a temple, perhaps initially dedicated to the goddess Concordia and then to the Capitoline Triad (Jupiter, Juno, Minerva). This building, with a rectangular plan, is in the Etruscan-Italic style, with terracotta decorations (covering slabs, antefixes, a frieze with a battle scene). Imposing in size, it stands on a podium. It is accessed by a flight of steps between two foreparts, in front of which there are several statues of magistrates. One of the characters represented is Titus Annius Luscus, one of the triumvirs who led the second contingent of settlers who arrived in the city in 169 BC and the one who would have built and consecrated the building, perhaps in the dissolution of a vote. The monument dates back to the years 130–120 BC. At the base, it bears an inscription, engraved in the 2nd century BC, which lists the functions of the magistrate:[7] drafting the laws for the administration of the colony, updating the local Senate (about the administration of the colony), and building a temple.[8]

At the center of the southern side of the square, a forepart with a propylaeum protrudes, which constitutes the solemn entrance to the Civil Basilica.

For the Romans, a basilica is a large two-story building, considerably longer than it is wide, where public meetings take place, business is negotiated, and justice is administered. Usually, in this type of building, the interior is organized in three central naves, separated by rows of columns, while the exterior is also formed by a colonnaded portico, which develops along the sides. Under the vaults of the external portico, there are many shops, where everything is sold, and many places where you can eat and drink, as well as the entrances to the building, which lead to the stairs that go up to the upper floors.

The Civil Basilica of Aquileia overlooks the *decumanus* of Galla Aratria (which we will deal with later) with two entrances, while on the opposite side, a monumental entrance connects it to the porticoes of the Forum. It is about 90 m long and just over 29 m wide. It was built in the early Augustan Age and will be radically refashioned at the end of the 2nd century with the addition of an apse on each of the short sides. Inside, it is divided into three naves paved with marble slabs, which also turn on the short sides, forming a sort of corridor paved with slabs of Istrian stone. It was probably erected on an already public space used for counting votes in local elections by an exponent of the entrepreneurial bourgeoisie of the city who counted construction among his activities and (perhaps through his freedmen) produced and exported bricks. This would explain the proud signature of the work inscribed on a lintel of the building, good for delivering the builder's memory to history and, if necessary, for making him undertake a political career. That patron would have built and donated the building to the city at the end of the 1st century BC. A relative of him—perhaps his daughter, Aratria Galla—had a long section of one of the inner streets of the city paved at his expense in the first half of the 1st century AD, which features large paving stones (the first southern *decumanus* south of the Basilica that separates the latter from the Forum) (*Inscr. Aq.* 842 and 3495).

The amphitheater

One of the most impressive and grandiloquent buildings in the city is located in the southwestern corner of the urban area, next to the Via Sepulcralis. It is a structure intended for public performances, called an amphitheater by the Romans. It has an elliptical plan, has several floors, and its facade is characterized by a sequence of arches. It encloses a flat, circular space covered with sand (arena), which is surrounded by tiers divided into sectors and also includes a tribune for the authorities.

The shows offered to the public in the amphitheaters consist of circus games, the hunting and killing of wild animals, and gladiator fights. Therefore, in the basement of the building and in other parts of the structure, there are numerous service rooms used for storage, the detention of animals, and the quarters of the gladiators. The animals exhibited in the arena are imported from distant countries—there are lions, tigers, leopards, elephants, bears, deer, wild boar, wild goats, and camels—and are on the one hand ostentation of the wealth and power of those who offer games and, on the other, a great opportunity for the plebeians to see exotic animals that they would never have seen otherwise.

Another form of entertainment offered in amphitheaters is the execution of low-ranking inmates in the form of death at the stake, crucifixion, or fatal encounters with wolves or other wild beasts, to which the condemned is exposed without weapons or armor.

The shows staged in the amphitheaters attract large masses of spectators, including from neighboring cities and the countryside. To facilitate the movement of the crowd, the structure is placed outside the city walls. Moreover, amphitheaters are usually located near a school of gladiators. The duelists are prepared for combat in a special school, which is also a barracks and prison, and is assiduously frequented by wealthy Romans in search of talent and popularity, usually aspiring candidates for public office. Visitors agree with the owner and manager (in Latin, *lanista*) to hire gladiators to be employed in the shows they intend to organize in Rome or in other important cities. Usually, the *lanista* is a Roman citizen of a noble and rich family. He does a very rewarding but despised job because he is halfway between a butcher and a pimp (gladiators are often requested by madams for sexual encounters). His gladiators are former prisoners of war, mainly Gauls or Thracians, but there are also Germans, Italics, or those of other origins. Particular attention should be paid to those who come from Thrace. Thracians are strong, bold, and cheerful men, full of life, life-loving, spontaneous and original. They live in a region in the southeast of the Balkan Peninsula (southern Bulgaria, European Turkey, northeastern Greece) that took the name of Thrace from them and in some areas adjacent to it, which extend north to the lower reaches of the Danube. Their distribution range is between the Danube in the north and the Strymōn (the Struma, a Macedonian river that flows into Bulgaria and Greece) in the west, and is bathed by the Black Sea in the north, the Sea of Marmara in the east, and the Aegean Sea in the south.

With its dimensions of 148 m in length and 112 m in width, the amphitheater of Aquileia is one of the greatest examples of this type of building in Italy, second in the *Regio X Venetia et Histria* only behind that of Verona (152 × 123 m). From the arches of the facade, it is possible to directly access the stairs leading to the top parts of the *cavea* or to the 16 radial corridors. The tiers have a capacity of 21,000 seats. The arena is a space of 72 m by 42 m, covering an area of 2,600 m². It was built in the mid-1st century AD, most likely in the Julio-Claudian Age. Therefore, it is contemporary with the new Forum of Aquileia and the amphitheater of Verona.

The port system

The wisdom of the Romans in hydraulic engineering is reflected in the port system of Aquileia, understood as an integrated system of commercial terminals and waterways at which men, goods, and raw materials from all over the Mediterranean land. The system consists of a seaport, located at the mouth of the Natissa river, in the lagoon island of Grado;[9] a series of secondary moorings in the Lagoon of Grado between the coast and the city; a river port, connected with the seaport; and also the Canale Anfora, which, together with other waterways, makes Aquileia completely circumnavigable. It is open to and guarantees all communication. It is the gateway to the Roman West for goods from Egypt, Greece, and the Near East and the terminus of maritime trade for the entire area of Caput Adriae (the arched northern end of the Adriatic Sea) in connection with Noricum, Illyria, Greece, Byzantium, Asia Minor, the South Levant, and Egypt.

The river port has evolved since the 1st century AD to meet the needs of growing merchant traffic, which reflected the prosperity of the local economy, which had its strengths in the trade and export of handicrafts. It develops along the Natissa river, which flows along the east side of the city, touching a stretch of the walls.[10] It has *horrea*, markets, and production-handicraft areas and is equipped with piers (the main one being 450 m long), ladders, lifting machines, shipyards on one side of the river and on the other. The *horrea* are warehouses that guarantee the storage of large quantities of grain destined for the local community, troops stationed in the city, passing troops, and other communities. Merchant ships load and unload agricultural products, raw materials, slaves, animals, and all sorts of goods. There are two piers placed one in front of the other. The one on the right bank of the river is 300 m long and consists of two mooring docks, one higher and the other lower to compensate for the unevenness of the water due to tides and flooding; this makes the port usable in any tide, in any season and in any weather. The highest quay is made up of protruding blocks, equipped with horizontal mooring rings; the lower one has vertical rings. The blocks used for the construction are of Istrian stone, which is a limestone rock that takes its name from the fact that it is quarried in Istria. This material is white when freshly mined, with shades ranging from pink to white, but tends to turn light gray with exposure to air, wind, and precipitation. Being compact and not very porous, it is highly resistant to both compression and saline corrosion. Starting from the stairs that interrupt the pier and going through any of the three cobbled and sloping streets, you arrive at the Forum-Basilica complex—in practice, the city center—through passages through the city walls, which lead into the *decumani*. The northern and central streets are at an angle so as to limit the rise of water during floods. Some warehouses and port structures, located between the pier and the walls, are connected to the roads by perpendicular ramps, paved and tiered, for loading and unloading. Every day, when the activity resumes after the night break, this pier registers the comings and goings of wagons, men carrying baskets and packages of various kinds, types, and sizes, donkeys loaded with goods, and the coming and going of merchants and slaves along the quays and along the streets that lead from them to the city center. The pier built along the left bank of the river has a neighborhood of modest houses behind it, inhabited mainly by port workers: sailors, dockers, customs officers, etc.

The Canale Anfora is an artificial watercourse, created in Aquileia during the reign of Claudius (AD 41–54) to connect the city with the lagoon and the sea. The work is

6 km long, has a flat bottom, and has an embankment supported by wooden poles, driven more than 1 m into the ground.[11] The part of it closest to the city is a real port around which commercial and artisanal activities develop. Among other things, there is an open-air market (Latin: *macellum*) specializing in the sale of the meat of animals: cattle, pigs, goats, horses.

The maritime port of Aquileia is the first port facility encountered when going up the western Adriatic coast north of Rabenna (Ravenna). As we noted earlier, it is located at the mouth of the Natissa, in the lagoon island of Grado.[12] Among the merchant ships that drop anchor at Grado, there are some that come from far away: Greece, Asia Minor, Egypt. If the boat, in size and draft, is suitable to go up the Natissa, it will continue its journey toward the river port of Aquileia, which it will reach after 10 km. Otherwise, its cargo will be transshipped on a boat of lower tonnage and draft, and the merchant will continue his journey to Aquileia aboard the latter.

The port system of Aquileia also serves military ships that play the role of the coast guard, also for the purposes of compliance with customs legislation, as well as an escort role for convoys against the ever-looming threat of Illyrian pirates, traveling up and down the coast and inspecting every bay and inlet. Those ships check all the fishing and pleasure boats they encounter on the sea and in the ports of the Upper Adriatic and ascertain the intentions of any vessel that has potentially aggressive behavior; if necessary, they attack hostile vessels as a preventive measure in order to counteract piracy.

Ships carry not only luxury goods, and therefore business and wealth, but also information. Their arrival in a port is an opportunity for meetings between distant worlds, which talk to each other and intertwine relations. The excitement of the moment is reflected in the faces and gestures of sailors and merchants, in the barges and rowing boats that parade around the arriving ships, and in the slaves who move along the rickety walkways when the disembarkation is over and the unloading has started.

Tombs and cemeteries

The funerary ritual of the Romans is a cremation until the middle of the 2nd century AD, when it becomes a burial. Only small children, those who do not yet have teeth, are never cremated. In a cremation, the body is placed on a wooden pyre doused with pitch, possibly wrapped in a sheet, with open eyes, a coin in the mouth or in the hand, and a funeral kit. The pyre is of regular shape and varies in height according to the social status of the deceased. After shouting the dead man's name, a relative or friend of the latter sets the fire, looking away. The fire is extinguished with water and wine, the semi-burnt bones are collected, and the ash is cleaned and deposited in an urn, possibly mixed with precious objects. The funeral urn is buried in the bare earth or locked up in a box of tiles or bricks. It can be in terracotta, stone, or lead. If it is made of stone, it is mostly cylindrical or square, occasionally in the shape of a chalice. Sometimes the urns are ornate. Sometimes they also have a lid. Often a glass urn is inserted into the stone or lead urn. Because the deceased is believed to remain in contact with the living for a certain period of time, for a few days after the funeral, relatives make offerings of food and drink, pouring wine and milk on the ground and putting solid food in the grave through a hole or pipe. The tomb is visited by relatives and friends on special occasions when libations and banquets are held in joy in honor of the dead.

In Aquileia, the graves are located outside the city for reasons of public hygiene (the ban on burying the deceased in the urban area is unobserved only in a few mandatory cases). Usually, they are arranged on the sides of suburban roads. Those that flank the main arteries stretch for over 4 km. Sometimes they consist of privately owned enclosures, separated by stone or brick walls, which enclose monuments and burials. See, for example, what is arranged along Via Annia, including five funerary enclosures belonging to as many families (Statia, anonymous, Giulia, Trebia, Cestia). These enclosures have been used since the 1st century AD. The Statia family is also known from other Aquileian sources (about 40 inscriptions). Inside its funerary enclosure, there is an altar with decorated steps and crown, which commemorates the deceased for whom the tomb was set up. Around the altar, there are other minor monuments and cinerary urns, including the sarcophagus of a child—Lucius Statius Fermus, son of Lucius—and a small altar-ossuary, dedicated by the parents to the 16-year-old Fabricia Severina, hosted by the Statii in their family tomb.

A vibrant community

Aquileia, in its first 150 years of life, gradually grew in size and population. In the Early Empire, its inhabitants number some tens of thousands. They are Veneti, Celts, Illyrians, Etruscans, Italics from the center-south of the Peninsula, Greeks, Levantines, above all Syriacs, and other individuals of various origins. They are merchants, entrepreneurs, artisans, construction and transport operators, agricultural entrepreneurs, land workers, garrison soldiers, passing troops, etc. In Aquileia, therefore, different languages are spoken, and people dress according to the dictates of Roman and Italic fashion or according to those of their country of origin, meaning different visions of the world are expressed. Despite the differences, the various ethnic components of the population manage to understand each other very well and form an integrated community, which reflects the characteristic features of Roman society: traditionally cohesive, liberal, and flexible, but animated by the spirit of free trade and founded on collective piety and, therefore, tolerant and attentive to all aspects of law, in particular to customary law deemed common to all peoples or nations (Latin: *ius gentium*).

Among the residents, there are free Roman citizens, freedmen, and slaves. The latter are very numerous, perhaps as many as there are inhabitants of a free condition if not more, as happens almost everywhere in the imperium of Rome and in every other contemporary society. The slaves of the Romans are in fact innumerable. It is said that Julius Caesar alone, returning from the conquest of Gaul, brought a million with him. Aquileia is—together with Rome—the largest slave market in Europe, where the slave trade is exercised above all by Romans and Italics, united in religious brotherhoods. Thousands of unfortunate people pass by that market. Sometimes those who have been deprived of their liberty come to Aquileia and other slave markets after they have already been bought and sold. Usually, in fact, prisoners of war are sold shortly after being captured to merchants who follow the legions and camp outside the entrenched camps. After being bought by the military, who had received them as a reward, as part of the spoils of war, they are resold at a higher price. Slaves are not part of society but contribute as goods, as things, to form their master's patrimony. They are employed as a workforce in every branch of economic activity in Italy, Spain, Asia Minor, and in the islands, as well as in the work of managers in the context of farms with centralized organization, large estates with a composite and diversified structure, in their villa, vineyards, gardens, smallholdings, and farms. They can be privately or publicly owned. If educated, they are usually employed by families or in public offices as tutors, doctors, or scribes. Some manage to acquire freedom by having a special legal institution applied to them called *manumissio*, which can also lead to the attribution of Roman citizenship. The enslaved person who has been released from slavery by legal means is called *libertus* and remains linked to his former master and his descendants. Depending on their abilities and fortune, freedmen can even enjoy enormous success and become wealthy.[13]

The port area is the beating heart of the city's economy. It is a densely populated and very popular neighborhood, inhabited by people of humble rank and a few infamous ones too. It is home to carters, dockers, shopkeepers, workers, etc. In part, these are foreigners, mainly oriental. If they have blond hair, it is likely that they are Gauls or Germans. Usually, those with red hair are Britons. Others are Serbs or Dalmatians, or Greeks, possibly Greeks from Asia. Still others have oriental features and a deep gaze: in this case, they are probably Syrians. There are also dark-skinned individuals, perhaps Mauritanians, Egyptians, or Sudanese.

The first foreigners who came to Aquileia to stay there were slaves (they became such because they were prisoners of war), placed at the service of rich families to carry out the humblest jobs, such as by becoming servants, masseurs, gardeners, laborers, etc., or Roman citizens of free condition who had deep scientific and technical knowledge, such as teachers, Greek merchants, and Syrian craftsmen. The latter came to Italy in search of fortune and opened schools, shops, and laboratories or offered themselves as service providers. For example, one of the trades practiced in the river port by the Syrians is that of carrying a litter, practiced by the *lecticarii*. Most of those workers offer transportation to those who get off the vessels. Over time, foreign entrepreneurs and workers have gathered in professional associations. Furthermore, foreigners usually form communities of compatriots or co-religionists.

The Jewish community is homogeneous and compact, while the Greeks and the Syrians form heterogeneous groups of people who speak the same language (but in a slightly different way); however, they maintain their own individuality, linked to their own, different origins. The Greek community began to form in the main cities of Italy after the Roman conquest of the Hellenistic world. The other foreign communities began to form after the conquest of the southern Levant, which was conducted by Pompey the Great between 66 and 63 BC, and that of Jerusalem by Emperor Titus in AD 70.

Foreigners have introduced not only the foods and dishes of their homeland to Aquileia but also traditions, customs, and religious beliefs. The Romans behave toward them in a peaceful way, but there is no lack of prejudices, especially toward the orientals, whom the Romans accuse of not keeping their word, of not having rigor and seriousness, and of coming from sites which are capitals of vice, like Antioch on the Orontes, where the suburb of Daphne has this reputation. The Jewish community, for example, is perfectly integrated into the city and in its daily life, but the Romans often accuse the Jews of wanting to isolate themselves because they are averse to other peoples and of showing a lack of willingness to adapt.

It is noteworthy that Publius Cornelius Tacitus (AD 55/58–117/120), the Roman historian, orator, and senator, speaks of the prejudice of the Romans toward the Jews in his work *Historiae* (see, for example, the third to fifth chapters of the fifth book). Tacitus's *Historiae* is subdivided into 12 or 14 books. The first four books are dedicated to the political events of AD 69, "The Year of the Four Emperors" (Galba, Otho, Vitellius, and Vespasian). The fifth deals with the events of the Jewish war, starting with a historical, geographical, and ethnic excursus.

It must also be said, however, that the Romans, since they consider themselves superior to all other peoples, subdue, criticize and make fun of all foreigners, including Jews. One thing that the Romans do not compromise on is their observance of the duty imposed on foreigners to abide by the organizational rules of the Roman state and Roman law in public life (at home, they can behave according to the culture to which they belong, provided this is not in conflict with Roman law).

The fact that it is an international port and at the center of land trade currents that come from afar—from continental Europe, southeastern Europe, Asia, or Africa— definitely makes Aquileia a cosmopolitan city, or better, a city inhabited by a multi-ethnic society.

Production of food

Over time, the territory of Aquileia has enlarged. In the Early Empire, it corresponds to the extreme northeastern part of *Regio X Venetia et Histria* and Istria. Its eastern part includes the Julian Alps, the city of Tergeste (Trieste in the Venezia Giulia), and the cities of Pietas Iulia (Pula, Croatia) and Tarsatica (Rijeka) in Istria. The territory in question is partly flat and partly hilly or mountainous, though rich in fertile soils and pastures, woods, surface waters, and biodiversity. Its agricultural areas are dotted with rural villages and farms with adjoining fields. Farms are equipped with oil mills and have cellars full of potbellied barrels. Large quantities of food are produced there that will be marketed in the city, and the part that exceeds local needs will be exported.

Aquileia's countryside is a territory where agriculture, pastoralism, livestock breeding, hunting, fishing, and the harvesting of vegetables and shellfish are combined with industrial craft activities and the supply of services (trade, construction, transport, etc.). Mainly, the local agriculture consists in the cultivation of cereals and vines, but also in the production of flour, bakery products, and wine, as well as in the cultivation of vegetables, legumes, and fruit (figs, walnuts, almonds). Cattle breeding and pastoralism are favored by the abundance of pasture. Their contribution to the local economy is very significant both for the production of milk, dairy products, meat, and sausages and for the production and processing of raw wool, which employs numerous dyers, domestic weavers, tailors, and hatters.

Mainly, sheep, goats, and pigs are raised; more rarely, cattle. Pig breeding and processing are common activities throughout the *Venetia et Histria* and are a legacy of the Celts. The Celts preserve pieces of pork in salt or after having smoked them, and they are famous for it. An ingredient of their recipes is suckling or recently weaned pig, which is emptied, stuffed, and roasted. There are two pig breeds raised by the Romans, one pink and one black. One of the types of pigs raised in *Venetia et Histria* is the same one already raised by the Celts (the Iberian?). Geese and ducks are also raised to obtain meat, liver, feathers, and lard. In this case too, the activity is favored by the particular characteristics of the territory of Aquileia, which is rich in marshes and ponds. Furthermore, in every rural settlement, whether small or large, there is a breeding of hens and capons, possibly even of peacocks or ostriches, aimed at obtaining meat and eggs (and from peacocks and ostriches, even feathers). Another form of agriculture is that of nurseries. In Aquileia, this is practiced in large fenced areas where animals destined to become hunting prey live in a state of pseudo-freedom.

Food production activities are supplemented by predatory activities aimed at obtaining food by hunting, fishing, and gathering. Hunting is practiced exclusively or on the sidelines of other work activities, especially on game in the woods and in the mountains (roe deer, deer, wild boar, hares, wolves, bears, foxes), poultry (pheasants, mallards, birds), geese, wild birds, partridges, pigeons, thrushes, turtledoves, etc. Fishing is practiced both in the Natissa river and in the sea that bathes the island of Grado, including for baby octopuses, and the same can be said for the collection of crustaceans. The woods that cover the colony's territory offer a variety of edible wild plants: mushrooms, fruits, aromatic herbs, etc.

Crafts and industry

Both in the urban area and in the surrounding area, there are numerous ovens and potters' workshops, where clay is molded and fired to obtain construction materials (tiles, bricks); jars and containers for the cooking, preparation, and conservation of liquids and food products and, at the table, for the service and consumption of meals; sculpted clay artifacts (theatrical masks, statuettes, cinerary urns, oil lamps); jars and vials for ointments and perfumes; and clay coatings for structures still predominantly wooden in their form, according to the Etruscan-Italic tradition, such as heads in relief, telamons, and acroteria auras. The rich Romans use fine tableware cups and plates, made in shapes and with trendy decorations, usually in imitation of Italic productions, and therefore they often replace them. The artisan workshops of Aquileia also produce sculptures in relief or in the round, glass objects, refined jewelry, artifacts in bone or finely carved ivory, mosaic tiles, marble inlays, and architectural elements. The jewelry uses gold, silver, and semi-precious stones.

Stonework
Stone sculpture started in Aquileia at the end of the 2nd century BC. In the 1st century BC, it makes a leap in quality and the first important products appeared, namely funerary urns, steles, and portrait heads. The stonecutters work blocks of Piasentina stone (a very compact gray limestone from the quarries of Aurisina, located between Trieste and Monfalcone) or of Pietra d'Istria, a softer material, and create vases, relief or round sculptures, architectural elements, tiles, plates with inscriptions, urns, steles, and funerary monuments. They make copies of masterpieces of the Greek tradition, intended for the decoration of public buildings and to furnish the houses and villas of rich individuals with a classic taste. We refer to bas-reliefs, statues, statuettes, head portraits, and herms. An unfinished portrait head, for example, portrays a Hellenistic prince, perhaps Caius Julius Caesar Octavianus Augustus or Marcus Vipsanius Agrippa. A series of portraits of the Julio-Claudian family was also painted in the 1st century AD. Among other products, we may point out a statue of Octavianus, not yet Augustus, and a bust of Caius Caesar, designated as the successor of Augustus. One of them might represent Drusus, in another one can perhaps recognize Claudius, yet another, perhaps, portrays Livia, consort of Augustus. Two statues depict Claudius, and another depicts a young man dressed in a toga, with his head covered, engaged in an act of worship, which could represent the Genius Augusti. Also in Aquileia, during the reign of Augustus, a vast repertoire of funerary monuments is produced, ranging from statues, mostly inserted in small mausoleums, to carved and inscribed steles, to urns decorated in relief, and to altars, tritons, lions, and sphinxes. The medallions with busts, the *plutei* with cherubs and festoons, the bas-reliefs, and other architectural decorations should not be ignored either. The architectural elements produced comprise blocks of squared stone, entrance thresholds, steps, manholes, drips, channels, jambs, architraves, shafts and bases of columns, capitals, balustrades, and marble inlays.

Metallurgy
Numerous foundries and metallurgical workshops are active both in the urban area and in the surrounding area. There, minerals are melted to extract the metal (copper,

tin, iron), the raw metals are mixed together to obtain alloys (for example, bronze, an alloy of copper and tin) and transformed into semi-finished products, and the latter become finished products. The metallurgical industry uses copper, bronze, iron, and steel and melts metal ores. For smelting, metallurgists use different types of furnaces, but more frequently a "vat" furnace, formed by two overlapping parts connected by a rather narrow neck (the lower, smaller part is filled with coal, the upper one with the mineral) and with a natural draft, which is sometimes obtained with the use of bellows. The molten metal is poured into a mold or matrix, where it solidifies as it cools and takes the desired shape. The casting is performed by various systems: "closed mold", "with the core", or "lost-wax". Finally, the artifact is embossed or chiseled. The finished products are mainly work tools, hunting and war weapons, ornaments, pipes, hydraulic devices, tools, nails, studs, buckles, and fibulae. In Aquileia, the artistic craftsmanship of the metal sector produces furniture, ornaments, worked bronzes, tripods, candelabra, chandeliers, and oil lamps. In the 1st century AD, some bronzes depicting divinities are produced. In the 3rd century AD, imitations of metal cups in terracotta and decorated in relief, widely used, will also be produced. The steel comes from Noricum through the Carnic and Julian Alps (Monte Croce Carnico pass and Tarvisio pass). In particular, it comes from mines located on the Norican side of the Carnic and Julian Alps and from others located just north of these mountains (for example, in Carinthia, in the Magdalensberg area), which are very rich and easily exploited. Steel arrives in Aquileia in the form of semi-finished products.

Production of glass
Aquileia is a center for the production of glass items, intended both as common glass articles, of green or blue color, blown into shapes suitable for use in canteens, kitchens and, in some cases, for the transport of liquids, and as products of high quality and refined taste, reserved for wealthy buyers, such as blown glass bottles and vitreous *balsamarii* for perfumes (the latter belong to the Aquileian perfume industry, which uses raw materials mainly from Arabia, but also from India, passing through Alexandria in Egypt). The products use natrium and silica imported from Egypt and Istria, respectively. They are characterized by the transparency, lightness, and variety of their bright colors, as well as by the elegance of their shapes. Some artifacts are small masterpieces. The oldest glass working techniques are that of blown glass shaping and that of mosaic. The first consists of taking a quantity of molten material and blowing into it with an iron rod, then giving the bubble its final shape with the help of spatulas, pliers, and other tools. It was invented in the 1st century BC and then gradually perfected in the Syrian-Palestinian area, probably in Jerusalem. The blown glass shape has enjoyed great and lasting success, quickly entering the daily life of the population. This happened for two reasons: because glass blown into shape can replace terracotta and base and precious metals and because, due to its unique qualities, it is preferable to these metals for the production of certain artifacts (containers for food, beverages, cosmetics, or medicines, as well as window glass, funeral urns, and fine

crockery). Glass can be blown into any shape and color, it does not require the use of molds, it is transparent (therefore it allows one to evaluate the state of conservation of its contents), it is waterproof, it is neutral (it does not interfere with its contents), and it is elegant, light, economical, and recyclable. Of course, its defect, common to the finest terracotta, lies in its fragility.

In the beginning, the Roman West, to satisfy its own need for blown glass, limited itself to importing it from the Eastern Mediterranean; by around 50 BC, however, alongside finished products, it also began to import techniques and masters of processing. Some glass factories thus opened their doors in various centers of the Peninsula, but above all in Rome, in the Vesuvian area (Herculaneum, Pompeii, Puteolis), and in Aquileia, above all on the initiative of craftsmen from Sidon, a city located in Phoenicia (Lebanon). Glass processing began in Aquileia between the end of the 1st century BC and the beginning of the 1st century AD in the context of the direct relations that the city had by sea to the Eastern Mediterranean (glass art is very ancient in Syria and Phoenicia; in Cyprus, it was only recently introduced). The first glassmakers to open a shop in Aquileia were some Phoenician and Syriac masters, frequently Sidonian (the blown glass produced by the Sidonian masters in Aquileia can be recognized by the small epigraphs, almost signatures). One of those Syriacs, named Ennion, signed his products with Greek letters. Thus began a great craft tradition, which will have a strong development at least until the 2nd century and will survive the collapse of Roman Aquileia.[14] Currently, the art of glassmaking is practiced in Aquileia by Egyptian masters, skilled in the processing of "mosaic" glass, of Alexandrian origin

Goldsmithing

Goldsmiths and silversmiths in Aquileia produce an abundant and varied quantity of ornaments and jewels, artifacts in bone or finely carved ivory, luxury silverware and crockery, and artistic mosaics, all destined for high-ranking personalities, who will use them as ornaments for themselves and their homes. Their precious and refined jewelry use gold, silver, semi-precious stones, pearls, and amber. Those in gold include necklaces in golden mesh with pearls and emeralds, rings with a large and smooth surface, and "cluster" earrings or with pearl pendants, all inspired by the models produced in the same period in the cities of the Vesuvian area, as well as amber pendants, large rings, tools, and carved gems. Where does the gold worked in Aquileia come from? From the mines of the Alps, not far from Aquileia itself, very rich and easily exploitable. Among the silver objects made in Aquileia in the 1st century AD, we point out a cup decorated with a ring and a slightly concave patera, with a border decorated in embossed and chiseled relief with mythological figures and scenes; the latter is one of the first examples of Roman celebratory art known to date.

Pearls are imported into the Roman world from India and Arabia via Alexandria in Egypt, which is a sorting center for the whole Empire. They are considered to be the most precious material after diamonds. Therefore, their commercial value is very high. The lucrative pearl trade attracts buyers or sellers to Aquileia. An epitaph recalls a pearl merchant named Lucius Valerius Primus, who lived in the second half of the 3rd century. He carried out his business in Rome and was on a business trip to Aquileia when he died. No one knows what the cause was. However, there are those who say that he had transferred the business and was exercising it in Aquileia at the time of his death.

The jewelry with semi-precious stones, possibly linked in gold, that is made in Aquileia use stones imported from Asia Minor, if not from further away, such as the Iranian plateau and the Indus valley. Semi-precious stones are translucent or opaque. Translucent ones are the most valuable. We refer, for example, to amethyst, chalcedony, and nicolo (onyx). The raw material arrives in Aquileia in the form of blocks to be cut, sanded, and finally assembled. From the beginning, in Aquileia, hard stones are also used to obtain seals. In the 1st century BC, these stones were also used to make pendants and ring mounts. Sometimes they were mounted on glass pastes, obtained by mold, in different colors. Lastly, before assembly, a final chisel work was performed, engraving images onto them of deities, portraits, ideal rural life scenes, parades of chariots or fantastic beings, such as Capricorn, indefinite living beings, or hybrids, partly human, partly animal. Often, the decorative motif of the closing of two right hands is engraved on wedding rings. In many cases, the incision is made in the negative, that is, it is hollowed out in the gem or metal.

Amber products
Aquileia, since the beginning of the 1st century BC, has been the main global center for processing and exporting finished products that use amber (it will remain so until the end of the 2nd century AD). Amber arrives there from the southern shores of the Baltic Sea through Central Europe in the form of an ingot or bead and is worked to obtain pendants and rings with a chiseled setting in order to represent cupids, crouching dogs, and busts of women with a fashionable hairstyle, all used as good luck charms to ward off nightmares, delusions, and diseases, including sore throats, and to detect the presence of poisons in food. The processing of amber, as well as that of semi-precious stones, requires the use of a drill and grinder; therefore, both amber and semi-precious stones are worked in the same workshops. In Aquileia, amber is also processed to obtain items to be used by women: perfume bottles, display cases for mirrors, wing-shaped or shell-shaped cups in which to dilute creams and make-up, as well as tools for mixing cosmetics, styling the hair or perfuming the hands.

Other artifacts
In other workshops in Aquileia, wood, wool, animal and vegetable fibers, leather, and stone are processed. The carpenters make beams, chests, chairs, finely wrought beds adorned with busts and statuettes, barrels, carts for oxen, irons, and harnesses for horses. Other artisans work wool, vegetable fibers, and leather to obtain fabrics, ropes, lacings, and belts.

Imports and exports

Aquileia is located at the intersection of various currents of merchant traffic and different roads, which connect it with the Po valley and Transalpine Gaul, central Italy and the Tyrrhenian Sea, Central Europe up to the Baltic, and with the Balkan Peninsula, up to the Black Sea. This makes it a natural outlet to the entire transalpine, Norican, and Pannonian hinterland and an intermediation point for a great variety of products, and it is an emporium also frequented by merchants from elsewhere: Latins, Italics, Veneti from the Adriatic, Galli Carni, Istri, Taurisci, and Illyrians.

In Aquileia, slaves, goods of all kinds produced locally or imported by sea or from the hinterland, and raw materials are traded with the cities of the Po-Venetian Plain, Noricum, and other cities of the Mediterranean. From the end of the 1st century AD onward, in particular, amphorae for oil and wheat and fine crockery, all from North Africa,[15] are imported to Aquileia, it being understood that the buyers of precious table ceramics that are currently enjoying the greatest success among the Aquileians are Italic ones.[16] Very often, raw materials are imported that will be transformed in the metallurgical workshops and in the craft shops. We refer above all to steel, gold, amber, semi-precious stones, and pearls. The market for these goods attracts intense traffic to Aquileia from the transalpine regions and from the East. In the 2nd century, Aquileia also imports aromas of oriental origin (from Arabia and/or India, through Alexandria) to be used in the local perfume industry,[17] as well as Greek sarcophagi, coming mainly from Attica (Aquileia is the largest market for these artifacts in Italy, larger than Rome itself). In the first half of the 3rd century, Aquileia will import Corinthian ceramics, decorated in relief, which imitate metal vases, textiles from north-western Italy and foodstuffs—wine from Veneto, oil from Spain, oil and wheat from Cyrenaica, and oil from Istria—since, during the reign of Marcus Aurelius, it is a supply base for the army.

With the progressive conquest and organization of the transalpine territories between the Alps and the Danube and of the Illyrian-Danube ones south of this river, and with the creation of military settlements along the same river, Aquileia has seen the opening of new and important markets. Hence, the city plays the role of an emporium for the Danubian populations and that of intermediary, which it played in the transalpine trade during the Late Republican Age, on the initiative of important Aquileian families such as the Barbii, Caesernii, Cantii, Didii, etc.

In exchange for the sale of their products, the Aquileians also receive slaves, cattle, and skins. Strabo (5.1.8) writes that Aquileia is "the place where products of the continent meet those coming from the sea", and then he adds: "Aquileia opens its market to the Illyrians of the Danubian regions: those buy goods that come from the sea, loading wine and oil on wagons, in wooden containers; the inhabitants (receive in exchange) slaves, cattle, skins."

One of the goods offered for sale in the Aquileian market is humans. The slave market of this city is, together with that of Rome, one of the largest in the Western

Mediterranean. Usually, former prisoners of war of Celtic, Illyrian, or Pannonian origin are bought and sold there. Generally, purchases are sent to Gallia Cisalpina, Gallia Narbonensis, Hispania Citerior, and Hispania Ulterior (the eastern provinces supply slaves to the entire Empire and do not need to import them).

Where Aquileia's production of common and luxury artifacts and imports, including agricultural products, exceeds local needs, the additional products are forwarded to other Italian and other markets, in particular to Veneto, Central Europe, the Western Balkans, the Danube region up to the Black Sea coast, Greece and its islands, and the Eastern Mediterranean coastline.

The wine produced in Cisalpine Gaul is exported to Noricum, Istrian oil to Greece, and skins to the Eastern Mediterranean.[18] The handcrafted textile products of Gallia Cisalpina and Aquileia are very popular everywhere; they also find a market in southern Italy, where they are preferred to the local, albeit valid, products. Those that are exported by sea from Aquileia are also directed toward Syria.

The imported livestock serves local needs and, at most, is partly forwarded to *Regio IX Liguria* and *Regio VIII Aemilia*.

The merchant trades that originate or take place in the extreme northeast of Italy and head toward the neighboring transalpine regions follow at least three routes: 1) the goods are transported by wagons to Nauportus (Vrhnika in Slovenia), where they are loaded onto riverboats and then travel up the rivers Ljubljanica and Sava up to Segestica (near Siscia, Sisak in Croatia), through the mountain pass of the Okra, and then to the Danube and the neighboring region; 2) they cross the Monte Croce Carnico pass, traveled since the second quarter of the 2nd century BC by Italic and Latin operators (especially from Aquileia) to reach the mining center of Magdalensberg (Noreia?[19]) and are then taken up the road that connects Aquileia to Aguntum (near Lienz in Austria); and 3) they are transported via the route that uses the Camporosso saddle and connects Aquileia to Virunum (Magdalensberg in Austria). The shipping option is represented by buyers coming from outside or by Aquileian traders, whose commercial activity is favored, as well as by the position of Aquileia on the right bank of a large navigable river, by the connection with the port of Grado and the Adriatic Sea.

Notes

1   We refer to the specimen that emerged from the excavations of Giovanni Brusin (1929–1934) in the southeastern corner of the urban layout, near the modern cemetery, that was unearthed and then buried again. Its construction seems to go back to the Late Republican period (171 BC and after). It certainly dates back to prior to 131 BC—the year of the construction of the Via Annia—because the road that crossed it appears to be inserted obliquely in a pre-established system of doors and roads.

2   This can be seen both from the fact that the elevation was not preserved due to the reuse of building materials after the destruction of the ancient city and from the fact that the foundations preserved are thin and therefore unsuitable to support a multi-storey building.

3   This is demonstrated by some plans of dwelling houses dating back to the 1st century preserved in the National Archaeological Museum in Aquileia.

4   The house was inhabited continuously until the 6th century, albeit with transformations and renovations. The owners' standard of living is evidenced by a beautiful gold ring and glass paste dated to the 2nd–3rd century AD. Over 1,200 coins were returned from excavations, among which the sestertius of Maximinus Thrax (AD 235–238) stands out. A hoard of 560 coins was later found in the atrium area, hidden by its owner in a hole in around 460 AD in the turbulent years following the capture of Aquileia by Attila, king of the Huns, and never recovered.

5   The colonnaded portico ran on at least three sides. The layout of the fourth side (north side) is almost completely unknown, except for a circular building with steps, which is identified as the Comitium, used for popular meetings, from the Republican Age.

6   The architectural fragments found, however, may not belong to the portico but to a temple, located in the center of the Forum.

7   After the Social War (91–89 BC), the self-governing bodies of the colonies of Rome (previously different from colony to colony, but very close to those of Rome) have changed and now consist of four civic magistrates—quattuorviri—and the local Senate. The quattuorviri, as the name implies, number four: two *duumviri iure dicundo* and two aediles. They are elected by the *comitia* (popular assemblies) for one year, have different competences and have the *toga praetexta* and the *sella curulis* as distinctive signs. The duumviri administer justice, award public works and public supplies contracts, call citizens to arms, and are responsible for local politics. Every five years, they carry out a census and review the electoral lists and the register of decurions (on the decurions, see below). They are the major local political and administrative authority, in a superordinate position to the aediles. Their seat is therefore that of the supreme city authority. Like the building site, it houses offices and archives. The aediles have administrative duties. They deal with annona, worship, roads, markets, sanitation and public order and organize the games. The Senate, or *ordo*, or *curia*, is made up of 100 citizens, called decuriones, usually ex-magistrates, who advise the executive power on the management of public resources.

8   The exact location of the temple mentioned in the inscription is unknown, but the building must have overlooked the square.

9   *Gradus* is the Latin term that defines a landing at the mouth of a river or at the mouth of a lagoon.

10 Impressive remains of the river port of Aquileia are now visible on the right bank of the river, largely attributed to the reign of Claudius, but heavily remodeled, and therefore are not easy to read.

11 They were replanted at the beginning of the 3rd century, replacing the previous ones, which were in need of maintenance.

12 The existence of a *macellum* in this part of the city is suggested by the fact that numerous animal bones have been found in the layers of soil deposited in the riverbed, as well as tree trunks, still green leaves, peach, cherry, and olive stones, grape seeds, pine nut shells, acorns, chestnuts, walnuts and hazelnuts, leather shoes, wooden objects, and a large fragment of a boat made up of three boards still "sewn" together. These bones are mainly those of cattle and horses, with a fair presence of pigs and perhaps goats, almost all whole. They show traces of skinning or slaughter and appear to belong to selected anatomical parts.

13 The relationship between a freedman and his patron is similar to that between father and son, so much so that the former takes his patron's family name and even his *praenomen* while retaining his own slave name as *cognomen*. It implied that the freedman had to respect his patron and his ancestors and that he accepts his authority as *paterfamilias* in the context of the *familia* (the whole of the *paterfamilias* and his cohabitants, including the servants). The reciprocal rights and obligations that arise from the establishment of that relationship are regulated by law.

14 The modern glass masters of Murano, a locality located in the Venice lagoon, are rightly considered as the heirs of their Aquileian counterparts.

15 From the beginning of the 2nd century AD onward, the fine tableware consumed in Aquileia will mainly be imported. We refer to terra sigillata products, two-handled vases with high rims, glasses and cups with very thin walls and even figurative decoration, and large decorated vases. Terra sigillata products arrive in Aquileia from central and central-northern Italy (one of the major centers of sealed ceramic production is Arretium [Arezzo]). They are typically red in color and are modeled on the lathe and by stamping. The two-handled, high-rim vases come especially from northern Italy; the name of the manufacturer is placed on the outside of these vases among the decorative motifs impressed. The glasses and cups mentioned come from the Po area. The large decorated vases are imported from southern and central France.

16 It was not always like this: those productions gradually lost ground and, at the beginning of the 2nd century AD, ceased to have a market in Aquileia, as they are no longer able to withstand the competition of Corinthian bowls decorated with pastoral or ritual scenes, amphorae with Dionysian representations from Cnidus (Greece), large decorated vases from Gaul, and especially ceramic tableware from North Africa, of simpler shapes than the Italic ones, without a trademark and with decoration limited to a few applied or imprinted motifs (pagan or Christian symbols and some biblical scenes).

17 That a perfume industry existed in Aquileia is demonstrated by an epigraph in memory of a *thurarius,* L. Gallonius Corinthi lib. Primigenius (CIL V 1042, cfr. P. 1025) and from the abundant local production of small glass containers used to store balsams and perfumed oils (*balsamarii*).

18 In the 1st century BC and the 1st century AD, it was Italy that exported oil, and some of the traffic passed through Aquileia (previously, it was one of the terminals for the import by sea of oil and wheat from Cyrenaica); later, the oil production destined for Italy decreased, and already by the 1st century AD, Italy imported oil from Spain and, later, it would also import it from the African provinces.

19 Noreia, we recall, was the main center of the Taurisci, one of the tribes that formed the federation or confederation of the Norici, which was called *regnum Noricum* by the Romans. It was located in southern Austria, perhaps in the same place as the modern city of Klagenfurt in Carinthia or Magdalensberg, the main archaeological site in southern Austria, once occupied by the Roman city of Virunum. Magdalensberg Hill was a place from which iron and gold were mined, and the metal was smelted into ingots. The ingots exceeding the local need were exported, often to Italy.

Chapter 5

In the whirlwind of the Marcomannic Wars

A tragedy of the sea[1]

A vessel with an unknown name is sailing in the Upper Adriatic, proceeding with difficulty in a sea that boils under the whip of the wind, which blows in gusts. It is a typical boat for coastal navigation—15 to 18 m long, 5 to 6 m wide, and weighing at least 22 tonnes—with a few crewmen, one of whom has light brown hair,[2] perhaps the same who maneuvers a single oar located at the stern, which acts as a rudder. It has a mainmast, crossed by the flagpole of a heavy square sail, and is equipped with cleats, connecting pins, blocks, and pulleys, which, together with the three-strand hemp ropes, and the "rudder" of which we said earlier, are the tools with which the crew operates the sail and steers the ship (the pulleys are used to maneuver the heavy sail). The on-board equipment also includes an instrument with a hollow base, which catches sediment from the seabed and allows the crew to understand what type of seabed they are navigating (echo sounder), as well as an anchor, whose main weight comes from a block of lead, and a bilge pump, which uses a lead pipe. Also on board are some terracotta oil lamps, a bronze lantern, some bronze inkwells and jars, and some styluses and a spatula, all bone. In the space of the ship reserved for the pantry and the kitchen, there are some bronze pots of Aegean manufacture, some terracotta dishes of North African production, some bottles, a glass flask of North Adriatic production, and some jugs, which are used to draw water from a large terracotta vase stowed in the bow. One pitcher has a trefoil rim, and the others have a handle. They are all of purified common ceramics and were manufactured in the territory of Aquileia. Inside the hull, there is also a series of bronze artifacts: a small scale, a tripod with lion's paws, some fishing hooks, and a statuette.

It is worthwhile to dwell on the scale and the statuette. The first has a counterweight slider in the shape of a bust of Minerva and a small graduated rod. The second is a small replica of a famous iconographic model, made in bronze in the 4th century BC by the famous Greek sculptor Lysippos for the sanctuary of Poseidon at Isthmia, about 16 km east of Corinth in Greece. It is 21 cm high and represents Neptune, understood as the tutelary deity of the ship (in each boat, the captain and the sailors entrust their life and their possessions to a deity, who is usually the god of the sea and earthquakes, to whom horses are sacred). In this effigy, this god is a mature man, with thick hair and a rich beard, with his right leg bent and resting on a iconic element,[3] with his right forearm resting on the left thigh and his left hand raised to hold a trident.

The cargo of the ship is distributed in a wooden barrel, placed next to the yard, and in a number of terracotta amphorae of different types, in all almost 600, carefully stowed according to their dimensions, with the large ones in the center and the small ones in the stern and bow. Each amphora has a tag tied around its neck indicating the contents. The large amphorae are crammed with sardines and a kind of fish similar to mackerel, all in brine. Each fish is about 30 cm long and weighs 3 oz. There are up to 430 in each container for a total weight of over 100 kg. The small amphorae contain garum, a liquid with a decidedly spicy and savory flavor.

Garum is obtained by filtering the mush resulting from the long fermentation and frequent stirring of fish of various qualities, which are arranged in alternating layers together with salt in a large jar until it is filled. The Romans learned to do this from the Greeks. They use it as a seasoning for food, for many preparations based on fish, meat, eggs, or fruit, and they go crazy for it, despite the fact that it emits an odor that is anything but delicate, unmistakable, and pungent. The qualities of garum available on the market differ according to the fish used and the place of processing. Due to the high concentration of salt, this preparation keeps for a long time and makes the use of salt in dishes unnecessary.

The wooden barrel contains broken glass, which used to be plates, cups, trays, glasses, and bottles, and is intended to be remelted in the workshop to obtain a mass of glass necessary for the creation of new products. By recycling glass, you save not only on the raw material but also on energy, since the amount of fuel required is radically less than what is needed to produce it starting from the raw material (because the temperature to be reached is less high). There are also some pieces in glass pasta to play *latrunculi,* the backgammon of the Romans: probably, the only entertainment of the crewmen in moments of break from work, when they are stationed in port or are at sea.

It is unknown from which port the ship sailed at the beginning of its voyage, but it must have made its last stop in Clodia (Chioggia), a port located at the southern end of the Venetian Lagoon, found in a group of islets divided by canals and connected by bridges. This hypothesis is supported by the fact that the inhabitants of Clodia live off fishing and the extraction of sea salt, and one of the typical products of the place is salted fish.

Sailors traveling up the western Adriatic coast stop in Clodia as a late stop before arriving in the port of the lagoon island of Grado. From Clodia onward, they skirt a coastal plain densely furrowed by rivers and canals, one of which is the Natissa river that flows into the Adriatic Sea just south of Grado. That coast is well populated and is home to commercial structures and residential settlements. The production plants and the burial areas near Grado are arranged on parallel lines. In the future, that stretch of coast will become a lagoon and the seat of the settlement of Marano, from which it will take its name.

Perhaps, after leaving Grado, the ship will go upstream of the Natissa and end its journey in the river port of Aquileia. At the moment, it finds it hard to proceed. The wind has risen, the sea is rough. The weather conditions are typical of the "Bora".

The Bora is a northeasterly wind, cold and dry, sometimes icy. It arises from a combination of a low-pressure center and a surrounding high-pressure system. It blows in gusts, sometimes extremely violent, and causes a lowering of the temperature of up to 10°C. The phenomenon lasts from three to seven days, occurs most often between October and April, and causes the formation of storm clouds, such as cumulus clouds. The best-known Bora in Italy is the one that sweeps the city and the Gulf of Trieste, where it can reach speeds of up to 150 km/h (hurricane), sometimes even greater. Before reaching Tergeste (Trieste), it blows into a valley between the Italian Alps and the Dinaric Alps and then falls toward the sea from the edge of the Karst (a high plain behind Tergeste). A few kilometers before reaching the sea, it crosses hilly areas. The phenomenon appears suddenly and develops rapidly. In the sea, it raises irregular, steep, short, and low waves covered with spray. It can create dust clouds that reduce visibility. The sea is whipped up, bubbling and foaming. When the Bora is blowing, it is best to stay sheltered in a safe place.

The ship sailing toward Grado is tossed about by the waves, which hit it sideways, and she risks overturning. Meanwhile it has become dark, the sky is crossed by lightning and thunder, it is raining heavily, and the sea is foaming. The captain and sailors frantically try to save themselves and the boat, shouting at the top of their lungs as the wind hisses and the rain thunders down. But their efforts are in vain. The ship sinks, taking the crew and cargo with it. The sea swallows it up, then closes over it like a grave. As the men drown, the ship settles at a depth of 16 m, scattering part of the cargo. It will remain there for a long time, undisturbed. The statuette of Poseidon will remain half-buried in the sand, sadly testifying to the powerlessness of the god, who did not save those trusting in him from death.

The tragedy of the sea we have reported really happened, but we don't know exactly when. It seems probable that it occurred between AD 98 and 161, the apogee period in the history of the Roman Empire, which embraces the reigns of Trajan (AD 98–117), Hadrian (117–138), and Antoninus Pius (138–161). Most likely, it occurred during the reign of Trajan (Auriemma 2000: 27–51).

Trajan (AD 98–117)

Marcus Ulpius Nerva Traianus is a tall man, robust with austere habits, passionate about hunting and other sports, skillful, courageous, just, moderate, and a great expert in military matters, and thus very popular among the legions. He was born in Spain into an aristocratic family (his father was a former consul, governor of Syria, and proconsul of Asia). He was lined up for the throne by Emperor Nerva in October 97 and succeeded him three months after his death with the approval of the army, the Praetorians (the bodyguard of the emperor), and the Senate of Rome.

Trajan's imperial proclamation is very significant for at least three reasons: 1) Nerva, who had been placed on the throne by the Senate of Rome, had adopted a soldier and designated him as his successor; in this way, the alliance between the senatorial order and the army, which formed the basis of the Principate, had been recovered and strengthened after a long period of progressive weakening (under Tiberius, Caligula, Domitian, and Nero); 2) after the death of Domitian (AD 81–96), the Flavian Dynasty had been extinguished; and 3) for the first time, the new Augustus is a provincial; before him, all the emperors had come from Roman and Italic groups, prevalent in the army and in the Senate of Rome. This is a sign of the times. By now, many servants of the state, both civil and military, come from the provinces, and the same can be said for most of the senators.

It was the people, under Vespasian (AD 69–79), who established that the emperor is the absolute center of power. However, the condition that guarantees the internal peace of the Empire consists in an unbalanced relationship between the highest public institutions; the emperor must not behave like an autocrat, like Caligula (AD 37–41), Nero (AD 54–68), and Domitian (AD 81–96) had, but it is not good for him to give too much voice to the Senate of Rome, as Tiberius had. Trajan will satisfy this condition and solve the problem, becoming the protagonist of an authoritarian, conservative, and expansionist but balanced policy, with government activity that respects the role and prerogatives of the Senate. He is personally interested in the administration of the state, sometimes taking paternalistic attitudes toward the provinces, and he expands the scope of the bureaucracy's competence. Furthermore, he pays much attention to Italy and the need for the assistance of the weakest and promotes many public works. Among his measures, it is worth mentioning the one that obliges the provincials who aspire to hold a magistracy in Rome and to enter the Senate to invest a large part of their assets in the purchase of land in Italy, so that they consider this as their homeland and not as the *hospitium* or the *stabulum* of a wayfarer.[4]

The conquest of Dacia

The transfer of power from Nerva to Trajan took place peacefully, so much so that the incoming emperor was able to postpone going to Rome for the investiture ceremony for a year because he was held back in Germany by the need to strengthen the border defenses along the Danube and strengthen the land and river communication channels in the border area, especially to facilitate the movement of troops. During that period, since the Prefect of the Praetorian tended to assume a disproportionate political weight, he got rid of him, and after he resigned, he was executed.

The strengthening of the defenses along the *limes germanicus* became necessary after the winds of war began to blow. Indeed, in the early years of his reign, Trajan fought a war in the Carpathian region in two phases. In 101–102, his army crossed the Danube on a pontoon bridge at Lederata, near Viminacium (Kostolac, Serbia), the capital of the Roman province of Moesia, and occupied the city of Sarmizegetusa (the residence of Decebalus, the tribal king of the Dacians, who rules in a condition of semi-independence from the Empire) and other positions of strategic-military interest. He later built a large bridge over the Danube, resting on stone pillars, based on the design of the most competent of his great engineers, the brilliant Apollodorus of Damascus.

The war has a flashpoint in 105–106 when the Dacians rebel against Roman rule. The Romans counterattack and destroy Sarmizegetusa, and Decebalus takes his own life. The severed head of the latter is brought to Rome and shown to the crowd, enthusiastic about the victory to the point of delirium. The Dacian kingdom is suppressed, and its territory becomes a new Roman province, called Dacia, and is garrisoned by two or three legions (which in the future will be reduced to one, headquartered in Apulum). Sarmizegetusa is re-founded as a Roman colony. The rich gold mines of Dacia are now exploited on behalf of the new Roman masters by Dalmatian miners. The spoils of war are immense: 5 million pounds of gold and 10 million pounds of silver, to which must be added the proceeds from the sale of 500,000 prisoners to slave traders (some, however, say that this estimate is exaggerated and should be divided by 10 for a more realistic picture). Trajan uses it to cover war expenses, to finance four months of uninterrupted games in the Circus of Rome with 10,000 gladiators, to distribute free food and other gifts to the people of Rome, and to promote an extensive public works program. The latter also includes a gigantic aqueduct in Segovia in Spain, a new port north of the mouth of the Tiber, four new consular roads, the amphitheater of Verona, and a new Forum in Rome. It is worthwhile to dwell on Trajan's port and the Forum.

The former is built in front of Ostia. It is shaped like a hexagon, each side being 370 m long, and includes a *palatium*, a theater, a building destined for thermal use, and a lighthouse. From now on, it will be the main port of the urban area of Rome.

Trajan's Forum

Trajan's Forum will be the last of the great monumental squares built by the emperors in the 1st and 2nd centuries to expand the civic center of Rome. It is built from 107 to 112 under the direction of Apollodorus of Damascus to express the immensity of Rome and the glory of its emperor. It will rise in an area between the Quirinale hill and the Suburra district (to the west) and the Arx, one of the two peaks of the Campidoglio hill (to the east); it is adjacent to the Forum of Augustus (to the north) and, to the northeast, to that of Julius Caesar. It occupies an area of 5.5 ha, equal to that of all the preceding forums put together (not only those of Julius Caesar and Augustus but even those of Nerva and Vespasian as well). At 300 m long and 190 m wide, the area of Trajan's Forum is divided into four parts: a large public square, accessible to the Roman people; the Basilica Ulpia; a small rectangular courtyard with arcades; and the Temple of the Divine Trajan. The square is a rectangle 116 m long and 95 m wide, paved with marble and with an equestrian statue of Trajan in the center. It is delimited on the extreme sides by Corinthian colonnades, behind each of which there is a hemicycle with two orders, with niches and marble statues, while the facade of the Basilica Ulpia rises on the short side opposite the entrance (a monumental triumphal arch with three arches, opening on a slightly arched floor facade and surmounted by a quadriga in gilded bronze led by the emperor).

The Basilica Ulpia is a place where justice is administered and public activities take place, and it takes its name from the emperor's family. It will be the largest civil basilica ever built in the Empire. It has a colonnaded facade with three entrances, two of which are surmounted by two chariots (the lateral ones) and the central one by a quadriga in gilded bronze, and a rectangular room, 104 m long and 52 m wide divided into five naves and flanked on the sides by exedras. The central nave is surrounded by a double Corinthian portico with two apses placed at the ends, preceded by a third order of columns. Its pillars and columns, all in white marble, its upper attic galleries, its roof covered in wood, its bronze tiles, and its colossal statues of the emperor make it a sumptuous building of unattainable grandeur and elegance. The small rectangular courtyard with arcades, adjacent to the north of the rear facade of the Basilica Ulpia, features a majestic column in the center and two libraries on either side, one Latin and one Greek.

The column is 40 m high and will become famous for the relief that celebrates the victory over the Dacians, wrapping around the trunk for a length of 200 m. Each library consists of a room about 30 m long, flanked inside by two colonnaded floors and covered by cross vaults. Adjacent to the north of the majestic complex, after the rectangular courtyard, is a vast semicircular esplanade bordered by arcades. In that area, after Trajan's death, the great Temple of the Divine Trajan will be built by his successor Hadrian. Trajan's Forum will become one of the major administrative centers of Imperial Rome and one of the major attractions of this city. It will arouse the admiration of visitors for its grandeur, its architectural elegance, and the refinement of the building materials used for centuries.[5]

The Roman Empire reaches its maximum extent
Meanwhile, the Roman armies have pushed further into the east: beyond the Euphrates river, fighting against the Parthians from Mesopotamia,[6] into the Caucasus (Kingdom of Armenia), and up to the edge of the deserts of Arabia (Kingdom of the Nabataeans). The Kingdom of Armenia will be the subject of endless disputes between Rome and the Parthians. The Kingdom of the Nabataeans was annexed to the Roman state after the death of its last ruler, who was already a client king of Rome. These inclusions increased Roman possessions in Asia to the south and east, making Rome the mistress of all lands between the Mediterranean Sea and the Zagros Mountains and from the Taurus Mountains to the deserts of Arabia. This was the completion of a strategic plan begun in the times of Julius Caesar and Marcus Antonius.

The new provinces of the Empire are therefore Dacia, i.e. the former kingdom of the Dacians (Romania); Arabia Petraea, that is, the former Kingdom of the Nabataeans; Lower Armenia, between Cappadocia and Assyria; Adiabene, with the cities of Edessa, Charrae, Resana, Nisibis, Singara, etc.; Assyria; Mesene; and Mesopotamia, with the cities of Seleucia-on-Tigris, Ctesiphon, Babylon, etc. The province of Mesopotamia was created in the Tigris and Euphrates region between the Syrian desert, the Taurus Mountains, the Zagros Mountains, and the shores of the Persian Gulf.

At the moment, no one can know for sure, but, with the establishment of those provinces, the Roman Empire reached its maximum territorial extent; from now on, it will no longer grow, but will gradually shrink.

The Roman Empire now encompasses much of Europe, Western Asia, and Saharan Africa, and is one of the largest political organizations in the ancient world, larger than the Achaemenid Persian Empire of the 5th century BC, and even more so than the Macedonian Empire, founded by Alexander the Great in 336 BC. Specifically, it extends from the Atlantic coasts of Western Europe to the Zagros Mountains, from the Atlantic coast of North Africa to the Red Sea, from Great Britain and the Rhine to Sicily, from the Danube and the Carpathians to the Aegean islands, from the Caucasus to the Euphrates, from the Syrian coast to Mount Sinai and the edge of the deserts of Arabia. It includes 2,000 urban communities and is populated by 50–60 million people. Its outer edges, which are a total of 16,000 km in length, are manned by 400,000 soldiers, who are involved, in addition to the surveillance of border crossing points and the defense of borders, in the suppression of revolts and the maintenance of public order and social peace. As it embraces all the lands bathed by the Mediterranean Sea, the Roman Empire is the first political organization that unifies all the populations living in this area of the world (it will also be the last). It is destined to last for 500 years (27 BC–AD 476) and to form the basis of the culture of the entirety of the West.

Trajan also divides Pannonia into two provinces: Lower Pannonia and Upper Pannonia. The management center of Lower Pannonia becomes Sirmium (Sremska Mitrovica in northwestern Serbia), a city located in the center of a vast and fertile plain near the Sava river.

An unimportant settlement had existed in the Sirmium area since the Neolithic Age. Under the Romans, it grew and developed to become a city, a crossroads of connections between the western and eastern parts of the Empire, a position of strategic-military importance, from which it is possible to monitor the Danube border, and a base for the launch of military operations across borders. Sirmium is in contact with the cities of the *Regio X Venetia et Histria,* mainly with the closest ones to it, which are Aquileia and Tergeste. It was the place of residence of Domitian before Trajan established his headquarters there during his Dacian campaign. Trajan probably stopped in Aquileia several times during that campaign.

Aquileia and Tergeste in the Early Empire

Aquileia currently enjoys peace and well-being. It is a large city, where both Latin and Greek are spoken and various oriental divinities are honored, mainly Artemis Ephesia. There is an air of the East due to the relations that the local community has developed with Greece, Anatolia, Cyprus, the southern Levant, and Egypt, and this air radiates toward the Danube region. The inhabitants live on agriculture, crafts, industry, and trade. Exports of glass, amber, gems, and iron and steel artifacts are thriving. The urban layout is still the one that was established between the end of the 1st century BC and the 1st century AD, with the restructuring of the Forum and the river port, the first phase of the Civil Basilica, the construction of the theater (in the Late Republic or in the Augustan Age) and of the amphitheater (in the Julio-Claudian Age), and perhaps also the establishment of a new food market (Tiussi 2009: 66–81, esp. 66–72). Under the paving of the Forum, in a gallery, passes a lead pipe 20 cm in diameter belonging to the aqueduct, which leads to the water tower north of the Forum. Currently, the main public building interventions are concentrating on the existing ones. Among other things, a particular building has been redone, perhaps a building used as a spa.

The city tends to expand outside the walls of the Republican Age, which have now lost their defensive function. The enclosure was demolished in some sections, for example, in the port area and in the southern area included in the bend of the Natissa river. A section of the north wall, the northern city gate, and at least one of the city gates persist. The main suburban residential expansion area is that of the Natisone loop. To the east of the port, across the river, two new neighborhoods are developing or consolidating. A third expansion area is extending east of the Republican walls in the locality of Marignane.

Further south of Marignane, there is a theater and an amphitheater. The latter is located outside the walls. Outside a stretch of the Republican walls that encloses the northwestern part of the city runs a 15–20 m wide canal, bordered by banks or quays. Mosaics referable to both the 1st and 2nd centuries decorate a large *domus* (in the former Cossar Fund, now state property). In the same house, an intermediate space (11 × 9 m), arranged as a garden, is surrounded on four sides by a porch paved with a mosaic with fairly large, black tiles, interspersed with white tiles. A large dining room (13 × 7 m) is all paved with a white mosaic with a thin black thread at the edge. Three large atriums retain, respectively, a white mosaic, a mosaic with a checkerboard decoration, and a mosaic with a black diagonal weaving to form lozenges.

During the reign of Trajan, Tergeste reaches its maximum flourishing. The city has about 12,000 inhabitants and, in the middle of the century, has a typical physiognomy, which it will maintain in the future. It has a typical triangle shape, where the vertex is the top of the San Giusto Hill, while the catheti are the city walls, which descend toward the sea. Among the internal streets, some rise from the port to the top of the hill, while the others follow the terraces and cross the former. Under the roadway run the sewers, which flow into two large collectors under the main streets. The water supply of the city is guaranteed by wells and the aqueduct that brings the water of the Fonte Oppia, in Val Rosandra, to the city, with an underground route of 17 km. On the top of the hill, enclosed within the fortification walls of the acropolis and accessible by an uphill road, are grouped the main public buildings, which form an articulated complex with a monumental and cultural character: the Forum, the center of public life, and the adjoining Civil Basilica; the Curia, seat of the local Senate; and the Temple of Capitoline Jupiter, dedicated to the Capitoline Triad (Jupiter Juno, Minerva). The Temple of Capitoline Jupiter has a double row of columns on the facade.[7] It is accessed through a majestic monumental entrance, made up of two side projections, equipped with Corinthian columns, and a central staircase, which leads to a colonnaded portico. A large public building with apses overlooks a paved square (Forum?). Lower down, on terraces, there are residential districts made up of houses of various types, which are usually built with the use of sandstone blocks bonded with mortar. Only sometimes are the thresholds and other structural elements in Aurisina stone (a type of limestone, which looks like marble), which is the building material with which public buildings are usually made. Both of these materials are available in the area; limestone in the Aurisina quarry and sandstone on the hills close to the city, including the San Giusto Hill. The use of bricks is rare; the roofs are covered with tiles and may have a terracotta antefix at the corners. Often, the houses are built at different altitudes, taking advantage of the slope going up to the acropolis, and these allow you to enjoy a splendid view of the Gulf. The homes of wealthy families are the *domus*, "atrium houses". Usually, they are adorned with mosaic floors, wall paintings, and stucco decorations. The residential districts are intersected by an internal uphill street, which, as it continues, meets two arches, similar to a triumphal arch. The first of the two marks the transition from the artisan-commercial district to a residential district at a point where the steepness of the ground increases, and the other, higher up, marks a point where the same street bends to the right. At the base of the hill, along the seashore, there is a theater, a commercial forum, and the port area, with installations, warehouses, and craft workshops. The point of arrival of the aqueduct is also in that part of the city.

The theater is located outside the city walls by the sea, from which it is separated by the coastal road. Its semicircular *cavea* takes advantage of the natural slope of the hill, in the Greek style, and is divided into sectors by five stairs and two shelves by corridors. A wooden gallery runs along its upper part. The steps descend to the orchestra floor and can hold from 3,500 to 6,000 spectators. A mighty semicircular wall supports the cover, which is unfolded during the shows, to shelter the spectators from the sun's rays. The scene is on two floors, with three doors for the actors, columns, and statues within niches. A portico pillar runs to the rear of the scene, along the facade; under its vaults, there are entrances for the public. Apparently built at the beginning of the 1st century AD, the building was renovated between 92 and 102 by the Tergestine Quintus Petronius Modestus, a *procurator Augusti* and a *flamen*.[8]

Along the coastal road, at the point where it crosses the road that goes up to the acropolis, there is a large rectangular-based structure, about 5 m high, which accentuates the importance of the place. It rests on four pillars decorated in relief, on the outside of which there are fluted columns that rest on a molded relief, which, in turn, overlaps a base in concrete. Still on the seashore, but outside the city walls, there is a necropolis and the Campus Martius. The latter is a large parade ground used for popular assemblies and military exercises.

Villages, farmhouses, luxurious villas, artisan facilities, places of worship, and extensive necropolises are distributed in no particular order outside the city walls, on the Karst plateau, and along the two extra-urban streets that originate from as many city gates, one of which leads to Aquileia and the other to Istria. A suburban shrine is dedicated to Bona Dea, an ancient Lazio deity (sometimes identified with Cybele, the Great Anatolian Mother), whose mystery cult is reserved for women. A suburban villa, arranged on several terraces, extends for 200 m on the seafront along the road to Aquileia. It contains numerous representative and service rooms, spas, a garden, a gym, and a nymphaeum and is adorned with mosaic floors and statues, including a mosaic with a rose window motif and a marble statue portraying an athlete (Diadumenos), a Roman copy of a Greek original by Polykleitos (5th century BC). It is said that it was owned by the very wealthy Calvia Crispinilla, a favorite of Emperor Nero (54–68). Another villa, also located along the road to Aquileia, contains a large room paved with black and white mosaic tiles and an adjacent room with a mosaic floor with red tiles. The necropolises are arranged along the extra-urban streets, with burials inside an urn or stone box, arranged within enclosures with cornerstones and funerary steles.

The war against the Parthians and the smallpox epidemic

Antoninus Pius (138–161), who succeeded Trajan and Hadrian, and his court visit Aquileia. Moreover, during the reign of Marcus Aurelius (161–180), the successor of Antoninus Pius, Aquileia once again becomes a logistical base and plays a strategic military role. Three episodes are relevant in this regard.

The first occurs in 166 and is the passage through Aquileia of the legions returning to Italy from the East, veterans of the war fought against Vologases IV (147–191), King of the Parthians (the reconquest of Mesopotamia and subsequent retreat). This news may seem insignificant, but this is not the case at all, because those legions carry the contagion of smallpox together with the spoils of war. Aquileia thus unknowingly becomes the gateway to Italy of what will prove to be a great "plague", destined to mark the Antonine age. The scourge will rapidly spread across vast territories and continents and will go down in history as one of the most serious pandemics to hit the ancient world. A detailed illustration of this painful chapter requires a preliminary summary of the historical picture.

As we noted above, the reign of Marcus Aurelius lasts from 161 to 180. His early years are dominated by the rekindling of the dispute between the Romans and the Parthians (this has already given rise to a war, which lasted from 114 to 123). As in the time of Trajan, the *casus belli* is the question of Armenia. In 161, Vologases IV ousted the pro-Roman king of Armenia, Soemus, and replaced him with his brother Pacorus (161–163). Subsequently, he invaded Cappadocia, defeated the legion of

Marcus Sedatius Severianus, governor of Cappadocia, at Elegia (near Erzurum in Turkey), and occupied the city of Edessa (Sanliurfa in Turkey). Finally, since Atidius Cornelianus, governor of Syria, had concentrated all his forces in Antioch on the Orontes (Antakia in Turkey), demilitarizing the positions on the Euphrates, Vologases broke into Syria, carrying out massacres, devastation, and looting, and chased Atidius out. These successes appear all the more remarkable if we consider that the Romans were not taken aback by the initiative of Vologases but instead were overwhelmed by the vastness of his strategic plan and by the grandeur of the means he deployed.

Marcus Aurelius reacts to Vologases' offensive by sending Marcus Statius Priscus to Cappadocia and his own adoptive brother Lucius Aurelius Verus to Antioch on the Orontes (he will remain in Rome to deal with other important affairs of state). Verus arrives in Antioch in the spring of 163. During the journey, he has shown that he is not in a hurry to arrive. In Antioch, he spends his time in the suburb of Daphne, playing and hunting.

Daphne takes its name from a grove of laurels located in its vicinity, where festivals in honor of Apollo Daphne are celebrated every year. It was a favored destination of the Seleucids and is reputed to be a place of debauchery.

Marcus Aurelius is patient and hardly complains about the carefreeness of Verus. In practice, the plan of military operations that Verus should have conducted against the Parthians has been prepared by Marcus Aurelius himself and implemented, with skill and luck, by the commanders of the legions of Verus, one of whom is Caius Avidius Cassius.

The war takes place in three phases: Armeniaca (161–163), Partica (163–165), and Medica (165–166). The final stages see Priscus and Cassius go on the offensive, the former in Cappadocia and Armenia, and the latter in Syria and beyond the Euphrates. In 163/164, Priscus leads the legions from Syria to Armenia, destroys Artaxata, the capital of the Kingdom of Pacorus, occupies the whole country, and put a prince of the Emesa dynasty on the throne. Therefore, the Kingdom of Armenia becomes a Roman protectorate once again. In 164, Cassius oversees the reorganization and intense training of the Syrian legions. He defeats the Parthians at Dura Europos and occupies this city. Later, he also occupies Edessa, which thus returns to the hands of a friendly prince. Vologases tries in vain to sign an armistice. He flees to Parthia, and the Romans chase him beyond the Tigris. In 165, Cassius occupies Carrhae, Nisibis, and Seleucia on the Tigris. He conquers Ctesiphon, the capital of Parthia, and sets fire to the royal palace. Then he conquers Media.

By this point, Armenia and northern Mesopotamia have returned to the possession of the Romans, Vologases has been defeated and humiliated, and the commercial horizons of the Empire have widened to the east. But Seleucia rebels. In 166, Cassius reconquers it and sacks it. But shortly thereafter, he must evacuate Mesopotamia because his troops become infected with smallpox during the sacking of Seleucia. He is appointed governor of Syria, with competence extended throughout the Roman East. Lucius Verus, undeservedly, receives the *cognomen ex virtute* of Armeniacus. On

13 August 166, in Rome, Marcus Aurelius and Lucius Verus celebrate the triumph over the Parthians.

Meanwhile, smallpox begins to spread in Rome and throughout the Empire. It is the second time that an epidemic of this type has hit the Mediterranean world (the first time, in AD 65, the disease was imported from Africa). The scourge hits families like a ghost. It throws houses and buildings into gloomy sadness. Every day there are hundreds of deaths, up to 2,000 on the worst days (Dio Cass. 83.4.3). The lifeless bodies are loaded onto carts and taken away by family members to be buried or burned, without coffins carried on shoulders or in procession. The bodies of slaves and those who have remained without relatives are thrown onto the streets, where they are collected by special agents, loaded onto wagons, and taken away. To prevent the dead from causing new epidemics, the obligation to bury them outside the city is established.[9] Those who can afford it isolate themselves in the countryside or in the hills, convinced that, by doing so, they will be saved. But the incubation of the disease lasts for about 40 days and often foils those who escape.

It is commonly believed that the epidemic is a divine punishment for Cassius having attacked Seleucia despite the fact that the city had already agreed to surrender and for the further sacrilegious act performed by a Roman soldier, who opened a chest of gold in the Temple of Apollo during the sacking of the city, unleashing the wrath of the god. Therefore, priests from all sides are called, rites are officiated, prayers are raised, and animals are sacrificed to any divinity, even foreign ones. But it's all in vain. Smallpox spreads mourning and desolation everywhere, and this is accompanied by famine since, in the countryside, there are no longer those who sow and reap. To appease hunger pangs, people are reduced to eating anything, not just figs and olives but also tubers, seeds, and spontaneously growing cereals, such as millet and rye. Hunger grips mainly cities, and many of those saved from smallpox die of hunger, vitamin deficiency, food poisoning, or gastric complications. Statues are raised to the most illustrious victims of the contagion, as is customary for military commanders who died in combat. Marcus Aurelius has the bodies of the poor buried at the expense of the state. But the state budget is in disarray: the war against the Parthians has bled the Treasury dry, and years of idleness and too much prosperity have passed in pleasant apathy, without the underlying problems of public finance being addressed. The money runs out. It is no longer possible either to buy grain for the population or to pay the salaries of officers, much less prepare for war. Marcus Aurelius chooses not to burden the provincials with new taxes. Instead, he orders all the furnishings of his palace and all the precious objects of the Imperial office to be sold: gold and crystal cups, ceramics, evening dresses, gems. At the end of the war, once normality is restored, he will authorize anyone who wants it to resell the goods purchased and get their money back, without putting pressure on anyone.

In Rome, the epidemic lasts for three years, causing—it seems—300,000 deaths out of a population of over 1 million, killing almost 30% of the population. Outside Rome, the disease will spread from Mediterranean Europe to continental Europe, as far as the Rhine. It will rage for 15 years and will affect 2% of the entire population of the Empire, causing 1 million deaths overall (Fundling 2009: 122, 251 n. 91), and one-third of its most populous centers, contributing in no little way to the constant process of demographic decrease in the Mediterranean area. The effects will last for nearly 500 years. In 251–266, another epidemic will break out, of proportions equal to the first, but in a less bloody way in Rome, as a result of the same infectious (previously dormant) strain.

A second, significant episode that occurred in Aquileia under the rule of Marcus Aurelius is the siege that the city suffers in 167 by the Quadi and the Marcomanni.

The Quadi and the Marcomanni besiege Aquileia

A new war front opens in Europe, along the Danubian border of the Roman Empire, in the winter of 166/167, by which time the "pestilence" has now reached the Rhine and is circulating among the Gauls, carried by the troops who returned from the East.

There have already been raids by the Germans across that border, between the Rezia and the Danube. But now it's different. What the Romans have to face is not an occasional and sporadic invasion as in the past but the emigration/invasion of entire peoples, who move south in search of a new territory in which to settle because they are being pressed by the Goths and the Vandals who are advancing from the Asian steppes and are, in turn, pursued by the Huns and other peoples who are migrating from Central Asia. The phenomenon is enormous, nor does each people go alone, as there is common coordination, direction, project, and strategy as has never been seen before. Among the migrants/invaders, the Quadi and the Marcomanni stand out for our purposes. Some are on the move from Moravia and others from Bohemia, under the guidance of Ballomarus, a Marcomannus.

They pour like a rising tide on the border garrisons between the Saale and the Lower Danube and on the new legions sent to strengthen the former; they overwhelm them and open a passage for Italy. In the meantime, the Lombards and the Ubii have also crossed the Danube and invaded Upper Pannonia. That province is governed by Claudius Quintianus Pompeianus and is frequently subject to attacks by bands of Goths, Catti, and Dacians coming from the southeast of the great Elbe and Danube basin.

The Quadi and the Marcomanni inflict two disastrous defeats on the Romans, after which they penetrate deeply into Italy, besiege Aquileia (the defenders and the whole population, increased by the masses of refugees from the countryside, resist the attacks, sheltered by the strong walls), destroy Opitergium (Oderzo), and sow terror as far as Verona. Tergeste is saved, probably because it is located in a secluded position with respect to the main access road to Italy through the Julian Alps.

Aquileia, under the reign of Marcus Aurelius, is still the capital of the *Venetia et Histria*. It is a very large and populous city, opulent and well organized, a center of artisanal and industrial production, and a large emporium, where the wine produced in great abundance in the surrounding countryside finds its market (Herodian. 8.3).

The city has expanded beyond the Republican walls, mainly within the bend of the Natissa river. Those walls have lost their defensive function because the *pax romana* made them superfluous for over two and a half centuries; after the Iapodes' raids (52 BC), in fact, Aquileia no longer needed it, as no one threatened it anymore. Two new urban districts have been built east of the river port, beyond the Natisone: one along the Canale Anfora, the other in Monastero. Another area into which the new buildings have extended is that of Marignane, west of the Republican walls.

The barbarians have therefore invaded Friuli Venezia Giulia and Veneto, reaching the river Adige, which descends from the Eastern Alps and flows into the Po. This means that they swarm across the entire northeast of Italy, devastating, plundering and killing. The walled cities resist, but the towns not protected by walls are indefensible, while the countryside is lost and lies abandoned and deserted.

Marcus Aurelius does not falter. He calls upon the army of Armenia, mobilizes the armies of Cappadocia and Egypt, and concentrates the army of the Rhine further south. He undoubtedly considers the prospect of a long war. First of all, control of Aquileia must be maintained at all costs because, if the barbarians overwhelm this bulwark, there will no longer be anything that can prevent them from safely descending through Italy and reaching Rome. The danger is therefore to the maximum degree. The safety of Italy and Rome depends on Aquileia.

Marcus Aurelius and Lucius Verus leave for the front together because for the war against the Germans the presence of both Augusti is necessary (this is the official motivation, but it is evident that Marcus Aurelius does not place great faith in the suitability of Verus to conduct war operations). It is the first time that a Roman emperor has led an army into war in the last 35 years (that is, since 134, the year of the presumed participation of Hadrian in the Jewish war), if not in the last 50 (Trajan's campaign against the Parthians in 117). In this case, there are actually two emperors directly engaged on the war front, with it being understood that the commander-in-chief of the army is Marcus Aurelius, while Verus is the deputy.

The march of the two Augusti to the north causes the enemy to be reduced in number, at the cost, however, of many deaths, due to both the clashes with the enemy and the epidemic. Some tribes withdraw, others kill the promoters of the insurrection. The besiegers of Aquileia abandon their intention to conquer the city and retreat, only to disappear just beyond the Alps. The besieged breathe a sigh of relief. They are safe!

Marcus Aurelius retakes all the positions that the Romans lost in the north of Italy and founds the *pretentura Italiae et Alpium,* a temporary military district located in the extreme northeast of Italy, the region most exposed to the barbarian invasions. This implies the fortification of the mountain passes and the strengthening of the walls. The works begin immediately (they will be completed in 171). In all probability, the seat of the *pretentura* will be established in Aquileia.

The two emperors plan to cross the Alps to liberate Noricum and Pannonia and colonize the whole of Germany. But then something unexpected happens. Verus is hit by a stroke while traveling in a carriage with Marcus Aurelius on the stretch from Concordia to Altinum, near Aquileia. At the time, the stroke makes him mute, but three days later, it kills him. Marcus Aurelius, consumed by grief, brings the body of Verus back to Rome for funeral honors and his apotheosis and orders that the deceased be deified.

The third of the episodes we mentioned above is the concentration of the legions led by Marcus Aurelius at Aquileia and their departure from there for Germany to fight against the Quadi and the Marcomanni, which takes place in 171. The commander-in-chief of the Roman army, reporting to Marcus Aurelius, is Tiberius Claudius Pompeianus. He was born in Syria in around 125, and is the son of the *eques* and *homo novus* Tiberius Claudius Quintus. He was alternate consul in 162 and governor of Lower Pannonia in 167. He distinguished himself in Verus' campaigns against the Parthians from 161 to 166 and was noticed by Marcus Aurelius. He then defended the Danubian border, repelling the invasion of a few thousand Lombards, and is alongside Marcus Aurelius when, shortly after, the first attacks of the Marcomanni begin.

The Marcomannic Wars will be very expensive and complicated for the Romans, especially due to the smallpox epidemic, which thins the ranks of the army.

New military expeditions from Aquileia

Marcus Aurelius establishes his headquarters in Carnuntum (Petronnel in Austria), as Tiberius and Trajan did before him. Carnuntum is an important legionary fortress. It occupies an area of 17.6 ha and is the seat both of the fleet of Pannonia and of the governor of Pannonia Superior.

Later, Marcus Aurelius goes up the March valley to face the Quadi and defeats them on the banks of the river Thaya. The enemies flee, but the emperor chases them into their territory, catches them, and defeats them again, then takes possession of all the cattle and horses of those who surrender. Thirteen-thousand prisoners are settled in the already depopulated cities and countryside of Italy with the obligation to cultivate the land and perform military service as part of a project of "forced colonization". The Quadi must also undertake not to offer military support and food aid to the Marcomanni; rather, they must prevent the latter from accessing their land. Peace is granted on two conditions, one of which is to evacuate a strip of land beyond the Danube, 10 miles deep, which will be garrisoned by the Romans.

In 173, Marcus Aurelius defeats and subdues the small people of the Germanic Suebi, settled in the Main basin, after which he confronts the Marcomanni and overwhelms them. The conditions of peace imposed on the Marcomanni are the same as those already imposed on the Quadi.

Fifteen-thousand prisoners in chains take the road to Italy, heading for Rabenna (Ravenna) to repopulate it. Once they have arrived in the Adriatic city and have been freed from their chains, instead of working the fields, they rebel against the officers and occupy the city. Marcus Aurelius has them all killed.

Military exploits do not distract the emperor from his study of philosophy. In the vicinity of Vindobona (Wien), during the long campaign against the Quadi and the Marcomanni, he wrote a philosophical work in Greek that was to be greatly appreciated for its expressive power and its relevance. This work is called "To myself" or "Thoughts", and it is a collection of reflections on the destiny of man and the inevitable desire to fight for vainglory.

Marcus Aurelius, after defeating the Marcomanni, meets a tribe of the Germanic people of the Lacringi and another Germanic tribe, the Cotini, who submit to him. In the near future, both will join the legions on an expedition to the East.

The emperor-philosopher subdues the Naristi, then confronts the Ermanduri in the Bohemian Forest and makes deals with groups of Vandals, Charii, Victuali, and Asdingi. In 174, he goes to Dacia (Romania), severely punishes the Costobaci, the Sarmatians, and also the Quadi, the latter because they are not respecting the peace treaty. Meanwhile, a threat from the barbarians has also emerged in the East. In 170, the Bastarni carried out raids for the purpose of robbery in Asia Minor, and the Parthians did the same in Greece. Furthermore, the Costobaci broke into the Lower Danube.

In 180, Marcus Aurelius contracts smallpox. He is very worried, both for his illness (which will lead to his death) and because his son Commodus is still too young and immature to exercise such great power as the imperial one, and there is a risk that he will stray from the teachings and education he has received. Furthermore, the war against the Germans is not yet over, and he fears that Commodus's inexperience could compromise the results achieved.

Marcus Aurelius, aware of the imminence of his earthly existence, prepares the succession to the throne. He marries his daughter Lucilla, widow of Lucius Verus, with his old but trusted adviser and collaborator Claudius Quintius Pompeianus, then adopts the latter as a son in the wake of the tradition born in 98, when Nerva adopted Trajan and elevated him to the rank of Caesar. This means that, in the event of the death of Marcus Aurelius, Pompeianus will succeed him on the throne. But Pompeianus rejects the purple. He will be in charge of the supreme command of the Marcomannic Wars, together with another war veteran: Pertinax.

Seven years after the death of Marcus Aurelius, with the war almost over, Commodus, who in the meantime has succeeded his father, makes a hasty peace and retires to Rome, much to Pompeianus' regret. Two years later, Lucilla, Pompeianus' wife, is involved in a palace plot to kill Commodus, but the attempt fails and costs her her life. Pompeianus does not suffer retaliation because he was recognized as a stranger to the events, but nonetheless he retires to private life. Commodus was assassinated on 31 December 192, the victim of yet another plot hatched against him, this time by some senators, some praetorians, and his lover Marcia. After escaping poisoning, he is strangled by his fighting master, the former gladiator Narcissus. The Senate of Rome will arrange for his memory to be damned (cancellation from the public register of a previously known, disgraced person, known as *damnatio memoriae*).

Pertinax, the prefect of the city, offers the throne to Pompeianus, but the latter refuses again, knowing that the Praetorians have already caused Pertinax to overcome his reluctance to become emperor himself. Indeed, the Praetorians hail Pertinax as the emperor. But after only 87 days, they assassinate him because they are disappointed by his attitude against corruption, which does not allow them to get rich. One of the darkest periods in the history of Rome begins when the Praetorians auction off the title of emperor. The one who grabs it is the rich senator Didius Julianus. He obtains the imperial acclamation at the price of 25,000 sesterces for each Praetorian. Didius Julianus would like to associate Pompeianus with the power, given his great experience in the military field, but Pompeianus refuses for a third time, arguing that he is old and has severe vision problems. Pompeianus dies the same year, leaving a son named Lucius Aurelius Commodus Pompeianus (the latter will become consul in 209, under the reign of Septimius Severus, but will be assassinated on the orders of Caracalla a few years later).

The act of Didius Julianus has aroused the aversion of the rest of the army to him. In this climate, the legions of Pannonia acclaim their commander Septimius Severus as emperor in Carnuntum.

The usurper goes to Italy to fight against the rightful emperor. While the latter declares the former a public enemy and the Empire is sinking into chaos, the legions of Syria proclaim Pescennius Niger emperor, and those of Britain do the same for Clodius Albinus. A four-year civil war ensues.

In 194, Septimius Severus defeats and kills Pescennius Niger near Issus. In 197, he triumphantly enters Lugdunum (Lyon). In the meantime, Clodius Albinus commits suicide.

Septimius Severus (193–211) dies in February 211 in Eburacum (York in England) during an expedition against the Britons. He is deified by the Senate and buried in the mausoleum of Emperor Hadrian in Rome. His successors are his sons Publius Septimius Geta and Lucius Septimius Bassianus—the latter will become better known as Caracalla—born from his marriage to a Syrian woman, Julia Domna. In 212, Caracalla kills Geta. From now on, he will reign alone.

Caracalla's campaign in Germany

Under the reign of Caracalla (189–217), the Romans administratively organized the territories they controlled in Germany into two provinces: Germania Superior and Germania Inferior.

Germania Superior, also called Agri Decumates, is located in the Upper Rhine. Germania Inferior is located in the Lower Rhine. The former also embraces the regions between this river and the upper course of the Danube and is separated from the territories not controlled by the Romans by the state border called *limes germanicus*. This is a wide strip of land with roads, fortresses, watchtowers, and outposts, manned by legions of Roman citizens and support troops. It coincides for a while with the middle course of the Main, a river that joins the Rhine at Mogontiacum (Mainz in Germany), and is constantly and carefully monitored. Light, fast boats with sails and oar propulsion—such as of the *liburna* or *drakkar* type—continuously move up and down the current, gliding silently among the waves.

Mogontiacum is a river port in the vast region adjacent to the east of Transalpine Gaul and is separated from Germany by the Rhine. It is a large military base, where the Legio XXII Primigenia and the fleet of the Rhine have their seat. The upper reaches of the Main remain outside the border. It is an area covered by dense forests and is inhabited by hostile and ferocious populations, including the Chatti, Naristi (or Varisci), Hermunduri, Juthungi, and some of the Semnones—all permanent farmers, who have a history of being shepherds and hunters, nomads or semi-nomads. In the beginning, the Romans used those populations as suppliers of support troops. Later, the Germans allied themselves with each other, and the Romans collectively called them Alemanni.

In 213, Caracalla takes advantage of the Alemanni's weakness by colonizing their territory, changing the name of their settlements, and killing their most valiant warriors. The Alemanni curse him, and Caracalla falls ill. To counteract the influence of evil, the emperor first calls the spirits of his ancestors to help, then sends the army against the gangs of Alemanni who have raided Germania Superior.

During that campaign, which lasts from 213 to 214, Caracalla defeats some of the Alemanni and strengthens the border fortifications of Germania Superior and Raetia to enable them to withstand further barbarian invasions for the next 20 years. Legio II Traiana Fortis, having successfully accomplished its mission, is called Germanica. A period of relative tranquility follows.

In 217, Caracalla dies near Carrhae in Mesopotamia (Harran, southern Turkey), where he went to fight against the Parthians. He is stabbed to death, in an act of treason, by an officer of the imperial bodyguard, Justin Martialis, who is driven by personal reasons. Shortly after committing the crime, Martialis is himself killed by an archer.

Macrinus, and his successor Elagabalus

Caracalla's successor is the praetorian prefect Marcus Opellius Severus Macrinus (217–218), a Berber from the Roman province of Mauretania Cesariensis and a member of the equestrian order. Macrinus is the first Roman emperor who does not come from the senatorial order. He is proclaimed emperor on 11 April 217 while he is in Mesopotamia. Subsequently, he is confirmed by the Senate (but for the entire duration of his reign, albeit a short one, he will never have the opportunity to return to Rome). He reigns from Antioch on the Orontes in Syria. On 8 June 218, he is defeated at the Battle of Antioch by Elagabalus' tutor, Gannys, near Immae, in a village located approximately 24 miles from Antioch.

Elagabalus, 14, is the high priest of the Phoenician divinity of the sun, Elagabalus (or El-Gabal), in Emesa (Homs in Syria). He is proclaimed emperor in place of Macrinus on 16 May 218 by the Legio III Gallica, which is camped in Raphanea, near Emesa, thanks to the maneuvers of his mother, Julia Mesa. Upon the revolt of Elagabalus, Macrinus goes to Apamea, a Hellenistic city located on the right bank of the Orontes river in Syria, and he confers the title of Augustus on his 10-year-old son Diadumenian (who thus becomes co-emperor). After the battle, Macrinus retires to Antioch, but fighting breaks out in the city and he flees to Rome, but he will never arrive there. He is captured in Chalcedon in Bithynia. Meanwhile, Diadumenian is killed in Zeugma (Balkis in Turkey). Macrinus attempts to escape captivity but is wounded in the attempt and then is recaptured and executed. His and Diadumenian's heads are sent to Elagabalus as trophies. Their memory is condemned. The usurper Elagabalus is recognized by the Senate of Rome as the new emperor.

Elagabalus (about 204–222) moves to Rome, where he arrives in August or September 219 and makes a ceremonial entrance to the city at the head of a multicolored procession. His reign will last for 18 years and will be characterized as that of the most corrupt and most eccentric emperor that Rome ever had.

On 11 March 222, the Praetorian Guard murder Elagabalus and his mother. Their heads are torn off their torsos and their naked bodies are dragged around the city. Finally, Julia Mesa's body is thrown into the Tiber. Elagabalus is also subjected to *damnatio memoriae*. The successor of Elagabalus is his cousin: Marcus Aurelius Severus Alexander.

Notes

1   What we are about to tell is a true story, based on the discovery of the wreck of a Roman merchant ship, which took place in 1986 in the Adriatic Sea, about 6 miles off the island of Grado, at a depth of 16 m. The wreck was recovered from the seabed, together with a quantity of material connected to it, and restored and studied. To house the remains, the construction of the National Museum of Underwater Archeology of the Middle and Upper Adriatic started in Grado. The true name of the ship is unknown. The archeologists called it Iulia Felix for propitiatory purposes.
2   The presence on board of a sailor with light brown hair is suggested by the human hair of this color that was found among the planking of the ship.
3   The "iconic element" vanished. Possibly, it was a rock, a bow of a ship, or a dolphin.
4   Pliny the Younger, *Epistulae* 6.19.4: *Occurrit; nam sumptus candidatorum, foedos illos et infames, ambitus lege restrinxit; eosdem patrimonii tertiam partem conferre iussit in ea quae solo continerentur, deforme arbitratus - et erat - honorem petituros urbem Italiamque non pro patria sed pro hospitio aut stabulo quasi peregrinantes habere.*
5   Trajan's Forum remained standing and in use until 801, when it partially collapsed due to an earthquake, an event that paved the way for the subsequent reuse of the area. Today, only Trajan's Column remains. This has been preserved almost intact. It originally had a gilt bronze statue of Trajan on top, depicted wearing armor.
6   Ancient Mesopotamia corresponds to modern Iraq. It was divided into three parts: Iraqi Jezirah (the former Kingdom of Osroene, which included Edessa), Northern Mesopotamia (Assyria,

formerly Adiabene, found between the courses of the Little and Great Zab, with Arbela (today's Erbil) as its capital), and the Mesopotamian Plain (Mesene).

7   Some of the columns are now visible inside the Cathedral of San Giusto in Trieste.

8   A *procurator Augusti* was a man of proven confidence of the emperor, who came from an equestrian military career and was well-versed in accounting and finance, which the Augustus used to manage branches of the administration. The *flamines* were priests of the traditional Roman religion, in charge of the worship of a specific deity from which they took their name and for whom they celebrated the rites and holidays.

9   The aforementioned provisions remained in force for a long time. It seems they were still in effect in the 4th century.

Chapter 6

Aquileia's War

Alexander Severus' death (235)

The Greek goddess Tyche is the personification of fortune and of the prosperity and destiny of cities. Her Roman equivalent is Fortuna. She assists births, makes people, plants, and animals grow, heals them if they get sick, presides over war and the administration of justice, determines life and death, and is in charge of fate and good and bad luck. She was brought to Rome by King Servius Tullius (578–535 BC) and is currently the subject of a variety of cults in a great number of temples and sanctuaries (26 in the city alone). One of her qualities is that of being *primigenia*, "original, primitive". The center of the cult of Fortuna Primigenia is a large, impressive oracular sanctuary with scenic architecture located in Praeneste (Palestrina), a city located in Lower Lazio in a dominant position over the Campagna Romana.

Fortuna Primigenia is the tutelary deity of the Twenty-Second Legion of the Roman army. This unit was established in AD 39 by Emperor Caligula (37–41) in view of a military campaign against the Germans. In AD 69, "The Year of the Four Emperors", it took the side in favor of Vitellius. In 213, it participated in Emperor Caracalla's (198–217) campaign in Germany. After being established in Mogontiacum (Mainz)—the capital of the Roman province of Germania Superior and a large military base—it contributed to the defense of the Upper Rhine sector of the *limes germanicus*. *Limes*, in Latin, means state border. With reference to the German border, this word identifies a series of structures of various nature and size—legionary fortresses, forts, fortified river ports, watchtowers, ditches, embankments, and palisades—all lined up along or close to a military road.

The Twenty-Second Legion has recently been chosen to be part of the expeditionary force of Emperor Alexander Severus (222–234) in Mesopotamia and is now fighting the Parthians. The conflict broke out in 230, when the Sassanid Ardashir I (224–241), in order to re-establish the ancient Persian empire of the Achaemenid dynasty (about 560–330 BC), invaded Armenia and Mesopotamia. Currently, the Parthians are threatening Syria and Cappadocia. The Twenty-Second went to Mesopotamia reluctantly, and its discontent grew as the war stretched far beyond what was expected, and it demanded an increasing toll of blood. In particular, it attributed the failures of the army to the military incapacity of the young emperor.

Alexander Severus is a modest and respectful young man but is dominated by his mother, Julia Avita Mamaea, a woman with a strong-willed and intrusive character. In 227, Mamaea, jealous of the title of Augusta of her daughter-in-law, Sallustia Orbana, removed the latter from the court. She later had her father, Praetorian Prefect Lucius Seius Sallustius, killed, and she exiled Sallustia to Libya. All this happened against the will of Alexander Severus, who did not have the courage to oppose his mother. Mamaea followed her son to the East and now influences his tactical and strategic choices, with disastrous results. Alexander Severus, supreme leader of the army, is perpetually indecisive, either because of the fear of putting his own life on the line or because of his mother's "feminine fears".

In 233, while Alexander Severus directs the campaign in Mesopotamia from his palace in Antioch on the Orontes (Hatay Antakya in Turkey), a horde of Alemanni crosses over into Germania Superior and attacks cities and countryside. Upon hearing the news, the Twenty-Second and the other Roman troops in Mesopotamia demand (successfully) that Alexander Severus settle matters with the Parthians and bring them back to the banks of the Rhine to drive back the Alemanni and punish them. It is noteworthy that Alexander Severus brings back with him some specialized units, recruited in Syria and Mesopotamia, including some contingents of Osroene archers and some heavy cavalry.[1]

Before returning to Germany, Alexander Severus celebrates a splendid triumph in Rome, despite the fact that his campaign in the East barely managed to restore the status quo ante, the morale of the army is in pieces, and Alexander is now branded in all military circles as a "coward". Once back in Germany, Alexander Severus re-establishes his own headquarters in Mogontiacum, has a bridge of boats set up across the Rhine, and enjoys some small local successes. It should also be noted that Mamaea again followed him to the front.

Once again, the emperor shows his indecision. He hesitates to cross the river in strength to face the Germans in their woods and take revenge on them. The troops quiver and wait impatiently to be able to cross the river. They are eager and ready to fight, but they must restrain themselves. The more time passes, the more impatient they become. When it clearly emerges that Alexander Severus, on the advice of his mother, is getting ready to solve the problem of relations between the Empire and the Alemanni in a bloodless way, granting the latter a subsidy, the tension in the camp skyrockets. The soldiers feel humiliated and offended. Now they believe they have one more reason to consider their emperor inadequate with respect to his high responsibilities. They also complain of their interests being damaged because they are being deprived of the possibility of accumulating the spoils of war and the money the emperor could have given them goes to the enemy instead. In short, they distance themselves from Alexander Severus. Even the specialized units from the East abandon the emperor.

The drama breaks out suddenly. The Twenty-Second mutinies under the leadership of its commander-in-chief, Caius Valerius Maximinus, a man with an imposing physique and Herculean strength.

Maximinus was born in 173 in Thrace (or in Lower Moesia) into a peasant family mixed with barbarian elements. He is rough, arrogant, proud, but also courageous and daring, very close to the soldiers. Moreover, his military path is very respectable. He served in Egypt, Mesopotamia, and Persia. From now on, we will call him Maximinus Thrax.

The outcome of the affair is bloody. On 18 March 235, in vicus Britanniae (Bretzenheim, near Mainz), during a meeting with the generals, Alexander Severus is killed together with his mother and some advisers (the other advisers will be removed from office).[2] Immediately afterward, the Twenty-Second acclaims Maximinus Thrax as the new Augustus at the cost of a generous donation from the interested party. Therefore, the death of Alexander Severus puts an end not only to the life of the young emperor but also to the Severan Dynasty (193–235).

The reign of Alexander Severus marked the rebirth of the prestige, if not the power, of the Senate of Rome, but recent events have shown that the army is now the real and only force of the Empire, and, due to the risks and sacrifices to which it is exposed, it demands adequate rewards. The Senate of Rome understands the antiphon and acts accordingly, despite the "scandal" represented in its eyes by Maximinus Thrax, due to the fact that he is the first soldier emperor, he comes from a border area, his ways are unbearable, hasty, and arbitrary, and there is the widespread suspicion that he was directly involved in the murder of his predecessor. Therefore, it accepts Maximinus' elevation to the imperial throne and openly acknowledges his achievements.

The successor: Maximinus Thrax (235–238)

Maximinus Thrax hurries to raise his son Caius Julius Verus Maximus to the rank of Caesar, then leads the army to the opposite bank of the Rhine, using every boat available to ferry men, equipment, weapons, and horses, including some large and capacious barges. He penetrates deep into the lands of the Alemanni and systematically devastates them. He fights among the soldiers and slaughters the enemy. The expedition is not a walk in the park, though: the Alemanni inflict heavy losses on the Romans, but they are defeated. In the end, the legions themselves give Maximinus a *cognomen ex virtute* to be added to the family name. The adjective is Germanicus Maximus. This episode also represents a break from the practice as, previously, it has always been the Senate of Rome that awarded the victorious commander with his *cognomen*.

But another emergency is looming. A barbarian horde is making it clear that they want to cross the Danube and invade Pannonia. It is formed by populations settled in the plain between the Tisza and the Danube: the Sarmatians-Iazyges and the free Dacians, that is, the Dacians not subject to the authority of Rome.

Pannonia, we recall, embraces the western part of Hungary, the northern part of Austria, the most eastern part of Austria, the northern part of Croatia, and part of Slovenia. After becoming a Roman province in AD 14, it developed a flourishing urban life in centers such as Carnuntum, Aquincum, and Sirmium, each of which evolved from a Roman fortified camp thanks to their involvement in commercial traffic between the cities of *Venetia et Histria*, the coastal centers of Illyricum, and the Danube area, gaining impetus especially from the activities of the merchants of Aquileia and Tergeste. In the 2nd century, it was frequently subject to attacks from bands of Goths, Catti, and Dacians. Marcus Aurelius (161–180) freed it from the Quadi and Marcomanni who had invaded it.

Maximinus attacks in advance. Thus begins the first of two military campaigns, which will see the use of the two legions stationed in the Roman province of Pannonia Inferior (the First Adiutrix and the Second Adiutrix), some Germanic support troops, and some specialized units, of which one comes from Emesa (Homs in Syria) (this one is one of those that were brought with him to Germany by Alexander Severus from the East), one from Mauritania, and one from Thrace. The first campaign takes place in the summer of 236, the second by the end of 237. Maximinus definitively defeats the enemy in a battle that takes place around Sirmium.

Sirmium (near Sremska Mitrovica, now in northwestern Serbia) is a city located on the banks of the Sava River. It grew and developed from a fortified village of the Scordisci and Amantini. It was conquered by the Romans during the Dalmatian-Illyrian campaigns in the years from 13 to 9 BC. Under the Flavian dynasty, it became a Roman colony. Subsequently, it retained an important strategic role. In 103, after the conquest of Dacia by Emperor Trajan (98–117), Pannonia was divided into Pannonia Superior and Pannonia Inferior, and Sirmium became the capital of the latter, while Carnuntum (Patronel in Austria) became the capital of the former. It remained so until, in 212–214, it was replaced in the role by Aquincum (Budapest in Hungary), a legionary fortress created to face the Germanic Quadi and the Sarmatians-Iazyges. It was the headquarters of Emperor Marcus Aurelius (161–180) in the Marcomannic Wars. In 236–237, it began to play a strategic-military role once again.

After the victory over the Sarmatians and the Dacians, Maximinus establishes his headquarters there. The presence of the emperor makes Sirmium a second capital of the Empire, with all the administrative, economic, cultural, and religious implications that this entails. It is already equipped with fortification walls. From now on, it will be enriched by a palatium, baths, and granaries.

In recognition of his achievements, Maximinus Thrax, between 237 and 238, receives the double *cognomen ex virtute* of Sarmaticus Maximus and Dacicus Maximus from the Senate of Rome.

In all, he holds power for three years. During them, in order to face the continuous, enormous military expenses, he drastically increases the taxes that weigh on the wealthier classes, bleeds the state treasury, and confiscates the public funds of the municipalities and even the votive offerings of the temples. Moreover, he persecutes the Christians.

The persecution of Christians

Christianity is a universalistic religion born during the reign of Augustus (27 BC–AD 14). Over a span of the intervening two centuries, it has made many proselytes throughout the Empire, unlike Judaism, which in the same period has characterized itself as "national" and anti-Roman. In the beginning, the beliefs of Christians found acceptance in the subordinate social classes, not only as a religion but also as a culture and discipline. Later, they were welcomed even among the ruling class.

Periodically, Christians become the targets of the repressive measures of the Roman authorities, such as imprisonment, torture, deportation, and even death, basically due to their refusal to sacrifice to the emperor—that is, to recognize him as a god—understood as a crime against the state. This happened for the first time under the reign of Nero (54–68). When they were already victims of acts of aggressive intolerance on the part of the pagans, they were falsely accused by the emperor of having started the great fire that destroyed much of Rome. Many of them were burned in the emperor's gardens so that bonfires would light up the parties he threw while he entertained his guests.

Maximinus believes that it is essential to restore the religious tradition of the Empire by requiring anyone to sacrifice to the Soldier-Emperor and, therefore, to propitiate the fortune of the army, of which the Augustus is an expression (since the Empire depends on the army, the fortune of the army is the fortune of the Empire). Therefore, he issues an edict authorizing further persecution of Christians, which will have an effect mainly on the heads of local churches, starting with the bishop of Rome.

The persecution of Christians by Maximinus Thrax is not regulated according to a plan, however. It takes place in Rome and perhaps elsewhere. But not in Aquileia, apparently.

The origin and the first martyrs of the Church of Aquileia

Paganism is still dominant even in Aquileia, where the traditional Roman religion (the worship of Mars, Mercury, etc.) is flanked by a series of ancient local cults, which the leveling action of Latin culture has not managed to obscure, and other cults that were welcomed into the Roman Empire in the 1st and 3rd centuries. We refer to the cult of Apollo Belenus, perhaps of Gallo-Carnic origin; to that of the Sources of Timavo; to that of the River Esontius; to that of Silvanus, a divinity of the wood; to the Hellenistic one of Mithras, a solar god; and to the Egyptian cults of Isis and Serapis. It should also be said that one of the ethnic groups that make up the cosmopolitan population of Aquileia is that of the Jews, who are very influential, while another is that of the Christians.

At this stage, probably, there is already an *ecclesia*, "church", in Aquileia, understood as an organized community of Christians. Indeed, it seems that we can speak of an Aquileian church from the 3rd century when the diocese of the same name was formed and began to dialogue with the evangelization poles of Poetovium (Ptuj in Slovenia) and Salona (Solin in Croatia), and perhaps also with that of Sirmium.

It is reasonable to assume that its primitive nucleus was formed in the 2nd century, at the latest during the reign of Antoninus Pius (138–161), when the Church of Aquileia still depended on the Church of Rome.[3] This hypothesis is supported by the letter of Saint Paul to the Romans and by the fact that Pope Pius I (140–155) was a native of Aquileia. It is also noteworthy that in Aquileia, at that time, the ritual of burial, typical of the funerary customs of the Christians, was practiced alongside the rite of cremation, distinctive of the Roman tradition.

Perhaps Christianity was introduced to Aquileia by Jews of the Christian faith, who, however, kept sacred respect for the prescriptions of the Mosaic Law, especially for the Sabbath. This would have happened several times: first by merchants and artisans, and then by land workers. The first Aquileian Christians would have formed a "closed" community, governed collegially, by the bishop, presbyters, and deacons, according to the provisions of the Church of Alexandria in Egypt. Only later—in the first decades of the 2nd century—would the community have opened it to the Catholic Church (Biasutti 2005: 58–59).

It is uncertain what weight pagans currently have in Aquileia and its territory and what relationship they have with the local Christian community. In general, in the Empire, the pagan world still gathers the great families of the senatorial aristocracy, the intellectuals, the military, and the rural masses, and, if Christians are divided among themselves, there is an even greater division between pagans and Christians.

Gordian I (238)

In 238, the rich landowners of the Roman province of Africa Proconsularis (Tunisia) enter into conflict with the Roman tax authorities, which have become overly rapacious. A rebellion breaks out in Thysdrus (El Djem), a rather prosperous olive oil production center located near Carthage. The governor of the province is killed in the riots. To save themselves from the consequences of that murder, the insurgents— acting against Maximinus Thrax—acclaim a rich *eques* (an enriched plebeian), one of the local landowners, as emperor: the 80-year-old Marcus Antonius Gordianus Sempronianus Romanus Africanus (from now on Gordian I), commander-in-chief of Legio III Scythica when it was stationed in Syria, governor in Britannia in 216, proconsul of Achaea under Emperor Elagabalus, and proconsul of Africa Proconsularis under Emperor Alexander Severus.

Gordian I (March–April 238) associates his son Marcus (born *c.* 192, from now on Gordian II), a consul under Alexander Severus and a womanizer, lover of the fine arts and author of literary compositions, though completely devoid of any military experience, as commander-in-chief of Legio III Scythica, and, on 19 March 238, they enter Carthage together triumphantly.

The Senate of Rome—in whose eyes Maximinus Thrax now appears as a tyrant, especially because of his fiscal policy—recognizes the two Gordians. The episode marks the beginning of a series of events that will shed blood in Rome, where the people will join the Senate in rising up against Maximinus and will lash out against everything that recalls the "tyrant". Maximinus' statues are demolished, his followers are hunted and killed, their homes are set on fire. Similar events also occur in other parts of Italy.

A follower of Maximinus—the senator Capellianus, governor of the Roman province of Numidia, bordering Africa Proconsularis to the east—confronts the two Gordians. He commands a legion of the regular army—the XIII Augusta—reinforced by support troops, while his opponents lead a muddled and ill-equipped army. Therefore, the outcome of the clash is taken for granted. Gordian II falls in the Battle of Carthage on 12 April 238. The remnants of his army, having fled, are chased to a nearby city and massacred there in front of their own families. Gordian I cannot bear the loss of his son and commits suicide. Retaliation follows. All those who sided with the Gordians, starting with the people of Carthage, are put to death and their assets are confiscated (Herodian. 7.9.7-8, 7.9.10).

Maximus/Pupienus and Balbinus (238)

On hearing the news of the Battle of Carthage, the Senate of Rome does not hesitate to regain possession of the ancient prerogative of electing the Augustus and elevates two of its members to the throne: Marcus Clodius Pupienus Maximus and Decimus Coelius Calvinus Balbinus. The former is a man of humble origins who was able to step forward in the administration of the state and currently holds the position of *praefectus urbis*. The latter is a member of a noble family; he was consul twice.

The population takes to the streets to protest against the election of Pupienus and Balbinus and presses the Senate to designate in their place as emperor Gordian I's 13-year-old grandson, Marcus Antonius Gordianus Pius (Gordian III), he also being of senatorial extraction. The Senate of Rome does not accept this, declares Gordian III a public enemy, and instructs a commission of 20 senators to mobilize the citizens and provide for everything that is necessary for Rome's defense (in the meantime, Maximinus Thrax has left Sirmium with his legions, heading for Rome by land). The Roman state thus falls into a new civil war, which will have devastating consequences on the political and social life of the Empire, from Rome to the provinces.

Maximinus Thrax's army is composed of a large number of Germanic support troops, javelineers from Mauritania, and archers from Osroene. He crosses abandoned and deserted countryside, where there is nothing to plunder, much less provisions to commandeer. Also, Iulia Aemona (Ljubljana in Slovenia), where he arrives on 10 May 238, is empty. The inhabitants took away everything they could, starting with the food supplies, and set the rest on fire. Maximinus stops there for one night and leaves the next day, taking the Via Gemina, which leads to Aquileia. He crosses the Julian Alps at ad Pirum, without encountering resistance, and goes down to the plain of Lower Friuli, descending through the Vipava valley and then the Frigidus (Isonzo) valley. But the melting of the snow in the mountains has caused the Frigidus river to break its banks. A bridge with stone arches has collapsed, and the plain is flooded. In their attempt to cross the river, many Germanic soldiers are swept away by the current. Eventually, Maximinus has a bridge set up across the river, made of wine barrels, and manages to cross it (Herodian. 7.22.4). Finally, he arrives in sight of Aquileia.

Aquileia: the hub of a well-kept territory

Under the Severan Dynasty (193–235), Aquileia was renamed Colonia Septimia Severa Clodia and underwent an intensive building phase, with renovations of the Forum area. The civil basilica has been reconfigured completely and assumed a plan with two opposing apses in a quadrangular outer structure. Otherwise, the urban layout of Aquileia is still as it was under the reign of Marcus Aurelius (161–180), with a notable exception. In the last 50 years, the city has expanded beyond the Republican walls. Moreover, in the same period, the Republican walls have been largely dismantled, mainly in the area of the river port and in the loop of the Natissa. The reason is found in the fact that there had been no threats to collective security from which the local community had had to defend itself for a long time. Perhaps, also, they had been demolished in part by the violent earthquake that hit the Veneto region in 238, which caused very serious damage, mainly in the city of Vicentia (Vicenza) and its surroundings.[4]

In the field of private construction, some houses with mosaic floors have been built. One floor has a mosaic in the center that gives the idea of a carpet of flowers, and the rest is all in white mosaic, framed by black stripes. Mosaics datable to the 1st and 2nd centuries adorn the floors of a rich *domus*, the large peristyle of which—a portico that runs around the internal garden measuring 11 m by 9 m—is also paved with mosaics, with fairly large black tiles, interspersed with white tiles. A 13 m by 7 m dining room is all paved in white mosaic with a thin black thread at the edge. The large atriums of three other houses retain, respectively, a white mosaic, a mosaic with a checkerboard decoration, and a mosaic with a black diagonal weave to form lozenges.

The city is the hub of a well-kept territory. The surrounding countryside, well cultivated, "seems to be garlanded with parallel rows of trees, and by the shoots of vines that intertwine on all sides, forming arches similar to those that are erected for the holidays" (Herodian. 3.6).

Maximinus Thrax besieges Aquileia[5]

On hearing the news of the approach of Maximinus Thrax and his army, many people flock to Aquileia from the surrounding countryside, trusting they would find safe refuge there. The refugees join their forces with those of the residents and the military garrison. Thus a spontaneous defense was formed, which, refusing to welcome the "barbarian" Maximinus and to negotiate with him, now try to save the city. The defenders are coordinated by Tullius Menophilus and Rutilius Prudens Crispinus on behalf of the local Senate, of which they are part. They prepare to withstand a long siege. Among other things, they restore and/or raise the surviving sections of the Republican walls, already heavily compromised, and rebuild the demolished sections, then reinforce everything with the construction of towers and other fortification works (Herodian. 8.2.5). All this happens in great haste and with the reuse of architectural elements taken from buildings intended for civil or religious use, even prestigious ones, such as a splendid marble entablature with inscriptions that belonged to a portico.[6]

A masonry curtain, reinforced by pillars incorporated into the wall, from which they protrude only slightly, is erected ex novo along the quay of the river port, further east of the Republican walls. Three small doors allow access to the river (Fozzati 2013: 85–90). The intervention required the sacrifice of the port, which played a major role in the life of the city. The bulk of the port traffic has moved to Aquae Gradatae (Grado) on the seashore, and it has thus become the sole port of Aquileia. Aquae Gradatae is connected to Aquileia both by the navigable course of the Natissa and by road.[7] The town has also become a holiday resort for wealthy Aquileians.

The vanguard of Maximinus' army attacks Aquileia repeatedly, but to no avail. The defenders resist. A shower of stones, javelins, and arrows forces the attackers to retreat. When Maximinus arrives in Aquileia, he camps at a safe distance from the walls. He decides to besiege the city and, to justify his choice, he says that his trip to Rome would not be glorious if he did not succeed in conquering the first city of Italy that resisted him. In doing so, however, he involuntarily allows Pupienus to go to Rabenna (Ravenna), who directs the defense of Aquileia from there (Balbinus remains in Rome).

Rabenna is a city located on the Adriatic coast, north of Ariminum (Rimini). It is surrounded by swamps, which isolate it from the mainland and represent an effective natural defense, and it has direct access to the sea, from where it can receive supplies and reinforcements. This makes it a position of great strategic-military importance. Classified by the Romans as *civitas libera et foederata*, Rabenna remained faithful to Rome when, in 217–216 BC, other Italic cities passed under the banner of the Carthaginian general Hannibal Barca. In around 100 BC, its inhabitants, grateful to Caius Marius, magistrate and military commander, for having freed them from the nightmare of the Germanic invasion, erected a statue in honor of him.[8] In 89 BC, Rabenna received the *ius Latii*, "Latin law", like many other city-states located in Italy, outside Lazio. On that occasion, one of its citizens, Publius Caesius, obtained full Roman citizenship. Octavianus Augustus had important hydraulic works carried out in the Rabenna area, such as the excavation of the Fossa Augusta—a canal that connects the Po with the large body of water south of the city—and in this stretch of sea, he founded a major naval base at Classis (Classe), a port located 4 km east–southeast from the city. Since then, that port has housed the Adriatic fleet, charged with monitoring the Adriatic Sea, the Aegean Sea, and the Eastern Mediterranean (the Western Mediterranean is supervised by the Tyrrhenian fleet, which has its base at Misenum in Campania). It can house up to 250 triremes and 10,000 sailors. Under the Empire, Rabenna became increasingly important. The port of Classis has also become commercial and currently acts as its emporium.

Before attacking Aquileia, Maximinus orders his soldiers to execute important maintenance and restoration works on two main extra-urban roads that converge on the city from different directions because they have been damaged due to long neglect to such an extent that, beaten by the marsh waters, they are now impassable for travelers. The roads are the Via Gemina and the Via Annia, and they both have an essential strategic-military and political role. We have already described the Via Gemina. It links Aquileia to Iulia Aemona (Ljubljana in Slovenia), passing through the Julian Alps, which—together with the Carnic Alps, further north—mark the northeastern border of Italy. It is continuously frequented by troops on the move, the emperor, his family, and his court, as well as imperial officers, traveling from Italy to the Roman provinces of the Danube region or the Balkan Peninsula, and vice versa. As for the Via Annia, this connects Aquileia with Hatria (Adria) in the Po delta, touching the main centers along its route, such as Concordia (Concordia Sagittaria), Altinum (Quinto d'Altino), and Patavium (Padua). In Patavium, it joins other roads that connect the most important cities of Cisalpine Gaul—above all, Mediolanum (Milan), the capital of the Western Roman Empire since the reign of Maximian (286–305)— and northern Italy to Rome. Through this wide road network, the nerve centers of the Roman state in Italy are connected to Aquileia. The Via Annia, therefore, is a fundamental route in *Regio X Venetia et Histria*. It was designed mainly for military purposes to facilitate the movement of the legions, but also to support a sprawling naval complex located along the main rivers that flow into the Adriatic. In fact, it guarantees easy penetration toward the most important inland locations, thanks to a series of secondary capillary connections.

The works ordered by Maximinus regard the Via Annia from the seventh milestone to the city and include numerous and systematic drainage interventions, functional for the reclamation of marshy lands. They are carried out in order to facilitate the passage of troops in an east–west direction and to obtain a favorable attitude from the inhabitants of the city. The works on the Via Gemina, in turn, are carried out on a stretch that goes from the city to the bridge over the Frigidus River (Vipava).[9]

Maximinus intimates the Aquileians to surrender, on pain of the destruction of the city and horrible reprisals. For this purpose, he uses a local military tribune whose wife, children, and relatives are in the city. However, the defenders refused to surrender after senator Crispinus urged them not to trust the promises of a liar and hypocritical tyrant and revealed to them that he has learned from the haruspices that Maximinus will be defeated. That prediction is based on the divine signs that emerged from the ritual sacrifices to Apollo Belenus, the tutelary deity of the city, around the cult of which the population has tightened. The role of Apollo Belenus and the oracular prophecies emanating from his sanctuary in the siege of the city clearly emerges from this episode, and there is a close identification of this indigenous god with the destinies of the city.

Maximinus launches continuous attacks on the city, also using some siege machines, built from the timber obtained from the destruction of some buildings that were standing in the surroundings, and he makes great efforts to bombard the walls, smash them, and rain projectiles on the city. The defenders respond in a similar way by throwing incendiary stones covered with pitch and olive oil at the attackers and pouring a fiery liquid, composed of bitumen and sulfur, on them, as well as firing incendiary arrows amid the screams and smoke. Among Maximinus' soldiers, many burned to death. Many siege engines were destroyed by flames. Maximinus conducts the operations himself. He urges the army to attack, circling the walls, giving orders to the soldiers, and railing against the defenders.

The siege continues with continuous bombardments, furious assaults on the walls, courageous sorties, fires, and massacres. The Aquileians defend themselves by any means. Women, the elderly, and children also participate in the defense as best they can. Crispinus and Menophilus place many armed men along the walls. They keep watch day and night. They show portraits of Pupienus, Balbinus, and Gordian III to the besiegers and throw the dead in the river, in the port area, in order to pollute the water and make it undrinkable.

Time does not play in Maximinus' favor, because the emperor is short of food and his troops have become discouraged. The same cannot be said for the Aquileians, who, in view of the siege, have accumulated large stocks of food, can draw drinking water from wells located within the city, and have faith in victory. The situation of the besiegers becomes more and more difficult. They fear that the besieged have Apollo Belenus on their side. In their eyes, therefore, it is not a question of fighting only against the Aquileians but also against a god. Powerless, Maximinus takes it out on his officers, accusing them of inefficiency, if not negligence, and punishes them severely, indeed with cruelty, even putting the generals to death. Discontent courses through the ranks of the soldiers. Finally, exhausted by the resistance of the besieged and weakened by hunger and disease, the soldiers become hostile to the emperor and mutiny. A bloody revolt suddenly breaks out, whose "causes are to be found in the prolongation of the war action, in the harshness of living conditions, in the shortage of food, [and] in the rigid discipline of Maximinus, who has engaged the soldiers in various jobs, including road works involving the Via Annia and the Via Gemina, which we talked about earlier, performed by the recruits". Maximinus is murdered by the soldiers of the Legio II Parthica in his camp together with his son Maximus and his ministers. His head, detached from his torso, is impaled on the tip of a spear. It will be brought to Rome by messengers on horseback and exhibited during the journey as a trophy through the cities of northern and central Italy. Maximinus' body is left to dogs and birds.

Now that the siege operations have ceased, the troops gathered in the camp of the late emperor, attracted by all that the city can offer, take advantage of the market that the inhabitants organize "on the walls" for a long time, being offered food, drinks, clothing, and footwear (Herodian. 8.3.8).

Pupienus and Balbinus do not survive the death of Maximinus for long. The same year, they are assassinated by the Praetorians, the soldiers who form the bodyguard of the emperors. The reason for the crime lies in the fact that the Praetorians feel humiliated by the new course of events. They did not tolerate having Germans as colleagues, nor being assigned to support troops, much less being tried by the plebeians. Therefore they incited riots, causing casualties and devastation. Finally, they managed to capture Pupienus and Balbinus (their Germanic bodyguards do not intervene) and killed them both at Castro Pretorio, the Praetorian barracks in Rome.

It is the Praetorians themselves who acclaim the new emperor in the person of the 13-year-old Gordian III (238–244). The Senate of Rome is faced with a *fait accompli* and must accept it in spite of itself. Thus escalates the most terrible and risky crisis that the Roman Empire has ever known, far more serious than the one that occurred from 193 to 197, from which Septimius Severus finally emerged as the winner. The "Crisis of the 3rd Century" will be much longer, more chaotic, more tormented, and immeasurably more damaging for Italy and the whole Roman world.

Gordian III will die at the age of 19 during a military campaign against the Parthians; it is uncertain whether this occurs at the Battle of Mesiche (Falluja), which ends with the victory of the Parthian Shapur I (*c.* 240–270), or at Circesium, located more than 300 km to the north of Mesiche, under mysterious circumstances. He will be succeeded by the Praetorian Prefect, Philip (244–249), who will be called "the Arab" (because he was born in the Roman province of Arabia) and will often be indicated as the instigator of the assassination of his predecessor.

The Crisis of the 3rd Century (*c.* 235–284)

The historical period that goes from the violent death of Alexander Severus (235) to the rise to power of Diocletian (284) witnessed numerous changes in Roman society, economy, and politics. The number of Roman people grew very considerably after Caracalla (198–217) granted citizenship to all the free-standing inhabitants of the Empire (Constitutio Antoniniana, 212). The Empire is no longer divided, as in the past, into patricians and plebeians, rich and poor, powerful and humble. Indeed, some plebeians are very rich and now have access to the highest civil and military offices. We refer to bankers, factory owners, merchants, artisans (goldsmiths, shoemakers, luthiers, furniture makers, etc.). Therefore, within the rich and powerful, a new aristocracy has formed, that of the "services", which is made up of administration officials and military commanders.

The ruling class is distinguished by more than one peculiar connotation, but what is most striking is its extraordinary homogeneity. The culture, tastes, and language of the Romans that matter is now the same everywhere: whether you are in Great Britain, Africa, continental Europe, the Aegean world, the East, or Egypt. Culture derives from the study of classical letters, tastes are strongly influenced by the most refined current fashions, and while the spoken language is Latin in the West and Greek in the East, the Western aristocracies also speak Greek and are as steeped in Greek culture as the bourgeoisie of the East is. The forma mentis of the social class of which we speak also has a tolerance toward local races and religions, but it does not admit any alternative to one's own culture; furthermore, the members of this class fail to understand why the barbarians (in the sense of those who cannot speak Greek or Latin) persist in keeping their language and their customs rather than "civilizing". Finally, they cannot bear it if people speak badly of the institutions, religion, and civilization of the Romans, much less if the divinities of traditional Roman religion are "offended".

The ruling class also shows a total uniformity in the way of life. Its members wear clothes woven with gold threads and precious jewels and make use of perfumes and cosmetics, and they feast with guests in a large room overlooking a central courtyard, surrounded by a colonnaded portico. In their "peristyle houses"—which can be splendid in their finishes and furnishings—the rich owner welcomes the clientes.

Clientes are those Roman citizens who, as free men, place themselves at the disposal of a patron, generally a nobleman, and therefore a senator, and maintain a very close relationship with him in fulfillment of a sacred bond based on loyalty and fidelity without limits. The patron-client relationship does not violate the law and is not subject to social reproach, except for some isolated criticisms, which arise from the fact that patrons accept any client, without distinguishing between good and bad, and that the poor are not free but must sell themselves to the powerful. On the contrary, it is highly appreciated, because it is the basis of political power and serves to create bonds between classes and social strata based on common interests. Every day, early in the morning, clients visit their patron in his home to say good morning, take an interest in his health and that of his family, express or renew their willingness to take responsibility for his every need, such as to be his armed escort, intervene with economic aid, vote in elections according to his instructions, work in the fields, attend to any type of commission, mobilize to fight, and to follow the patron at public events. The slave-guardian makes them sit in the entrance hall, which for this reason must be large and imposing and express the wealth, nobility, and power of the master of the house in its architecture, furnishings, and decoration. The patron receives clients one by one in his study, whose entrance door opens into the atrium. He shows that he appreciates the treatment and takes care of them (if necessary, he defends them in court, helps them financially, recommends them for the most varied purposes), and he pays them a modest sum of money every day, not by way of compensation, but to show his generosity.

A huge percentage of the Empire's wealth comes from agriculture. In practice, most of the population lives off the work in the fields. Thus, among the poor citizens, there are traders, fishermen, and fortunetellers, but above all, smallholding owners, farmers, settlers, and laborers. The poor and humble are normally without any education. If their mother tongue is Latin or Greek, then they express themselves in this language, particularly in their dialect; if not, they use another language. In the Roman provinces, it is mainly those who live in the countryside who ignore the classical languages, except in Greece, in the lands already colonized by the Greeks, and in the Roman colonies outside the metropolitan territory. In Gaul, peasants speak the language of the Celts. In North Africa, Punic. In Cyrenaica and Tripolitania, Libyan. In Asia Minor, ancient dialects are spoken, such as those of Lycaonia, Phrygia, and Cappadocia. In Syria, Aramaic, which is Syrian, is spoken. In Egypt, Coptic.

The proletarians, the poor, and the destitute congregate mainly in the big cities where they literally live on the street, living off illegal expedients and activities, or, if they can afford to pay the rent, inhabit large condominiums of up to six floors high, with shops on the ground floor and small apartments on the upper floors, which are grouped in regular blocks and bordered on each side by streets (*insulae*).

If we consider that there are large masses of poor and unemployed people, which can be made up of hundreds of thousands of individuals (300,000 in Rome alone), and that the normal living conditions of this numerical majority in society are characterized by poverty, lack of freedom and oppression, it clearly emerges that we are faced with an unstable social element, fundamentally turbulent and politically maneuverable, and it is easy to understand why the emperors and the administrative authorities try in every way to maintain control over it, not only through the adoption of public order measures and law enforcement repression but also through forms of entertainment and assistance. This is demonstrated by the concern of the rulers to provide the cities and smaller centers with public baths, arenas, racecourses, and theaters, access to which is free or subject to the payment of a modest sum, and to implement, at least in Rome and in other large cities, such as Alexandria in Egypt, periodic and free distributions of food to needy heads of families, who are issued a certificate of poverty. Wheat and, from 200, oil, are distributed free and daily. The grain comes from Africa or Egypt and accounts for a large part of the grain distribution of these provinces; in practice, it is required as part of the property tax. It arrives aboard a special fleet in Rome via Ostia—the first colony of Rome, a large commercial center located at the mouth of the Tiber, about 25 km from the capital—whose Portus district has become important also for this reason, or via Puteolis (Pozzuoli), an important port in Campania that serves the great city of Capua (Santa Maria Capua Vetere). The grain ships, depending on whether they have set sail from North Africa or Egypt, call at Lilybaeum (Marsala, at the northeastern end of Sicily) or cross the Strait of Messina.

One of the greatest "entertainment" venues of the Romans is the Flavian Amphitheater (Colosseum), a magnificent structure for mass performances, which can accommodate 50,000 people, covers 3,500 m², and has a canopy that can be retracted if necessary. In the large arena of this immense building, gladiator fights, hunts, and naval battles take place, which greatly fascinate the inhabitants of the city. Another colossal structure used for public events is the Circus Maximus, a wide horseshoe-shaped track lined with rows of seats, where chariot races take place. It is 600 m long and can hold 25,000 spectators.

The new aristocracy has joined the old, but without supplanting it. The latter is formed by the families that have their own members in the Senate of Rome. These number a few hundred families, almost all of Roman or Italic origin, often less ancient than they would like to believe, but are owners of immense assets and constitute an exclusive elite.

The Senate of Rome is housed in the Curia, an austere building located in the area of the Forum that has been rebuilt several times, first by Faustus Sulla (a son of the late dictator for life) and then by Julius Caesar, who significantly made it an extension of his own Forum. The Curia Julia (so-called because it was built by Caesar as part of his building redevelopment project in the Forum area) has been restored several times: by Pompey, Augustus, and Domitian.

The Senate of Rome was once regarded as a council of kings. Currently, it has been ousted from the competencies that made it great in the Republican Age. It does not designate the Augustus, nor does it appoint most of the provincial governors, the legates in charge of the military provinces, the urban prefects, or the legion commanders anymore. Its main function is to express the continuity of the old aristocracy. In fact, normally, those who access it are members of the great Roman families. Only exceptionally do you become a senator by imperial decree.

The imperial institution itself has changed. The one who, from Augustus (27 BC–AD 14) onward, was the *princeps*, understood as the First Citizen of Rome (*princeps*, in Latin, means "first one"), has been transformed into a new figure, whose power, which is defined propagandistically as being of divine origin, is absolute, that is, it absorbs that of traditional political forces. Moreover, the emperor is now almost always a career soldier of provincial origin and peasant class. He often comes from the ranks of the army and even ignores, or in any case does not love, the great Roman tradition. He is a hard and determined man, far from the cultural ideal represented by Marcus Aurelius (161–180), and has been continuously exposed not only to the risks of war but also to that of being the victim of military sedition, or of a plot, perhaps ordered by his most trusted men. He travels through the Empire with a large following, called a *comitatus* (from *comites*, "comrades"). His procession is made up of the staff of the imperial secretariat, the managers and workers of the imperial mint, and a crowd of servants, whose sumptuous parades proceed along the large extra-urban roads, carrying all kinds of luggage and the treasure of the imperial mint, made up of gold and silver ingots. The protection of both the emperor and the *comitatus* is ensured by a military escort, composed of about 3,500 armed men, including *equites singulares*, or *equites comites* (cavalry units), Praetorian infantry, and *vexillationes* (detachments of legionary infantry). During the reign of Gallienus (253–268), *protectores* were added to the escort listed above. These are the real bodyguard of the emperor. They are not simple soldiers but high officials (tribunes who were chosen from among the Praetorians, legion commanders, or centurions of high rank). They come from different *vexillationes* and constitute a sort of general staff of the army.

The historical period we are talking about is politically characterized by the alternation on the throne of 18 "legitimate" emperors (without considering the sons associated with the throne by their fathers or by their colleagues and the usurpers, who form an unspecified number), whose domination lasts on average less than three years and usually ends in their violent death: whether in battle, as a result of a plot, or at the hands of a hitman or the victim's soldiers. The continuous and rapid succession of emperors, however, is only one of the factors of the crisis from which the Empire struggles. The phenomenon is in fact linked to the almost permanent state of war, the increase in the political weight of the military, the collapse in value of the silver coin, and the state's recourse to collections of taxes in kind. Meanwhile, the large landed property class does not end but gains sway at the expense of both smallholders and the state, the gap between rich and poor widens, and serfdom begins to form in the context of a more general phenomenon, which arises from the constraint of the populace to remain bound to their profession.

Therefore, the upheaval is at the same time social, economic, demographic, and institutionalized, and it will go down in history as the "Crisis of the 3rd Century". The general situation is very serious. It undermines the strength of the Empire and jeopardizes its very survival. The western provinces pay the price (all except Africa, which will remain unscathed), as demographic decline and the shortage of manpower causes the regression of industry and trade, the decline of cities, and the weakening of city life. However, Diocletian's rise to power introduces the establishment of a new order.

Diocletian (284–305) and the Tetrarchy

Diocletian was born in around 245 in Illyricum into a family of humble conditions with the name Diocles. He was a career soldier. During the reign of Carinus (283–285), he commands the *protectores*, the imperial bodyguard. In 284, he is acclaimed emperor by the soldiers, the last of a long line of usurpers. In 285, he overthrows Carinus, who is murdered. In the same year, he elevates one of his former comrades in arms, Marcus Aurelius Valerius Maximian Herculius (hereafter Maximian, 286–305), to the rank of Caesar. In 286, he associates him with the throne by appointing him as Augustus, though in a subordinate position to him. Furthermore, in 293, Diocletian appoints two more Caesars: Caius Valerius Galerius and Flavius Valerius Constantius Chlorus.

The two Augusti and the two Caesars embody a new political system called the Tetrarchy. This system implies the division of the Empire into a *pars orientis* and a *pars occidentis*, each ruled by an Augustus, who has equal dignity with respect to his colleague and is able to govern and legislate separately and autonomously in the exercise of his own territorial competence. Diocletian and Galerius rule the East, the former from Nicomedia in Bithynia (Izmit in Turkey), the latter from Sirmium in Pannonia (Sremska Mitrovica in Serbia), while Maximian and Constantius Chlorus rule the West, the one from Mediolanum (Milan) and the other from Augusta Trevirorum (Trier in Germany). Nicomedia thus becomes the capital of the *pars orientis*, while Mediolanum becomes the capital of the *pars occidentis*.

Diocletian and Maximian each reign for 20 years. The former, in addition to the reform of the political system, implemented through the Tetrarchy, also introduces other reforms, which affect the organization of the state, the economy, and the army. Also, he restores paganism. His first reforms consist of increasing the number of provinces by splitting the existing ones and grouping them in dioceses and of separating the civil administration from the military one, with the strengthening of both. The provinces increase from 47 to 85 and are grouped into 13 dioceses.

Italy, which also becomes a diocese (this is the first time this has happened), is divided into provinces, as follows: *Venetia et Histria, Aemilia et Liguria, Alpes Cottiae, Graiae et Pontinae, Flaminia et Picenum Annonarium, Raetia prima et secunda, Tuscia et Umbria, Campania, Apulia et Calabria, Lucania et Brittii*. It is noteworthy that, under Diocletian, the Augustan *Venetia et Histria* has been divided into two: *Venetia et Histria* and *Aemilia et Liguria*. The capital of *Venetia et Histria* continues to be Aquileia, and Mediolanum becomes the capital of *Aemilia et Liguria*.

The direct collaborators of the emperor are the Praetorian Prefects, one of whom is the commander of the *protectores*. The highest-ranking central administration officials are the *magistri* (central administration managers). The governors of the dioceses are the *vicarii*.

The provinces are entrusted to the *duces*, with the exception of Italy, whose provinces are governed by *correctores*, civil officials of equestrian rank. The *corrector* charge is not new but has changed form over time. Originally, the *correctores* were senators and were in charge of the Roman government of the cities of Greece. Under Caracalla (198–217), some of them also appeared in Italy. In some moments of the "Crisis of the 3rd Century", there was a *corrector totius Italiae*. During the reign of Marcus Aurelius Probus (276–282), there were two *correctores Italiae*, one competent for Gallia Transpadana and the other for Italia Propria (all the regions south of the Po). The army reform consists of the creation of smaller legions and the introduction of a new military hierarchy: *praepositi limitum* (commanders of sectors of the state borders), prefects, tribunes, and other *praepositi* (commanders of various units).

Another Diocletian reform concerns the monetary system. This aims at overcoming the difficulties of monetary circulation and consists of the introduction of a silver-plated copper coin, the *follis*. Further reforms are made in the reorganization of the tax authorities and in the issuance of an edict that sets a limit on prices and wages.

Aquileia in the Tetrarchic Age (293–324)

Aquileia, in the Tetrarchic Age, receives a new stimulus. This gives safety and impetus to the traffic and life of a vast area, and the phenomenon of urbanism begins to manifest itself. Similar effects will occur in the future with the reorganization of the city by Constantine I.

In 294, or at the latest in 296, a public mint (different from the Comitatense mints) is established in Aquileia, with three workshops to mint gold, silver, and copper coins under the direction of a *procurator monetae aquileiensis*. It arises in the area of the *palatium* (Callegher 2007: 327–362). It will remain in operation until 425, when it is transferred to Arelate (Arles in Provence, southern France). In its first phase of activity (294–310), it will produce, continuously and in considerable quantities, gold and silver coins and bronze *folles*, which will circulate throughout *Venetia et Histria* and the East. The most precious exports bear the names of the Tetrarchs. A substantial part of the production is used to pay the army. Many troops, let us remember, are headquartered in Aquileia. Some are those who guard the city, others are passing troops, coming from areas of operations in the Danube region and the Balkan Peninsula.

On 31 March 296, the Tetrarchs promulgate a constitution in Aquileia. This presupposes the presence of an imperial chancellery in the city (Sotinel 2005: 20). Aquileia is also home to important tax officials in charge of collecting taxes.

Furthermore, under the Tetrarchy, Aquileia becomes the seat of the *comes Italiae*, the commander-in-chief of the army in Italy, and of the *praefectus classis Venetum*, the commanding admiral of a fleet of warships. Among other things, these commanders have the task of ensuring the connections and supply of the legions that guard the Danube border and those that cross the eastern Alpine passes in both directions.

The city is also the main hub of the defensive system of northeastern Italy (Claustra Alpium Iuliarium) and a vital part of the communications system between Italy and the provinces of southeastern Europe. The Claustra Alpium Iuliarum is a chain of fortifications that has the purpose of facing possible barbarian invasions from the northeast, such as those that affected Italy from 259 to 271, and of blocking the corridor that leads from Pannonia and Dalmatia to Italy through the Julian Alps. Since those invasions, the region has been manned by soldiers. Within that system, garrison troops deployed along the border are flanked by mobile military units, which can be used in the event of the enemy crossing fortified lines. The system finds further support in the defensive potential of the cities of *Venetia et Histria*, in the military factories of the region, responsible for the supply of weapons, clothing, and food—see, for example, the Concordia arrow factory (in present-day Concordia Sagittaria)—and, finally, in the prefectures of Opitergium, Patavium and Verona, where the presence of troops is more modest, but which are invested with similar defensive tasks. From a commercial point of view, Aquileia is a market, as it is the terminal for maritime traffic in the Adriatic and the main place of exchange for goods that go to the Italian, Illyrian and Danubian hinterlands. It will retain this role for the next few decades.

Between 293 and 296, the betrothal ceremony of Constantine, son of Constantius Chlorus, to Fausta, the daughter of Maximian, takes place in the *palatium* of Aquileia, in the presence of Maximian. Constantine is only a boy and Fausta little more than a child. At the occasion, Constantine receives a splendid gift from Fausta: a sparkling golden helmet, with gems, crested with the feathers of a beautiful bird, probably a peacock.[10] The episode is reported in the panegyric for Maximian and Constantine, which will be pronounced by an anonymous person on the occasion of their wedding, which takes place in 307 in Augusta Trevirorum (Trier in Germany). In the meantime, it is immortalized in a painting or mosaic in the *palatium* of Aquileia.[11]

In 297, Diocletian and Maximian visit Aquileia, each with his family and the court, though it is not certain whether they visit separately or jointly. Diocletian certainly stays in Aquileia together with Maximian in 303–304. The last official act of veneration of Apollo Belenus dates to that occasion. It is performed in antithesis to Christianity and in homage to the traditional pagan cult. It probably aims to obtain political consensus in favor of the two emperors and their religious policy (Zaccaria 2005: 91–125). This can be seen from a dedicatory inscription from them to Belenus.[12]

The Great Persecution

During and after the "Crisis of the 3rd Century", the gap between pagans and Christians widened in conjunction with the rise of Christianity, the refusal of Christians to recognize the emperor as a god, and the persecutions carried out by the Roman authorities against Christians. In fact, the imperial visit to Aquileia we mentioned earlier takes place while the Great Persecution of Christians is underway, which was desired by Diocletian but carried out by Maximian in particular and, even more, by Galerius (Constantius Chlorus is more moderate). At first, this takes its victims from the army, then it extends to the organized communities of Christians. In 303 and above all in 304, four edicts are issued, which provide for the seizure of sacred books, the demolition of churches, the arrest of community leaders, the release of repentants, and the organization throughout the Empire of ritual sacrifices, dedicated to the gods of traditional Roman religion.

This is not the first time that the organized community of Christians in Aquileia has been hit by the Roman authorities. A legend, perhaps born during the reign of Diocletian, tells of the martyrdom of two Aquileians—Hermagoras, first bishop of Aquileia, and Fortunatus—which took place under the reign of Trajan Decius (249–251). At that time, the proselytism of Christians must have made progress, given that Decius, a supporter of paganism, decided to intervene to force the government of Aquileia to relocate a statue of Neptune, which had been removed and lay in ruin, in the port area. This occurred while the second wave of the Antonine plague was underway; this was known as the "Cyprian Plague" (251–266) after Cyprian, who was bishop of Carthage from 248/249 to 258 (Carthage is a city where both the plague and the persecution of Christians manifested themselves in particularly serious forms). The plague was so virulent that, in 250–262, at the height of the epidemic, it was said that it killed 5,000 people a day in Rome.[13]

The edicts of Decius were renewed under Valerian (253–260) in 253 and repealed under the latter's son, Gallienus (263–268), in 260–261. Later, however, Christians were persecuted again. Another tradition, in fact, refers to the martyrdom of Hylarius, the first successor of Hermagoras, and Tatianus, the presumed deacon of Hylarius, which occurred in Aquileia. It seems that this episode took place under the reign of Numerian (283–284). At that time, Aquileia would have been able to influence Istria, Venetia et Histria, and Noricum (Hylarius would have carried out missionary activity in these areas). Certain individuals named Felix, Largo, and Dyonisius, all otherwise unidentified, also suffered martyrdom in Aquileia, while a certain Fortunatus, also mentioned in the Aquileian episcopal catalog, was a bishop who died a martyr in Pannonia and was transferred to Aquileia (Biasutti 2005: 83; see also Paschini 1909).

In 303–305, the Great Persecution of Christians claims some victims in Aquileia, Aquae Gradatae (Grado), and San Canzian d'Isonzo, a place located about 21 km from Aquae Gradatae and about 12 km from Aquileia: the Cantiani brothers—Cantius, Cantianus, and Cantianilla—and Protus, presumed tutor of the Cantiani, as well as the Roman senator Chrysogonus.

The *Cantiani* is a high-ranking family but not yet particularly flourishing, as it will do in the future, between the 4th and 6th centuries. It is probably linked to the gens Anicia, a clan of the Roman aristocracy, formed by the Praenestinus, Gallus, Faustus, Paulinus, Auchenius, Bassus, Proba, Faltonia, Iulianus, Hermogenianus, Olybrius, Maximus, Boëthius Albinus families. One of its members—Lucius Anicius Gallus—was consul in 160. The Cantiani must have converted to Christianity no later than the middle of the 3rd century because an Anicia Anatolia was martyred in 249 (in the Great Persecution by Decius).

The last hours of the lives of the Cantiani brothers and Protus can be summarized as follows. They all leave Rome to escape the persecution of Christians in the capital. Once in Aquileia, they are arrested by order of the governor Dulcidius and sent to trial, but they are acquitted and released by the intervention of eminent personalities, who hold them in esteem. Diocletian instead orders that they be arrested and executed. The four are captured at San Canzian d'Isonzo and beheaded.

Aquae Gradatae, we recall, is a small town 12 km from Aquileia. In 303, some of its houses are decorated with mosaics, like many houses of wealthy people of Aquileia. The locality touches the territory of Aquileia, and one of the nine dyeing plants operating in Italy by imperial concession for the production of purple is found there. In addition, there is a terracotta tile factory.

Senator Chyrsogonus also undergoes martyrdom in Aquae Gradatae, though it is uncertain whether he dies together with the Cantiani and Protus or separately.

In the same period, Chrysogonus, the bishop of Aquileia, was put to death because of his faith. Chrysogonus is a native of Dalmatia and the spokesman for the communities of both Aquileia and Dalmatia. He will be buried in Aquileia, publicly venerated by the faithful of that zone, and will become the patron saint of Iader (Zadar in Croatia) and be venerated as a saint and martyr by the Roman Catholic Church and the Orthodox Church.

The Great Persecution also claims victims in Illyricum. In 304, an Aquileian named Anastasius is put to death in Salona (Solin in Croatia), the main center of the only diocese in Dalmatia.

Diocletian falls ill and, on 1 May 305, abdicates in favor of Constantius Chlorus (305–306), while Maximian does the same in favor of his son Maxentius (305–311). Diocletian retires to his palace in Aspálathos (Split in Croatia), where he will remain until his death, which will occur in the spring of 313. In the meantime, the Tetrarchy collapses, but Diocletian always refuses to take back the reins of power, unlike Maximian, who will come out of his retirement in southern Italy to take to the field to favor Maxentius, who is at war against Constantine I, the son of Constantius Chlorus and a concubine, Helen, who is said to have served tables in a tavern.

Constantine I (306–337) was born in around 280 in Naissus (Niš in Serbia), a city located in the Roman province of Moesia on the banks of the Nišava river. He fought in Egypt in 295–296 and later against the Sarmatians. He is a pragmatic type, not an intellectual at all.

Maximinus Daia (305–313)

In 306, Constantius Chlorus dies in Britannia during a military campaign. Constantine is acclaimed emperor by the soldiers. In Rome, the Praetorians do not accept the *fait accompli* and, in turn, acclaim Maxentius (306–312) as emperor. Then, Severus—the Caesar of Constantius Chlorus (the Caesar of Galerius is Maximinus Daia)—is assassinated.

Maximian comes out of his retirement in southern Italy to support his son. To prevent chaos, Galerius organizes a conference in 308 at Carnuntum in Pannonia (Petronell in Austria), at which he, Maximian, and Diocletian participate. Thus an agreement is reached: Galerius will continue to reign in the East and will have Maximinus Daia as his Caesar; Constantine will continue to reign in the West and will have Licinius as his Caesar. However, Maximinus Daia and Maxentius maintain their claims (Maxentius remains master of Rome, Maximinus Daia proclaims himself Augustus), while a seventh protagonist, Domitius Alexander, advances his own claims in Africa.

In 308, Maximian attempts to depose Maxentius but fails to do so and takes refuge with Constantine in Augusta Trevirorum (Trier in Germany). In 310, however, he attempts to overthrow Constantine while he leads a military campaign on the Rhine border. But the revolt receives little following, and it ends the same year in Massilia (Marseille), with the capture and suicide of Maximian. In the same year, both Domitius Alexander and Galerius die.

In 312, Constantine gets the better of Maxentius at the Battle of the Milvian Bridge in Rome (Maxentius drowns in the Tiber). In 313, Maximinus Daia is defeated by

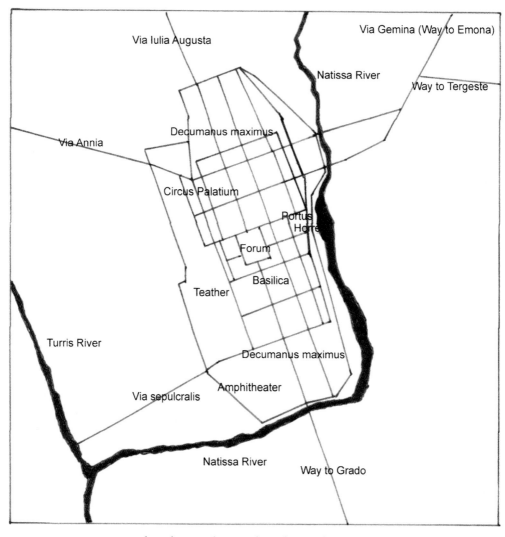

Map 3. The urbanistic layout of Aquileia in the Late Antiquity

Licinius at the Battle of Tzirallum and retires to Tarsos in Cilicia (Tarsus in Turkey), where he commits suicide.

In 313, Licinius defeats Maximinus Daia at Adrianopolis in Moesia (Edirne in Turkey). Finally, in 316, Constantine clashes with Licinius at the Battle of Mardia and, following the peace signed on 1 March 317, forces him to give him Illyricum.

The peace agreement lasts for seven years. In 324, Constantine I and Licinius clash again at Adrianopolis. Licinius wins, but he doesn't know how to take advantage of the success and, with too much confidence, it ends in disaster for him. He is defeated twice: the first time by Crispus, Constantine's son and the Caesar of his rival, in a naval battle (in the Aegean Sea, at the mouth of the Strait of the Dardanelles), and for a second time, definitively, by Constantine at the Battle of Chrysopolis (a city located on the Bosphorus Strait in Asia Minor; from this city, it is possible to see Constantinople, located on the opposite coast). Taken prisoner, he is pardoned by Constantine, who confines him to Thessalonica in Macedonia (Thessaloniki in Greece). But he plots against the emperor with the help of some tribes of barbarians from the Danube region. Discovered, he is executed (325). Constantine I is thus the only living Augustus remaining.

Notes

1   A region of Mesopotamia was once called Osroene. When it was conquered by the Romans, in around 116, it was an independent kingdom, with Edessa as its capital. Under the reign of Marcus Aurelius, after the war against the Parthians, the Romans built forts there, established a garrison in Nisibis, and incorporated some fighting units formed by locals and specialized in archery into their army. In 216, Osroene became a Roman province.

2   The bodies of Alexander Severus and of his mother were moved to Rome and buried together in a mausoleum.

3   A tradition reported by Paulus Diaconus (8th century) says that the evangelization of the church of Aquileia would have been brought about by Saint Mark. This does not correspond to the truth. It is probably a legend that was formed between the 6th and 7th centuries as an expression of the autonomy proclaimed by the Church of Aquileia with respect to the Church of Rome, when a large group of bishops, mainly Western, broke off relations with other bishops and the Pope, rejecting the decisions of the Second Council of Constantinople of 553. The separation lasted for about a century and a half and involved a vast territory, including Northern Italy, Dalmatia, Illyria, and North Africa (the Three-Chapter Controversy).

4   The Vicenza earthquake of 238 is perhaps one of the earthquakes that have always originated along the Insubric Line, which extends for about 1,000 km in latitude from the Canavese to the Carnic Alps, and is responsible, among other things, for the telluric upheavals that have their epicenter in the Middle Friuli. Hence the hypothesis according to which that earthquake could also have hit Aquileia, causing damage to the city walls, among other things. For the Vicenza earthquake of 238: Piovene 1888: 45–57, esp. 47.

5   Herodian of Syria (170–240) is the author of a history of the Roman emperors in eight books, from the death of Marcus Aurelius (180) to the accession to the throne of Gordian III. This work is called the *Historia Augusta* and is the main source available today regarding the War of Aquileia.

6   The entablature we are talking about, dating back to the second half of the 2nd century, was reassembled after its discovery on the Viale degli Scavi del Porto.

7   It seems that the road we are talking about was destroyed in 682 by a Lombard duke named Lupus.

8   Plut. *Mar.* 2.1, with reference to a statue of Caius Marius, seen by Plutarch in Rabenna.

9   On the maintenance and restoration works carried out along the Via Annia and Via Gemina by the soldiers of Maximinus Thrax: *Inscr. Aq.* 2893a-b, 2894a-b. See also Guerra and Ventura 2010: 27.

10 A reconstruction of Constantine's helmet is kept at the Diocesan Museum in Milan.

11 The *palatium* mentioned in the panegyric became the residence of the emperor. Or, perhaps, another *palatium* was built to house the emperor, his family, and his entourage on their stays in the city.

12 A block of a large funerary altar from the imperial age was reused to house the dedication of Diocletian and Maximian to Apollo Belenus. The monument is currently being held in the National Archaeological Museum of Aquileia. The dedication is as follows: [Apollini] Beleno / [Imperatore] s Caesares / [C. Aur (elius) Val (erius) D] iocletianus et / [M. Aur (elius) M] aximianus / [Pii Fel (ices) Invi] cti Aug (usti duo) / [- - -] dedicaverunt.

13 We learn this from the biographer of Cyprian, Pontius, and from Cyprian himself, who speaks of it in his work *De mortalitate.* Accounts of the plague date it from around 249 to 262. There was a subsequent incident in 270 involving the death of Claudius II Gothic, but it is not known whether this was a result of the same plague or a different epidemic.

Chapter 7

The Great Constantinian Aquileia

An extensive program of urban and monumental renewal

Aquileia, during the reign of Constantine I (306–337), has recovered its condition of economic prosperity and architectural and urban magnificence and is tending to expand toward the east, west, and south, but especially on the southern and western sides, including toward the port on the Natissa to the southwest and the theater to the west, already external to the urban area. A whole new neighborhood began to form in the northwest area after the suburb was leveled and the terminal section of the Canale Anfora was closed. A new, grandiose city wall, 4 km long, is under construction. It is intended to functionally replace the old one, except for the northern side of its perimeter, significantly expanding it, especially on the southern and western sides. This is just one of the initiatives that make up the monumental renewal program of the city, which begins under Constantine I. It is accompanied by the construction of a racecourse (from now on: circus), an amphitheater, large baths, a food market between the Forum and the port on the Natissa, and some public markets and warehouses further south. The implementation of this program will continue during the reigns of the sons of Constantine I (from now on: the Constantinians): Constantius II (337–361), Constantine II (337–340), and Constans (337–350).

The new walls[1]

In 361, when an army of Emperor Julian, commanded by Iovinus, besieges the city, as we will see later, the Constantinian walls will have been completed and enclose an urban area extending for 83.5 ha, almost double that of the previous ones.

The elevation of the new walls stands on foundations that rest on wooden stilts. It is 0.7 to 3.3 m thick, depending on the features, and is made up of a conglomerate that reuses architectural and sculptural elements from other contexts. The external cladding is a double facing in bricks, in which stone blocks are inserted. On the eastern side of the perimeter, the new curtain runs parallel to the old one and ends on the outer edge of the quay. On the eastern side, a long stretch of the circus, a facility that we will deal with later, is attached to the wall. On the northern side, it is accompanied by a protective rampart, located 12 m away. The entire circuit is interspersed with towers, which can have a quarter-circle plan (with a radius of about 6 m), semicircular, or quadrangular, depending on the situation.[2] Along the western side of the perimeter, the towers are more frequent and follow each other at intervals of 25–30 m. In this enclosure, there are six gates, one more than in the past. The new gate opens on the northwestern side, north of the circus, and marks the entrance to the city of the Via Annia, a major suburban road. That road enters the city from the northwest, strongly defining and influencing the sector of the urban area that it passes through, in spite of its decentralized position with respect to the heart of Aquileia, which consists of the Forum and the Civil Basilica. In turn, four of the five remaining gates mark the entrance and exit from the city of the two main suburban roads: Via Augusta and Via Gemina.

Via Augusta enters the city from the gate that opens on the north side of the walls, crosses the entire urban area, of which it constitutes the *decumanus maximus*, in a straight line, and leaves the city through the gate that opens on the southern side of the wall before continuing in the direction of Aquae Gradatae (Grado). The Via Gemina originates from the urban gates of Aquileia located in the northeastern part of the wall and connects the city to Iulia Aemona (Ljubljana). One of its branches arrives in Istria, passing through Tergeste (Trieste). In the 4th century, the redevelopment of the Via Annia is underway. A local road originates from it: the *via sepulcralis.*

Usually, Roman city gates are not large: a chariot can hardly pass through them. They have a solid wooden door at street level and a crenelated balcony above. The former serves to close access to the urban area for the defense of its inhabitants. The latter serves as a military checkpoint. The guardhouse is housed under the vault. It opens the gate at dawn and closes it at sunset. During the hours the gates are open, many people enter or leave the city on foot, on horseback, or aboard a wagon. Some go on foot while pushing a flock or herd. Guards scan passersby, inspect wagons, stop suspicious travelers, accept a gift to turn a blind eye, and let the traveler pass; sometimes they ask for it.

The *circus*

The *circus*[3] is located in line with the amphitheater, along the east side of the urban area and the new walls, in connection[4] with a luxurious residence (henceforth: *palatium*) intended to house the emperor, the members of his family, and all their entourage during their stays in the city. Like all other structures of the same type, it has the shape of an elongated horseshoe and, due to its grandeur, reflects the great importance of circus games for the Romans, who are more interested in horse racing than in any other form of entertainment, including gladiator duels. The straight side is that of the starting blocks of the racing chariots (*carceres*). On the straight eastern side, it has a facade with open arches. The structure, on its western side, rests on the walls, while it has a more monumental aspect on its eastern side, which looks toward the city. Its entrances are distinct and, inside, the steps are divided into sectors. The best seats are reserved for magistrates, senators, *equites*, and army officers. A short distance from these sectors, near the finish line, is the imperial stage, with embellished coats of arms and marble columns; here the emperor shows himself to the people. The emperor presides over all the events that take place in the circus, meaning not only the public games but also the celebrations of victories and jubilees (these are the occasions when the Senate of Rome calls for the celebration of sacrifices and games to ask for the preservation of the health of the emperors; they coincide with the completion of the 5th, 10th, 20th, and 30th year of the emperor's reign, known in Latin as *quinquennalia, decennalia, vicennalia,* and *tricennalia,* respectively). The rest of the audience settles into the upper levels.

Two large entrances with bronze doors are placed at opposite ends of the circus. Through one of these, the great procession that inaugurates the days of the competitions enters the arena, preceded by heralds and bearers of banners. The arena is an expanse of beaten earth with a linear structure in the center, which is called a *spina* and is covered with marble, statues, *aedicules,* and gilded bronze figures.

All of Aquileia and many foreigners, who come from the surrounding area, flock to the circus on the days of the races. The show starts early in the morning when people have been pushing at the gates for hours. The influx is so massive also because admission costs very little, if not even free. As the spectacle is about to begin, tens of thousands of people, perhaps 100,000, flock to the steps—a vibrant, multicolored crowd—waving flags and handkerchiefs.

At an agreed signal, given by the person who finances the race, 12 chariots, each being steered by a charioteer, leave the *carceres* at full speed. Each charioteer miraculously balances himself on a low step with small wheels and incites and whips the horses, to which he is tied at the height of his bust by a leather bridle. He and his colleagues try to hinder each other in an unbridled carousel. The chariots must circle the plug seven times. With each turn, the shapes we mentioned earlier are lowered, marking their completion. The show is thrilling. The roars of the crowd can be heard from afar.

The circus is not only an entertainment facility but also a shopping center. Many shops, *popinae* (bars), and *tabernae* (taverns)[5] are located on the ground floor, under the external arcades. A lot of people frequent them, even women, who mainly visit clothing and footwear stores. Bookmakers, barber-dentists, shoemakers, and street food and souvenir sellers, with their stalls lined up, mingle with the crowd that fills the sidewalk and the street front and is made up of traders, shop assistants, transporters, *clientes*, prostitutes, fortune tellers, pickpockets, and slackers. Their shouts add to the confusion as the fragrances of freshly baked bread and sizzling pancakes waft through the air, along with the foul smells of boiled cabbage and broccoli. Among the individuals who gravitate to the area, many are slaves and many other foreigners. Their languages and dialects mingle with the Latin of the Roman citizens, making it increasingly seem like Babel.

The *palatium*[6]

The *palatium*-circus association is typical. In fact, in addition to Aquileia, it also appears in other Roman cities, such as Thessalonica, Mediolanum, Rome, Augusta Trevirorum, Sirmium, Antioch on the Orontes, Nicomedia, and Constantinopolis. It seems to have been done on purpose to allow the emperor not to have to travel far to go to the races.

The *palatium* of Aquileia stands immediately east of the circus.[7] Erected at the latest in 295, it is decorated with statues of the emperor and some large shields with bust-portraits of divinities on white stone and hanging on the facade, which is probably the work of stonecutters linked to the school of Aphrodisias, a Hellenistic city in Caria (southwestern Turkey) (Sperti 2003: 181–286). Its interiors include numerous rooms embellished with mosaics and paintings.

Nazarius, a Roman rhetorician and historian, active during the reign of Constantine I (306–337), describes one of those mosaics and paintings,[8] which portrays Constantine I in the act of receiving a precious helmet from his future wife Fausta as an engagement gift (we have already talked about this in the previous chapter). Nazarius also wrote a panegyric in praise of the emperor, focusing on the celebration of the victory he won over Maxentius at the Battle of the Milvian Bridge (312) and using the artifices of Gallic rhetoric. In that context, Nazarius recalls that Aquileia submitted to Constantine I in 311, sending him legates and supplications (*Pan. Lat.* IX [12].11.1) (in the conflict between Constantine I and Maxentius, the city had sided with the latter, perhaps because the father of Maxentius, Maximian, had been a benefactor of the city, or perhaps because Maxentius was the bearer of the traditional Roman pagan ideology). He then lists the many advantages that Aquileia has drawn from that choice,[9] certainly in relation to its own importance, including even its strategic-military role. Aquileia, we remember, is the capital of *Venetia et Histria*, it is the second most important city in northern Italy after Mediolanum, and its control of the northeastern border is essential for the security of Italy.

With the decision of Maximian to establish his residence in Mediolanum (Milan in Italy) and with that of Diocletian to reside in Nicomedia (Izmit in Turkey), Rome ceased to be the capital of the Empire, in the sense that it is the place of residence of the emperor. The Augusti now go to Rome only on rare occasions, usually celebrations, and do not permanently reside there. One of Constantine I's favorite places to stay is Aquileia. He certainly stays there in 318, 320, 324, and 326 (Bonfioli 1973: 477–527). In 326, he returns to Aquileia in the spring and stays there for a long time, departing only to go to Rome in order to attend the celebrations of his *vicennalia*. He will return to Aquileia in 333 and 337. If we consider that Constantine, during all the years of his dominate, goes to Rome only twice, his numerous stays in Aquileia emerge as a very significant fact.

Constantine is so far, both mentally and physically, from Rome that, in 330, he inaugurates the construction works of a new capital of the Empire: Constantinopolis (Istanbul in Turkey, from now on Constantinople). This is located on the shores of the Bosphorus Strait—the strait that connects the Sea of Marmara to the Black Sea—not far from Nicomedia.[10]

The mint

The area of the *palatium*-circus is also occupied by a mint. This is very active during the reign of Constantine I, before 322, with coins issued in gold, silver, and bronze.[11] Its first gold Constantinian releases depict a shining sun, first with a prisoner at his feet, then with the globe and victory in hand. The subsequent ones, after the Edict of Mediolanum of 313—this act is also called the Edict of Tolerance, because it proclaimed the neutrality of the Empire toward all religious faiths, paving the way to the definitive affirmation of Christianity throughout the Empire—reflect the conversion to Christianity symbology and depict a banner with an inscription and two prisoners seated on the sides of the same flag.

The mint we are talking about is closed in 322 or 324 due to the needs of an evolving political framework. Meanwhile, the imperial coinage has changed due to a reform introduced by Constantine I in 324. A new gold coin, the *solidus,* has replaced the *aureus.* The new coin is lighter and thinner than the old one. It will have great luck. It will remain in use until the fall of the Western Roman Empire, and in the Eastern Roman Empire until the 10th century. The mint of Aquileia reopens in 334, when Constantine I is still the reigning sovereign, and will remain in operation under the Constantinians. In particular, it will issue gold, bronze or silver coins (respectively, *solidi, folles,* and *multiples*) up to 340, when a *multiple* in silver is issued for Constantine II after his military invasion of the Prefecture of Italy, ruled by his brother Constans, and his occupation of the *palatium* of Aquileia. This takes place just before Constantine II's death, as we will see later.

The Great *Thermae*

The practice of hot baths enjoys extraordinary favor with the Romans. It constitutes a fixed occupation of the day, perhaps the most important one, for those who can afford it; certainly the most pleasant, which no one would want to miss out on. It is much more than a need dictated by the absence of running water in most houses (as a rule, with the exception of the *domus,* the homes of the Romans are not equipped with toilets; sometimes, there are some in the tenements, but they are rudimentary and shared by all the tenants of the building). It is a custom, an expression of a particular conception of life and of the way of living itself, or at least of the way of enjoying free time, linked to the fact that the baths offer everything that can make life enjoyable. "Going to the *thermae*" means both taking care of body hygiene and giving it refreshment, because it relaxes the nerves and frees the spirit, and many other things: keeping fit through physical and sporting exercise, dealing with business, building relationships, meeting acquaintances and friends, enjoying the walk, sunbathing, visiting art exhibitions, attending a theatrical or musical performance, a lecture or a poetic declamation, studying, writing, playing, betting, eating and drinking, and even remaining inactive. Often, in fact, the baths are grandiose architectural and monumental complexes that use all the best elements of the great Roman architecture (concrete, glass windows, arched vaults, etc.), and they include several rooms that both have different uses—from those for bathing to terraces, gyms, theaters, auditoriums, libraries, reading rooms, and rooms for exhibitions—and are splendidly decorated with columns, polychrome marbles, other precious materials, statues, murals, and mosaic floors. Furthermore, they are commonly inserted in a green space equipped with fountains, water lilies, and water features. There are *thermae* in every corner of the Empire, not only in cities but also in small towns, rural villages, and ports. For those that are open to the public, you can enter by purchasing a ticket that costs a *quadrans*: a bronze coin that is worth a quarter of the bronze *as*. Four *asses* form a *sestertius*, a small silver coin. One of the most imposing public bathing complexes is the *Thermae* Constantinianae, built on the Quirinal Hill in Rome by Constantine I, probably before 315; they were possibly started by Maxentius. The similar complexes of Constantinople and Arles are known as *Thermae* of Constantine.

In Aquileia, the *Thermae* Felices Costantinianae are located in the southwestern part of the city, immediately north of the amphitheater. They extend for 20,000 m² and include, in addition to the functional environments typical of Roman *thermae*, entrances, changing rooms, gyms, massage rooms, saunas, corridors, courtyards with arcades, latrines, and other rooms. Begun during the reign of Constantine I (306–337), they are completed during the reign of either Constantine II (337–340) or Constantius II (337–361), though definitely by 350. With their vast rooms, light vaults, and precious mosaic decorations and marble inlays, the *thermae* constitute one of the most important architectural complexes of Aquileia and are an emblem of the city, like the walls and the river port (Rubinich 2013: 85–90).

The public warehouses

Usually, the public warehouses of the Romans (Latin: *horreum*, pl. *horrea*) consist of a massive rectangular building, with thick perimeter walls of stone or brick, narrow entrances, and gates closed with chains and bolts, and they enclose a series of rooms, aligned on several floors, and large internal courtyards with arcades. The interior is semi-dark and the climate is dry if the building is used to store grain. The Aquileia specimens of the Constantinian Age are placed in connection with the river port, unlike those of the Republican Age and the Principate, which are instead linked to the terrestrial road system, and are therefore located in the northern area of the city and on the outskirts. Two of them arise in an area that was occupied in the past by a private *domus* and a building with a portico, forming a large architectural complex. A third public warehouse is located immediately south of an open-air livestock market along the Canale Anfora. It is 99 m long and 66 m wide and consists of two large parallel halls, divided internally into aisles by rows of pillars, separated by a central uncovered area. The external perimeter walls are marked by pilasters ending with blind arches. The structure is similar to the corresponding buildings in Mediolanum and Augusta Trevirorum. Additional warehouses, with central courtyards and wooden arcades, are located further south.

The *horrea* of Aquileia store the wheat imported from the eastern provinces of the Empire, which arrives by sea through Aquae Gradatae (Grado). The cereal unloaded in that port continues its journey on barges, flat-bottomed boats, which go up the Natissa current to the river port of Aquileia, where it is pulled up to the *horrea* from the shore by men or oxen. Crowds of porters, usually slaves, go back and forth between the barges full of grain, lined up along the quays of the river port, and the *horrea,* walking bent under the weight of the sacks they carry on their shoulders. They go through the front door of the building, open under a wide arch, and drop the sack on a plank. The grain will remain in the *horreum*—protected from the humidity rising from the floor by being crammed into large terracotta jars—under the careful supervision of the staff who manage the warehouse until its distribution.

The part of the stored grain that was bought by private wholesalers is resold in the city at retail, at market price, with good earnings. The remainder is used for payment in kind for the tithe, the indirect tax on agricultural production, which is levied in colonies under Latin law and in federate cities. Part of it is distributed to the army. Another part is set aside to prevent stock manipulation and price speculation. The remainder is sold to the public at a controlled price. The distributions of public grain rations are called *frumentationes.* The fathers of families or their delegates, on the appointed days and in the appointed places, line up in front of a raised counter, behind which an employee delivers the rations, in grain, after weighing them with a bushel and leveling the grain with a splint. The bushel is a barrel-shaped container with an iron cross that is used to connect four points on the edges of the container. Its content is equal to 6.6 kg. Before the Age of the Gracchi (133–122 BC), the *frumentationes* had an extraordinary character and took place on the initiative of the Senate, which entrusted their care to the *aediles curuli* or to individual magistrates. In 123 BC, the tribune of the plebeians Caius Sempronius Gracchus introduced a principle according to which the urban plebeians (to whom he wanted to bind himself) have the right to be maintained, at least in part, by proceeds from the taxation of the provinces, and he gave his name to the *lex Sempronia frumentaria.* That law made the *frumentationes* a permanent institution, charged to the state. It established that public wheat was to be sold to adult Roman citizens (Tantillo 2014: 90) at the price of 5/6 per bushel (8.73 liters), equivalent to 1/4 or 1/5 of the market price; that special warehouses have to be built for the storage of cereals; that the purchase of wheat at a controlled price must be made by the citizen concerned in person; and that the distribution is made monthly. In 100 BC, the tribune of the plebeians Lucius Apuleius Saturninus promoted and passed a law that reduced the price of wheat to 5/6 of an *as* per bushel, thus making the *frumentationes* almost free (*lex Appuleia frumentaria*). But that law imposed a huge expense on the state; therefore, after the killing of Saturninus (which took place for other reasons concerning his political activity), it was repealed. A further *lex frumentaria,* approved in 91 BC on the proposal of the tribune of the plebeians Marcus

Livius Drusus, was canceled due to a formal defect after the murder of its proponent. The *frumentationes* were then abolished by Lucius Cornelius Sulla, dictator from 82 to 79 BC. But a new *lex frumentaria*, introduced into the system on the initiative of the consul Marcus Aemilius Lepidus in 78 BC, restored the distribution of wheat at controlled prices. The quantity of public grain that a Roman citizen could buy each month was set at five bushels. Until the last years of the Republic, anyone who was physically in Rome, not just Roman citizens residing in the city, could probably have bought public wheat at a controlled price. In 73 BC, the consul Caius Cassius Longinus and his colleague Marcus Terentius Varro Lucullus promoted and brought to approval the *lex Terentia et Cassia frumentaria*, according to which the state would buy grain in Sicily and sell it at a controlled price in Rome. In 58 BC, another law, approved on the proposal of the tribune of the plebeians Publius Clodius Pulcher (*lex Clodia frumentaria*), established that the grain distributed by the *frumentationes* should be given to the less affluent population free of charge by a *curator annonae*, who would be responsible for the management of the lists of entitled persons. In the imperial era, there was a shift from the sale of grain at a reduced price to the free distribution of grain and, in the 3rd century, to the free distribution of oil, salt, and pork. One of the places where the *frumentationes* take place in Rome is the Porticus Minucia, a quadrilateral portico that encloses a square with two temples in the center, located in the Campus Martius, near the Circus Flaminius.

The outdoor markets

In addition to the port and warehouses, the city's economic importance is reflected in its markets. These each consist of an uncovered area delimited by square-based blocks whose through-holes house the supporting poles of a roof that covers the sales area. A portico, probably with two naves, surrounds the square, which is occupied by stalls. A commercial area adjoins a large store with blind arches 20 m in height, located near the Theodorian Halls (which we'll deal with later) and is in close connection with the nearby Natissa River, which can be reached through some gaps in the city walls, which are landing places for the supply of the points of sale. It consists of three small paved areas, intended for the sale of goods, where merchants display their goods inside masonry structures or simple wooden arcades. Similar areas—at least four—are located in other points of the city. At least two are in the southern part of the city, on the seaward side. These structures, in particular, show that the location of the loading and unloading of goods and the marketing of these have been moved from the river port to the southern part of the city. They are accessed to the north by a road and to the south directly from the Natissa, which bends west at this point. As before, the boats coming from Aquae Gradatae go up the Natissa to here, land, and, using ramps and passages, found between the two lines of the late-ancient city walls, deliver the food directly to the sales structures. In at least one of the areas mentioned above, live and slaughtered animals are sold, together with vegetables, wine, eggs, cheeses, and even cooked foods. In that space, which is teeming with men and animals and enveloped in a din of voices, screams, bellowing, and grunts, the goods on sale consist of reared animals or hunting or fishing prey, including exotic species such as monkeys or giraffes, as well as wild animals, poultry, fish, mollusks, crustaceans, etc. The market day (Latin: *nundina*) falls every eight days. Each time, there is real bedlam. People scream, laugh, and crowd and push around the animal enclosures, the cages of roosters, hens, geese, and hares, and the butchers' counters. Someone takes advantage of the confusion to steal someone else's purse, secretly.

The Forum

The Forum is still that of the Late Republic. Therefore, it is centrally located in relation to the rest of the city and has preserved the appearance of a rectangular square paved with limestone slabs, surrounded by prestigious buildings (including a basilica) and colonnaded porticoes with shops, and is adorned with statues of magistrates and officials on pedestals with inscriptions. The columns of the arcades have grooves filled up to a third of the height with *rudenti*. They have a Corinthian capital and support an architrave decorated with pedestals with protomes of Jupiter Ammon and Medusa—symbolizing the western and eastern borders of the Empire (Casari 2005)—alternated with slabs with garlands supported by cupids. At the end of the 3rd century, or the beginning of the 4th, an inscription with the names of some characters linked to the history of the city will be added to the upper band of the pluteus of the eastern portico.

Domestic housing

The public interventions that aim at the urban and monumental renewal of the city are accompanied by those of private owners of residential properties. Mainly, the latter consists in the construction from scratch or the renovation of residential and representative environments, with particular emphasis to their dining rooms.

A beautiful, very large house from the Constantinian era (now in the Fondo Cossar) has both a mosaic-paved peristyle with white tiles and a Christian oratory (the so-called "of the Fishing" one). One of the rooms, probably a bedroom, is decorated with a mosaic depicting a deer. In another room, larger than the others, perhaps a dining room, there is a mosaic of white tiles within a black frame.

Three dwelling houses, built in the Augustan Age (27 BC–AD 14) in the southwest of the urban area between the *cardo maximus* and the amphitheater,[12] are still in use today. One of them, the one closest to the amphitheater, encloses a rectangular garden, surrounded by a portico with plastered brick columns, overlooked by some rooms, paved with white tiles. Some rooms in the house are decorated with mosaics and frescoes.

The cemeteries

The positioning of cemeteries continues to be outside the urban area, along the main roads. In the case of the main arteries, mainly along Via Annia, they extend for more than 4 km. The one at Ponterosso has been in use since the second half of the 1st century BC or the beginning of the 2nd century. Its tombs consist of simple earthen pits of an elliptical shape or brick masonry boxes in which a stone urn has been inserted, containing the ashes of the deceased. Sometimes the pit is lined with limestone blocks and fragments of tiles, placed side by side without the aid of a binder. Another cemetery is located in a southern area of the city (today's Beligna locality), along a road that goes toward the sea of Grado. It has been in use since the 1st century. Dating from the beginning of the 4th century, there will be some deposits in different forms: a simple pit, possibly covered with stones and bricks, a brick box, with a possible capuchin covering, and amphorae, usually of an African model. Thus a vast Christian cemetery was formed.

Luxury craftsmanship

Constantinian Aquileia is an important center of luxury artifacts. Its shops churn out glass, jewels, and sculptures. The common glass of local production, already of a natural green/blue color, is now practically colorless, with green or yellow shades. Imports of precious glassware from the Eastern Mediterranean continue, as evidenced by some examples of Cypriot origin.

The production of jewelry with engraved semi-precious stones has begun. This includes both the local production of hard stone seals and the production of pendants with semi-precious stones and bezels, introduced in the 1st century BC. The shapes have become heavier and richer. Goldsmiths seek chromatic effects by inserting more than one gem. In addition, they make use of the *opus interassile*, a Roman goldsmithing technique that has been in use since the 3rd century and consists of the fretwork of a gold sheet. There is a fashion to engrave an inscription in the rings, which might be a loving dedication or a spell, according to the circumstances.

Aquileia's portraiture is made up of full-length statues and busts, all in marble, made to commemorate the dead. Since the end of the first 30 years of the 3rd century, it has been characterized by a note of "existential anguish", of "suffered inner crisis", of "pain of living", common to all contemporary Roman portraiture.[13]

In this phase, Aquileia is, along with Rabenna (Ravenna), a notable center of production of sarcophagi sculpted in high relief. Often, the relief reproduces the motif of spouses meeting with a gaze, already typical of the funerary shrines of the Late Republic and the early centuries of the Empire.

The consolidation of Christianity in Aquileia

The persecutions of Christians ceased with the Edict of Galerius of 311, confirmed by the Edict of Milan of 313 between Constantine I and Licinius (308–324), which were carried out after the definitive defeat of Maximinus Daia (305–313). This allowed Christianity to establish and consolidate itself throughout the Empire. In this context, Aquileia has become—and will increasingly be from now on—a stronghold of the Catholic Church. This is demonstrated, among other things, by the multiplication of religious buildings, all embellished with biblical stories and Christian symbols, which takes place during the reign of Constantine I. We refer in particular to the Octagonal Baptistery; to the Basilica called "of Beligna", dedicated to the martyrs Felix and Fortunatus; to the Basilica of Monastero; to the Basilica of San Giovanni in the square; and to the Martyrium of San Hylarius.[14] The Theodorian Halls and the Paleochristian Oratories also reflect the vitality of the Church of Aquileia during the reign of Constantine I.

The Theodorian Halls

The Theodorian Halls—named after Theodore (312?–323?), the first successor of Chrysogonus, third or fourth bishop of Aquileia—are a rectangular episcopal complex, 68.5 m long and 38 m wide (about 2,500 m^2), with three main rooms, which serve to meet complex needs related to religious rites, some smaller rooms intended for residences (perhaps bishopric) and sacristies, and some corridors. They are located close to the late antique walls on the southeastern edge of the city and reflect a unitary and organic architectural project. The main rooms are arranged in a "U" shape and are all rectangular and supported by pillars. The north room and the south room are parallel and are connected with each other through the third room. The former have walls frescoed with geometric motifs in imitation marble; the ceiling is supported by six pillars arranged in two central rows, flat and also frescoed; and the floor is mosaic. The Northern Hall is superimposed on a *domus* of the Augustan Age with mosaic floors, which could be accessed from the port area, about 45 m away, and on those of other buildings of the same period as the *domus*, perhaps warehouses or an arsenal.

The hall arranged transversely has frescoed walls with the same geometric motifs as the others, from which, however, it differs for a number of reasons: apart from the transverse arrangement, it is narrower and shorter, it has four pillars arranged in two parallel rows instead of six, and the floor is in cocciopesto rather than mosaic. The north room and the south room are probably intended for liturgical celebrations, while the third, perhaps, is a solemn access space or serves as a room for catechesis in preparation for baptism. Perhaps, more likely, it is a hall for the administration of confirmation by the bishop, if not an entrance or the place of the presbytery where the preparation of the liturgy takes place in the Eastern Orthodox Church and in the Eastern Catholic Church.

The Theodorian Halls were built immediately after the Edict of Tolerance as the first local seat of Christian worship, probably as a reconstruction of an ancient place of worship that existed before the Edict. This took place on the initiative of Bishop Theodore with the financial support of the faithful, including some very wealthy members, who are remembered in the portraits of the south room and the north room,[15] and, at the same time, marked the official entry of the Church into the panorama of the city, its official recognition, and its participation in imperial power (Cuscito 2013: 27).

The mosaic floors were added when Theodore was already dead. They were probably made by at least three masters or groups of craftsmen. The one in the Northern Hall includes the inscription THEODORE FELIX HIC CREVISTI HIC FELIX, while the one in the Southern Hall bears the inscription THEODORE FELIX ADJUVANTE DEO OMNIPOTENTE ET POEMNIO CAELITUS TIBI TRADITUM OMNIA BAEATAE FECISTI ET GLORIOSE DEDICASTI. This latter wording is found at the base of a Christological symbol—a P superimposed on an X—which is the celestial sign to which Constantine I attributed his victory over Maxentius. These inscriptions refer to the fact that Theodore, in the rooms that have taken his name, has progressed in the ecclesiastical hierarchy.

The structure of the rooms, the didactic richness of the symbolism of their floor mosaics, and the opulence of their decoration indicate that the Christian community of Aquileia, at the time of Theodore, is anything but negligible.

The mosaics of the Northern Hall, in particular, suggest that the group of Christians who unite there are oriented toward asceticism, believe in the millenarian eschatological conception, and constitute an elite who know the so-called "revelation" of the great mysteries, reserved only for a few. These Christians believe in the spiritual survival, that is, in the soul alone, of a select few, while much of humanity is destined to perish, except some who are capable of reaching a very low level of salvation. The representation of the path of asceticism through the heavens was, among other things, readable only by those who knew the texts and the "seals" and the formulas that accompanied it. All this is part of the cultural baggage typical of Alexandrian Hellenism of the 2nd century. Its main feature consists of a syncretism of Jewish, Greek, Iranian, Egyptian, and Christian cultures (Iacumin n.d.: 4).

The early Christian oratories

In the urban area of Aquileia, there are several early Christian oratories, places intended for divine worship by a community or group of the faithful that can also be accessed by other members of the faithful with the consent of the competent superior. Usually, these oratories each consist of an isolated, small chapel adjacent to a monastery or church. There are at least five, all decorated with polychrome floor mosaics. One is decorated with a mosaic of the Good Shepherd, another with the mosaic of the Peach, a third with another mosaic of the Good Shepherd in a singular dress. A fourth oratory is decorated with the Pheasant mosaic and the fifth with the mosaic of the semicircular table.[16]

The participation of Theodore, bishop of Aquileia, at the Synod of Arelate (314)

In 314, Constantine I convenes a synod of bishops in Arelate (Arles in Provence, France),[17] insisting that he be an "external bishop" of the Church, despite not even having been baptized.

Arelate is a city located in the south of Transalpine Gaul, at the intersection of the Via Domitia (which connects Italy to Spain) and the Rhone River.[18] After being an emporium of the Greeks of Massalia (Marseille), it became a settlement colony of the Romans (118 BC). In 104 BC, the consul Caius Marius, commanding general of the Roman army on the Cimbrian front, made it his main logistical base and had a canal dug there through the marshes to connect the Rhone to the Gulf of Fos. In 46 BC, Arelate welcomed the veterans of the Legio VI Ferrata, changing its name to Colonia Iulia Paterna Arelate Sextanorum. With the passage of time, the economic exploitation of its territory intensified, and its river port increased the volume of its trade, surpassing the port of Massilia (Massilia is the Roman name of the Greek Massalia). By 314, it is a thriving agricultural center that exports oil, wine, cured meats, meat, and rice. It is home to an imperial mint. It is one of the main religious centers of the Roman West and is the capital of Gaul (the diocese that embraces Spain, part of France, and Britain). In practice, it is one of the capitals of the Empire. At least, it is when Constantine I stays there. The Gallo-Roman poet Decimus Magnus Ausonius (about 310–393), writing between 379 and 388, will speak of Arelate in his short poem *Ordo urbium nobilium*, into which he pours his knowledge of the most illustrious cities of the Empire: Rome, Constantinople, Antioch on the Orontes, Augusta Trevirorum (Trier in Germany), Mediolanum, Capua, Aquileia, Arelate itself, Merida, Tolosa (Toulouse), and Burdigala (Bordeaux), his hometown. He will describe Arelate as follows: "Open your ports, Arelate, sweet hospitable land and little Rome of Gaul [...]. You are cut by the rushing course of the Rhone, in the middle of which a pontoon bridge forms a square where you receive merchandise from the Roman world; do not hold them back and enrich the other peoples and other cities that Gaul and Aquitaine guard in their vast bosom" (Auson. 67 in Pastorino 1971: 539–553).

The initiative of the "external bishop" Costantine I happens at a time when the churches of Christians, throughout the Empire, are in great tension and confusion, as they are being torn apart by internal struggles linked to ecclesiastical discipline, to the doctrinal interpretation of the Holy Scriptures, and to the different ways of understanding Christianity (the eastern way is more Hellenizing and philosophical, while the western one is more pragmatic and centralistic). This gave rise to the spread of asceticism, which sometimes results in fanatical monasticism, and to some particular interpretations of Christian dogma (Pelagianism, Arianism, Donatism), branded as heresies.

Donatism, in particular, is a schismatic movement with a rigorous and pauperistic character, headed by the theologian Donatus Magnus (c. 270–c. 355), bishop of the

Diocese of Casae Nigrae in Numidia (the oasis of Negrine in Algeria). This position arises from the fact that, in compliance with the edicts of Diocletian that had unleashed the Great Persecution, some Christians of the Church of Africa had handed over books and sacred furnishings, and a party of hardliners asked that they be excluded from the Christian community, arguing that Christian clergy must be flawless for their ministry to be effective and for their prayers and the sacraments administered by them to be valid. One of those Christians was Cecilian, elected in 311 as bishop of Carthage, while another was Felix of Aptonga, who had consecrated Cecilian. The intransigent did not want to recognize Cecilian and appointed their own bishop: first Maggiorinus and then Donatus. The Donatist schism took its name from the latter. A council held in Rome under the presidency of the city's bishop, Militiade, ruled in favor of Cecilian. The Donatists contested that conclusion, arguing that the council fathers had not taken into consideration the position of Felix of Aptonga, and they appealed to the emperor.

In 314, therefore, Constantine convenes a new and more numerous council of bishops in Arelate in order to determine whether Donatism is heresy or not. Representatives of 44 Western Churches from Italy, Gaul, Britain, Hispania, and Roman Africa participate in the synodal works. Among the participants who came from Italy, there are two members of the by now large Christian community of Aquileia: Bishop Theodore and the deacon Agathon. After the examination of the theses of the Donatists and the subsequent discussion, the majority of the defendants condemn the Donatists as heretics. It is interesting to note that both Theodore and Agathon sign the concluding acts as follows: "*Theodorus episcopus, Agathon diaconus de civitate Aquileiensium provincia Dalmatia*", that is, "Theodore bishop, Agathon deacon, from the city of Aquileia, from the province of Dalmatia". Thereby, they probably want to emphasize that the missionary momentum of the Church of Aquileia is reaching out toward the East. Therefore, a year after the rescript of Constantine with which freedom of worship was granted to Christianity, the bishop of Aquileia participates in a leading position (he is the fourth signatory out of the 44 present) at a council dedicated especially to disciplinary and internal organization issues of the Churches.

But the Donatists do not give up. Therefore, Constantine calls Cecilian and Donatus to appear before his court in Mediolanum, where he decides in favor of Cecilian, after which he orders that the churches occupied by the Donatists be seized and that the schismatics be condemned to exile and undergo the confiscation of their estates. But not even these measures serve to end the schism. The next five years are plagued by unrest and strife. Eventually, Constantine decides to tolerate the schismatics and postpones the solution of the problem until better times.

The difference between the religious policy of Constantine, who reigns in the *pars Occidentis*, and that of Licinius, who reigns in the *pars Orientis*, should be noted. The first remains the greatest pontiff of paganism, but is approaching, albeit slowly, Christianity, of which he has already accepted the fundamental principle of faith in the one God and is making Christianity an instrument of his policy. The second has abandoned his position of neutrality and approached paganism: he has forbidden men and women from participating together in the religious services of Christians and bishops preaching before women; he also forbade Christians to assemble within the city walls and expelled Christians from his court and state administration.

In 325, a synod of bishops that takes place in Antioch of Syria excommunicates the bishop of Nicomedia, Eusebius, for his closeness to the Berber theologian Arius (256–336).

Arius is the author of one of the many interpretations of Christian dogma that currently divide Christians. He admits that Jesus Christ is the son of God, but, unlike Catholics, who see in Christ the double divine and human nature, he claims instead that Christ is only a man and is therefore of a different nature to his father. This theory gives rise to a Christian theological current called Arianism.

The First Council of Nicaea

Arius was trained at the school of Lucian of Antioch, where he met Eusebius, a native of Berythus in Phoenicia, with whom he became friends. He later went to Egypt, where he was ordained a priest in the Church of Alexandria. Preaching his creed and proselytizing set him against orthodoxy. In 300, the patriarch of Alexandria, Peter I, condemned Arianism as a heretical doctrine and excommunicated Arius. In 311, however, Arius was rehabilitated by the new patriarch of Alexandria, Achillas. He resumed preaching his creed, and, after Achillas' death in 312, he became Alexander's main antagonist in the race for the succession, which was however won by Alexander.

In 318, Alexander summons a synod of bishops to condemn Arianism and excommunicate Arius. This is held in 321, with the participation of 100 Egyptian and Libyan bishops. It confirms the condemnation of Arianism and calls for the convening of a council, to be held in Ancyra (Ankara) in central Anatolia. Arius flees to Palestine, from where he later moves to Syria, where he continues to preach and proselytize, finding hospitality with Eusebius, then bishop of Caesarea ad mare, a port city in Judaea, founded by Herod the Great between 25 and 13 BC.

In 325, as we noted earlier, a synod of bishops that takes place in Antioch on the Orontes excommunicates Eusebius for his proximity to Arius. Eusebius, on the other hand, is on excellent terms with Constantine I, so much so that he becomes bishop of Nicomedia in Bithynia.

Arius joins Eusebius in Nicomedia, where he will be protected by the emperor. Constantine I establishes that the council requested by the Libyan and Egyptian bishops will see the participation of all the bishops of the Christian world and will not take place in Ancyra but in Nicaea (Iznik in Turkey), a city on the Sea of Marmara, because the latter is easier to reach for the bishops of the West. The intent of Constantine is to unite the Church, because this will put an end to the unrest and violence born of theological disputes and will guarantee order and stability in the Empire. The council records a learned discussion between the supporters of Catholic orthodoxy and the followers of Arianism. The emperor personally follows the discussion and attends all the sessions. The work ends with the condemnation of Arianism. Eusebius and Arius are exiled. Arius moves to Illyria, but his doctrine will continue to form proselytes. In 328, Eusebius is officially recalled to his homeland and reinstated to the office of bishop of Nicomedia, and he pleads the cause of Arius, ensuring that, in 331 or 334, he is rehabilitated and recalled from exile. A new council takes place in Tyre in Phoenicia in 335, which ends with the condemnation of the exile of one of Arius' most strenuous opponents, the bishop Athanasius of Alexandria. Arius dies in Constantinople in 336. Meanwhile, Constantine has also died, and the Empire has been divided among his sons.

The death of Constantine I

Constantine dies on 22 May 337, the day of Pentecost (the descent of the Holy Spirit on the Apostles), in Nicomedia, while he was preparing to go to war against the Sassanid Shahpur II. On his deathbed, he was baptized by Eusebius. He receives extreme unction and dies peacefully. He is buried in Constantinople.[19] Previously, the two Caesars appointed by Constantine, Crispus and Licinius Junior, had also died, both in 326.

Crispus was the son of Constantine I and his first wife, Minervina. As a Caesar, he was based in Augusta Trevirorum (Trier in Germany). He had been consul twice and had fought against the Franks and the Alemanni. He had been the main architect of the victory that his father had won over Licinius at the Battle of the Hellespont in 324. He was married to Helena and had a son. He was executed in 326, in Pula, Istria, on the orders of Constantine at the height of a dark affair, shortly before his stepmother Fausta was also executed. The reasons for these executions are unknown, but it is suspected that they had been in an incestuous relationship, or that Fausta had unjustly accused Crispus of having molested her, and Constantine punished both after discovering the deception.[20]

Successors: Constantine II, Constantius II, Constans

The late emperor has neither said nor left anything written about the succession. However, he had made it known that he wanted a hereditary succession and that he wanted the unity of the Empire to be preserved (under him, the concept of the Empire as the patrimony of the *princeps*, transmissible to his descendants, had returned; according to Eusebius, God would reward Constantine I for his loyalty, making sure that, after his death, he continued to reign through his heirs and successors). It seems that he thought of designating his second son, Constantius, as his successor, and his other sons—the first-born Constantine and the second-born Constans—as Caesars, flanking the latter with other Caesars, Hannibalianus and Dalmatius, who were his nephews and the sons of Flavius Dalmatius, or Dalmatius Il Censor. The latter was the half-brother of Constantine I because he was born from the marriage of Constantius

Chlorus and Maximiana Theodora (Constantine I was the son of Constantius Chlorus and of a concubine, Helena; Constantius Chlorus divorced the latter to marry Theodora in order to strengthen his bond with the Augustus Maximian).

A four-month interregnum follows the death of Constantine I. In the course of it, more precisely in July 337, all those who can claim succession rights and an unspecified number of senior officials and commanders are assassinated by the military in Constantinople. We refer to the Caesars Hannibalianus and Dalmatius; to Julius Constantius, born from the marriage of Constantius Chlorus and Maximiana Teodora, and therefore the half-brother of Constantine I; and to the eldest son of Julius Constantius. The other two sons of Julius Constantius—Gallus and Julian, respectively 16 and six—are spared, given their young age, but are sent to confinement. It is said that the massacre depended on the fact that the soldiers wanted the only sons of Constantine I to reign over the Empire, but it is suspected that this was actually wanted by Constantius, the future Constantius II. He was in Constantinople and did not lift a finger to prevent the massacre; moreover, he was one of the massacre's main beneficiaries.

On 9 September 337, the three sons of Constantine I ascend to the imperial throne as his heirs and successors: Constantine (Constantine II) and Constantius (Constantius II), both born in 317, and Constans, who is just 17. Therefore, from now on, there will not be only one Augustus but three. The imperial proclamation of these emperors is the origin of the Neo-Flavian dynasty. More commonly, however, the first successors of Constantine I, up to and including Julian, will be called the Constantinians.

Shortly after the proclamation, the three emperors meet in Viminacium in Pannonia (Kostolac in Serbia) and share the inheritance (Iul. 1.19a.; Lib. 59.75). The operation presupposes a reorganization of the Empire, which has already been arranged by the will of Constantine I and is currently being implemented. The empire is divided into four prefectures: Gaul, Italy, Illyricum, and the East. In turn, each prefecture is divided into dioceses and each diocese into provinces. The Prefecture of Gaul embraces three dioceses—Spain, the Seven Provinces, and Britain—for a total of 29 provinces. The Prefecture of Italy is composed of three dioceses—the City of Rome, Italy, and Africa—totaling 40 provinces in all. The Prefecture of Illyricum includes the dioceses of Dacia, Macedonia, and Achaia, in all 11 provinces. The Prefecture of the East is made up of four dioceses—Egypt, Asia, Pontus, and Thrace—for a total of 46 provinces, including the city of Constantinople. The Prefecture of Gaul goes to Constantine II. Constans keeps the Prefecture of Italy and the Prefecture of Illyricum for himself. Constantius II receives the Prefecture of the East.

The death of Constantine II

The Prefectures are large enough to satisfy the brothers' appetites, but Constantine II asks for more. He tends to exercise *de facto* protection against Constans, taking advantage of the fact that he is older than him. But Constans claims autonomy. In

January–February 340, while Constantius II fights in the East against the Sassanids, Constantine II waits for Constans I to go to Dacia (a province where there are many men loyal to him), then leads the army to Italy, claiming to be headed for the eastern front to support Constantius II. Constantine II makes a stop in Aquileia and takes up residence in the *palatium*. Constans is informed of Constantine II's invasion of the Diocese of Italy and orders the army, which is in Italy, to oppose the invader, trying to slow him down while awaiting his arrival, after which he sets out to join him.

Between the end of the winter and the beginning of April 340, Constans' generals feigned an attack on Aquileia and retreated. Constantine II chases them and falls into an ambush in Cervenianum (Cervignano del Friuli). He fights, loses many men, and meets death himself. He was 23, and his reign had lasted just three years. He is beheaded and his body is thrown into the river Aussa (*Epit. De Caes.* 41), perhaps near the bridge over which the Via Annia passes, in the place where a *tetrapylon* will be erected in the future (a *tetrapylon* is a cubic monument with a door on each of its four sides, and is usually erected at road junctions).[21]

The emperors visit Aquileia

Constans takes possession of his brother's inheritance undisturbed and establishes his residence in Mediolanum, but he will often go to Aquileia, thus confirming the existence of a special bond between this city, Constantine I, and the Constantinians. As we have seen previously, Constantine I stayed in Aquileia several times. The second wife of Constantius II, Flavia Eusebia, belongs to the Eusebii family, who are originally from Thessalonica, but she owns a villa in the territory of Aquileia.[22] The signature of Constans at the bottom of a law certifies his presence in Aquileia on 9 April 340. In 342, Constans returns to Aquileia. During his stays in Aquileia, the city was the western capital of the Roman Empire. From there, the Augustus governs a patchwork of territories extending from the Danube to the Atlantic coast of the Iberian Peninsula, from northwestern Europe to Hadrian's Wall in Great Britain, and from the border of the Rhine to North Africa.

Meanwhile, the controversy between Arians and Catholics continues in many cities of the West, aroused by the declaration of the consubstantiality of the Son with the Father (Jesus Christ is identified as being of the same substance or essence as God, despite the difference in appearance), according to the Nicene Creed and the condemnation of Arianism pronounced by the First Council of Nicaea in 325. The discussions are very heated and often degenerate into violence and disorder.

Theological conflicts

In general, after the First Council of Nicaea, the Churches of the West turned mainly in favor of Catholicism, therefore in favor of the pope of Rome and the patriarch of Alexandria. In the East, however, Constantius II is caught between an ever-expanding Christianity and a paganism that is still tied to ancient values, but he was educated in Christianity. His religious policy proceeds in the wake of that of his father. His is based on the tolerance of paganism, on the fight against magical practices, exorcisms, etc., and on the propensity to favor Catholicism among the religions of the Empire. Among the measures he adopted to this end, the recognition of tax exemptions for the Christian clergy and the confirmation of the exclusive jurisdiction of Christian bishops over crimes committed by clerics are worthy of note.

The expansion of Arianism in the West mainly originates in the Western Balkans and is directed toward Mediolanum, and therefore it passes through Aquileia, where it leads to great discussions within the local church, traditionally oriented toward Alexandrian-style religious orthodoxy. Theological conflicts in the community are quite frequent. In 343, two bishops of Pannonia—Ursacius of Singidunum (Belgrade in Serbia) and Valens of Mursa (Osijek in Serbia)—inflame the debate in the Aquileian church. The discussion takes place in harsh tones, in a climate of heated controversy. A riot breaks out. The bishop of Aquileia, Viator, is killed. The Theodorian Halls are devastated. Fortunatianus (342–368?) is chosen as Viator's successor in consideration of his tendency to exercise a role of religious mediation and pacification.

Fortunatianus, bishop of Aquileia from 342 to 369

Constantius II, following the example of his father, aims to ensure the unity of the Christian faith in the unity of the Empire through the convening of councils that aim to facilitate a settlement of the differences between Arians and Catholics.

In 345, Fortunatianus participates in the Council of Sardica (Sofia in Romania) and signs the final conclusions, which confirm the condemnation of Arianism. Upon returning from the council, he offers hospitality in Aquileia to Athanasius, the exiled bishop of Alexandria. The origins of the theological formation of the Church of Aquileia, we recall, reveal an Alexandrian influence, undoubtedly due to its maritime relations with Egypt.

Athanasius, during his stay in Aquileia, attends the Easter rites in a building under construction, in the presence of the Augustus Constans, and he gives an account of it in a letter about him (Athanasius 3.25, col. 597 *et passim*). The works to which Athanasius refers are aimed at the construction of a grandiose basilica with a large quadrilateral portico. The great work, undertaken under the initiative of Fortunatianus, rises above the demolished Theodorian Halls,[23] whose reconstruction in larger and more solemn forms was necessary to hold masses for the faithful, which in the meantime has increased considerably. Among the other works started after the death of Constantine I in an Aquileia already rich in temples, there are therefore also those aimed at the construction of a large Christian basilica.[24]

The death of Constans and the subsequent usurpations of the title of Augustus

Constantius II and Constans jointly share the rule of an empire which appears to be a political unit, with some distinctions, due to the diversity of their characters. The former is commonly considered as a good commander and administrator, reducing the weight of the imperial bureaucracy and the tax authorities, and he faces the incursions of the barbarian peoples across the Germanic and Danubian borders. He is a Christian of Arian faith and, like his father before him, takes part in the doctrinal controversies and removes and appoints bishops. Under his reign, the ecclesiastical hierarchy consolidates its power and privileges, and Christianity asserts itself as the main religion in the eastern part of the Empire.

Constans, however, is a little-loved sovereign, both by the people and by the army, because of his sexual tastes and above all the excessive influence of his favorites and the corruption that reigns at court. Moreover, he despises the soldiers.

In 350, a military revolt breaks out in Augustodunum (Autun in the Saone-et-Loire department in the Burgundy-Franche-Comté region in France) due to the growing discontent that had been brewing for some time in the imperial court and in military circles. Augustodunum is a city founded by Augustus on the same site as a pre-existing Gallic settlement. Surrounded by walls, it is accessed through two monumental gates. Among the buildings in the urban area, the famous theater—the largest structure of its kind in Gaul (150 m in diameter)—and a temple of Janus are worthy of note.

The rioters declare that Constans has fallen from the throne and in his place acclaim Magnentius, a Franco-British soldier, born in 303 in Samarobriva (Amiens), and commander general of the Herculians and the Jovians, the units of the imperial guard. Constans flees towards Spain, but is chased and caught by Gaiso, general of Magnentius, in a church in oppidum Helena in the Pyrenees. He is dragged out of the building and killed (18 January 350).

The usurpation of Magnentius is an expression of Gallic separatism, which has already emerged in the 3rd century, on the occasion of the birth of the *Galliarum Imperium*, a state born in 260 from the secession of the provinces of Gaul, Britannia, and Spain from the Roman Empire (this existed up until 273). On hearing of this, Vetranius, general commander of the legions stationed in Illyricum, and Julius Nepotianus, nephew of Constantine I and consul in 336, each separately claim the title of Augustus of the West for himself.

It is important to note that Nepotianus is the son of Virius Nepotianus and Eutropia, half-sister of Constantine I, and that therefore he is the nephew of Constantius Chlorus and Maximiana Theodora. After Constans' death, he proclaims himself as his successor on the basis that, with the death of the Augustus, he remained the only living member of the family of Constantine I in the West. He assembles a *militia*, made up of a certain number of gladiators, brigands, and other criminals, and, on 3 June

350, he goes to Rome. He shows himself dressed as an emperor in public, and he is acclaimed as such by the population, especially by the Senate.

The prefect of the city, Titianus, loyal to Magnentius, in turn, recruits a militia and attacks Nepotianus and his men outside the city. Nepotianus' men are disorganized and undisciplined. They are defeated and flee toward the city. Titianus orders the city gates to be closed, surrounds the fugitives, and massacres them. The most notable victim of the clash is Nepotianus himself. His head, severed from his torso, is stuck on the tip of a spear and carried around the streets of the city. Magnentius then sends his trusted *magister officiorum* Marcellinus to Rome and, in the following days, carries out a massacre among the population, especially among the senators. It was probably in these circumstances that Eutropia, half-sister of Constantine I and mother of Nepotianus, was killed.

Meanwhile, Magnentius has rushed to Aquileia with a retinue of Celtic, Gallic, Frankish, and Saxon troops (Iul. 1.28). He has occupied the city, has been proclaimed Augustus, and has established his residence there. In some gold, silver, and bronze coins minted by the Aquileian mint, he has defined himself *liberator rei publicae* and *restitutor libertatis*, but also *conservator militum et provincialium* (Bastien 1964). Interestingly, those coins carry the Christogram. In all likelihood, Magnentius wants to refer to Constantine I and his religious choice; perhaps he is turning to the God of Christians, the only one who can guarantee him the victory and the support of the Orthodox communities of Gaul. More likely, he wants to appropriate the Christological symbol for reasons of expediency, as he is uncertain whether he is a Christian. Two further reasons for Magnentius' propaganda are the emphasis placed on the primacy of Rome over Constantinople and the restoration of nocturnal sacrifices, in contrast to the anti-pagan legislation of Constantine II and Constans.

The *Claustra Alpium Iuliarium*

Aquileia, we recall, has always played, and currently plays, the role of a rearward stronghold with strategic functions within the defensive system of the Eastern Alps. The fulcrum of that system is the chain of fortifications guarding the Julian Alps passes called *Claustra Alpium Iuliarium.* The reason why Magnentius chose to reside in Aquileia, therefore, is his strategic interest in maintaining control of the Claustra and, consequently, of the Julian passes. The system has been increased and strengthened over time, and today it consists of 14 linear defenses (long stone walls with towers) and eight forts, which close each valley and isolate each hill, integrating themselves with the many natural defenses of the region (ravines, rivers, woods). These structures are divided into three groups. The first group goes from Tarsatica (Rijeka) to Iulia Aemona (Ljubljana). It resembles a broken line of walls, sometimes several kilometers long, and aims to block the route that connects Tarsatica with Tergeste (Trieste), passing through Istria. The second group focuses on Via Gemina. This includes most of the fortifications, among which there are several checkpoints: Vrhnika; the two secondary watchtowers of Lanusce and Martiny Hrib; ad Pirum (Hrusica), the most imposing and the central fortress of the Claustra, which controls the homonymous pass; and Castra (Aidussina) at the entrance to the road that leads to Aquileia. Castra and ad Pirum are impressive fortresses. They were built after 284, during the reign of Diocletian (284–305) or Constantine I (306–337), if not in the 270s at the same time as some urban walls of northern Italy. The third group includes five forts north of Castra between Forum Iulii (Cividale del Friuli) and Iulia Aemona (Vannesse 2007: 314–339). In the context of the Claustra, Aquileia plays a complementary role to the fortifications. All the Claustra were certainly garrisoned in the years 306–314, and they will remain so throughout the 4th century.

The death of Magnentius

Magnentius (350–353) resided in Aquileia for more than a year between 351 and 352. At that time, he asks Constantius II—who is residing in Constantinople—to grant him the hand of his sister Constantina, widow of Hannibalianus. If he obtained it, he would become the designated successor and legitimate heir of Constantius II. Constantius II recognizes that the situation has reached the limit of his endurance and decides to go to war against Magnentius. Before leaving for the West, having no children (although he married three times), he marries Constantina to his cousin Constantius Gallus (one of Julius Constantius' sons, who with his brother Julian survived the massacre of his family in 337), and then he designates the latter as Caesar and sends him to Antioch in Syria to govern the Prefecture of the East (351). Gallus thus becomes the designated successor and legitimate heir of Constantius II.

The emperor then moves from Constantinople at the head of an army of 80,000 men, of which 50,000 are a new, powerful specialty: heavily armored cavalry, which imitates the Parthian cataphract cavalry. As the Augustus of the East approaches, Vetranius gives up his claim to the crown, goes to meet him on the plain of Serdica, and kneels before him, asking for forgiveness (which is granted to him, including because he has the merit of having prevented Magnentius from occupying Illyricum). He later joins his forces with those of Constantius II and marches alongside the latter against Magnentius.

Constantius II quarters his troops for the winter in Sirmium. On 28 September 351, he defeats Magnentius at the Battle of Mursa Major (Osijek in Croatia), thanks to errors by Magnentius and the betrayal and desertion of a Frankish cavalry unit, commanded by the tribune Claudius Silvanus. The Battle of Mursa Major is one of the most bitter and bloody in Roman history. Magnentius and Constantius II lose thirty thousand and twenty-four thousand men respectively, equal to two-thirds of the strength of the former and half of the strength of the latter (Zonar. 13.8.17). One of the missing is Marcellinus. He probably also fell in combat, but his body will not be found.[25] Magnentius escapes and returns to Aquileia, from where he will unleash a campaign of terror throughout the Prefecture of Gaul, calling all his supporters together on the understanding that those who do not show up are against him.

Constantius II is unable to fully exploit the success achieved in the Battle of Mursa Major due to the heavy losses suffered. Therefore, he remains in Illyricum, where he takes advantage of the winter to recruit troops and recapture the city of Siscia, occupied by Magnentius.

With the return of spring, Constantius II penetrates into the heart of the Claustra Alpium Iuliarum by secondary roads. A battle takes place in ad Pirum and lasts for two days. The first day of fighting ends with the defeat of the infantry of Constantius II, who are sent ahead without any protection. The next day, the enemy are taken by surprise by Constantius II's heavy armored cavalry as they are celebrating the victory.

Magnentius is taking advantage of the luxury and delights of Aquileia, spending his time amidst games and effeminate pleasures. He learns that the enemy is at the gates while he is watching a horse race in the Circus. He quickly leaves the city and takes refuge in Transalpine Gaul. With the entry of Constantius II into Aquileia, many people are arrested for political reasons and put into chains to be transferred to Mediolanum to be tried (one man, to escape torture, commits suicide in a tavern). They will be sentenced to death and executed.

Constantius II chases Magnentius and, on 11 August 353, defeats him definitively at the Battle of Mons Seleucus (La Bâtie-Montsaléon in the Hautes-Alpes in southeastern France). Magnentius flees to Spain, with Constantius on his heels. When he sees he has lost, rather than surrender to the enemy and have an indecent death, he takes his own life (10 August 353). Constantius quarters for the winter in Arelate and persecutes the last supporters of Magnentius. Mere suspicion is enough for his officials and bodyguards to act against them.

With the death of Magnentius, Constantius II becomes the only living heir of Constantine I, and the Roman Empire is once again united in name and in fact. Again, therefore, there is only one Augustus for the whole Empire.

The death of Constantius II and the rise of Julian

In 354, Constantius II's confidence in his brother-in-law Constantius Gallus, Caesar of the East from 351 and consul from 352, fails, not so much (or not only) for the failures of his governmental activity, bankruptcy, and hate (excesses of cruelty were recently committed in the repression of revolts that broke out in Antioch on the Orontes and in Palestine) as for the accusations of high treason made by some high officials of the imperial court, including the great chamberlain Eusebius, who has already been in the service of Constantine I in this capacity and exerts great influence on the Augustus of the East (among the other officials involved in the conspiracy, Pentadius, Apodemius, and Lucillianus are mentioned).

Eusebius follows Constantius Gallus to Gaul (353–354) and is in Mediolanum when the latter is arrested in Poetovium in Pannonia (Ptuj in Slovenia) while, in the company of the Comes Lucillianus, he is traveling to Constantinople, to which he had been summoned. Gallus is imprisoned in Pietas Iulia (Pula in Croatia).

Pietas Iulia is the current name of the ancient capital of the Istri, Visace, later called Nesactium and then Alba Iulia. The city has risen after the destruction suffered in the civil war between Octavianus, Marcus Antonius, and Marcus Aemilius Lepidus on the one hand and the assassins of Julius Caesar, led by Brutus and Cassius, on the other, in which it had taken the side of the latter. Located in *Venetia et Histra*, on the border with Pannonia, it is a thriving city and an important port, and it administers a vast territory. It has a large forum, a triumphal arch, an amphitheater, two theaters, and several Christian temples and basilicas.

Constantius II sentences Gallus to death. With the execution imminent, Constantius II grants pardon to the condemned, but the imperial messenger, who is carrying the order to suspend the execution, is hindered by Eusebius and arrives in Pula just after Gallus has been beheaded in prison. At the time of his brother's execution, Julian, 24, is in Constantinople.

Julian and Constantius Gallus, after the death of their parents, spent their childhood and adolescence together, changing domicile several times. First, they lived in Nicomedia (Izmit in Turkey), a city located in the province of *Bithynia et Pontus*, halfway between Constantinople and Nicaea, under the tutelage of the city's bishop and their relative, Eusebius (not to be confused with the eunuch of the same name). In 340, they move to Constantinople, where Eusebius had been appointed bishop and where Julian then studied grammar and rhetoric. From 341 onward (341 is the year of the death of Bishop Eusebius), they were forced to live in Macellum in Cappadocia, a fortified post in an imperial estate by order of Constantius II.

As a child, Julian was educated in Christianity by Bishop Eusebius. In Macellum, he was a reader in the Christian community: he proclaimed the word of God and also read other texts in liturgical celebrations without being able to exclude the performance of other tasks in the pastoral field. In 351, with the elevation of Gallus to the rank of Caesar of the East, Julian regained full freedom of movement and completed his studies, first in Pergamum (Bergama in Turkey), where he attended the circle of the Neoplatonic Herdesius, and then in Ephesus (near Selçuk in Izmir Province, Turkey), where, under the influence of the Neoplatonic Maximus, he abjured Christianity and embraced the religion and polytheistic cults of the classical world, that is, paganism.

Julian, like Gallus, is also in the sights of Eusebius and his companions. In 354, on the death of Gallus, he finds himself in danger. Augusta Eusebia intervenes on Julian's behalf with her husband and gets him sent to Athens to improve his studies. Augusta Eusebia is a daughter of the Greek governor of Thessalonica in Macedonia (Thessaloniki in Greece) and the consort of Constantius II. She is a young woman, beautiful and of great culture.

Julian takes advantage of his stay in Athens to be initiated into the Eleusinian mysteries and the mysteries of Mithras. When Julian has been in the City of the Acropolis for three months, Constantius II distracts him from his studies, appoints him as the Caesar of the East as the successor of Gallus, and puts him in charge of the Prefecture of Gaul, with the priority tasks of putting an end to the raids for the purpose of robbery of bands of Franks and Alemanni that are crossing the Rhine and of suppressing a revolt of the Saxons in Britain. First of all, Julian has Palatine officials tried for involvement in Gallus' death. Eusebius and Apodemius are found guilty, sentenced to death, and executed. Pentadius is acquitted. Lucillianus is deposed from office and forced to retire to private life.

Constantius II's trust in Julian is well placed. Although he has done nothing but study all his life, Julian turns out to be a very talented general, gifted with great leadership and organizational skills, and is both prudent and fair. In 355, he annihilates the Franks and the Alemanni in a bloody battle close to Strasbourg, then stifles the rebellion in Britain in blood. Relations between Constantius II and the Caesar of the East could not be better.

Since 352, Constantius II has lived in Mediolanum, which has been the capital of the *pars Occidentis* since 286, when Emperor Maximian established his own residence there. Maximian made it the object of an urban, architectural, and monumental development program, in which an imperial palace was also built. The latter is located in the western part of the city. Together with the neighborhood that surrounds it, it occupies an area of 80,000 m². It includes residential districts, representative rooms, offices, spas, military posts, places of worship, etc. The rooms are organized in groups around a porticoed courtyard and are often decorated with floors in *opus sectile* or with black and white tiles (or, in the future, with figured mosaics). As in other cities of the Roman Empire, the imperial palace of Mediolanum has direct access to the hippodrome or circus so that the emperor can go there without going out into the street but instead through a covered and protected passage.

Mediolanum, under the Constantinians, is a city where "everything is worthy of admiration".

> There are great riches and numerous noble houses. The city has grown and is surrounded by a double circle of walls. There is the circus, where the people enjoy the shows, the theater with wedge-shaped steps, the temples, the fortress of the imperial palace, the mint, the district that takes its name from the Erculee baths. The colonnaded courtyards are decorated with marble statues, the walls are surrounded by a belt of fortified embankments. Its buildings are one more imposing than the other as if they were rivals, and neither does their proximity to Rome diminish their size (Auson. 7).

The Council of Mediolanum

We have already said that Constantius II is used to getting involved in religious matters, in imitation of his father, the deceased Constantine I. He is a Christian of the Arian faith and therefore basically rejects Catholic thought, which is Orthodox, that is, based on the conclusions of the Council of Nicaea of 325 (Nicaea I), which condemned the theologian Arius, who, since 321, had preached that Jesus was not both man and god but only a man, created by God. His plan is to unite all Christians in a modified form of Arianism. It is supported by the Eastern Church, which is predominantly of Arian inspiration, but is opposed by Athanasius, bishop of Alexandria, who is of the Orthodox faith. Athanasius, after being acquitted by the Council of Sardica in 345, insisted with strength and continuity on opposing Constantius II.

The bishop of Rome is currently Pope Liberius. He has held the Chair of St Peter since 352. He, like his predecessor Julius, is a Christian of the Nicene faith and shared and made his own conclusions at the Council of Sardica. In 353, after the death of Magnentius, he asks Constantius II to assemble a council in Aquileia, since he had received letters from many oriental bishops (against Athanasius) and from many others, including Egyptians (pro-Athanasius). Why does he choose Aquileia? Because the Church of Aquileia is a point of reference for about 20 dioceses in Italy and 10 on the other side of the Alps for the authority it exercises and its doctrinal elaboration, and it is also making a vigorous contribution to the development of Christianity in the West. Its bishop is currently Fortunatianus. He is an important prelate who enjoys great prestige. He participated at the Council of Sardica and signed the condemnation of Arianism. The council, to be held in Aquileia in 381 and which will affect all the churches of the West, will be decisive in the fight against Arianism.

The emperor convenes the council in 355, though not in Aquileia but in Mediolanum, in the sumptuous *palatium*. During the work, Dionysius, the orthodox bishop of Mediolanum and friend of Constantius II, pronounces himself in favor of the condemnation of Athanasius, but conditions his signature of the sentence on the preliminary signs of the Nicene Creed by those present. He is about to sign the text of that profession of faith when Valens of Mursa snatches the formula from him, declaring the whole procedure unacceptable. Athanasius is therefore condemned by all the bishops present, except by Dionysius and two others: Eusebius, bishop of Vercellae (Vercelli, in Lombardy), who represents the Pope, and Lucifer, bishop of Caralis (Cagliari in Sardinia). Athanasius and the three dissidents are dismissed from the offices they hold and exiled by Constantius II. The Arian Aussentius becomes bishop of Mediolanum in place of Dionysius. Therefore, Arianism conquers the stronghold of Mediolanum with the consent of the emperor.

Pope Liberius deplores the condemnation of Athanasius, Dionysius, Eusebius, and Lucifer. In the summer of 356, Constantius II has him arrested and transferred to Mediolanum. The capture takes place at night to prevent the people of Rome, who are devoted to their bishop, from rising up against the emperor. But the Pope does not renounce his position. Constantius II ends up exiling him to Beroea in Thrace and has the Archdeacon Felix (Felix II), of Arian faith, elected in his place. However, he will have to send Liborius back to Rome in 358 because the Romans rose up against Felix II and threw him out of the city.

In 358, Fortunatianus, the bishop of Aquileia, risks being exiled like Dionysius, Eusebius and Lucifer, albeit for the opposite reason. To escape this, he changes his opinion on Arianism and signs the Arian Creed of Sirmium together with other bishops. He thus assumes an attitude opposite to what he showed in 355 on the occasion of the Council of Mediolanum. For this reason, he will be accused of Arianism and of having convinced the Pope to move in this direction too. Raising his voice against him is Eusebius Sophronius Hieronymus (347–412/420), a priest, confessor, theologian, and historian, who is quite well known in the ecclesiastical environment for having translated most of the Bible into Latin and for his comments on the Gospels. The accusation is totally unfounded. Fortunatianus never adhered to Arianism, nor did he ever incite Liberius to do so. He only tried to mediate toward moderate Arians (Iacumin n.d.: 4).

Eusebius Sophronius Hieronymus, also known as Jerome, is a native of Stridon in Illyria (Zrenj or Sdrin in Istria, Croatia). At the time of the Council of Mediolanum, he lives in Rome, where he is a student and pupil of Caius Marius Victorinus and Aelius Donatus, Latin grammarians and teachers of rhetoric; Victorinus is also a Neoplatonic philosopher, and he translated two books of Aristotle from Greek into Latin. After his death, Jerome will become a saint of the Catholic Church (Hieron. 97).

The ideal climate of collaboration between Constantius II and Julian fails in 359 for reasons we will now describe. However, it is best to provide a premise first.

Julian's usurpation

In 337, immediately before the death of Constantine I, the Sassanid Shāpūr II (309–379), emperor of the Persians, broke the truce that had been agreed in 297 between Diocletian and Narses (293–302). He invaded the Prefecture of the East and, in Mesopotamia, contended with Constantius II for control of the fortress-cities of Singara (Sinjar in Iraq), Nisibis (Nusaybin in Turkey), and Amida (Diyarbakir in Turkey), which are typified by always being involved in the ups and downs of the eastern border of the Empire, which is the theater of the eternal conflict between Rome and the Parthians (before) and between Rome and the Sassanids (after). The conflict experienced a pause from 353 to 358 because the Persian Empire was under attack from the East by some nomadic, Arabian, and Hunnic tribes. Eventually, Shāpūr II managed to subdue those tribes and make them allies.

In 359, Shāpūr returns to the offensive against the Romans. His objective is Amida, a walled city located on a basaltic plateau (660 m above sea level) along the right bank of the Tigris (which from this point becomes navigable) and dominates the valley bottom from a height difference of about 100 m, which ensures, toward the east and southeast, a powerful natural defense. It was originally very small (Amm. Marc., *Res Gestae* 18.9.1). Amida was enlarged and fortified by Constantius II between 324 and 327 and is currently a strategic point for the defense of northern Mesopotamia and the satrapies controlled by the Romans up to the distant Corduena (Kurdistan).[26]

The city is the target of a night attack, carried out simultaneously on several fronts, with use made of siege towers and fire arrows. It resists and is besieged. Its defense is directed by the *magister equitum* Ursicinus. The battle is fierce and bloody. It takes over 73 days, during which Ursicinus loses six legions and a *vexilatio comitatensis* in battle, a total of 4,000 infantry and 300–400 knights.[27] Finally, the city is captured, though Ursicinus escapes by fleeing. In the future, he will be held responsible for the defeat and dismissed. The siege of Amida will be described by the Roman historian Ammianus Marcellinus in book 19 of his *Rerum Gestarum*, or more simply, *Res Gestae*. That of Marcellinus is a first-hand account. In fact, its author is an eyewitness, having served in the defense of the city.[28]

Constantius II learns of the fall of Amida while in Nisibis, a great city of Jezirah, which, after the victories of Emperor Galerius (293–311) and the peace that was signed there in 298 (Peace of Nisibis), has become a hub for mercantile traffic between the Roman East and Persia. Nisibis resisted Parthian sieges in 338, 346, and 350 thanks to the valor of its defenders and its mighty walls. It is currently defended by the Legio III Parthica. It is full of buildings that refer to the Christian religion and houses the tomb of St James, who died in 338.

Constantius orders Julian to reach the eastern front as soon as possible to fight against the Persians, but the army that Julian brings with him mutinies and, in February 360, in Lutetia (Paris), acclaims Julian as Augustus of the West. Julian did not expect this. At first, he hesitates, then accepts (perhaps he already suspects that Constantius played a role in the massacre of his family when Julian was a child; in 361, he will define Constantius as "the killer of my family"). Constantius II asks Julian to renounce the title, but Julian resists. This inevitably leads to war between the Augustus of the East and the Caesar of the East. Constantius leaves Nisibis for Europe at the head of an army. Shāpūr takes the opportunity to continue the advance and conquers Singara and Bezabde (360).

In turn, Julian leads an army from Transalpine Gaul to Illyricum. He goes up the Sava to Sirmium (Sremska Mitrovica in Serbia), lands near the city, and captures Lucillianus, the leader of the troops who were gathered there by Constantius; the city falls into his hands soon after. Later, Julian goes to Naissus in Moesia (Niš in Serbia), establishes his headquarters there, and awaits the arrival of Constantius.

Julian besieges Aquileia

Constantius II's two legions and the cohort of archers who surrendered in Sirmium and whom Julian sent to Transalpine Gaul take refuge in Aquileia, confident that the emperor will come to their aid. The local population supports the mutineers, rising in turn against Julian, on the instigation of some members of the senatorial aristocracy. Julian, from Naissus, orders the *magister equitum* Flavius Valens Iovinus and his cavalry, which are probably located in Iulia Aemona, to take control of both roads that connect this city to Aquileia and which touch the nerve centers of the Claustra Alpium Iuliarium—namely, in order of succession from Iulia Aemona (Ljubljana in Slovenia) to Aquileia: Nauportus, ad Pirum, and Castra—and also to take control of Aquileia to prevent the insurgents from barring the passes of the Julian Alps and thus blocking the supplies that Constantius II himself needs to fight against the Parthians. While Iovinus approaches along that road of fundamental strategic importance, the mutineers and the Aquileians close the gates of the city and prepare to withstand a siege. Their resistance is tenacious: for two years (from 361 to 362), the besiegers cannot break through. Among the many and useless attempts to conquer the city, one is that which consists in attacking the walls on the side of the port, with huge towers mounted on three ships. But, due to the presence of the river, "[Aquileia] is not a suitable place either to approach rams, or to fix machines, or to dig tunnels" (Amm. Marc., *Res Gestae* 21.11–12). There is also an attempt to divert the course of the Natissa, which feeds the port.[29] It is noteworthy that, at this stage, in the port, the eastern quarter is no longer operational (the area has been abandoned and is now used for burials), and the western quarter has masonry defenses along the quays, reinforced by towers made with reused materials. Meanwhile, the countryside of Aquileia is devastated and sacked. The soldiers of Iovinus carry out raids in the nearby countryside, as they have plenty of necessities, and they share most of the loot with their fellow soldiers (Amm. Marc., *Res Gestae* 21.11–12).

In the meantime, Julian, having placed himself at the head of the army, leaves Naissus and goes to Thrace, ready to confront Constantius. There will be no confrontation. Unpredictably, Constantius dies during the journey, on 3 November 361 in Cilicia. It will be said—it is uncertain whether rightly or wrongly—that Constantius was in favor of the idea that Julian could succeed him. In any case, the sudden death of Constantius effectively places the Empire in the hands of Julian, who, having obtained the recognition of the army, triumphantly enters Constantinople and succeeds the deceased emperor.

Only in February 362, when they are convinced of the death of Constantius, do the mutineers and the Aquileians open their doors to the new emperor.[30] The praetorian prefect Mamertinus can thus enter the city. No looting or massacres are ordered, but the officer who pushed the legions to rise up is condemned to die at the stake, and two members of the Aquileian Senate, Romulus and Sabostius, are put to death as punishment. The fact remains though that Aquileia suffered serious damage due to the siege. The walls have crumbled, some suburbs have been destroyed, and the surrounding countryside has been devastated and looted. The Circus is still in operation (at least, it was under Magnentius), but the same cannot be said about the Great *Thermae* due to a lack of water, given that, during the siege, the aqueducts were destroyed.

Meanwhile, Julian, on 4 February 362, officially recalled all those who had been exiled by Constantius II to their homeland. But Dionysius, former bishop of Mediolanum, is not able to benefit from the provision. He retired to Cappadocia, where he led an ascetic life, soon becoming a symbol of fidelity to the true faith, and died in the odor of sanctity.

In May 362, Julian issues an edict with which he permits any cult in the Empire, and he makes a public pagan profession of faith. In the past, he has avoided openly cultivating his faith. But religion and faith have now become one of the main themes of politics, and no one should have doubts about the emperor's position in this regard. The gesture does not please the Catholic Church, and in fact it is very disappointed. It blames Julian for repudiating his own religious beliefs. This explains why Julian will go down in history as the Apostate, that is, the Renegade.

The Flowered Carpet

A large *domus* of Aquileia is probably of this age (it would have been built in around 350 and renovated around 370). It is located on the second island northeast of the Forum, between the latter and the river port, in an area occupied by numerous *domus* built since the beginning of the 1st century (former Cassis area). It is so large that it occupies the entire *insula*.[31] It is made up of three groups of rooms gathered around three courtyards, connected by corridors, but separate and with different destinations. It has several entrances. One opens onto the *decumanus maximus* (the stretch of Via Germina that crosses the city) and is decorated with murals, statues commemorating the glory of the landlord's family on Greek marble pedestals, and beautifully crafted mosaic floors. One of those mosaics, splendid, polychrome, with cupids within flower garlands, is commonly known as the Flowered Carpet. It is a star composition of eight lozenges and squares, with deer, fish, and plant elements.[32] It seems that the building we are talking about belongs to Septimius Theodulus, governor of *Venetia et Histria*.

Theodulus, shortly before 361, probably on the encouragement of the central authority, relocated three 2nd-century sculptures of Hercules and Minerva to the Forum, placing them on pedestals. The same sculptures had been set aside in 331 or later, in compliance with the imperial edicts that had led to the closure and confiscation of pagan temples, the prohibition of making sacrifices to the gods, the suppression of festivals and anniversaries of the pagan calendar, and the interdiction of all non-Christians from public office. Theodulus brought them back to light as mere artistic manifestations and a sign of the past to enrich the city center with ornaments that recalled and reaffirmed the great traditions and history of the city. In doing so, he became the architect of a gesture of fidelity to the institutions and memories of his homeland.[33]

The House of Wounded Beasts

It is also worth paying attention to another house of Aquileia. This one is located in the northern part of the city, specifically in the *insula* that is bordered to the west by the *cardo maximus* and, to the south, by the urban stretch of Via Gemina, and it is a high-level residential building. It evolved from a primitive structure from the Augustan Age (27 BC–AD 14) with refined tessellated coverings and geometric decoration of central-Italic tradition, going through subsequent interventions, consisting in the raising of some floors with remaking of the mosaic decoration and in the addition of a central paved courtyard, which the living room and reception areas overlook, as well as a large room decorated with a mosaic depicting hunting scenes and wounded animals[34] and, next to this, a room with a mosaic floor depicting a female character between fish and birds, perhaps the mistress of the home. The latest interventions, carried out in the second half of the 4th century, consisted, among other things, of adding an apse to the main reception room and new mosaic, geometric, and figurative decorations. In addition, the inner courtyard was repaved.

Notes

1   For the walls of Aquileia: Bonetto 2003: 151–196; 2009: 83–92.
2   Some towers are contemporary with the curtain while others were later reinforced, and it is difficult to distinguish the former from the latter. Therefore, not all towers are from the Constantinian age. Some must have been erected in the Theodosian age, when steps were also taken to reinforce the curtains. Furthermore, in the 5th century (it is not known whether at the time of the siege of Attila in 452 or later), some protective ramparts were erected along the southern stretches of the western and eastern sides, as well as along the entire southern side, at a distance of between 8 and 20 m.
3   The Circus of Aquileia was a gigantic construction, but its dimensions remain unknown. The structure was perhaps 380 m long, if not 450 m or 520 m. Most likely it was between 460–470 m long and 76–90 m wide. It may be interesting to compare these estimates with data referring to the major circuses of the Roman world: the Circus of Maxentius, on the Via Appia in Rome, was 503 m long. The circus of Antioch on the Orontes (near Antakia, Syria), 460 m. That of Augusta Trevirorum (Trier, Germany), perhaps 440 m. That of Sirmium (Sremska Mitrovica, Serbia), 430 m. That of Thessaloniki (Greece), between 400 and 500 m. The circus of Aquileia, therefore, is in third place in the ranking of the largest circuses of antiquity, after that of Maxentius in Rome and that of Antioch.
4   But perhaps separated from the gate and the ancient walls.
5   What differentiates *tabernae* from *popinae* is that people gather there not only to drink alcoholic beverages (wine, beer) but also to be served food and receive lodging. Other differences are the more spartan and rustic decor and the opening hours, which are mainly in the evening.
6   The existence of a *palatium* in Aquileia and the location and decoration of this structure as indicated in the text are hypothetical. The suppositions are based, respectively, on the panegyric for Maximian and Constantine I pronounced by an anonymous person on the occasion of Constantine I's wedding to Fausta in AD 307; on the fragments of statues and clypei found; and on the fact that the binomial Circopalatium also appears in other cities of late antiquity.
7   Alternatively, it has been hypothesized that the palace was built outside the late ancient walls, precisely in the locality of Marignane, where archaeologists have excavated the remains of a large suburban villa that underwent significant extensions and renovations in the Constantinian era. In this case, the building would not have been located immediately east of the circus, but in the northwestern sector of the city.
8   The work of art we are talking about is mentioned in *Pan. Lat.* 6.6.2.
9   *Pan. Lat.* IX [4].27.1: *praetera te, Aquileia, te, Mutina, ceterasqua regiones quibus insecutas incredibilium bonorum commoditates gratissima fuit oppugnationis iniuria.*
10 Constantinople was the capital of the *pars Orientis* of the Roman Empire from 330 to 395. From 476 to 1204, it was the only capital of the Roman Empire, now deprived of its *pars Occidentis*.

11 This too is a hypothesis, based on coins found in archaeological excavations.

12 The structures considered are known from the foundation walls and from a series of superimposed floors that emerged from the excavation to the west of the Via Iulia Augusta.

13 There are no entire statues of this age in Aquileia but instead a gallery of portraits made for the commemoration of many deceased persons, in marble or Aurisina stone, the "all-roundedness" of which may suggest they originally belonged to statues or busts.

14 All the buildings mentioned have been preserved only at the level of their foundations, but often with splendid mosaic floors. The ancient Basilica of Monastero is currently the Museo Paleocristiano.

15 It has not been proven that the emperor also contributed to the financing of the work.

16 We have already mentioned one of the three private houses whose foundation walls and a series of superimposed floors emerged from the excavation to the west of the Via Giulia Augusta, to the southwest of the Republican walls, between the *cardo maximus* and the amphitheater, all built in the Augustan Age and which had remained in use for all this time. The other two houses, at the beginning of the 4th century, each contained a private Christian oratory. Excavations at the northern oratory returned a polychrome mosaic floor, the so-called "of the Good Shepherd" mosaic. The southern oratory also restored a mosaic floor, but unfortunately this was very damaged, except in the apse.

17 Several monuments, such as the amphitheater, the remains of the circus, a necropolis, a large cryptoporticus or underground passage, and parts of the walls tell us about the Roman past of Arles, as well as a large amount of sculptures, inscriptions, mosaics, and other objects, all preserved in the Musée de l'Arles antique.

18 The Via Aurelia we are talking about connected Colonia Claudia Ara Agrippinensium (the Roman colony in the Rhineland from which the German city of Cologne developed) to Massilia (Marseille) and Aquae Sextiae (Aix-en-Provence).

19 In the following centuries, Constantine I was called "the Great" for the help given to the Catholic Church. His tomb was honored as that of a saint, while his name was invoked as that of a martyr to obtain graces. The first, great Roman emperor to convert to Christianity became the perfect model of the Christian prince. Eastern princes, especially in Russia, were compared to him. The fact that he had his son Crispus and stepmother Fausta put to death was not considered a noteworthy fact for the purpose of raising the altars to glory. Even today, Constantine I is revered as a saint in the Eastern Churches. In the calendars of the Orthodox Christian religion, the feast of St Constantine falls on 21 May, together with that of his mother, St Helena, who died in approximately 329.

20 It is unknown what happened to Crispus' wife and children. Crispus' memory was damned.

21 For the violent death of Constantine II: *Epit. de Caes.* 41.21; Socr. 2.5; Zonar. 13.5. For the location of the episode and the possibility that the *tetrapylon* was erected to commemorate it: Buora 2008: 155.

22 The existence of the villa in question is indicted by the discovery of the tomb of a child belonging to the Eusebii family in San Canzian d'Isonzo.

23 The Theodorian Halls vanished after the superimposition of two successive basilicas, which today constitute the original nucleus of the Basilica of Poppone, the first of which was built in around AD 400 and destroyed by the Huns in AD 452. The center of Christian Aquileia evolved in three architectural phases: 1) Theodorian Halls, 2) Primitive Basilica, or "Post-Theodorian" Basilica, and 3) the "Post-Attilian" Basilica, with its connected floors between the baptistery rooms. The excavation area is located in front of viale Patriarca Popone. A complex of residential houses has been unearthed there, some of which date back to the end of the Republican period, with floor mosaics, pipes and wells, as well as two small early Christian oratories with apses, being found there. Another excavation area is located on the left of the Basilica, with access

from Piazza del Capitolo. The little that remains of the Primitive Basilica is partly visible today in the so-called "crypt of excavations", and partly lies buried to the east of today's bell tower. The latter was built in the 11th century, when the abandonment of the site had lasted for five centuries and the surviving structures of the rooms lay under a few meters of alluvial sediments.

24 The basilica we are talking about, which no longer exists today, stood above the north Theodorian Hall and alongside and parallel to the Primitive Basilica; it is to the viewer's left from today's square at the Popponian Basilica, which is to the north.

25 The Battle of Mursa Major is described and commented on in Iul. 1.35–37 and 58. On this subject see also: Eutrop. 10.12 and Zos. 2.51.2–3.

26 Amm. Marc., *Res Gestae* 18.9.3–4: *Cuius oppidi praesidio erat semper quinta Parthica legio destinata cum indigenarum turma non contemnenda. Sed tunc ingruentem Persarum multitudinem sex legiones raptim percursis itineribus antegressae muris adstitere firmissimis. Magnentiaci et Decentiaci quos post consummatos civiles procinctus, ut fallaces et turbidos ad orientem venire compulit imperator, ubi nihil praeter bella timetur externa, et Tricensimani Decimanique Fortenses et Superventores atque Praeventores cum Aeliano iam Comite, quos tirones tum etiam novellos hortante memorato adhuc protectore erupisse a Singara Persasque fusos in somnum rettulimus trucidasse complures. Aderat comitum quoque sagittariorum pars maior, equestres videlicet turmae ita cognominatae, ubi merent omnes ingenui barbari, armorum viriumque firmitudine inter alios eminentes.*

27 Two legions of *comitatenses* (the Tricensimani and Decimani Fortenses) and four legions of *auxilia comitatenses* (the Magnentiaci, the Decentiaci, the Superventores, and the Praeventores). The *vexillatio* could have been formed by the *comites sagittarii seniores*, the *comites sagittarii iuniores*, or the *comites sagittarii Armenii*. Colombo 2008: 124–161.

28 Ammianus Marcellinus (325/330–*c*. 400), a Latin historian of Greek origin, wrote a historical work—*The Histories*—in 31 books, of which 18 have been preserved. Eleven books are dedicated to the events of the Empire under Julian. To describe Julian's siege of Aquileia, Ammianus drew inspiration from Herodian's account of the siege of Maximinus Thrax in 238.

29 It is commonly known among scholars that, at some point in the ancient history of Aquileia, the course of the Natissa river changed, but it is not known whether this was due to human or natural causes. It cannot be excluded that the change began in 361.

30 There is no agreement among scholars regarding the precise point when the defenders of Aquileia opened the gates of the city to Iovinus. According to Tantillo (2001: 71), this would have happened upon the news of the death of Constantius II. However, Conti (2002: 16) places the surrender of the city in February 262.

31 We are referring to the House of the Cupids (or Putti) Dancing.

32 The house in question was renovated again in the 5th century.

33 For Septimius Theodulus and his dedication to statues in the Forum of Aquileia: Bakker 1993–1994: 274–277; Maselli-Scotti 1999: 360–367, esp. 361–362 and fig. 1; Orlandi 1999: 575–594, esp. 583 n. 29; Pietri 1982: 89–137, esp. 104; Zaccaria 2000: 91–113, esp. 98; 2001a: 475–494, esp. 463–475.

34 The building is now known as the House of the Wounded Beasts. It was abandoned in the 5th century after a phase of reuse and refunctionalization, perhaps for economic and productive purposes.

Chapter 8

A residence of emperors and an evangelizing Church

Jovian (363–364)

Julian probably thought that the problem of selecting his successor had to be solved by choosing the best, as in the days of the great adoptive emperors: Trajan (98–117), Hadrian (117–138), Antoninus Pius (138–161), and Marcus Aurelius (161–180). But he didn't have time to choose. With his death, which occurred in 363, all male descendants of Constantine's family disappeared. The Empire needed to find a successor and quickly because a war was underway on the eastern front, where the latest Augustus passed away. The general staff of the army unanimously designates Saturninus Secondus Salustus, a Gallo-Roman, as the new emperor. Salustus was a friend of Julian, who had appointed him *prefectus praetorium* in 361. Before becoming *prefectus praetorium*, he was an official of the state during the reigns of Constans I and Constantius II.

He is a Neoplatonic philosopher; that is, he adheres to that particular interpretation of the thought of Plato (428/427–348/347 BC) that was elaborated by Plotinus of Lycopolis (AD 204–270) and has since been the main philosophical doctrine.

But Salustus renounces the purple for reasons of health and old age.[1] Consequently, the general staff fell back on the 32-year-old Flavius Claudius Iovianus (363–364), son of Varronianus, the *comes domesticorum*, commander of the *protectores domestici* (the imperial guard), of Constantius II, and himself a commander of the *protectores domestici (primicerius)* from 361.

All this was done by passing over the right of succession of Procopius, the only remaining living member of the family of Constantine I.

Procopius is a general of the army of the *pars Orientis*. He was born in Cilicia (southeastern Anatolia). His mother was the sister of Basilina, Julian's mother. He is therefore a cousin of the latest emperor. In 358, at the behest of Constantius II, he participated in an embassy to the Sassanids, led by Lucillianus. In 363, he participated in Julian's campaign against the Sassanids. Arriving at Carrhae in Mesopotamia (Harran in Turkey), Julian entrusted him with part of the army, giving him the task of leading it to Armenia, joining King Arsaces, and reuniting with him in Assyria. On that occasion, Julian allowed his cousin to wear the imperial robe—it is unknown why. Julian died before Procopius returned. When Procopius arrived in Tilsafata, between Nisibis and Singara, the army had already chosen Jovian as the new Augustus. Procopius took leave of the army, saying that he wanted to devote himself to agriculture and the administration of his own goods, and he went with his wife and children to Caesarea in Cappadocia (central Anatolian plateau), where he had a property. Many consider him to be Julian's legitimate heir and successor. In fact, his propaganda relies heavily on his belonging to the family of Constantine I.

Jovian is a tall individual and has gray eyes, a dignified bearing, a serene expression, and a gentle, sometimes joking manner. He is careful in his choice of collaborators, but he is greedy, devoted to women and wine, weak, and indolent. He was born in 311 in Singidunum (Belgrade in Serbia), a city located in Moesia (central Serbia, parts of Northern Macedonia, northern Bulgaria, part of Romania, parts of southern Ukraine).

Located on a hill overlooking the confluence of the Danube and the Sava, along the Via Militaris—an important road connecting the forests and settlements along the Danube border—Singidunum is a typical Roman city, with internal streets that cross at right angles. It has a Forum, some temples, internal paved streets, an aqueduct, a sewer network, etc. A rectangular-plan castrum occupies its highest part. It emerged as a high-sea fortress of the Celtic Scordisci in the 3rd century BC and was then conquered by the Romans for the first time in 75 BC and definitively in 29 BC.

With Sirmium (Sremka Mitrovica in Serbia) and Viminacium (Kostolac in Serbia), Singidinum is one of the most important centers in the Balkans south of the Danube River. From AD 46 to 69, it was the seat of the Legio VIII Augusta. Since 86, the Legio III Flavia Felix has been located there. After 86, it first became a municipium and then a colony. It played a fundamental role in the war for the conquest of Dacia (Romania and parts of Hungary and Serbia). Later, with the abandonment of Dacia by Aurelian (in about 270–274), it returned to being a frontier city. In 285, the Battle of the Margus was fought near Singidunum, in which Diocletian defeated Carinus (who died shortly after, possibly due to a conspiracy by his generals). Constantius II stayed there in 359.

Jovian enters into peace negotiations and accepts conditions to halt hostilities in order to be able to withdraw safely and quickly, despite the fact that the Romans have an advantage in the war against the Parthians and their morale being high. Specifically, he agrees to evacuate a large part of the former kingdom of Armenia and to abandon all the provinces east of Euphratensis and Syria Salutaris, acquired for Rome by Diocletian—Osroene, Mesopotamia, Gordiene, Arzanene—together with the cities of Edessa, Nisibis, Castra Maurorum, and Singara. His haste to make peace is dictated by the fact that he wants to go to Rome as soon as possible to receive his investiture and for fear that Procopius could claim the throne and get it before him.

With that peace treaty, the border of the Roman Empire in Asia shifts to the west. Amida (Diyarbakir in Turkey) becomes the new capital of Roman Mesopotamia. Conquered by Shāpūr II in 359, this city was taken over by Julian in 363. It welcomes refugees from Nisibis. The arrival of these leads to the creation of a suburb on the plain west of the city. Jovian has the walls enlarged so that that suburb becomes part of the urban area. The works will be completed by his successors—Valentinianus, Valens, and Gratianus—between 367 and 375.

It is common opinion that the agreement made with the Parthians was not necessary and that it is dishonorable. Therefore, when Jovian brings the army back to Antioch on the Orontes in Syria (Antakia in Turkey), he is challenged by the population, who accuse him of having abandoned his positions.

Unlike Salustus, who had shared Julian's program of restoring paganism, Jovian is a Christian and is moved by the anxiety to restore a Christian physiognomy to the Empire and to unite the Christian episcopate, divided between Athanasians and anti-Athanasians. He revokes the anti-Christian decrees of his predecessor, restores the subsidies granted by Constantine I to the Catholic Church and revoked by Julian, and declares himself tolerant toward all religions. But then he contradicts himself, because he closes some temples and forbids ritual sacrifices.

It is still the middle of winter when Jovian leaves for Rome. Once he arrives in Tarsos in the Roman province of Cilicia (Tarsus in Turkey), he visits the temporary tomb of Julian. The next stop on his journey is Tyana, a city located in Cappadocia, at the foot of the Taurus and near the Gates of Cilicia. There, Jovian learns of riots in Durocortorum (Reims in France), in which two senior officers lost their lives. He then goes to Ancyra in Cappadocia (Ankara in Turkey), where he receives the consulate and chooses his son Varronianus, who is little more than a child, as a colleague. Jovian's journey ends unexpectedly. On 17 February 364, the emperor suddenly dies in Dadastana (Karahisar in Turkey), a city located in Bithynia, on the border with Galatia. The cause of his death is uncertain. Perhaps Jovian was killed by the carbon monoxide emitted from a brazier while he was sleeping or a form of mushroom poisoning. Possibly, he was killed by his own soldiers, furious at him for his ignoble and pusillanimous behavior toward the Parthians. He was 32, and he left behind a son at an early age.

The accession to the throne of Valentinian I (364–375) and Valens (364–375)

Once again, the problem of choosing a successor arises. A new *consilium* made up of the higher ranks of the army and holders of high civilian positions meets in Nicaea (Iznik in Turkey), a city located in the Roman province of Bythynia et Pontus, in a fertile basin at the eastern end of Lake Ascanius, bounded by ranges of hills to the north and the south. Nicaea hosted an ecumenical council of Christian bishops in 325, convened by Constantine I (first Council of Nicaea), which concluded with the resolution of the question of the divine nature of the Son of God, the relationship between the Son and the Father, the definition of the first part of the Nicene Creed, the uniform observance of the date of Easter, and the promulgation of ancient canon law.

The *consilium* proclaims as Augustus a career soldier, Valentinian, who is 44 years old (born in 321). Valentinian is an energetic and austere man, of strong and muscular build, of good stature and very well proportioned, with shiny hair, gray eyes, and robust complexion. He was born in Cibalae in Pannonia (Vinkovci in Croatia) into a modest family. He is not very educated, but he knows how to move, has political flair, and knows how to deal with situations and solve problems. He was a military tribune in Mesopotamia under Constantius II and the commander of a unit of javelin throwers under Julian. In 362, because he professed himself a Christian of the Arian faith, he was sanctioned with a transfer to Thebes in Egypt. Later, thanks to the revocation of the discriminatory measures against non-pagans ordered by Jovian, he was reinstated to a position of responsibility and assigned to the Viennese diocese.

The Viennese diocese is part of the Prefecture of Gaul (which also includes the dioceses of Gaul, Spain, and Britain), which has its seat in Augusta Trevirorum (Trier in Germany). It embraces seven provinces: Aquitanica Prima, Aquitanica Secunda, Novempopulana (Aquitanica Tertia), Narbonense Prima, Narbonense Secunda, Gallia Viennense, and Alpes Maritimae. In practice, it corresponds to the regions of France that are located south and west of the Loire River and to Provence. It is based in Arelate in Narbonensis Secunda (Arles in Provence). In the future, it will be renamed the Diocese of the Seven Provinces.

The task that Jovian assigned to Valentinian was to bring the legions of Gaul back to order, as, under the *prefectus praetorium* of Nebridius, they had sided with Julian rather than with Constantius II, acclaimed him Augustus, and swore allegiance to him. Nebridius, since he did not feel like betraying the oath of loyalty he had made to Constantius II, dissociated himself from the choice of his soldiers. The latter wanted to kill him, but Nebridius threw himself at Julian's feet, who covered him with his own cloak, thus saving his life. Later, Julian removed Nebridius from office and allowed him to retire to private life wherever he wanted (Nebridius will retire to Etruria). He replaced Nebridius with Decimius, a German. Under the reign of Jovian, therefore, the *prefectus praetorium* of Gaul and the legions of Gaul come from having taken an oath of allegiance to Julian and are in turmoil. Valentinian completes his mission successfully. To reward him, Jovian promotes him, placing him in command of a unit of the imperial guard.

Valentinian is acclaimed emperor by the army on 26 February 364. He is convinced that he cannot govern such a large empire alone. Therefore, he accepts the purple (and takes the royal name of Valentinian I) on the condition that he can share the honor and the burden with his younger brother, Valens, who is 36 years old. Valens is a man who tends to get fat (he has a sturdy neck and a hint of a double chin), has bent legs and a bad eye. He has a less strong personality than his brother and is a little rough, but he is an honest and willing person who tries not to make a fool of himself. He is a Christian of Arian faith, more fanatical than his brother, who, in comparison, is a moderate.

After associating Valens with the throne, Valentinian I (364–375) marries him to Justina, the widow of Constantius II.

In the summer of 364, the two brothers meet twice, first in Naissus and then in Sirmium, and they share power, territories, capitals, commands, and troops. Valentinian entrusts the Prefecture of the East to Valens and keeps for himself the Prefectures of Gaul, Italy, Illyria, and Africa.

The Roman state in the Late Empire

In 364, the Roman Empire is a giant political subject that has its center in the Mediterranean but extends well beyond this basin, already immense in itself. It covers a large part of Europe, from the islands and mainland coasts to the Rhine and the Danube; the island of Great Britain south of Hadrian's Wall; a part of Asia, extending from the coasts of the Mediterranean to the southern and eastern coasts of the Black Sea, and from Anatolia to the Caucasus; the southern Levant, Arabia, and Mesopotamia; and North Africa, from Mauretania (Morocco) to Egypt, and from the sea coasts to the threshold of the internal Sahara. Within these political borders, manned by the army, there are populous cities, real metropolises, farms, estates, etc. The sea routes intertwine, are crossed by cargo ships and military fleets, and converge on Rome, a metropolis of one million inhabitants, and Constantinople, the Second Rome, the Rome of the East. The center of gravity of the Empire is no longer the former but the latter, as the most flourishing provinces are no longer those of Western Europe but those of Asia. Therefore, the Roman Empire is no longer, as originally, a world where Latin is spoken as well as Greek, but increasingly it is Greek that is spoken. It has recovered after the "Crisis of the 3rd Century", the economy has returned to grow and develop, capital circulates, cities prosper, especially the eastern ones, and continue to be the scene of an intense cultural life within the great tradition of oratory, philosophy, literature, and poetry in both Latin and Greek, and Christianity flanks paganism from a position of growing strength, with its own theological disputes and heretical movements, which fight each other. Constantine I established that all religions are tolerated, but he made it clear that Christianity is the most suitable for guaranteeing the happiness of the subjects of the Empire and that the Christian Church can count on the support of the emperor. After him, all the emperors were Christians, except Julian, and the time is now near when the Edict of Thessalonica, issued by Theodosius I (379–395), will establish that Christianity, in its Nicene, Catholic, that is, Orthodox version, is the only religion that can be practiced in the Empire. The main problems that the emperors have to face are four: the frequent usurpations of generals, who are acclaimed Augustus by the soldiers, perhaps after murdering the emperor; the raids for the purpose of robbery of the barbarians who live beyond the borders of Britain, the Rhine, and the Danube and in the deserts of Africa and the East; the pressure exerted on the borders by entire barbarian peoples who are asking to be admitted to the Empire; the ongoing rivalry with the Persian Empire, formerly Parthian and now Sassanid, from the name of the dynasty that governs it, which wants to get its hands on the rich eastern provinces, aiming to reconstitute the ancient Achaemenid

Empire (6th–4th century BC). What worries the Roman authorities the most is the barbarians who live in the country of forests and swamps that extends beyond the Rhine and Danube borders, with particular reference to the Germanic sphere.

But there are Germans and other Germans. Those who live beyond the Rhine border are as ferocious and dangerous as the others, but they are sedentary and well known by the Romans; moreover, they are often linked to the Empire by a treaty, which obliges them to provide support troops and which they usually honor, providing Rome with excellent and loyal soldiers, who come to be used by the emperors also as a bodyguard. Those who live beyond the Danube border, on the other hand, are a seething magma of nomadic peoples who are constantly moving between the steppes of Ukraine and the plains of Central Asia. Among the steppe peoples, those closest to the border are the Goths and Sarmatians. Before talking about these peoples, however, it is better to focus on another of the peoples of the steppes: the Alans.

It is likely that the Alans, at the beginning of their history, were not a people but a caste of warriors, who placed themselves at the service of several barbarian kings, from Pontus to Central Asia, for whom they fought. With the passage of time, the name Alans may have been adopted by the peoples for whom they fought. Pliny the Elder (AD 23–79) places them north of the Black Sea (Plin., IV, 25, 80). Seneca (4 BC–AD 65) mentions them as enemies of the Empire on the Danube (Sen., act. IV, scene I). Joseph (AD 37/38–100) speaks of the invasion of the Alans in AD 72, which started from the Maeotian Swamp, that is, from the Azov Sea, heading toward Transcaucasia and the Near East (Joseph. 7.7.4). In the 2nd and 3rd centuries, the Alans are a people of the Pontic-Asian steppes that include several Iranian-speaking populations of indigenous and oriental origin. It is uncertain whether they became so at the beginning of the Common Era, as a union of Sarmatian peoples, settled in the steppes of southern Russia, or if they became so later, arriving in Europe from Central Asia and subduing the indigenous Sarmatian tribes. What is certain is that they are the predominant people in the Pontic steppes and are in contact with Asian populations. In the period 230–250, they were the cause of unrest throughout the southern part of eastern Europe, together with the Germans (mainly the Goths) and other Sarmatian peoples. Among others, the cities of the Cimmerian Bosphorus, the population of Kuban, and the Scythians of the lower Dnieper are paying for this disorder (the Scythians will be forced to migrate westward, toward the steppes of the Dniester and the Danube).

Toward the middle of the 3rd century and in the first half of the 4th century, the Alans invade the Transcaucasian regions. As of the second half of the 3rd century, they are divided into two groups: those of the Don and those of the steppes between the Dniester and the Danube, which are part of the federation of the Goths.

The Goths are tall individuals with blond or reddish hair and are Germans native to Pomerania and Poland. Around the middle of the 2nd century, they moved to southern Poland, to the regions east of the Vistula. They later split into two large groups: Greutungi, "Shining Goths", and Tervingi, "Noble Goths" (in the future, these groups will be more commonly known as Ostrogoths and Visigoths, respectively, and so we will call them as such from now on). For the most part, they emigrated together with the Vandals to the south or southeast: first to the Polish part of Volhynia, then to Ukraine, Moldavia and Romania; the rest remained in the regions east of the middle Vistula, from where they will not move until at least 400.

The federation of Goths is a set of tribes and clans, loyal to different kings, chieftains, and magistrates. In the 4th century, it extends from the south of Russia to the Baltic coasts, including Pomerania and Mecklenburg, and is divided into two major ethnic groups, the Ostrogoths and the Visigoths, as well as other minor groups: Eruli, Venedi, Aestii, and Alans.

The Ostrogoths live west of the Dnieper, in particular in Oium (Scythia), or in a fertile part of it (Ukraine), and are the dominant component of the federation. Their leader is Ermanaric.

The Visigoths live north of the mouth of the Danube, on the eastern bank of this river, right on the border of the Empire (Dacia Ripense, Moesia II, Scythia), at the beginning of the immense steppe that is lost toward the Don and leads to Central Asia. They are farmers, cattle ranchers, and shepherds, but they maintain the nomadic tradition, so they are often on the move, on foot or on horseback, with carts, rolled-up tents, herds, flocks, wooden or stone idols, vases, cups, and ornaments bearing inscriptions in runic characters and entrusted to priests and priestesses. Unlike the Ostrogoths, who are pagans adhering to the Germanic mythological tradition, the Visigoths are Christians of the Arian faith (Arianism, we recall, was condemned as heresy by the First Council of Nicaea in 325 but was rooted in the pars Orientis of the Empire, where Emperor Valens is a Christian of the Arian faith). They got to know Christianity in the 3rd century through the Roman prisoners of war whom they held as slaves, or rather through those of them who were Christians. Their bishop is Ulfilas, a Romanized Gothic intellectual, inventor of an alphabet to write the language of the Goths and author of a translation of the Bible from Greek to Gothic. It should be added that Constantine I entered into a treaty with the Visigoths, according to which the latter were to provide support troops to the Empire in exchange for gifts, pensions, and regular supplies of food (grain, oil, meat). That treaty was observed up until the reign of Julian (contact with Rome is the reason why the Visigoths began to change their way of life, becoming less uncivilized than the other steppe peoples).

Beyond the Visigoths are the Heruli and, further east, the Sarmatians. Further east of the Sarmatians, between the Dnieper and the Volga and between the marshes of Pripyat and the coasts of the Black Sea, live the peoples of the steppe: a mass of Germanic, Indo-Germanic, Iranian-Sarmatian, Ural-Altaic, and proto-slave peoples. East of the Volga, on the other hand, live the Hsiung-nu, meaning "ferocious slaves" or "screaming slaves" or "evil slaves", a people originally from Mongolia, creator of the first great nomadic empire, and enemy of the Han of China. The Romans call them Huns.

The Huns are individuals of short stature, have almond-shaped eyes, and a face covered with scars, caused by the cuts they make to express the pain of bereavement.

They are cattle breeders, they speak a language incomprehensible for the Romans, and they know no other home than the tent and the cart; in practice, they live on horseback. Forced by an atavistic and endemic hunger to wander relentlessly in the harsh environment of the steppe, they are accustomed to fatigue and discomfort, but they are strong warriors: they use the bow and arrow or the sling and the javelin, fight on horseback, move at great speed, and are fearless in hand-to-hand combat.

Valentinian I (364–375) strengthens the Germanic border

Hadrian's Wall is a 117 km long stone wall, 2.5 to 3 m thick and 5 m high, reinforced by towers, fortresses, and forts, also made of stone, running from the River Tyne to the Solway Firth in the province of Britannia Superior, part of the Roman diocese of Britannia. It was built by the Roman emperor Hadrian (118–138) and marks the political border between the Roman state and Pittavia (eastern and northern Scotland), the land of the Picts, also known as Caledonia.

The Romans use the name "Picts" for a group of tribes of uncertain origin, perhaps pre-Celtic, confederate with each other, who live in Great Britain, north of the Forth and Clyde rivers. This name, like that of the region they occupy, derives from the Pictish habit of tattooing their bodies (the Latin adjective *pictus*, pl. *picti*, means "painted"). Strenuous opponents of Rome, the Picts have already crossed Hadrian's Wall several times: before 180, between 196 and 197, and subsequently.

That fortification was erected precisely to defend Roman territory from incursions by the Picts. It is guarded by a mixture of legionary *vexillationes* (cavalry units) and auxiliary units of the Roman army, in all about 9,000 men, including infantry and knights, many of whom, with the passage of time, have integrated into the local communities.

In the 4th century, one of the units stationed along Hadrian's Wall is the *pseudocomitatensis legio Defensores Seniores*, created with the Pact of Naissus (365) between Valentinian I and Valens (*Not. Dign. (Occ.)* 5 and 7). The *pseudocomitatenses* are those *limitanei* —"the soldiers in frontier districts" (from the Latin phrase *limes*, "political border")—who have been "loaned" to the *comitatus* (a mobile army, located close to the limes) to repel an invasion or raid for the purpose of robbery by enemies of the Empire, or to participate in a cross-border campaign, and were subsequently kept there permanently. The *pseudocomitatenses* have lower status and pay than the *comitatenses*; on the other hand, they enjoy the advantage of not being in the front line but at the rear, in an area where the movement of troops and coordination of services takes place.

At the beginning of 365, the Picts overwhelm the border troops along the Hadrian's Wall and invade the Roman province of Maxima Caesariensis (southeastern England), just as the Saxons, coming from the region between the Rhine and Jutland, wash by the North Sea, they invade the Roman province of Britannia Prima (southern England and possibly Wales). In the same days, the Franks, and the Bucinobanti, a tribe of the Alemanni, headed by Macrianus, cross the Rhine and invade Gallia Belgica. They annihilate two Roman legions and their support troops, devastate the border districts (the French department of Alsace and German land in the Rhineland-Palatinate in the province of Germania Prima of Diocese II-Viennense), and take Mogontiacum (Mainz in Germany).

Valentinian I sends Iovinus, the *magister equitum*, "cavalry commander general", against the Franks and the Alemanni, and the general Theodosius against the Saxons.

Theodosius is a Spanish native and comes from a Galician family of landowners. From now on, we will call him Theodosius the Elder to distinguish him from his son, the future Theodosius I (379–395), emperor of the *pars Orientis*.

Both Theodosius and Iovinus will defeat the enemy multiple times.

To better follow the operations along the *limes germanicus*, Valentinian I moves to Lutetia (Paris in France), from there to Samarobriva (Amiens in France) in the land of the Celtic tribe of the Ambiani, and later to Augusta Trevirorum (Trier in Germany).

The usurpation of Procopius (365–366)

Emperor Valens fights against corruption, tries to reduce taxes, and builds public works. Among other things, the great aqueduct that supplies Constantinople is his work. Then, however, his good reputation turns into a bad one due to his fiscal policy, which has become atrocious and ruthless, so much so as to provoke riots.

In 365, a riot broke out in Constantinople, led by Procopius (the cousin of the deceased Emperor Julian, considered by many to be his legitimate successor, of whom we have already spoken). This occurs shortly after the Cretan earthquake, on which it is worthwhile to dwell.

On 21 July 365, a violent earthquake, of a magnitude of 8.3 or 8.5, with its epicenter in the sea to the southwest of Crete, hit this island and caused a tsunami that would travel across the Mediterranean. The earthquake is the strongest of the last two millennia in the Mediterranean. In Crete, it causes displacements of 9–10 m and the total destruction of buildings on the island, so much so that some cities will never be rebuilt. The earthquake is of such magnitude that it causes extensive damage on all the Aegean islands. Its disastrous effects are felt as far away as the island of Kythira in the Peloponnese (with destruction in Patras and Olympia), in the Ionian Sea near the border with the Aegean Sea, and in the Ionian coasts of Italy. Waves from 9 to 15 m high crash over the southern coast of Crete, spread in concentric circles, and spill over the coasts of Cyprus, of Lebanon to the east, and of Calabria and Sicily to the west, causing serious damage also in Tunisia, Libya (Leptis Magna, Sabratha, Apollonia, Cyrene), and Egypt. The phenomenon causes 45,000 victims, of whom about 5,000 are in Alexandria. The latter is almost completely destroyed. Many people, deceived by the temporary withdrawal of the waters from the shore, will be overwhelmed by the furious rise of these while they are collecting the fish that have remained exposed. Many ships anchored in the harbor will be sunk. Some other ships, grabbed by the waves, will be pushed onto the mainland, some a considerable distance from the coastline (Amm. Marc., *Res Gestae* 26.10.15–19).

In September 365, when Valens is absent from Constantinople, Procopius, with the help of the eunuch Eugenius, corrupts two legions, arms slaves and volunteers, and takes over the city without bloodshed. He is acclaimed as emperor by the troops and then crowned by the Senate of Constantinople. He puts his own men in positions of command, obtains an alliance with the Goths, reminding them of the commitment they had assumed toward Constantine I and his successors (the Goths accept and send troops, believing that the agreement they have made with the Roman state linked them to Constantine and his sons and successors, to whom they were loyal, though in fact it does not link them to Valens, who belongs to another dynasty). He takes Constantius II's wife and his daughters, Faustine and Constance, as hostages and manages to get some troops passing through Constantinople and headed to Thrace to join him. Instead, his attempt to associate the legions of Illyricum with his cause fails.

The first clash between Procopius and Valens takes place in Mygdos in Asia Minor and ends in favor of Procopius. Valentinian I cannot help his brother as he is engaged in a campaign against the Germans. But Valens ends up winning. Procopius resists Valens in Nicaea, Chalcedon, and Helenopolis (Hersek in Turkey) and forces him to leave Bithynia. Valens takes refuge in Ancyra. Procopius takes advantage of the subsequent break in the fighting (winter 365/366) to prepare for the spring offensive, collecting money and troops. But general Flavius Arbitius, previously a close collaborator of Constantius II, turns his back on him. This leads to the abandonment of Procopius by some troops. Later, Procopius is defeated at the Battle of Thyatira in Lydia (Akhisar in Turkey) due to the betrayal of his general Gomoarius. Later, history repeats itself. Procopius is defeated again due to the betrayal of his general Agilonius. Losing hope, he runs away with two collaborators but is also betrayed by them. Delivered to the troops of Valens, he is killed by order of the latter on 27 May 366, it is uncertain whether by beheading or quartering, together with those who had betrayed him.

Later, to punish the Visigoths who had mobilized to give support to Procopius (but who arrived too late, after Procopius had already been defeated), Valens has them taken prisoner and sold to slave traders, and then he invades the lands of the Visigoths and devastates them, destroying crops. When the Visigoths are already starving, he grants them peace, which they asked him for on their knees, on the condition that they provide support troops to use in the campaign he is preparing against the Persians, who, in the meantime, have advanced new claims. The previous agreement (the one that the Goths made together with Constantine I) is not restored. Therefore, in exchange for military aid, the Goths will no longer be supplied with food by the Romans, nor will they be able to trade with them.

For having made peace with the Goths, instead of conducting a massacre, Valens will be praised by the Greek rhetorician Themistius, one of the most influential politicians of Constantinople, who, in a famous speech, saw in that act of generosity the concrete application of the theory according to which the Romans have the right and duty to govern all peoples of the Earth and that their foreign policy has the value and significance of a historical mission, aimed at protecting all peoples, ensuring them peace and justice, and civilizing them, to make them a single *gens*, a single nation.

The origins of the Valentinian dynasty

Valentinian I has two children: Gratian, born from his marriage with Marina Severa, and Valentinian, born from his second marriage with Justina, a Sicilian noble. In addition, three daughters were born from this last marriage: Galla, Grata, and Giusta.

In 367, after being cured of a serious illness, to ensure a peaceful succession to the empire, Valentinian I associates his son Gratian (367–383). The latter is eight or nine years old and resides with his family in Augusta Trevirorum where he has Decimus Magnus Ausonius (310–394) as his tutor.

Ausonius is a Roman aristocrat who approached Christianity without renouncing pagan culture, with the throne.

At the same time, Valentinian I marries Gratian to Constantia, the posthumous daughter of Constantius II and Faustina, thus linking his own dynasty to that of Constantine I. The Valentinian dynasty will be particularly fortunate; it will remain in power for about 90 years and will represent one of the longest sequences of emperors of the same family in the history of Rome, a rare example of the continuity of power in a very troubled period such as the 4th century.

Meanwhile, Pope Felix II (355–365)—who had ascended to the papal throne when he was an archdeacon in Rome, replacing Pope Liberius (352–355), who had been exiled by Constantius II— has died. Two factions are contending for the election of the new pope. One is against any agreement with the Arians and is in the majority. The other is led by the Arian Auxentius, bishop of Mediolanum, and is more conciliatory, and therefore inclined to compromise agreements. Damasus (366–384) is chosen as the new Pope. His election shows that the Catholic-Orthodox faction prevailed over the Arian one. But the losing side does not accept the election. There are violent clashes with casualties. The blame for the riots is attributed to Damasus, a synod of bishops refuses to acquit him, and a criminal trial is even brought against him. The effects do not take long to manifest. In the same year (366), Pope Damasus excommunicates Auxentius. But the latter remains in his position. Valentinian, although he is a Christian of the Arian faith, is nevertheless on excellent terms with Pope Damasus and, through him, with the Roman aristocracy and the Catholic clergy. In 370, on the request of Hylarius (310–367), bishop of Poitiers and doctor of the Church, he asks Auxentius to resign and leave Mediolanum.

Meanwhile, the new *consularis Aemiliae et Liguriae*, the 25- or 26-year-old Aurelius Ambrosius (born around 339–340), has just arrived in that city. He was born in Augusta Treverorum into the noble and ancient Roman family of the Aurelii. After spending the first 20 years of his life in Rome, he moved to Sirmium together with his brother Satyrus to exercise legal aid, and he remained there for some years. There he met

Sextus Petronius Probus, *praefectus praetorii Italiae, Illyrici et Africae*. Probus also came from Rome, and he was linked to the same circle of the Aurelii. Since he admired Ambrosius' eloquence, he included him in his *consilium*. So Ambrosius was able to become familiar with the imperial bureaucracy. In 370, Probus boosted Ambrosius' career by promoting him to the office of *consularis Aemiliae et Liguriae*, which is based in Mediolanum.

The stays of Valentinian I in Aquileia

Valentinian I stays in Augusta Trevirorum for nine years (365–374). During this period, in the early years, he manages to attract the Germanic tribe of the Burgundi, historical enemy of the Alemanni, to his side, and he strengthens the defenses of the *limes germanicus*, from the sources of the Rhine in the Tyrol to the mouth of this river in the North Sea, by building a complex system of fortifications both in Roman territory and on the opposite bank of the river, which also implies the deviation of the Neckar River. In the same years, moreover, Valentinian strengthens the army, improves the economic treatment of the military, increases taxes (making the taxman more oppressive than it already was; this measure will place him in conflict with the Senate of Rome), multiplies the *frumentationes*, institutes the "defenders of the people", to whom he assigns the task of assisting the poor, and settles numerous Germans within the borders of the empire as colonists. Among other things, he also negotiates a peace agreement with Macrianus, under which the Bucinobanti will be welcomed in Britain (specifically in what is now the county of Norfolk in eastern England, bordered by the North Sea).

In 373 and later, Valentinian I fortifies also the border in Eastern Europe, which runs along the course of the Danube, from the Noric Alps to the mouth of the Black Sea. Thus, a continuous wall is built, reinforced by numerous forts and towers for the purposes of control and signaling. The provinces affected by the works are the following: the more northerly parts of Diocese V-Italy (Retia Prima, Retia Secunda, Noricum, Ripensis, Pannonia, Valeria Ripensis), those of Diocese VII-Dacia (Mesia Prima, Dacia Ripense), and those of Diocese XIII-Thrace (Moesia II, Scythia).

The measure will not be able to prevent some groups of Quadi from crossing the Danube in 374, facing and defeating two legions in battle, and devastating Pannonia. The prefect Probus, from Sirmium, sends a request for help to Valentinian I, which reaches the emperor in Augusta Raurica (Basel in Switzerland), a city located in the Raetia (the Roman province embracing Bavaria, Switzerland, and part of Austria), where he is supervising the construction of a fortress. In June 375, Valentinian leads an army to Carnuntum in Pannonia Superior (Petronell in Austria), has a bridge built over the Danube. He confronts and defeats the Quadi in the upper part of the Neckar River, and savagely plunders their lands. During this period, Valentinian I spends a lot of time in Aquileia. Thus the visits of emperors to the city resume, as they had ceased with the death of Constans (which took place in Autun in southern France on 18 January 350), excluding the stay of the usurper Magnentius between 351 and 352. Constantius II resided in Mediolanum, and his successor, Julian (360–363), never went to Aquileia (he probably never even went to Italy).

The religious life in Aquileia

In recent times, the religious life in Aquileia has entered in a new phase. In this regard, it must be said at the outset that the Church of Aquileia, probably since the beginning of its history, has been faithful to the organization and the ritual of the Church of Alexandria in Egypt, from which Catholicism (*i.e.* Orthodoxy) and anti-Arianism emanated, except in 355, when it changed its attitude with the signing of the conclusions of the Council of Mediolanum by Bishop Fortunatianus.

Under the reign of Constantius II (337–361), in fact, the Arians had in their hands the main episcopal sees of Illyricum—Sirmium, Salona—and Fortunatianus had to submit under their pressure.

The Arian faction prevailed for a decade, after which it lost ground. A gradual reversal of the trend occurred, starting in 366, when Bishop Germinius of Sirmium partially renounced Arianism. In 371, Fortunatianus was replaced in the office by Valerian.

Under the bishopric of Valerian, the Church of Aquileia has returned to its origins, that is, it once again and definitively has taken a position in favor of orthodoxy. Under Valerian, moreover, the community of Christians of Aquileia has become a point of reference for the churches of northern Italy (at least for those of the northeast) and those that have arisen in the meantime between the Adriatic and the Danube. All this is due to the enlightened guidance of Valerian himself, but also to the cenacle of lay people and religious figures that had formed around him, which includes, among others: Chromatius (a cleric oriented toward asceticism and presbyter in 370), his brother Eusebius, Jovian, Heliodorus (the future bishop of Altinum), Bonosus, Julian, Nicea, Crisocoma, Florentinus, Nepotianus, Rufinus, and, from 371, Eusebius Sophronius Hieronymus (347–419/420), a rhetorician and theologian from Augusta Trevirorum (Trier in Germany). It is worth dwelling on the latter.

Hieronymus (from now on: Jerome) is a native of Stridon (Zrenj or Sdrin in Istria, Croatia), a village located near Iulia Aemona (Ljubljana in Slovenia) on the border of Dalmatia and Pannonia. He was formerly a student in Rome and a pupil of Caius Marius Victorinus and Aelius Dotanus (the latter is a Roman grammarian, rhetorician, and Neoplatonic philosopher, also known for translating two of Aristotle's books from Greek into Latin). After having stood out as a good theologian in Rome, he studied law in Augusta Trevirorum. He arrived in Aquileia in 370.

In 374, after sharing the asceticism of the Aquileia clerics, which was accompanied by intense intellectual activity in the Cenacle, Jerome goes to Antioch on the Orontes in Syria (Antakia in Turkey), from where he then continues to Palestine. They are with him some companions of Aquileia and a rich noblewoman: Paola Romana (who would later be canonized). The latter will finance the foundation in the Holy Land of a monastery for herself, her daughters, and her friends, a convent for Jerome and his companions, and a hospice for pilgrims.

In this regard, it must be said that throughout the Near East, but especially in Cappadocia, Syria, and the Judaean desert, there is a dense presence of monasteries in the 4th century, which reflects the growth of monasticism, which has been going on since the end of the 3rd century, especially in Egypt. Many monks live in the desert in Egypt. The most famous are Pacomius and Antonius the Egyptian. Each of them founded a monastery: the former in Upper Egypt and the latter at the foot of Jebel Qulzum in the Thebaid.

In Palestine, Jerome is translating the Bible into Latin and commenting on the Gospels. He remained linked to the Aquileia group—he would remain such for the rest of his life—maintaining epistolary correspondence with them (he will also dedicate his biblical works to them). In one of his letters to Chromatius, Eusebius, and Iovianusus, he reveals his pleasure with them for having collaborated in the expulsion of the Arian heresy from the Church of Aquileia. We are referring here to the seventh of his *Epistulae*, which will often be cited in the future as proof of a common life of the Aquileian clergy in the years 371–374, and subsequently, and consequently as evidence of the existence of a *coenobium*. In reality, for Jerome, there was never a true monastery in Aquileia, nor a *coenobium* for ecclesiastics, even though he calls some clerics in that environment by the nickname *monachi*, "monks", and Jerome himself converted to monasticism only after his departure for the East (Spinelli 1982: 292, 294).

Jerome will die in Bethlehem (Palestine) in 419/420. He will be recognized as a saint and doctor of the Church by the Catholic Church, the Eastern Orthodox Church, the Lutheran Church, and the Anglican Communion (Hieron. 97).

The death of Valentinian I

On 17 November 375, Valentinian I receives envoys of the Quadi in the legionary fortress of Brigetium in Pannonia (Komarom in Hungary), garrisoned by the Legio I Adiutrix. The hearing is in progress when the emperor suffers a stroke and dies. Gratian, who is about 16 years old and is in Augusta Trevirorum, is thus alone in command of the Western Empire (the emperor of the East, we recall, is Valens, who lives in Constantinople). The army considers the possibility of acclaiming the general Sebastianus as emperor, but some high imperial officials, including Merobaudus, Maximinus, Romanus, and Petronius Probus, put Valentinian II on the throne, the second son of Valentinian I and Justina, a child of four years of age, and therefore an easily manipulated subject. The regency is assumed by Justina, who will exercise it under the control of the powerful general Merobaudus.

Merobaudus is a Roman general of Frankish origin. He served under the emperor Julian (361–363). After the latter's death, he took care of the transportation of his body. He was appointed *magister militum* by Valentinian I, probably in 375, and took part in the military campaigns against the Quadi.

Valentinian II (375–392) and Gratian (364–378) divide the Western Empire. The former receives the government of Italy, Africa, and Illyricum, and the latter, the government of Gaul, Hispania, and Britain.

Valentinian II and Justina establish their residence in Mediolanum. From there, Illyricum is monitored and Italy is protected.

It is probable that Valentinian II and Gratian are both in Aquileia in 379 due to the need to repel the bands of Goths who have broken into the rural villages of Istria and the mountainous area between Aquileia and Iulia Aemona.

Valerian remains in office as bishop of Aquileia from 371 to 387/388. This period is marred by a plague. The scourge is accompanied by an epizootic,[2] which exterminates herds and flocks, and terrible famine. It originated in the Danube region, south of the river, and also spread to northern Italy, first of all affecting the *Venetia et Histria*, where the most affected area is undoubtedly the eastern one. The population of Aquileia struggles to contain the spread of the infection, is in full economic crisis, and suffers from hunger.

The revolt of Firmus and the death of Theodosius the Elder

In the latest decades, serious problems have arisen in the African provinces. In 364, in the *Regio Syrtica* of the *provincia Africae* (Tripolitania in Libya), a league of indigenous peoples—that of the Austuriani—invaded the cities of Oea (Tripoli) and Leptis Magna (Khoms, 130 km east of Tripoli). In 372, in Mauretania (the territory stretching from northern Morocco and the Atlas Mountains to central Algeria), the Berber Firmus—son of the deceased Nubel, a warlord in the service of Rome—quarreled over a question of inheritance, had his pro-Roman brother Zamma killed, and, with the help of his sister Ciria, his brother Mascezel, and other brothers, rebelled against Rome with the aim of creating his own domain. His action arose from a mixture of indigenous demands, rebellion against taxes, and Donatist-style religious protest. Gildo, one of Firmus's brothers, instead remained faithful to Rome.

In 375, Valentinian I sends Theodosius the Elder to Diocese IV-Africa with the task of quelling the revolt of Firmus. Theodosius puts Gildo at the head of the army and leads a long campaign with him to suppress the revolt. Meanwhile, Firmus' cruelty and depravity have alienated him from the sympathies of the people. This favors Theodosius, who has no problem with driving Firmus out of the province. Firmus flees to the Libyan desert. When the tribal ruler with whom he found refuge agrees to hand him over to Rome, he commits suicide. Theodosius cannot enjoy his success, however. Shortly after, in fact, he is unjustly accused of treason. He undergoes a trial and is sentenced to death and executed by beheading.

In the meantime, the Goths have invaded Thrace, plundered it, and terrorized the population in order to induce them to flee and settle in their place. Valens defeated them in battle several times, without, however, obtaining a definitive victory.

Furthermore, the Sassanids attacked Syria and occupied Armenia and Iberia in the Caucasus. The Romans managed to drive them out of Iberia, but Armenia remained in the hands of the Sassanids.

Valens (364–378) admits the Goths to the Empire

In 375, the Huns embark on a mass migration to the West. They impose their supremacy over the Peoples of the Steppes between the Volga and the Dnieper, decimate the Alans of the Don, and force the survivors to follow them against the Ostrogoths. Attacked by the Huns and Alans, the Ostrogoths retreat and make desperate efforts to contain the advance of the enemy on the Dniester line. The Huns attack the Ostrogoths in their sleep, systematically ravage and pillage, and kill anyone they meet, as if to wipe the Ostrogoths off the face of the Earth. The pressure of the enemy proves uncontainable, and the defenses on the Dniester are overwhelmed. Ermanaric commits suicide to escape capture and an indecent death. His successor, Vithimiris, counterattacks with the help of some of the Alans and Hun deserters, but falls in combat. The group of survivors—formed by Ostrogoths, Huns, and Alans, and led by Alateus and Safrax— wanders the steppe and fights for a few months, then joins the Visigoths, with whom they try to resist the Huns.

In this phase, the Visigoths are divided into two parties, one of which is headed by Fritigern (369–380) and the other by Athanaric (369–381). When the Visigoths and their allies are about to be overwhelmed, Athanaric accepts Fritigern's proposal to leave the country—now uncultivated and strewn with unburied corpses and burned houses—and to seek asylum from the Romans, within the borders of the Empire. Therefore, a huge mass of Goths, hungry and pushed to their limit, camps at the mouth of the Danube on the opposite bank of the river to that garrisoned by the Romans. It is not a horde that is preparing to make a raid but an entire people, made up of warriors on foot or on horseback but also of women, old people, and children, who follow them on their chariots.

Through Ulfilas, the Visigoths ask Valens to be welcomed into the Empire, to enjoy its protection, and to be able to establish themselves as colonists, with the obligation to pay taxes and provide support troops. The request is presented to the commanders of the border garrison, who forward it to the military governors, who pass it on to the imperial government. Valens receives it in Antioch on the Orontes in Syria (Antakia in Tukey), where he is temporarily, due to a flare-up of tension with the Sassanids for control of Armenia, and examines it carefully. He knows Fritigern due to aiding him in his rebellion against Athanaric and is tempted by the opportunity offered to him to obtain bodies for the cultivation of wastelands and new recruits for his army at a time when these are more needed than usual (a transfer of troops to the Western Empire in 374 has opened many gaps in the Eastern defense lines and the Western emperor is seeking men to fill them), as well as by the opportunity to decrease his dependence on provincial conscripts and increase income from recruitment tax. Conversely, he is opposed to welcoming the Visigoths of Athanaric, against whom he has conducted various campaigns, which concluded with a peace agreement in 369 on a boat in the middle of the Danube. In the end, he decides to grant land for cultivation and subsidies only to the Visigoths of Fritigern and places the disarmament of the warriors and the delivery of a large number of children as hostages as mandatory conditions.

The crossing of the Danube is a dramatic episode that takes place in an atmosphere of great confusion, which prevents us from counting precisely how many Goths are crossing. The soldiers of the border districts (the *limitanei*) cannot prevent the group of Alateus and Safrax, and other minor groups, from crossing the border together with the Visigoths of Fritigern. Five hundred thousand barbarians encamp on the Roman bank of the Danube. Another 300,000 camp in Scythia. Still others in Moesia. All are controlled by the Roman army, which distributes food and blankets. This poor organization, however, means that the Romans cannot effectively disarm the warriors, nor feed the huge mass of refugees. It also proves impossible to install the Goths as colonists. Corrupt officials, ignoring the instructions of the imperial government, resell the foodstuffs that are intended to support the refugees and take advantage of the needs of the Goths, who are reduced to hunger and misery, by selling them by the thousand to slave traders at very low prices. The anger and despair of the refugees, starving and deprived of their dignity, gradually increase until they burst.

In 377, in Marcianopolis in Thrace (Devnja in Bulgaria), riots break out, and the Romans lose control of the situation. This is the first link in an unstoppable chain of events that will prove disastrous for the Empire and will lead the Romans to have bitter regrets—not so much for having welcomed the refugees into the Empire but above all for having treated them like dogs.

The Battle of Adrianople

Thracian barbarians and former slaves, condemned to work in mines, devastate and plunder the Thracian countryside and end up controlling the entire rural part of this diocese. Lupicinus, the Roman governor of Thrace, gathers 5,000–6,000 well-armed and equipped soldiers and engages 7,000–8,000 Goths in combat. The Goths are ill-equipped, but they attack with such force that the Roman army retreats and falls apart. Most of the Romans are killed. Lupicinus is saved by running away. The Goths take possession of their fallen enemies' weapons and equipment.

Informed of what has happened in Thrace, Valens sends a request for help to Gratian, then leaves Antioch on the Orontes and, on 30 May 378, reaches Constantinople. He has more than 20,000 men with him, all he could remove from the defense of the eastern dioceses, including heavy cavalry, cataphracts (knights covered in armor), and some units of Gothic auxiliaries. He leaves the outskirts of the capital and intercepts the Goths of Fritigern—who number about 10,000 and have come from Cabyle, a town in the interior of Thrace (near Yambol, in southeastern Bulgaria), which they have just sacked, thinking they can make their way to Constantinople—in the valley of the Tundzha river.

Valens camps near Adrianople in Thrace (Edirne, in European Turkey). There, Ricomerus, the *comes domesticorum* of Gratian (the *domestici*, we recall, are the personal guard of the emperor, and the *comes* is their commander-in-chief), tells him that Gratian is traveling with the requested reinforcements and that he is not so far away, and he advises him not to take the initiative before his arrival. Valens receives the same advice from his *magister equitum* (master of the cavalry) Victor, an officer of Sarmatian ethnicity and of the Christian religion. The other members of Valens' war cabinet, including his generals Frigeridus and Sebastianus, instead suggest to Valens that he attack without delay, having realized that this is what he wants, because he is envious of the successes reported by Gratian on the Rhine and does not want to share the success he expects to achieve over the Goths with his nephew.

On 8 August 378, Fritigern proposes to Valens that he negotiate an agreement that avoids the test of strength. To this end, he sends him an embassy, led by an Arian priest. In reality, Fritigern just wants to play for time, as he is waiting for his Alanian, Ostrogothic, and Hunnic cavalry, which have temporarily left him to look for provisions, to return to camp. But Valens distrusts Fritigern and refuses to receive his legates.

The next day—9 August—Valens moves with 40,000 soldiers against the Goths, who are more than double their number (50,000 infantry and 50,000 cavalry), leaving the baggage, the imperial treasury, and his civil advisers under guard in the city. After marching for 13 km in the sun, in the midst of scorching heat and a hilly, arid, barren, and desolate landscape, he comes within sight of the enemy chariots about 16 km north of Adrianople and 5 km east of the Tundzha river[3] and deploys the army, with the cavalry on the right and the light infantry in the front line, while the rest of the cavalry are behind and are hurrying to catch up. The cavalry of the Romans also includes a detachment of archers commanded by an Iberian "king" or "prince" named Bacurius and a unit of *scutarii*, part of the *schola palatina*, the imperial guard on horseback, commanded by an officer named Cassius. The enemy's fighters are lined up on a ridge, while the others have taken cover in a circle of chariots, formed by thousands of vehicles. The Goths have amassed themselves and are ready to fight, but they don't move. Fritigern stalls, awaiting the arrival of the cavalry (the Visigoths of Alatheus and Saphrax and the Alans) who had left the camp to look for fodder further north, along the Tundzha. Therefore, he renews the negotiation offer. This time, Valens accepts but rejects the negotiators sent by Fritigern because Ricomerus is of low rank. Fritigern offers to negotiate personally but asks for the delivery of a high-ranking Roman to be held hostage in exchange. Valens proposes to send one of his relatives, the tribune Equitus, but the latter opposes this, saying that he had been a prisoner of war and fears that the Goths want to take revenge of the fact that he had regained his freedom by fleeing. Ricomerus volunteers. The negotiation proceeds slowly. Perhaps Valens is no longer so sure of winning and, in turn, wants to buy time, pending the arrival of Gratian. Valens' army remains deployed out under the sun, waiting, without eating or drinking. The air is further heated by the shrubs being set on fire by the Goths for the express purpose of reducing the enemy to the extreme due to the heat.[4]

Suddenly, the situation unexpectedly worsens. The mounted archers of Bacurius and the *scutarii* of Cassius, who had come in sight of a unit of enemy cavalry—the Visigoths of Alatheus and Saphrax and the Alans, who were returning to the camp—launch an attack and engage the enemy with distant arrow shots and hit-and-run strikes. The Goths receive reinforcements and repel the attackers, and the incident begins the battle. The Alan cavalry intervene to defeat the mounted archers, putting the Romans to flight and now pursuing them, while the Visigoths of Alatheus and Saphrax throw themselves on the front line of the Romans, while the cavalry of the Romans that has been left behind delays on taking a position. The invasion of the battlefield of the enemy cavalry catches the Romans off guard and breaks the balance. The Roman infantry is attacked on the flanks, which have been left exposed. It can't take the pressure for long and ends up giving in. Valens orders the reserve troops forward, but these cannot be found; they had fled. The emperor is wounded, hit by an arrow, and he is carried to a farm, whose upper floor is fortified. The Visigoths attack the building, and, seeing that the defenders are resisting, they set it on fire, unaware that the Roman emperor is inside. The Augustus dies along with all the other occupants of the building, but his body will never be found. A survivor who managed to escape will recount the last dramatic moments in the life of the Augustus.

When everything is over, the Romans lament the loss not only of the emperor but also of the *comites* Trajan and Sebastian, high-ranking commanders and members of the emperor's entourage; three *duces* (commanders directly dependent on the *magister militum*); 35 tribunes (commanders of one unit); and as many as 30,000 infantry and cavalry. Two-thirds of the Roman army have been lost. What remains of it withdraws from the battlefield, at night, under the guidance of Ricomerus, while Victor brings the news of the defeat to Gratian, covering a distance of over 300 km at a gallop. There is no news about the losses of the Goths, but it is excluded that they were light. The battle was lost by the Romans due to a series of concomitant causes, such as a lack of coordination, a lack of discipline, and their considerable numerical inferiority. Also, the Romans were exhausted from heat and fatigue. This is probably what decided the fight.

The defeat of Adrianople is one of the worst in the military history of the Romans, comparable to that of Cannae, suffered in 216 BC at the hands of the Carthaginian general Hannibal Barca (on that occasion, the catastrophe was caused by the fact that the cavalry was forced to abandon the infantry, leaving them at the mercy of the enemy, who attacked them from all sides and annihilated them). The difference is that the defeat at Cannae was followed by the great victory at Zama in 202 BC, while that of Adrianople marks the beginning of the period of the barbarian invasions, which will last for about a century and will lead to the fall of the Western Roman Empire with the coup against Romulus Augustulus by Odoacer in 476.

The news of the catastrophe spreads like lightning across the Roman world, arousing anguish and dismay, both because the *pars Orientis* has been left without its supreme leader and its army and because the aura of invincibility of the legionary infantry has dissolved and the territorial integrity of the Roman state is no longer a certainty. The enemies of the Empire take advantage of it. The Goths and the Alans, galvanized by the victory, roam throughout the Balkan area, carrying out massacres and robberies and sowing chaos (this state of affairs will persist for years). The Sassanids return to the attack in the Caucasus and definitively appropriate Armenia and Iberia. The Quadi and the Sarmatians take advantage of the fact that the Danube border is partially unguarded to carry out raids for the purpose of robbery south of the river and plunder what little has been saved from the Goths and the Alans.

Theodosius I (379–395)

In 378, after Valens' death, Gratian takes particular care of the defense system of the eastern borders of the Empire. In this context, he strengthens the *Claustra Alpium Iuliarum* and calls into service an able general, Theodosius, appointing him to the post of *magister equitum* for Illyricum and assigning him the priority task of defending the *limes* of Moesia Superior and Dacia, which are again under threat from the Sarmatians. The Theodosius we are talking about was born in 347, in Hispania, into a noble and rich family of the Catholic religion. He is the son of Theodosius the Elder, the *magister equitum* executed in Carthage (near Tunis in Tunisia) in 375–376 after being found guilty of high treason in relation to the revolt of Firmus, which he himself had repressed (it was later discovered that the accusation was unfounded). In 368, he followed his father into the war campaigns against the Britons and the Alemanni. In 374–375, he was *dux Moesiae* and defended the province against the Sarmatians. When, in 376, his father was unjustly killed, he took leave of the army and retired to his property in Hispania; it is uncertain whether in Cauca in Galicia or in Italica in Betica. There, he married his countrywoman Flaccilla, who gave him two children: Arcadius and Honorius. He is a man with blond hair, an aquiline nose, and an elegant appearance. His behavior fluctuates from one extreme to the other: now he is hyperactive, now he is lazy, now he is austere and thrifty, now he is a lover of luxury and pleasure, now he is evil, cruel, and even ferocious, now he is good and lovable, now he is loyal, now he is treacherous, now he is contained, now he is excessive. He shares the life of his soldiers and, while loving magnificence and pleasures, he knows how to find all his strength and energy in moments of danger (Piganiol 1972: 230–231).

Returning to Moesia, Theodosius achieved important successes in the fight against the Sarmatians. To reward him, Gratian, on 19 January 379 in Sirmium, gives him his sister in marriage and associates him with the throne as emperor of the *pars Orientis*.

Gratian then returned to Augusta Trevirorum (Trier in Germany), while Theodosius I settled in Thessalonica in Macedonia (Thessalonica in Greece).

Emperor Theodosius (379–385) will go down in history as Theodosius I the Great for having made Christianity the only and obligatory religion of the Empire (Edict of Thessalonica, 380). Under his reign, the *pars Orientis* remains relatively quiet, while in the *pars Occidentis*, particularly in Illyricum and Pannonia, the group of Ostrogoths, Huns, and Alans led by Alatheus and Saphrax are a continuous cause for alarm. In 380, Gratian, unable to resolve the question otherwise, allows that group to settle on the banks of the Sava in Pannonia. To this end, he makes a pact (*foedus*) with them, the content of which is not known, but it can be guessed at from the *foedus* that will be stipulated two years later between Theodosius I and the group of Alatheus and Saphrax, the group of Fritigern, and the Visigoths of Alaric.

Under the aforementioned agreement, the Visigoths can settle in Moesia and the Ostrogoths in Pannonia as foreign members of the empire. They are autonomous (because they continue to depend on their tribal leaders), but they cannot marry Roman women or become owners of the lands that have been assigned to them, in which they live "under the same roof" as the provincials. They have to support themselves, working the land, but they will receive annual subsidies from the Roman state. In exchange, they must militarily help the Empire, in which, however, they can only hold positions of subordinate command. The phenomenon of the classification of the barbarian auxiliaries in the Roman army originates from this last clause. It will take on a regular rhythm and an increasing dimension with the passage of time, solving the problem of the lack of provincial recruits in a practical and effective way and ending up involving not only the Goths and the Alans, but also the Huns.

Their chieftain, Alaric, was born on the island of Peuce in the Danube (Claud. 105–106). He is a member of the noble lineage of the Balti (Jord. 146) that has ruled the Visigoths since ancient times. In the universe of the Goths, the Balti are second only to the Amali, Ostrogoths.

The leading role of the Church of Aquileia in the evangelization of the Goths

The Gallo-Roman poet Decimus Magnus Ausonius (about 310–393), who writes between 379 and 388, estimates that Aquileia is the ninth city of the Empire. He speaks of this city in his poem *Ordo urbium nobilium*, describing it as follows: "This would not have been your place, but nevertheless, since a recent glory has made you great, you will be counted ninth among the illustrious cities, O Aquileia, an Italic colony, facing the Illyrian mountains, famous for your walls and for your port" (Auson. 67 in Pastorino 1971: 539–553).

The city is famous for its harbor and walls. It is a large military base, a bustling market, and a thriving manufacturing center. In fact, the merchant traffic between Aquileia and the rest of the Mediterranean, North Africa, Asia Minor, Syria, and

Palestine is intense (it will remain so throughout the 4th and 5th centuries, although perhaps less so, compared to the past).

In addition, Aquileia plays a supplier role for the troops. For this purpose, it imports food, grain, oil, and wine from various places, for example, from Palestine.

The success of Amantius in the work of promoting and spreading Christianity in Western Illyricum lies in this period of the history of the city.[5]

Amantius is the first Aquileian missionary to become bishop in Pannonia, perhaps not only by the will of Valerian, bishop of Aquileia, but also of Augustus Gratian. He leads not only the Christian community of the city of Iovia[6] but the entire Christian community of the province.

That community is made up of two different groups, one of which is made up of resident Romans and the other of federated barbarians. We refer to the Ostrogoths, Huns, and Alans who appeared north of the Lower Danube in 376. These barbarians participated at the Battle of Adrianople in 378, after that they carried out looting in the Balkan-Danubian provinces and in the territories westward toward "the foot of the Julian Alps" (Amm. Marc., *Res Gestae* 31.16.7). After destroying the cities of Mursa and Stridon (the former located in Pannonia Secunda, the latter between Dalmatia and Pannonia), they were defeated in battle by Theodosius in 379, and entered into a federative pact with Gratian and Theodosius in 380. On the basis of that pact, they were able to settle in Western Illyria—for the most part, in Valeria and in Pannonia Prima—where they then came into contact with Christianity. The group is made up of about 20,000 armed men, extremely valuable militarily and politically active, and, during the reign of Theodosius I (379–395), it represents the greatest military force in Pannonia and the neighboring areas, where it will prevail for about 30 years until its Alan component, together with the Vandals and the Suebi, emigrate to Gaul (early 407), and the Gotho-Hunnic component will drop down into Italy (409). The same must be said for the early years of his successor Honorius (393–423). This group is to be distinguished from another, stronger group of federated barbarians, who are also exceptionally dynamic: the one led first by Fritigern and then later by Alaric, who took office under the *foedus* concluded with Theodosius in 382, first in Thrace and then in eastern Illyricum. The group of federated barbarians based in western Illyricum is led with equal authority by Alatheus (head of the Ostrogoth and Hun components) and Saphrax (head of the Alan component). The Aquileian cleric Amantius, who is on a mission in Pannonia as he is their spiritual guide, advises them and collects their confidences, and therefore he has a great influence on them.

Ultimately, the Church of Aquileia, through the missionary Amantius and in agreement with Gratian and Theodosius, exercises an active ecclesiastical policy in western Illyricum, replacing the Church of Sirmium. An implication of that apostolic activity is the exercise of control over Alatheus and Saphrax, considering that the group headed by them is a danger looming over *Venetia et Histria* due to both its geographical proximity and its political unreliability. Amantius' role is also of fundamental importance because it prevents the group of Alatheus and Saphrax from falling under the influence of Iulian Valens, the Arian bishop of Poetovium in Noricum (Ptuj in Slovenia), who also tries to take control of it (Iulian Valens establishes contacts with the Goths, but this has a negative impact on the interests of Poetovium's community, which rises up against him and forces him to flee; Iulian Valens will find refuge in Mediolanum, where he will continue his activity).

In the latest years (378–381), the Christological controversies ceased. This happened with the synod of Sirmium (before or in 378) and the dismissal of many Arian bishops, followed by the religious edict of Theodosius (February 380), the Second Ecumenical Council of Constantinople (spring of 381), and the Council of Aquileia (September 381).

In 381, Amantius participates at the Council of Aquileia as bishop of Iovia.[7]

The Council of Aquileia

Among the affairs of state not related to defense and war, the most important after the fiscal ones are those that pertain to religion. During the reigns of Gratian and Theodosius I, the taxation is invasive, oppressive, and rapacious, and paganism, which resists in some parts of the Empire, but especially in Rome and among the Italic nobility, is discouraged. In February 380, in Thessalonica, Theodosius proclaims the Nicene Creed as the only faith of all the peoples of the Empire, condemning both Arianism and any other religious faith other than the Orthodox Catholic one as heretical. He confirms the protection of the state to Judaism (traditionally, Jews are free to practice their religion, but they are second-class citizens), and he convenes the second ecumenical council in history. In 381, the Council of Constantinople concludes its work with the approval of the Nicene-Constantinopolitan Creed (an amended version of the Nicene Creed—in 325, the First Council of Nicaea affirmed the Creed of the same name to make use of it in the Christian liturgy), which summarizes the conclusions of the doctrinal elaboration carried out by the doctors of the Church during the 4th century and defines Nicene Christianity. In December 381, Theodosius issues an edict in which he punishes the performance of pagan sacrificial rites very severely. The following year, he forbids all sacrifices in the temples. In turn, Gratian—who is influenced by Theodosius, Pope Damasus, and Ambrosius, now the bishop of Mediolanum—convenes two synods of bishops: one in Aquileia and the other in Rome.

The Council of Aquileia begins on 3 September 381, under the guidance of the bishop Valerian. The Orthodox component of the group of participants is made up of 34 bishops from the Latin West—including Filastrus of Brixia (Brescia) and Iustus of Lugdunum (Lyon)—two delegates, one from Spain and the other from North Africa, five bishops from *Venetia et Histria*, one of whom is from Iulia Aemona, three bishops from the Pannonian provinces (Anemius of Sirmium, Constantius of Siscia, and Amantius of Iovia), and one from Dalmatia (Felix of Iader). It is a small number, but decisive for the resolutions that will be adopted (the Council will mark the final victory over Arianism in Illyricum). The Christian community of Salona, whose position toward Arianism in this period is not clear, is not represented, nor are the Christian communities of Istria.

The opposing party, the Arians, is represented by two bishops of Eastern Illyricum: Palladius, bishop of the diocese of Ratiaria in Dacia Ripensis,[8] and Secondianus of Singidunum in Moesia Prima (Belgrade in Serbia), as well as by the presbyter Adtalus from Poetovium, who represents the absent bishop Iulian Valens, who fled to Mediolanum even before the Council. It is worthwhile dwelling on Palladius. He is a follower of Photinus (300–376), bishop of Sirmium, considered by the Catholic Church as the head of a heretical movement because he denies the incarnation of Christ (he affirms that Christ has no divine nature and that the *Logos* did not exist before the conception of Jesus). Photinus was deposed in 351 for heresy, but he became Arian and retook the diocese, after which he asked the Eastern emperor to be able to defend himself from accusations before a general council (not before a council of only Western bishops, as Ambrose would like).

Ambrose, bishop of Mediolanum, firmly believes in the superiority of Christianity over any other religion, believes that the God of Christians is the true God, and supports the illegitimacy of any form of worship or religion other than Orthodox Catholicism. During the Council of Aquileia, he proposes that Palladius defend or condemn any heretical proposition of Arius that challenges Catholic orthodoxy. Palladius disputes the legitimacy of this way of proceeding, but all the other "Western" bishops take the side of the bishop of Mediolanum. In particular, eight Catholic bishops (Ambrose, Eusebius of Bononia, Sabinus of Placentia, Valerian of Aquileia, Constantius of Arausium, Iustus of Lugdunum, Felix of a seat in Gaul, and Anemius of Sirmium) take part in the discussion, including one bishop of western Illyricum (Anemius). Two presbyters also participate in the debate: Evadrius and Cromatius. The latter belongs to the Church of Aquileia, accompanies Valerian, and, like the latter, is a trusted follower of Ambrose. The presbyter Adtalus remains silent. The Council ends with a majority decision (including the bishops of western Illyricum: Anemius, Constantius of Siscia, Felix of Iader, and Amantius of Iovia) to condemn Palladius and to dismiss him and Secundianus as followers of Arius. This will mark the end of Arianism in Illyricum. On the other hand, Arianism will recover its strength in Pannonia, among the Ostrogoths, and subsequently in the Balkan provinces, among the Visigoth federates (380–408/409).

The Council also sends four letters to Gratian and Theodosius I. One contains a declaration of fidelity or respect toward the Church of Alexandria in Egypt. Another appeals to the emperor to ban the Fotinians of Sirmium from the meeting by law. Yet another is the request to convene a general council of all bishops in Alexandria to put an end to the Meletian schism, which has been underway in Antioch on the Orontes since 362. In the same year, the Synod of Rome also takes measures against the Arians. On that occasion, the Church of Aquileia, made up of numerous congregations and ascetic schools, clearly and explicitly confirms its orientation in favor of religious orthodoxy, which it has assumed since the election of Valerian.

While Aquileia is Catholic, Rome remains a pagan city. The Senate of Rome is the strongest supporter of the traditional Roman religion. The *prefectus praetorium* Vetius Agorius Pretestatus (*c.* 320–384) is a man of ardent pagan faith. The *praefectus urbis* Quintus Aurelius Symmachus, an orator, senator, and writer, is a pagan no less ardent than Pretestatus.

Symmachus (*c.* 340–402/403) descends from a Roman family of senatorial rank, which became pre-eminent under the reign of Constantine I. His family is closely linked to the Nicomachi, another noble and influential family, and is very wealthy. Symmachus is a personal friend of Virius Nicomachus Flavianus and owns three houses in Rome, another in Capua, and 15 suburban villas, three of which are in Rome. He was educated in Gaul and is a friend of the Gallo-Roman poet and rhetorician Ausonius, tutor of Gratian. He is a connoisseur of Greek and Latin literature. He is the author of 10 books of correspondence, including official letters (Book I) and private letters, three panegyrics addressed to the emperors Valentinian I and Gratian, five prayers, and about 50 reports. He is the most important Latin orator of his time, compared by his contemporaries to Marcus Tullius Cicero (106–44 BC). In his prayers, he appears as a defender of tradition and of the *mos maiorum*.[9] His oratory style is typical of the Gallic rhetoric school of the time, bombastic and refined. Furthermore, Symmachus is the bearer of an ideology inspired by pluralism and religious tolerance. Before becoming *praefectus urbis* (in 383, he will hold this office until 385), he was proconsul of Africa in 373. He will become consul in 391.

The controversy of the Altar of Victory

The official seat of the Senate of Rome is named Curia and located in the Imperial Forums. Inside that building, at the back of the hall where the senators gather, is located an altar of the goddess Victory, to which the pagan senators pay homage, considering it more as a symbol of *romanitas*, "the Roman identity", and state sovereignty rather than as a deity.

In 381, at the request of the Christian senators and following the example of what Constantius II had already done, Gratian—educated as an intolerant Christian— orders the removal of that altar, with reference to the fact that Theodosius I, with the Edict of Thessalonica (380), has established Christianity as the new state religion. He also revokes immunities for pagan priestly colleges and Vestal Virgins and proscribes heretics. In addition, he abolishes the office of *pontifex maximus* for the emperor and suppresses the funds destined for pagan worship and Roman priestly colleges, earning him the endorsement of Ambrose, bishop of Mediolanum (Ambr. 57.3).

In 383, the Roman senators make an attempt to restore the Altar of Victory: the *praefectus urbis* Symmachus goes to Mediolanum and, in front of Gratian, argues in favor of maintaining the traditional Roman religion in official state ceremonies and of the restoration of the Altar and the cult of Victory. The action proves to be useless and triggers the outbreak of a disagreement between Symmachus and Ambrose.

The dispute will be resumed after the death of Gratian, when Symmachus will renew his request to restore the Altar of Victory in front of his successor, Valentinian II (375–392). But Symmachus' expectations will be disappointed. Eventually, Valentinian, under the influence of Theodosius, will side with Ambrose, with the consequence that the Altar of Victory will be not replaced and Symmachus will be removed from public life. From now on, Symmachus will devote himself to philology and will continue to have frequent correspondence with authoritative personalities.

The usurpation of Maximus (383–388) and the death of Gratian (375–383)

The Goths were starved and forced to surrender by Theodosius with skilled tactics. In 382, they are forced to sign a peace agreement that grants them some territories in Thrace and northern Dacia, but it does not allow them to marry Roman citizens. In 383, the admission into the Roman army of some contingents of barbarians, especially Alans, recruited with high salaries, arouses protests from the Roman army in Britannia, which stems from them having fought victoriously against the Picts and the Scots. The protest degenerates into a military revolt, and this leads to the imperial acclamation of a commander named Maximus.

Maximus is originally from Spain, like Theodosius I. He probably knows the latter, if not even related to him. He fought under Theodosius the Elder between 363 and 373, then was sent by Gratian to Great Britain, where he distinguished himself in the fight against the Picts (probably in 368–369, when Theodosius had already defeated the Saxons and other Scottish and Irish populations).

Gratian refuses to recognize Maximus as Augustus and prepares to face him on the battlefield in Gaul. Maximus leads his troops onto the continent and clashes with Gratian near Lutetia (Paris in France), the capital of the Lugdunensis quarta or Senonia. The battle is decided by the defection of the Mauritanian cavalry and other troops and their passage under the flag of the usurper.

Gratian, with the few troops he has left, retires to Gallia Narbonensis, from where he hopes to be able to return to Italy to reinvigorate the army and launch a counter-offensive. Maximus assumes a large part of the Gallic diocese, and secures the support of many of Gratian's court officers and officials who charge Gratian of favoring an Alan cavalry regiment and of devoting himself to pleasures, neglecting his work (Goldsworthy 2011: 288 with 541, n.31; see Amm. Marc., *Res Gestae* 31.10.18–19; Curran 1988: 104–106; Potter 2004: 549–552; Williams & Friell 1994: 36–40).

Gratian discovers the other dissidents and sentences them to death. On 25 August 383, in Lugdunum (Lyon in France), the capital of Gallia Lugdunensis, he is killed during a banquet by Andragatius, the *magister equitum praesentalis*, "commander-in-chief of all the cavalry forces".

Andragastus is at the head of 388 *vexillationes* (cavalry units) between *palatinae* and *comitatenses*, each of which is composed of 300 and 100 men, respectively.

Gratian's end is so sudden that Theodosius does not have time to help him. Theodosius replaces him with his half-brother, Valentinian II, aged 12, who joins him in Augusta Trevirorum, coming from Mediolanum. Furthermore, since he fears a military invasion of the Roman territories in the East by the Sassanids, Theodosius decides to postpone the showdown with Maximus, and, for tactical reasons, both he and Valentinian II temporarily recognize the sovereignty of Maximus over the Gallic prefecture. They also recognize Maximus as consul in the West for 384 and agree that his name should appear in official documents and that statues of him be erected next to theirs.

Maximus converts to Catholicism and changes his name to Magnus Clemens Maximus (from now on, for short, Magnus Maximus). He then adds the Iberian Peninsula to his dominions, and—when Theodosius I, in 382, associates his eldest son, Arcadius, who is just five or six years old, to the throne—he, in turn, appoints his own son Victor as Caesar.

Magnus Clemens Maximus (383–388) foresees that Valentinian II, when he is of age, will affirm his right to govern the whole West, with the inevitable support of Theodosius I, but he does not dare go to war against him because the Augustus of the West has a strong army. Besides, he doesn't have a good excuse to do it. To get it, he tries to strain his relationship with him.

The army of Valentinian II is commanded by Bauto, a Romanized Frank, likely a Christian. Bauto, in 380, was Gratian's *magister militum* and advisor. In 383, after Gratian had died and Maximus had usurped the throne, he helped Valentinian II to defend the Alpine passes from the risk of an invasion by the usurper. Since Valentinian II is still a child, Bauto has become very influential at court, practically ruling instead of him. In 385, he will reach the apex of his career with his appointment to the consulate. Augustine of Hippo, the future "prince" of the Catholic Church, will dedicate a panegyric to him in Mediolanum.

In the 4th century, Mediolanum is a city where—in the words of the Gallo-Roman poet Ausonius, who wrote between 379 and 388—"everything is wonderful: abundant wealth, countless and sumptuous houses, fertile and intelligent population, pleasant customs". Ausonius describes it in his poem *Ordo urbium nobilium* as follows: "A double circle of walls also amplifies the appearance of the city and, for the pleasure of the people, there are a circus and the wedge-shaped mass of a covered theater, as well as temples, an imperial palace, an opulent mint, a district famous under the name of the Baths of Hercules; its colonnades, all adorned with marble statues, and the walls surround, like a bastion, the edges of the city. All these constructions, and their grandiose forms, seem to rival a magnificence and are by no means oppressed by the close proximity of Rome" (Auson. 67 in Pastorino 1971: 539–553).

Between 384 and 385, Justina, widow of Valentinian I, and her son Valentinian II frequent Aquileia. Usually, however, they live in Mediolanum.

Justina trained Valentinian II in the doctrine of Arius and shows the Arians of Mediolanum sympathy. It should be added that Valentinian II is more assertive than his predecessor Valentinian I in matters of religion, if not fanatics (Valentinian I was tolerant of all religious confessions, despite being a Christian of the Arian faith).

In 385, the Arians of Mediolanum—who feel protected by Justina and Valentinian II—forcefully ask that Bishop Ambrose allow them to practice worship in the Basilica Portia (present day's Vittoria ad Corpus), which is located outside the city. Ambrose refuses, and this triggers a conflict between the Arians of Mediolanum—supported by the emperor and the Queen Mother—and the Christian community of Mediolanum. The controversy escalates when Justina asks for another basilica for the Arians, this time inside the city. Upon a new and more forceful refusal by Ambrose, Justina first cites the Bishop of Mediolanum before the *consilium* of the emperor, then forces the Basilica Portia to be occupied. Ambrose calls for the people to demonstrate, and the latter forcefully protest. Valentinian II gives in to avoid a popular revolt and, at Easter in 385, goes to Ambrose to reconcile with him.

While in the Western Roman Empire the controversies of Mediolanum fuel the controversy between the Christians of the Orthodox faith and the Christians of the Aryan faith, in the Eastern Roman Empire Theodosius I perseveres in his fight against paganism, which still has strong support among educated members of the ruling class and rural populations. In March 385, he prescribes crucifixion as a punishment for the execution of divinatory sacrifices, without success (these will continue to be practiced in hiding until the 6th century, despite the harsh repression of state powers and the Church).

On 25 January 386, Theodosius I issues an edict that grants the Arians permission to worship in the East. At the news, Justina renews her request regarding the Basilica Portia. Ambrose refuses again, and a crowd of Orthodox Christians guard the Basilica in arms for several days and nights, determined to oppose any attempt at occupation by force. Ambrose receives an imperial order to hold a debate in public with the leader of the Arians under penalty of exile, but does not obey; he replies that, in religious matters, he does not recognize any authority that is different from that of the Councils.

Magnus Maximus joins the controversy between the Arians and Catholics of Mediolanum in support of the latter. To this end, he tries to accredit himself in the role of protector of Catholicism in the West, replacing the late Gratian, and writes to Siricius, the new bishop of Rome. In that letter, he professes himself as *defensor fidei* and protests against the claims of the pagans and Arians of Italy. In ecclesiastical circles, however, there is a widespread suspicion that Magnus Maximus converted to Christianity and supports the Catholic Church for reasons of personal utility (so much so that Ambrose, while expressing loyalty to him, avoids meeting him). In fact, the operation aims to create the *casus belli* that would allow him to invade northern Italy and drive out Valentinian II.

This succeeds precisely because—at least in words—its creator enjoys the support of the major exponents of the "Orthodox" clergy, first of all Bishop Ambrose. In fact, in October 386, Magnus Maximus suddenly invades Italy with an army. He has already crossed the Alps and is aiming for Mediolanum when Justina flees to Aquileia, where she will embark for the East, together with Valentinian II, her daughter Galla and the whole court.

Arriving in Constantinople, Justina asks Theodosius I to intervene militarily in Italy to restore Valentinian II to the throne, offering him her daughter Galla, aged 15 or 16, in marriage. Theodosius I cannot tolerate that Magnus Maximus has taken over northern Italy. But defending the rights of Valentinian II means siding in favor of an Arian and against the Catholics. The problem is solved when Justina dies while traveling and Valentinian, under the influence of Theodosius, adheres to the Nicene-Constantinopolitan Creed, that is, he abandons Arianism and converts to Catholicism.

In the spring of 388, Theodosius, who is 40 years old, marries Galla (this is his second marriage; he has already been married to Aelia Flavia Flaccilla, and two children were born from this marriage: Honorius and Arcadius). Soon after, he leaves for Italy at the head of a large army, which also includes thousands of barbarians, including a cavalry contingent of Huns and several units of Alans, Sciri, Rugi, and Goths. The army is commanded by the Frank Arbogastes. Meanwhile, Bauto has died and Arbogastes has become *magister militum* in his place.

Magnus Maximus goes to face Theodosius and clashes with him in Siscia in Pannonia (Sisak in Serbia), where he is defeated. He is later defeated again at Poetovium in Pannonia. He retires to Iulia Aemona (Ljubljana in Slovenia) since his army is undergoing many defections and he hopes to be able to resist better there; then he goes to Italy, heading for Aquileia. Aquileia will be far from a safe refuge for him. Theodosius, in fact, goes to Aquileia on a forced march, finds a way in with repeated assaults on the city gates, and overthrows Magnus Maximus from the imperial throne.[10] He captures him and hands him over to the soldiers. Maximus is put to death at the third milestone of Aquileia, and his body is dragged by the angry crowd through the internal streets of Aquileia.[11]

Victor, the son of Magnus Maximus and his Caesar, who is in Gaul, survive his father for a short time. He is hunted by Arbogastes, who has been sent to Gaul by Theodosius to govern it in the name of Valentinian II; and finally captured. He is brought to Aquileia, imprisoned, and executed (July 388).[12]

Cromatius, bishop of Aquileia from 388 to 407

With the conversion of Valentinian II and the death of Magnus Maximus, Arianism has received a severe blow in the West, while Catholicism has become so powerful that Ambrose can afford to say that the emperor is not above the Church but inside it. From now on, the Catholic Church will interfere more and more often in the affairs of the Empire and, through its own hierarchies, will impose its will on the Augustus himself. This is demonstrated, for example, by an episode that takes place in Callinicum, a town located on the banks of the Euphrates in Mesopotamia. In the fall of 388, the local bishop urges local Christians to destroy a synagogue and an Arian shrine. Since

Jewish worship is permitted, Theodosius orders that the bishop rebuild the destroyed buildings at his own expense and that the perpetrators of the destruction be punished. Ambrose stands in defense of the bishop and, in a letter addressed to Theodosius, addresses the emperor with these words: "I am writing to you so that you listen to me in your Palace, so that I am not forced to be heard in the Church". Theodosius I does not allow himself to be intimidated by the language of Ambrose, but he must give in when the bishop of Mediolanum declares that religious services will remain suspended until the emperor takes a step back. A second, significant episode will occur in the summer of 390. Thousands of people have been killed in the Circus of Thessalonica by order of Theodosius after a revolt in which the city's military commander, Butheric, a Romanized barbarian, had been killed. Ambrose harshly criticizes Theodosius without pausing on the fact that he has always been on his side in the fight against paganism and Arianism, and he goes so far as to excommunicate the emperor, who, in order to be readmitted into the communion of the faithful, will have to make public amends.

In 389, Valerian, the bishop of Aquileia, died and was succeeded in the office by Chromatius (388/389–408), a man with a strong character and a solid cultural background. Chromatius (Beatrice and Peršič 2011) was born and raised in Aquileia. He is one of the most famous prelates of his time. He is an erudite theologian in active correspondence with Ambrose, Jerome, and Tyrannius Rufinus. He is also active as an exegete and a preacher. He opposes Arianism with great zeal and gives loyal support to John Chrysostom, Archbishop of Constantinople, when he is unjustly oppressed. Chromatius builds a new basilica in Aquileia with three naves, and he establishes two new dioceses, one in Concordia (Concordia Sagittaria) and the other in Iulium Carnicum (Zuglio). During his bishopric, the art of mosaic flourishes, already being present in places of worship as well as in stately homes, with a transition from purely decorative and naturalistic elements in black and white to color and the narration of the Christian religion through images.

The rise of Alaric

In 391, Valentinian, while in Gaul, is informed that bands of Goths, Vandals, and Huns are approaching the eastern border of Italy and intervenes immediately. He acts with such resoluteness that the barbarians prefer to retreat after having freed many Italics whom they had previously captured and enslaved. The Claustra Alpium Iulianum are reinforced.

Meanwhile, some gangs of Gothic federates have settled in Moesia. In the late summer of 391, they cross the Balkans and enter Thrace, together with a horde of barbarians who have descended from the region north of the Danube, led by Alaric. Theodosius, who is in Constantinople, tries to stop them, but he will succeed only after three years of fighting (388–391).

The commander-in-chief of the army of Theodosius (*magister utriusque militiae*) is Stilicho, the son of a Vandal who served in the Roman army, and is therefore a

Romanized Vandal. Born in 359, Stilicho served in the past in the *protectores* (the emperor's bodyguard). He is related to Theodosius I, having married one of his nieces, Serena.

In 391, Alaric must renew the *foedus* of 382 under the same conditions. Meanwhile, under pressure from the barbarians, Theodosius had to evacuate the western edge of the upper Danube border, abandoning it to the Germans. He also established a new administrative structure, called the Prefecture of Illyria, resulting from the unification of the diocese of Dacia (Moesia Superior) and the diocese of Macedonia.

In 391, Theodosius returns victorious to Constantinople and discovers that, in the three years of his absence from the city, his wife Galla and his son Arcadius are divided by a profound incompatibility. He remains in Constantinople for a few years, during which time he intensifies the fight against paganism and Arianism (he forbids access to pagan temples). The same year, Galla gives birth to a daughter: Galla Placidia.

On 15 May 392, Valentinian II dies in Colonia Julia Viennensis (Vienne in southeastern France, south of Lyon, at the confluence of the Gère and the Rhône) at the age of 21 in dark circumstances. His lifeless body was found in the bedroom. It is said that he committed suicide. More likely, Valentinian II was killed by order of Arbogastes, with whom he had recently had stormy relations (Arbogastes was increasingly contemptuous of the Augustus; he had appointed himself as *magister militum* without even consulting him, and when the emperor had fired him from the post, he had replied that he could not do so). Arbogastes sends the body of Valentinian to Mediolanum and, at the request of Theodosius, Ambrose organizes the funeral and pronounces the funeral oration. The sarcophagus of the deceased is placed next to that of his brother Gratian, most likely in the chapel of Sant'Aquilino in the Basilica of San Lorenzo.

Theodosius and Arcadius are the only living *Augusti,* both from the East. Arbogastes tries in vain to propose himself before Theodosius as the new Augustus of the West, replacing the late Valentinian, but the discussions are cut off in the bud because Arbogastes is a barbarian and a pagan.

The usurpation of Eugenius (392–394)

Eugenius is an elderly former grammarian and Roman rhetorician, head of Valentinian II's bureaucracy, and a pagan who converted to Catholicism, albeit only formally. On 22 August 392, he is acclaimed by the army as Augustus of the West, returns to Rome and tries to be credited as the champion of the Roman tradition and the promoter of a pagan restoration. All this takes place with the support of the Senate of Rome, which is a stronghold of paganism and sees an opportunity to counter the growing power of the Catholic Church in the political developments now underway.

In November 392, Theodosius bans the cult of the pagan gods in all its forms, even if practiced in private. Shortly after (in January 393), he appoints his son Honorius as Augustus of the West and his son Arcadius as regent, and leaves Constantinople for Italy at the head of a strong army, commanded by Stilicho and comprising 20,000

Goths, led by Alaric. He brings with him the young Honorius and the very young Galla Placidia, both entrusted to the care of Serena, wife of Stilicho.

Eugenius establishes his headquarters in Aquileia and, together with Arbogastes and their Frankish and Alemannic allies, awaits Theodosius and his troops in the Claustra Alpium Iuliarum. This leads to the Battle of the Frigidus. The Frigidus (the current name of this river is the Vipava) is a left tributary of the Isonzo river that runs through Slovenia and flows into the Isonzo near Savogna, near Aquileia.

The clash takes place on 5 and 6 September 394 on the banks of that river (between the small centers of Vipava in Slovenia and Aidussina, near the city of Gorizia in Italy). It starts well for Eugenius' army, but then a detachment of this army, commanded by an officer named Arbitius, who is supposed to attack the troops of Theodosius, don't move (he betrays Eugenius for money and will pass over to the enemy). Meanwhile, a very strong bora rose up and hit Eugenius' troops head-on, throwing them into turmoil.

The bora is an icy wind blowing from the northeast. We have already talked about this before (see Chapter 3). The appearance of the bora decides the fate of the battle. The violent gusts snatch the shields of Eugenius' soldiers and turn the arrows at them, favoring the enemy. The fight goes on for two days, with ups and downs, and ends with the defeat of Eugenius, whose camp is stormed. Eugenius is taken prisoner and put to death on the spot. Arbogastes commits suicide to escape capture. On the side of Theodosius, the Goths distinguished themselves with their valor and fighting spirit, despite the considerable losses they suffered (10,000 fell) (Oros. 7.35.19). After the victory, Alaric was rewarded by being given the title of *comes rei militaris* (which makes him a member of the entourage of the emperor), notwithstanding the limitations introduced in the agreement of 382, renewed in 392.

Based on the ecclesiastical history of Tyrannius Rufinus (*c.* 345–411)—a monk, historian, and Christian theologian, the translator into Latin of works in Greek of some fathers of the Church, in particular those of Eusebius of Caesarea and of Origen of Alexandria—the Battle of the Frigidus will be cataloged as the last attempt to resist Christianity in the Roman Empire, since Eugenius is a sympathizer of the traditional Roman religion, and therefore of paganism, while Theodosius is a Christian. It is therefore a decisive point that marks the triumph of Christianity, as was the Battle of the Milvian Bridge (313), won by Constantine I over his rival Maxentius.[13]

The Battle of the Frigidus certainly marks the beginning of the end of the Western Roman Empire. From now on, in fact, the *Porta Orientis*, "Eastern Gate", of Italy will be crossed several times by invading armies, heading for Aquileia and the cities of the Veneto Plain, neglecting Tergeste, located in a secluded position. This will not prevent Tergeste from entering a dark period in its history though.

The division of the Empire into two parts

On 17 January 385, Theodosius—who has just abolished the Olympic Games—falls ill and dies in Mediolanum after entrusting the lives of his children to Bishop Ambrose.

He prepared his succession in time. He wanted to avoid his sons Honorius and Arcadius, after his death, competing for the inheritance. Therefore, he introduced a definitive reform of the Empire, dividing it into two parts—two parts of a single empire—with two emperors and two distinct seats, Rome and Constantinople.

The *pars Orientis* roughly embraces the territories of the future national states of Malta, Libya, Egypt, Lebanon, Syria, Jordan, Iraq, Turkey, Greece, Bulgaria, Albania, Montenegro, Serbia, Croatia, and Slovenia.

The *pars Occidentis* is made up of Italy and the adjacent islands, North Africa, Noricum, Retia, Gaul, Spain, and the Balearic Islands.

Theodosius I assigned the *pars Occidentis* to the 17-year-old Arcadius (383–408) and the *pars Occidentis* to Honorius (383–423), who, at just 11 years old, is in need of a tutor. Arcadius will reside in Constantinople, Honorius in Mediolanum. Both are very young and are exposed to the manipulations of their closest collaborators, who are, respectively: Rufinus, the ambitious, unscrupulous, and corrupt *praefectus praetorio*, in the East, and the Vandal Stilicho, brother-in-law of Thodosius, and the *magister militum,* in the West. Theodosius entrusted the latter with the protection of Honorius.

Stilicho has fought victoriously against the bands of Huns who were raiding Roman territories in Asia Minor, Armenia, Syria, and Mesopotamia. He has returned to Mediolanum, through Greece and Illyricum, bringing with him both the Western and the Eastern armies. From now on, Stilicho will act on behalf of Honorius, but with a very large degree of autonomy. He controls Italy, Spain, Gaul, and Africa. However, he does not control the diocese of Illyricum, which embraces Dalmatia and the four provinces of Pannonia: Prima, Secunda, Savia, and Valeria.

Arcadius will manage to keep his part of the Empire intact over time and even increase it with the acquisition of Macedonia and part of present-day Romania (Dacia), already attributed to the Western Empire. He will push the border of the Eastern Empire up to the middle and lower course of the Danube, north of which are the barbarians (Avars, Antes, Slavs, Gepids, Lombards, etc.). Initially, however, he quickly falls under the influence of Rufinus (Jones, Martindale and Morris 1980). In short, the latter tries to get Arcadius to marry his daughter. But Arcadius decides otherwise. On 27 April 395, Arcadius marries Aelia Eudoxia, daughter of the deceased *magister militum per Orientem* Bauto, who was introduced to him by Eutropius, the *praepositus sacri cubiculi*, "provost of the sacred bedchamber", one of the senior palace officials. The holder of this post is usually a eunuch (a man who has been castrated) and acts as the grand chamberlain of the palace, wielding considerable authority and influence.

Notes

1   Amm. Marc., *Res Gestae* 25.5.14. Zos. 3.36.1–2 also reports the offer of the purple to the son of Salustus, which was rejected on the basis of his young age.
2   A disease event in an animal population similar to an epidemic in humans.
3   McNab (2011: 308–309) leans toward the locality now called Muratçali, while Runkel (1903) suggests Demirhali, which he calls Demeranlinga, which is as distant from Adrianople as Muratçali but is a little further east instead of north.

4 For the Battle of Adrianople: Amm. Marc., *Res Gestae* 31.12–13.

5 The life of Amantius can be reconstructed on the basis of the inscription (now lost) on the sarcophagus of Beligna, near Aquileia.

6 As there were two towns in Pannonia called Iovia—Botivo near Ludbreg south of the Drava in northern Croatia (province of Savia, bordering Pannonia Prima) and, about 100 km northeast of this, Alsóheténypuszta (province of Valeria) in Hungary—its exact location cannot be established with certainty.

7 After two decades as the spiritual guide of this geographically and strategically exposed community of the Roman province and of the great group of federated barbarians, Amantius returned to Aquileia in around 400 for unknown reasons. The possible cause of his return could be identified in the revolt of the Pannonian federates (396) or, more likely, in the decline of the Roman military organization and in the violent barbaric devastation which, after 400, resulted in waves of refugees moving from Pannonia to Italy. Amantius died in Aquileia, where he was buried on 6 April 413. More than 10 years later (1 December 423), the deacon Ambrose was buried in the same sarcophagus; he was probably one of Amantius' collaborators. Amantius' work as a bishop and as a missionary among the federated barbarians in the Danubian Roman provinces, so strongly threatened, recalls the role that Niketas of Remesiana († after 414) played in Dacia and, more than half a century later, the ascetic Severinus in Noricum († 482)

8 An ancient city located near modern Archar in Bulgaria, refounded by the Romans with the name of Colonia Ulpia Traiana Ratiaria.

9 The expression *mos maiorum* identifies the set of rites and ceremonies that were already proper to the Latins before the foundation of Rome and that form the essence of the Roman tradition. But it was also a thought, notion or mental representation that went beyond the meaning that was made evident by the words that made it up, according to their connection. In fact, it also identified the set of values that inspired and guided the Roman citizen from birth and that had made Rome great: *auctoritas* (the prestige and trust one enjoys), *dignitas* (reputation, honor, esteem), *fides* (loyalty, good faith), *gloria* (recognition and praise from the community), *gravitas* (imperturbability in the face of adversity), *integritas* (consistency, honesty), *maiestas* (the pride of belonging to the Roman people), *pietas* (religious devotion and the feeling of homeland love, respect for the family, and the hierarchical order), and *virtus* (personal value, courage, fortitude, solidity of character). The *mos maiorum* was therefore the complex of beliefs, opinions, representations, and values that guided the Romans, linked them together, justified their common feeling about public affairs, and made them feel like a community of citizens.

10 Zosimus uses these terms in a passage of his *Historia Nova*, a history of the Roman emperors from Augustus (27 BC–AD 14) to Priscus Attalus (409–410 and 414–415). Zosimus is a Greek historian who lived in Constantinople during the reign of the Eastern Roman emperor Anastasius I (491–518), under whom he held the position of "lawyer" of the imperial treasury.

11 Hydatius (*c.* 400–*c.* 469), bishop of Aquae Flaviae in Gallaecia (Chaves, in the Vila Real district in Portugal), the author of a chronicle of his times, talks about this.

12 Hyd. 10 ("*Maximus tyrannus occiditur per Theodosium tertio lapide ab Aquileia quinto kalendas Augustas: et eodem tempore vel ipso anno in Galliis per Arbogastem comitem filius Maximi nomine Victor exstinctus est*"); Burgess 1993. Hydatius had one more reason to talk about Magnus Maximus because, we remember, he was a Hispanic, a native of Gallaecia.

13 It is possible that Eugenius and Arbogastes were not pagans at all, nor supporters of the pagans, and that they were falsely labeled in this way to justify Theodosius' campaign against them. The same can be said for Magnentius. See Cameron 2011.

Chapter 9

Aquileia in the sunset of the Empire

The Visigoths devastate southeastern Europe

Illyricum was established as a diocese in 314 with the provincial reforms of Diocletian and Constantine. In the beginning, it was part of the Prefecture of the Praetorium of Italy. In 337, it became the Prefecture of the Praetorium of Illyricum. After the Battle of Adrianople (378), it passed to the Eastern Roman Empire to allow Theodosius I to face the threat of the Goths. It borders *Venetia et Histria* in Italy, and this border is no longer manned militarily. Not only are there no more garrison troops along the northeastern border of Italy, but there are also none in all of northern Italy. Cities must defend themselves with their militias.

It is clear that both the Eastern Roman Empire and the Western Roman Empire are interested in what is happening in Illyricum politically and militarily. In order to avoid unwelcome surprises, Stilicho would like Illyricum to return to the Western Empire and therefore be under his command. Rufinus opposes that plan because he fears that Stilicho wants to take over the entire Eastern Empire, starting with Illyricum. He tells Arcadius that Stilicho is not to be trusted, especially since he is suspected of having embezzled the treasure of Theodosius (Claud., *In Ruf.* 2.156), and he gets heard. Therefore, not even the Augustus of the East trusts Stilicho.

In 395, Stilicho dismisses the federates—the barbarian support troops who fought alongside the Roman legions at the Battle of the Frigidus (5–6 September 394), contributing with their own blood to the victory—without rewarding them adequately and forcing them to return home to the East via the Julian Alps. That happens in the middle of winter. The mass splits into groups that do not have enough food supplies, and they know that they will be not able to find any on the route. Alaric leads a group of Visigoths. Of course, he and his men are dissatisfied with the treatment they have received. In addition, Alaric complains that the title of *comes rei militaris,* which he has been awarded, is not adequate. He aspires to a higher military rank that could guarantee him a command, as well as support troops, perhaps even some legions of Roman citizens.

When Alaric is encamped in the plain of Larissa in Thessaly (northern Greece), he decides to let his own dissatisfaction and that of his men be shown. And he does it in his way, that is, by making a show of strength. He leads his men to Constantinople through Macedonia and Thrace. Along the way, he carries out all sorts of violence against people and things, plundering and taking prisoners, who will be reduced to slavery.

The absence from the East of a large part of the imperial army—first Theodosius and then Stilicho have led most of the regiments to Italy, including the Gothic mercenaries commanded by Gainas, with whom Theodosius then prevailed over Eugenius at the Battle of the Frigidus—does not allow Arcadius to prevent Alaric from encamping under the walls of Constantinople. Also, what remains of the imperial army is necessarily being used by Arcadius to face other threats. Bands of Huns and Marcomanni roam freely in Thrace and Pannonia. Other Huns are raiding Cappadocia and destroying the many monasteries in the region. They come from having invaded and raided Mesopotamia, sacked and burnt numerous cities, and directly threatened Antioch on the Orontes in Syria, and crossed the Caucasus, and invaded Armenia.

All that remains is to try to appease Alaric. Rufinus takes charge of this. He personally meets the leader of the Visigoths. No one knows precisely what they agreed. The fact is that Alaric returns to Macedonia.

In the meantime, Stilicho has secured the northwestern border, ensuring that the Franks submit and contribute to the defense of the *limes germanicus*, "the German border". He leads an army against Alaric, made up of regular troops from the Western Empire, the regiments of the Eastern Empire, and the Gothic mercenaries, headed by Gainas. He leaves some contingents along the northeastern border of Italy to guarantee his retreat. He is victorious against the Visigoths in Macedonia, chases them to Thessaly, and ends up encircling them in the Peneus valley.

Arcadius, on the advice of Rufinus (Claud., *In Ruf.* 2.162–165), refuses Stilicho's help, orders him to stop, and calls the Eastern regiments and the Gothic mercenaries to him (Claud., *In Ruf.* 2.186–196). Stilicho obeys and returns to Italy, while the Eastern regiments and the Gothic mercenaries return to Constantinople. In the meantime, Gainas has been appointed as the *magister militum* for Thrace.

On 27 November 395, Rufinus welcomes the mercenaries of Gainas in the Campus Martius outside Constantinople. While he speaks, the Goths silently surround him and kill him, taking advantage of the fact that he does not have an escort. The event should probably be read as Stilicho's revenge for Rufinus having messed up his campaign in the Balkans. Stilicho would have made use of Gainas and his men, relying on their dissatisfaction at having been confronted with the prospect of receiving a lower salary in the East than they had enjoyed in the West.

With the death of Rufinus, power in the imperial court of the East passes to Licinia Eudocia, a sister of the Emperor, and to the *praepositus sacri cubicula* Eutropius. Therefore, Licinia Eudocia and Eutropius become advisers and/or guardians of Arcadius, who is too young and too weak to oppose them.

Eutropius is an avid person, who took over from Rufinus after collaborating with him. He is an Oriental, perhaps an Assyrian or an Armenian. After the death of

Theodosius II, he opposed Rufinus and arranged the marriage of Arcadius to Aelia Eudocia, the daughter of the general Bauto.

The Visigoths acclaim Alaric as their king

In 396, some Germanic populations—the Marcomanni, the Vandals, and the Quadi— make a pact with Stilicho and obtain permission to establish themselves in part of Pannonia (in the future, they will occupy all of it). A little later, Alaric returns to the scene. He claims land for his people, in analogy to what was granted to the Marcomanni, the Vandals, and the Quadi. He also once again puts pressure on the Eastern Empire to get himself integrated into the Eastern Roman army in a suitable position of command.

The two imperial courts have different ideas about the attitude to take toward the barbarians; Stilicho, who decides the foreign policy of the West, is inclined to seek a compromise, both because he is of barbaric origin and because he is aware of the weakness of the Empire, while the imperial court of the East rejects any plea bargain. Therefore, the response of Arcadius is disappointing for Alaric.

The latter reacts violently. He invades Greece. Some groups of monks follow Alaric with the sole purpose of plundering and destroying pagan sanctuaries. However, the hostility of the Visigoths also manifests itself against Greeks of the Christian-Orthodox religion. The Visigoths, we remember, are followers of the heretic Arius.

Alaric walks the main north–south route and, when he has arrived between Thessaly and Locris, moves through the Thermopylae pass thanks to the betrayal of both Antiochus, the proconsul of Achaea, and Gerontius, the commander of the garrison placed in defense of the pass.

The Visigoths bypass Thebes and head to Athens and the Piraeus. Before menacing Athens, they destroy the sanctuary of Demeter in Eleusis in Phocis, the seat of the ancient mysteries. This will never rise again.

Athens immediately capitulates and, to save itself from destruction, pays a heavy ransom. The Athenians, however, are unable to prevent the Parthenon from being set on fire by fanatical monks. The Parthenon is the most important temple in the city, dedicated to the goddess Athena Parthenos, "Athena the Virgin". It is the most important building in classical Greece. It is the zenith of the Doric order, and its sculptures are the highest achievements of Greek art.

The fire devastates the interior of the *cella* and heavily damages the rest of the structure. The wooden frame of the roof burns and collapses to the ground, falling with a crash from a height of 14 m and raising a cloud of ash and sparks. The precious metopes and the sculptures of the pediment of the eastern side and the cornices of the pediment of the west side are mutilated or removed and thrown to the ground.[1]

The Visigoths devastate the entire territory of Attica, from Cape Sounion to Megara. Subsequently, they cross the Isthmus of Corinth—the narrow strip of land that joins the Peloponnese to the mainland of Greece—breaking its defenses. All the cities of the Peloponnese, because they trust in the natural defenses of the isthmus, are not surrounded by fortification walls, so they must surrender to the invaders. Corinth,[2] Argos, and Sparta also surrender without resistance, but this does not save them from pillage; moreover, their populations are reduced to slavery. Corinth and Olympia are destroyed by fire. Argos too is sacked and burned. The Visigoths will remain in the Peloponnese for more than a year, wreaking havoc and pillaging everywhere.

The Eastern Roman Empire is in a tight spot. It cannot repel the enemy, because it does not have the necessary military strength; it can only negotiate, and that's what it does.

In April 397, while Arcadius and Eutropius are discussing with Alaric about the possibility of integrating him into the imperial army of the East in a position that suits him, Stilicho leads an army made up of regular units and support troops to Greece. A Germanic army crosses the Ionian Sea aboard a large fleet, lands near Corinth, which has already been sacked by Alaric, and reaches Arcadia (central Peloponnese), where it will fight for a long time against the Visigoths. Arcadius—on the advice of Eutropius, who "controls him as if he were a sheep"[3]—blocks Stilicho again. He orders him to leave Illyricum and return to within the borders of the Western Roman Empire.

This time Stilicho does not obey, at least not immediately. First, he attacks Alaric, defeats him repeatedly, and forces him to retreat to the north.

Alarmed more by Stilicho's behavior than by having the Goths at home and the Huns at the gates (the Huns have crossed the Danube, entered Thrace, and now threaten Illyricum), Arcadius declares Stilicho *publicus hostis*, a "public enemy", and confiscates his property in the Eastern Empire. All this happens after Stilicho has forced Alaric to retire to the Foloi mountains, near the sources of the Peneus and the frontiers of Elis (western part of the Peloponnese) (Zos. 5.7.2).

Stilicho has surrounded Alaric, but the news from Constantinople demoralizes him, and therefore he lingers to attack the Visigoths in order to finish them off. Alaric takes advantage of this: he breaks the encirclement and makes his way toward the coast. By the time Stilicho takes possession of Alaric's camp and sacks it, it has already been abandoned and deserted.

Alaric crosses the Gulf of Corinth safely and lands in Epirus, where he will carry out new, horrible devastations (Zos. 5.6.4). To stop him, Arcadius promises to give him what he asks for, namely the appointment as *magister militum* for Illyricum. The leader of the Visigoths thus becomes one of the most senior military commanders of the Eastern Roman Empire. He brings his men back to Thrace and Macedonia and settles in an area between the Haliacmon and Axios rivers. The Visigoths acclaim him as king.

Stilicho, therefore, leaves Illyricum. From now on, he will deal with other matters. First of all, he deals with the repression of the revolt that broke out in the province of Africa during the reign of Theodosius I, under the leadership of the Berber Gildo. This development has affected Italy's grain supplies. Gildo has a brother, Mascezel, his mortal enemy. Stilicho places the latter in command of an army and sends him to North Africa to quell his brother's revolt. Mascezel successfully completes the mission, then dies by drowning in a river, into which it seems that he was thrown by his own bodyguards, by order of Stilicho.

In 399, Eutropius becomes consul (the only eunuch consul in the history of Rome) as a reward for defeating the Huns. The same year, some Goths, who had been hired to fight against the bandits in Asia Minor, rebel against Arcadius and demand the dismissal of Eutropius. Gainas marches against the rebels but ends up making an agreement with them and gets Eutropius to be tried on the basis of a false accusation, that of having plotted against the emperor. Eutropius is found guilty and executed for high treason in Cyprus. With the death of Eutropius, the influence of Licinia Eudocia and her friends at the court of Constantinople grows.

Gainas is appointed consul for 400, but the population of Constantinople rises against the act, with many victims. Gainas flees to the Danube, but he is killed by a Hun chieftain.

In the same year, Honorius stays in Aquileia for some time, perhaps with the aim of supporting the troops who, under the command of Stilicho, oppose the hordes of Vandals who have invaded Noricum and Raetia.

Aquileia on the eve of the siege by Alaric

Late antiquity Aquileia is now a true metropolis. It is a large Mediterranean port where goods, people, languages, religions, and different cultures meet and coexist, helping to bring new ideas to an area that has always been of strategic importance, as a link and intermediary between East and West, between the Mediterranean and the northern and eastern regions of Europe. Decimus Magnus Ausonius (*c.* 310–395), a Roman poet of Gallic origins, placed Aquileia in fourth place in the ranking of the main cities of Italy, after Rome, Mediolanum, and Capua, and in ninth place in that of the main cities of the Empire. Therefore, Aquileia is competing with Mediolanum for the primacy of the most important city in northern Italy.

The late imperial wall of Aquileia encloses a rectangle approximately 1.8 km long, oriented from north to south with a certain inclination toward the west, derived from the centuriation, and lapped along the eastern and southern sides by the Natissa river, which is now a small stream when it was once a real river. The new fortification wall that stands in front of the old port, now practically in disuse, was erected during the reign of Theodosius I, while the walls of the southern side of the urban system were doubled with the construction of an external wall. The walls of the western side were reinforced with towers.

On the initiative of Bishop Crestomatius (388–407/408), Aquileia was enriched with a new, large seat of worship with a basilica plan.[4] The new structure is parallel to the one that was under construction at the time of Athanasius of Alexandria's visit to Aquileia in 345 and which, at the time of Crestomatius, can be said to be completed. The two basilicas have specific and distinct purposes; they rise on the grounds of the

Theodorian Halls and are decorated with significant floor mosaics. On the eastern side of the new structure are the port (to the north) and the area of the Basilica (to the south; the market is probably also located here). On the western side are, respectively, the circus, a large public building of uncertain function, and the amphitheater. In the center, there is the Forum.

Outside the walls and beyond the river, there are some factories and furnaces in the Monastero area (so-called because a monastery was built over an early Christian basilica); other furnaces are located in the area south of the city. Further west, still on the left bank of the river, there is a huge public market and a vast bath complex. To the west, near the curve of the circus, there is a large villa with splendid mosaics.

Some roads connecting with other centers, either paved or unpaved, pass through the city gates; once outside the city walls, the necropolises are arranged down the roads, consisting of funerary monuments and relative burials, enclosed within fences. The Via Annia exits from a gate on the northwest side, which leads to Concordia and Altinum. From another gate, on the east side, the road leads to Tergeste. A third paved road (nowadays called Petrada), exits toward the northeast, running along the right bank of the Isonzo river (crossing the modern towns of Gorizia and Gradisca), and then climbs up the Vipava valley, heading toward Iulia Aemona (Ljubljana).

Three other roads originate in Aquileia. Two leave the city in continuation of the *cardo maximus*, with their first connections, respectively, in aquae Gradatae (Grado) to the south and Iulium Carnicum (Zuglio) and the Alpine area to the north, while the third, directed westward, originates from the area of the amphitheater and descends toward the sea down the right bank of the river.[5]

Alaric besieges Aquileia

The fall of Eutropius and the violent anti-Germanic reaction of Constantinople leads Alaric to fear that the Eastern Empire will break its promises and get rid of him and his men by taking preventative action in the form of a show of strength. Probably, what happens in 401 must be seen in this light. Alaric leaves Thessalonica in Macedonia (Thessaloniki in Greece) for Italy. He leads a large and well-armed army, perhaps supplemented by contingents of native barbarians from beyond the Danube, but also—apparently—by the families of the fighters. This suggests not so much a military invasion as above all a mass emigration; in this case, Alaric's aim would be to take over a part of Italy and settle there. Perhaps he thinks that, in the end, he will be able to find an agreement with Stilicho.

Alaric invades Dalmatia and Pannonia, takes Sirmium, which resisted him, and, on 18 November 401, enters Italy from the northeast, "passing through an area that looks like a desert", that is, without encountering resistance.[6]

The community of Aquileia is the first to suffer the impact of the Visigoths in Italy. It closes up in defense, trusting in the protection of the city walls, after having welcomed the refugees from the countryside, who rushed to the city with carts loaded with household goods and livestock and camped in the shade of the temples and large civic buildings. The Visigoths fail to conquer the city, but they devastate the surrounding territory.[7] They then spread to the Venetian-Friulian plain, from where they will go on to the Po valley, heading west. In a flash, they are in Mediolanum.

Honorius quickly leaves Mediolanum together with the court. His plan is to flee to Transalpine Gaul. But he is chased by the Visigoths and besieged in Hasta (Asti), a town in Piedmont (the modern Italian region closest to the Western Alps) in the plain of the Tanaro river.

In the meantime, Stilicho has asked for all possible help from all the Western provinces. He reaches Hasta and manages to penetrate the city, of which he assumes the defense. In short, imperial troops flock to Hasta from all over. Alaric is surrounded, but he does not give up. In the Holy Week of 402, Stilicho attacks him near Pollentia (Pollenzo), on the banks of the Tanaro river. Pollentia is a strategic center between the Po valley, the Alpine passes, and the Ligurian coast. It is a renowned center for the production of black wool and precious ceramic vases. Emperor Constantine I welcomed Sarmatian refugees fleeing from the Goths there.

On Easter Sunday—6 April 402—the Alan cavalry of Stilicho invades the camp of the Visigoths with surprise and violence. Alaric defends himself, repels the Alans, and counterattacks, but Stilicho always throws new forces into the fray. At the end of a day of fighting, in what becomes known as the Battle of Pollentia, the Visigoths leave the field defeated. Stilicho finds the enormous booty that the Goths had accumulated in Thrace and Greece years earlier and appropriates it. Furthermore, he takes many prisoners, including women and children, and frees many Romans. Among the prisoners, there is the wife of Alaric.

Honorius will never return to Mediolanum. Between September 401 and December 402, he will move together with the court to Rabenna (Ravenna), an important city on the Adriatic coast of Italy, which is a much safer location than Mediolanum. Rabenna thus becomes the new capital of the Western Roman Empire.

Under Augustus (27 BC–AD 14), the post of Classis (Classe)—one of the three neighborhoods of the city—became the seat of a large military fleet in charge of overseeing the safety of the Adriatic Sea, and was connected to the Po delta by the Fossa Augusta. In the 2nd and 3rd centuries, that harbor could contain up to 250 warships, while the city was inhabited by about 10,000 people. From now on, Rabenna will be a city increasingly rich in large and precious monuments, artistic masterpieces, and military defense works.

Alaric has little infantry remaining, but the cavalry is intact. He does not return to the Balkan Peninsula but crosses the Apennines on his way to Rome. Stilicho offers him peace, promising him compensation. Alaric, under pressure from his generals, agrees to return to Dalmatia. Therefore, he crosses the Po river. Stilicho follows him at a distance. Unlike what has been agreed, however, the Visigoths enter the Adige valley. They want to cross the Eastern Alps to cross into Raetia (Alto Adige, southern Bavaria, part of Switzerland, western Austria), regather their forces, and plunder the province. Stilicho prevents them: he attacks them and defeats them in the Battle of Verona (at the end of 402 or start of 403). Alaric first retreats to the Julian Alps (he passes through Aquileia again, though without causing damage), then reaches Istria through these mountains. In the meantime, a minority of Visigoths have disassociated themselves from the remaining part, commanded by Alaric, and passed under the banner of Stilicho. Their leaders are Sarus and Ulfila.

Alaric returns to the attack in Italy in 403. He focuses on Rome, so much so that Stilicho completes a circuit of the urban walls and strengthens them here and there with the remaking of gates, the consolidation of towers, and the opening of loopholes. The *praefectus* Longinus supervises the works. Eventually, the defensive walls of the city will exceed 19 km in length.

But Alaric will not reach Rome. He retires after having reached an agreement with Stilicho, who wants to use him to wrest eastern Illyricum from the Eastern Empire.

The Ostrogothic Radagaisus invades Italy

But another danger looms on the horizon of the Western Roman Empire. In 405, a migrating multitude of Alans and Vandals, under the command of Radagaisus, pursued by the Huns, overwhelms the defenses of the Danube *limes*, destroys the Roman cities it encountered, and enters Italy from the northeast. Radagaisus is an Ostrogothic prince and a pagan, and he declares his intention to take Rome.

Estimates of the number of invaders range from 100,000 to 400,000. Throughout the Peninsula, there are rumors of dire, terrifying omens. Panic spreads. In Central Italy, large masses of refugees in search of a safe refuge flock to Rome. The Western Empire orders a general mobilization and enlists slaves as well as Roman citizens, promising them liberation and a decent wage (April 406).

In this case, too, Stilicho's intervention proves decisive. He gathers 30 legions under his command, for a total of 30,000 men, clearing the Rhine border and using Sarus' men as auxiliaries. He secures an alliance with the Huns, led by Uldinus, giving them a part of Pannonia in exchange; intercepts Radagaisus' horde as they march on Florentia (Florence), and confronts it in Faesulae (Fiesole), defeating it (23 August 406). Radagaisus is captured and beheaded. Some of Radagaisus' men are enslaved, while the rest become part of the Western Roman army. In Rome, the narrow escape is celebrated, including through the erection of monuments to victory. A statue of Stilicho is placed in the Forum. Honorius assumes the office of consul (1 January 407).

Meanwhile, several Germanic tribes—including Vandals, Burgundians, Alani, and Suebi—have crossed the frozen Rhine near Mogontiacum (Mainz) and invaded the Roman province of Gallia Belgica, overwhelming the *limes'* weak defenses (31 December 406).

At the beginning of 407, the Roman provinces in Britain acclaim the general Flavius Claudius Constantinus as emperor, and he assumes the imperial name of

Constantine III. The usurper crosses the English Channel with local mercenary militias and lands in Gesoriacum (Boulogne-sur-Mer in the Pas-de-Calais department in the Hauts-de-France region). Stilicho sends an army under the command of Sarus to fight against Constantine III. Sarus defeats two generals of Constantine III—Justinian and the Frank Nebiogaste—then meets Nebiogastes in Valence and kills him. Later, another contingent of Constantine III, commanded by Edobicus and the *magister militum* Gerontius, force Sarus to return to Italy. Sarus, we recall, is one of the leaders of those Visigoths who disassociated themselves from the remaining part of their people and passed under the banner of Stilicho at the end of 402 or start of 403 (the other leader is Ulfila). He had also had a career in the Roman army: in 407, he became *magister militum*.

Constantine III secures the Rhine border, establishes garrisons to guard the Alpine passes, which connect Transalpine Gaul with Italy, chooses to reside in Arelate (Arles in Provence, France), the seat of the *prefectus praetorium* of the Gauls, and appoints Apollinaris as *praefectus urbis*. Stilicho reorganizes the Western Roman army, while a revolt led by Didymus and Varenian, cousins of Honorius and loyal to the latter, breaks out in Spain. Constantine III feels caught in a vice and decides to launch a preemptive attack.

In this turmoil, Honorius's only concern seems to be to strengthen Catholicism and attract interest from the Catholic Church (the Church of Nicaea has been so-called for about a century). On 15 November 407, he issues an edict that exacerbates the penalties against heretics—Manicheans, Donatists, Priscillanists—confiscates and donates to the army the revenues that are due to the temples of the traditional Roman religion, uses the same temples for the use of the state, closes private places of worship, orders the removal of statues of the gods and the destruction of altars, burns the Sibylline Books, excludes non-Catholics from Palatine offices, and removes non-Catholic officials from office. The provision is valid for the entire Western Empire, except for Africa.

The exception we just mentioned is probably due to the work of Olympius, a court dignitary and *magister scrini,* head of one of the four offices that make up the Palatine secretariat and who deals with decisions of the emperor and petitions addressed to him, correspondence, appeals, petitions concerning the administration of justice, and documents in Greek. Olympius is an unscrupulous schemer who professes himself a Christian only because it suits him.

Olympius distributed the most important civil and military offices to his loyalists. The former went (or would go), among others, to the eunuch Terentius, *praepositus sacri cubiculi*; to Arsacius, *primicerius sacri cubiculi*; to Caecilianus, who will be *praefectus praetorio* of Italy in 409; and to Priscus Attalus, the *comes sacrarum largitionum*, "minister of finance". The latter, to Sextus Turpilius, *magister equitum* and then *magister peditum*; to the Persian Varanes, *magister peditum* (he will become *magister militum praesentalis* in Constantinople); and to Vigilantius, *comes equitum domesticorum*, then *magister equitum* in place of Turpilius.

The murder of Stilicho

Stilicho tries to establish an alliance with Alaric to send him to fight against Constantine III and recapture Transalpine Gaul. He, at the head of another army, will march on Constantinople to take possession of the Eastern Roman Empire, taking advantage of the fact that Arcadius had died on 1 May 408. Alaric is in the area of Iulia Aemona and accepts the offer, subject to his appointment as *magister militum* for Illyricum, the payment of 4,000 pounds of gold, and the authorization for him and his people to settle in Noricum. Stilicho gathers an army with a legionary majority in Ticinum (Pavia), to be placed under the command of Alaric, and asks for the ratification of the agreement in the Senate of Rome. Therefore, he goes to Rome.

Rome is no longer the capital of the Roman state, partly because there are now two Roman states, one in the East and one in the West, but it remains the heart of Roman civilization.

The Senate of Rome is dominated by the anti-barbarian party, headed by two senators, both natives of Mediolanum: Flavius Mallius Theodorus and his brother Lampadius. It considers the agreement as an act of submission, rather than as a way to safeguard peace, and rejects it.

Stilicho returns to Rabenna and tries to convince Honorius to take over the army gathered in Ticinum. Therefore, according to Stilicho's plans, Honorius should lead the army against Constantine III in place of Alaric. The men closest to the emperor oppose this and find support in Serena, wife of Stilicho. One of them is Olympius. Recently, he had been appointed as *magister officiorum*, "head of the Palatine secretariat", a position that also allows him to supervise the work of the feared *agentes in rebus*. The *agentes in rebus* are a body of people in charge of collecting information on everything that surrounds the emperor, both inside and outside the government and the court, in the capital and throughout the Empire (CTh 6.29.3 = CI 12.22.3). In practice, they are the secret agents of the Roman Western Empire.

At the court of Honorius, where Olympius weaves his intrigues, rumor has it that Stilicho wants to ally himself with the Goths to overthrow Honorius and place his son Eucherius on the throne. It is a slander, circulated by Olympius, who supports a policy of firmness toward Alaric (he was behind the refusal of the Senate to ratify the agreement between Stilicho and Alaric). But Honorius takes it at face value, and this marks the end for Stilicho. On 13 August 408, the troops gathered in Ticinum mutiny. The following 22 August, Stilicho and all the men closest to him are massacred in a church in Rabenna. Eucherius, the son of Stilicho, is also arrested and executed on the same day. Shortly after, the anti-barbarian wave takes other victims. The families of the German soldiers who served under Stilicho are exterminated.

Upon hearing the news of the killing of Stilicho, Alaric, frustrated and furious at the same time, returns to Italy to force Honorius to respect the pact he made with Stilicho. This time, his destination is Rome, the most ambitious goal he could have set himself.

It is not only his warriors who are with Alaric, but all his people. Alaric's warriors number 30,000, among whom are members of the elite and a much larger group of free warriors. The former wear long hair, finely decorated weapons, and metal armor; the latter, leather tunics or Roman breastplates and helmets. One hundred and fifty thousand men, women, old people, and children are added to them, divided between free and slaves. The multitude travels on foot, on horseback, or in wagons, bringing with them provisions and an arsenal of weapons: swords, spears, clubs, and shields.

Lastly, the survivors of the massacre of the German families who fought under Stilicho and the army of his brother Athaulf join Alaric from Pannonia Superior.

To prevent Athaulf from joining Alaric, Olympius sends Sarus against Athaulf with 300 Huns. Sarus defeats Athaulf in battle, but the latter still manages to reach Alaric with the bulk of his forces (CTh 5.35–37, 45).

Alaric enters Italy through the Julian Alps. Once again, Aquileia is not touched, but its countryside is devastated. The Visigoths cross the Po in Cremona, follow the Via Aurelia to Rimini, and then the Via Flaminia to Rome, through Picenum and Tuscany, plundering and devastating everywhere. In September (or November) 408, they reach their goal, camping in the shadow of the Aurelian Walls. Rome closes down in defense. Meanwhile, Constantine III, the usurper, recognized by Honorius as co-emperor in 409 and currently ruling in France, has raised his son Constans to the rank of Caesar and sent him to suppress the loyalist revolt that broke out in Spain, together with Gerontius, Apollinaris, and the *magister officiorum* Decimus Rusticus. Didymus and Varenianus, relatives of Honorius and both living in Spain, are captured and transferred to Arelate (summer of 408).

Honorius does not intervene in any way to prevent Alaric from exerting his fury on Rome. He prefers to keep his forces intact, more concerned with Constantine III possibly invading Italy than with Alaric taking over Rome. In practice, he abandons Rome to its fate. The Romans will not understand this immediately, only little by little.

The siege of Rome by Alaric reduces the population to starvation (winter 408–409). Disaster looms over the city. The Senate, to avert it, restores public sacrifices and other pagan rites. It is said, with no known basis, that the Pope consented to this reluctantly and on the condition that the rites were held in secret. Finally, the Senate proposes a negotiation to Alaric, who accepts. Therefore, a delegation led by Priscus Attalus, son of Ampelius of Antioch—who is the former proconsul of Asia and Africa, former *comes sacrarum largitionum*, and current *praefectus urbis*—is received by Alaric. The King of the Goths dictates the conditions. He asks for a ransom, the delivery of hostages (sons of different personalities), and the liberation of 40,000 slaves of Germanic origin (he has it in mind to enlist them in his ranks) (CTh 5.40–41).

The Visigoths enter Rome after a siege and sack it

The ransom consists of 5,000 pounds of gold, 30,000 pounds of silver, 4,000 silk tunics, 3,000 scarlet-dyed skins, and 3,000 pounds of pepper. In response, the delegation asks him what on earth he wants to leave to the Romans, and the King of the Goths replies: "life". Eventually, the Romans agree to pay. To obtain the necessary gold, the assets of the rich are confiscated and gold and silver statues are melted, as are the precious metal ornaments of other statues. Alaric receives the ransom and the liberated slaves of Germanic origin; while waiting for the requested hostages, he retires to Tuscany and reiterates his claims, forcing the Romans to speak for him with Honorius.

A delegation, headed again by Attalus, goes to Rabenna. But Honorius, yielding to the pressure of Olympius and the *praepositus sacri cubiculi* Iovius, another despicable opportunist, refuses to make peace with Alaric and to hand over the hostages. Nor is he willing to appoint Alaric *magister equitum* for Illyricum and give him Venetia et Histria, Noricum, and Dalmatia, as he had requested.

Not everyone at the court of Honorius shares Olympius' policy, contrary to any compromise with Alaric, much less approve of the instigating role he played in Stilicho's death. One of Olympius' opponents is Iovius. He was *praefectus praetorio* of Illyricum in 407, under Stilicho. In that situation, he would have forged ties with Alaric.

Before the end of 408, Honorius dismisses Olympius and has Turpilius and Vigilantius assassinated. Olympius takes refuge in Dalmatia (Zos. *Hist.* 5.46.1). Soon after, Iovius—probably one of the proponents of the fall of Olympius—becomes Honorius' most influential collaborator. He enters into negotiations with Alaric in Ariminum (Rimini) and presses Honorius so that he accepts the requests of Alaric. But Honorius insists on not wanting to invest the King of the Goths with any military position, and Iovius aligns himself with Honorius' intransigence.

Alaric reduces his claims. He renounces *Venetia et Histria* and Dalmatia; he will be satisfied with Noricum, or an equivalent province. Furthermore, he renounces the appointment to the post of *magister militum* for Illyricum. But Honorius and his advisers see in this a sign of weakness and oppose a new proposal. Alaric reacts in a rush: he returns to Rome, besieges the city for a second time, and asks the Romans to rise up against the emperor who had abandoned them (fall 409). The people accept, the Senate proclaims an emperor from its own members of oriental origin, Priscus Attalus, who accepts, and Attalus appoints Athaulf as commander of his bodyguard. Attalus is a pagan, but he is baptized in a hurry because a Roman emperor cannot but be a Christian, at least in name, if not in fact. He becomes a Christian of the Orthodox faith, therefore a Catholic. Alaric is appointed *magister militum*, and Athaulf becomes his first subordinate. Many other Visigoths also join the army in positions of command. Attalus and the Visigoths surround Rabenna and ask for the abdication of Honorius. But the latter limits himself to offering to share the empire with Attalus.

Iovius was sent by Honorius to negotiate with Attalus and Alaric, but he goes over to their side when he is offered the post of *praefectus praetorio* and the dignity of *patricius*. Perhaps he gives up Honorius not only because he is isolated in Rabenna, but also because Alaric has 30,000 warriors and Attalus was elected by the Senate, enjoys the favor of the people, and is a Catholic, that is, he is supported by the Church. Later, however, Iovius tries to separate Alaric from Attalus (he does not love Attalus, previously a close collaborator of Olympius). Thus, perhaps it is not true that, by deserting, he intended to betray Honorius. On the contrary, perhaps he wanted to help him by dividing his enemies.

Meanwhile, at the court of Honorius, effective power passed into the hands of the eunuch Eusebius, the successor of Terentius in the office of *praepositus sacri cubiculi*. But Eusebius died shortly after. Therefore, effective power changed hands again: this time, into the hands of Allobicus, one of Iovius' men, who took the place of Vigilantius. But when Iovius deserted, Allobicus was accused of being a supporter of Constantine III, arrested, and executed by order of Honorius. But the twists are not over yet. Honorius calls Olympius back into his service, and he thus returns to the position of *magister officiorium*.

Honorius is saved by the fact that 4,000 soldiers of the imperial army of the East have just arrived in Italy from Constantinople on board a fleet. The news encourages him. To put Alaric, who is in Rome, into difficulty, he orders the governor of the diocese of Africa, Heraclianus, who has remained loyal to him, to suspend the shipment of grain supplies to Rome. Therefore, the population of the city is again reduced to hunger.

In July 410, Alaric sends a contingent of soldiers to Africa. He would like to send 500 Goths, but Attalus insists that ordinary troops be sent. When the latter suffer a serious defeat, Alaric deposes him and reopens negotiations with Honorius, but the emperor does not yield. Honorius thus abandons Rome to its fate for a second time. Why does he do this? Probably, not because the former capital no longer counts for anything and can therefore be sacrificed (Honorius, unlike many of his predecessors, often stayed in that city, the Senate of Rome still embodies the Empire, and Rome is the seat of the Pope), but because he wants "to take the opportunity, on the advice of the most intransigent Catholics, to give the coup de grace to Roman paganism, weakening the pagan component of the Senate" (Lançon 2021: 79).

Probably in order to "torpedo" the negotiations, Sarus attacks Alaric (Philostorgius 12.3; Sozom. 9.9.3). The King of the Goths thinks that Sarus' initiative was in concert with Honorius and takes out all his anger on Rome. The city is not well guarded, the circuit of the walls is too long for everything to be monitored. On the night between 23 and 24 August 410, the Visigoths enter the city. Rome, which has taken the whole world, is itself taken. For three days, the Visigoths plunder it, stripping it of its wealth, accumulated over the centuries. The palaces of the aristocracy are looted. Those who resist the robbery are killed. Women are raped, either by the Visigoths or by family slaves, who take advantage of the circumstances to take revenge on their masters. Many buildings and monuments are set on fire, but Roman institutions, clergy, places of worship, and the treasures of Christians and the Catholic Church are respected. A group of Visigoths refrains from stealing vases of gold and silver when they learn that they belong to St Peter's Chair. By order of Alaric, the sacred objects are brought and placed in safety in St Peter's Basilica, accompanied by a crowd of faithful.[8] When he leaves the city, Alaric takes Galla Placidia (who will be treated with respect) with him. Galla Placidia, we recall, is the daughter of Theodosius I (378–395), wife of Constantius III (421), sister of Honorius (393–423), and mother of the future emperor Valentinian III (425–455).

The Sack of Rome sends a shiver of horror throughout the Roman world. The Western Roman Empire, in practice, no longer exists. This is a very strong psychological shock. Some Romans see the collapse as a consequence of the conversion to Christianity. Some contemporary Christian observers, on the other hand, recognize in Alaric—himself a Christian—the wrath of God that befell a still pagan Rome. On hearing the news, Honorius does not hide his feelings. He thinks the messenger is talking about his favorite hen, which is called Rome, and he bursts into tears, thinking she is dead. It is necessary to explain to him that he has misunderstood and that the disaster that has occurred is much more serious, even apocalyptic and epochal.

Alaric, having struck at the heart of the Western Roman Empire, wants to snatch one of its most flourishing dioceses from it in order to settle there with his people. His new destination is North Africa, and he plans to reach it through Sicily. Therefore, the Visigoths move along the Appian Way, slowly advancing south, with the immense booty and numerous prisoners they have taken as slaves or to be ransomed. They take and destroy some cities, especially in southern Italy. They kill everyone they meet on the street, young and old, without sparing women and children. They continue looting.

They descend the Peninsula as far as Calabria. They hope to arrive in Sicily, but they are unable to overcome the obstacle presented by the sea (the Strait of Messina). Forced to renounce his plan, Alaric decides to go back, that is, to go up the Peninsula again, but when the Visigoths reach Consentia (Cosenza), he falls ill with malaria and dies in a few days, aged about 40.

The King of the Visigoths is buried in a rich funerary outfit in the bed of the river Crati, though the precise place is kept secret, together with great wealth. Thus was born the legend of Alaric's Gold, a fabulous treasure, which will be sought in vain for many years. Alaric's successor is Athaulf. After negotiations with the Rabenna authorities, he leads the Visigoths to southwestern France, where they will establish their kingdom. In 414, Athaulf marries Galla Placidia, who thus becomes the Queen of the Visigoths.

The revenge against the usurper Joannes Primicerius (423–425)

Honorius dies on 15 August 423. The Eastern emperor, Theodosius II (408–450), son of Arcadius (383–408), delays the choice of a successor. The Senate of Rome, on the proposal of Castinus, one of the patricians of Honorius, proclaims Joannes, the *primicerius notariorum*, "dean of civil servants", as the Augustus. Theodosius II does not recognize Joannes and, under pressure from Galla Placidia, his aunt, he places on the throne Valentinian III (423–455), son of Constantius III (who died of illness in 421, after just seven months of his reign). In the meantime, Valentinian III was engaged by Galla Placidia to Theodosius II's daughter, Licinia Eudocia.

Valentinian is only five years old and is under the tutelage of his aunt. Therefore, the one who will hold power in the West from now on is Gallia Placidia, regent of the Empire on behalf of Valentinian.

On 23 October 424, in Thessalonica, Helion, *magister officiorum* of the Eastern Emperor Theodosius II from 414, elevates Valentinian III to the rank of Caesar. Subsequently, on behalf of Theodosius, he follows Valentinian, Galla Placidia, and the imperial army of the East on their journey to Italy. The army is commanded by the *magister militum* Ardabur and his son Aspar and has the task of repressing Joannes' usurpation.

Valentinian, Galla Placidia, and the Eastern army winter in Aquileia (424/425). Once again Aquileia is therefore the residence of the imperial family and a quartering place for the legions. The city and surrounding countryside are crowded with soldiers, who are lodging in constructions built in wood or masonry, instead of usual tents, and are dressing in heavy cloaks, heavy long-sleeved trousers, and tunics, as well as bands to protect the legs, instead of usual clothing. They train for combat, mix with the civilian population, and frequent the taverns and brothels. The local economy is positively affected, the food suppliers, the artisans, the merchants, the operators of the restaurants and entertainment venues all do good business. When spring arrives, Joannes is besieged in Rabenna. He will capitulate after having resisted for four months, due to the betrayal of the garrison. He will be captured, one hand mutilated, placed on the back of a mule, exposed to public mockery in the circus, and finally decapitated (June or July 425).

Notes

1 For an account of the destruction of the Parthenon by the Visigoths: Bouras 2012: 1–6.
2 Corinth, after being destroyed by the Romans in 146 BC, remained largely deserted until Julius Caesar, who refounded it as Colonia Laus Iulia Corinthiensis in 44 BC, shortly before his assassination, and it became one of the main cities of southern Greece or Achaea. It had a large mixed population of Romans, Greeks, and Jews. Prior to Alaric's invasion of Greece in 396, Corinth had been largely destroyed again by earthquakes in 365 and 375. The city had been rebuilt after these disasters on a monumental scale, but it covered a much smaller area than in the past.
3 Zos. *Hist.* 5: "The animosity between Eutropius and Stilico, object of general discourse, was evident from this period. Yet, although they disagreed with each other, they agreed to confidently insult the miseries of the people, the one who had given his daughter Mary in marriage to the emperor Honorius, and the other who ruled Arcadius as if he were a sheep, or any other tame animal."
4 The perimeter walls of today's basilica, up to a certain height, are those of the basilica of Crestomatius.
5 It is likely that, at the time of the usurpation of Magnus Maximus, the city walls of Aquileia underwent new interventions, including the construction of towers, which is mentioned in a very fragmentary inscription preserved in the local National Archaeological Museum.

6 Jord. 29: *Mox ut ergo antefatus Halaricus creatus est rex ... sumptu exercitu per Pannoniae, Stilicho et Aureliano consulibus et per Sirmium dextero latere quasi viris vacuam intravit Italiam.*

7 Christian sources (which are very numerous for this period) do not mention any fire or sacking of the city.

8 Saint Augustine mentions this episode in his *De Civitate Dei.*

Chapter 10

Aquileia's fall

Attila (434–453)

Attila is a coarse, ferocious, and cruel man (he was called "the scourge of God"), but also intelligent and charismatic, a crowd-puller. He became chief of the Huns in 434, the same year in which he obtained both the doubling of the tribute that Attila himself had imposed on Theodosius II (408–455) and the title of *magister militum* from Valentinian III (425–455). Subsequently, he crossed the Danube *limes* several times with his Huns, descended through the Balkan Peninsula, and went almost right to the gates of Constantinople. In 441, he took over Sirmium, Naissus, and Arcadiopolis, and established his winter camp—his capital, so to speak—at Sirmium (this city will never again be in the possession of the Western Roman Empire but will remain in the hands of the barbarians for a century, after which it will be conquered by the Romans of the East). Theodosius II, to stop him, had to submit to triple the tribute he owed him and to redeem the Romans who had been captured at a high price. In 446, the bands of Attila, which descended into Greece, passed through Thermopylae, and, in 449, they crossed the Danube again. It is at this point that an episode took place that would be defined as romantic if not for the consideration that it was pregnant with political consequences for the whole Empire.

The "engagement" to Augusta Honoria

The female protagonist is Justa Grata Honoria, born from the marriage of Constantius III (crowned emperor on 8 February 421) and Galla Placidia, and sister of Valentinian III. Honoria lives in Rabenna (Ravenna) and is currently staying in her residence, which is part of the imperial palace. She is an irreverent and unconventional woman, more energetic and more intelligent than Valentinian, compared to whom she is a year or two older, and aspires to play a much more important role than the one her brother has reserved for her and which tends to relegate her to the fringes of court life and exclude her from any political activity and even from any political information.

   A senior officer of Valentinian III is in charge of the safety of Honoria: Eugenius. Honoria and Eugenius become lovers. When it is evident that the Augusta has been made pregnant by Eugenius, Valentinian III fears for the stability of his throne and reacts: he decapitates Eugenius and forces Honoria to marry Flavius Bassus Hercolanus, a rich and respected senator, so that he can keep her under control. Honoria resents this a lot and, in the spring of 450, she takes the incredible initiative of asking Attila to intervene to free her from the bond of a marriage that she is living with the mental attitude of a recluse. She gives a eunuch named Hyacinthus, whom she trusts, a letter, a large sum of money, and her personal ring and instructs him to go to Attila as her personal ambassador and deliver it all to him. Hyacinthus fulfills his mission, but upon his return, he is arrested and tortured, reveals everything, and is beheaded.

Informed of the incident, Valentinian does not approve of Honoria's work at all and rejects the invitation that Theodosius II has addressed to him to deliver the Augusta to Attila so as not to irritate him. He instead hands Honoria to her mother, Galla Placidia. Attila warns him from doing any harm to his "betrothed" and asks for Gaul as a dowry, that is, a good half of the Western Empire. Valentinian replies that his sister is already married, that the succession to the throne with the Romans takes place in the male line, and that the territory of the Empire is the property of the state and not of the imperial family, which cannot sell it off against the law.

The Battle of the Campus Mauriacus

Attila is furious and decides to take Gaul by force. He moves from Pannonia toward the Rhine *limes* in the first months of 451 at the head of 30,000 Huns and their allies, crosses the river and overwhelms the Roman defenses along the banks, and occupies Mediomatrix (Metz in Lorraine, northeastern France). He then continues his advance toward the west, reaches the Loire, and surrounds Aurelianum (Orlèans, on the banks of the Loire River, central France) in a siege. But the city resists. While Attila is engaged in the siege of Orleans, the Roman general Aetius surprises him from behind.

Aetius is not only a military commander but also, since 433, the most influential man in the Western Roman Empire. His priority is rejecting the attacks of barbarians throughout the empire. His army is composed of some Roman legions and auxiliary troops that were made available to him by those barbaric kings of Gaul whom Aetius himself convinced to collaborate in order to defeat their common enemy. The enemies we refer to are the Salian Franks of Belgica, the Ripuarian Franks of the Lower Rhine, the Burgundians of Savoy, and the Celts of Armorica. Aetius also has the Visigoths of the old King Theodoric at his side.

Attila lifts the siege of the city and begins to retreat slowly, but he is attacked, not only by Aetius but also by other barbarians, in particular by the Alans, who, encouraged by the retreat of the Huns, have decided to give support to the Romans and their allies.

Attila is engaged in combat at Tricassis (Troyes in Champagne), more precisely at the Campus Mauriacus, where he had stopped. The clash is very hard and the outcome is contested, though it would have been resolved in favor of the Huns, had it not been for the damage that the Visigoths managed to inflict on them after Theodoric was killed in combat. The next day, the two armies remain stationary, then Attila resumes the retreat toward the Rhine, chased only by Aetius, who has sent the auxiliaries and his other allies home. The Huns cross the river again and head toward Central Europe, venting their anger in the territories they gradually cross, leaving behind cities in ruins, villages on fire, devastated fields, and massacres.

The following year, the Empire enters its 479th year of life, but it lives a troubled existence and is close to definitive collapse. The *pars Occidentis* will again be threatened by Attila, whose obsession remains settling his account with Marcianus (450–457) due to the non-payment of the agreed tax. Furthermore, Attila is still furious at the defeat he suffered the year before in the Battle of Campus Mauriacus and wants to take revenge on Aetius. Unexpectedly and lightning-fast, he leads a great mass of Huns, no less than that which followed him the year before in Gaul, from Pannonia to Italy, and penetrates into *Venetia et Histria*. Attila enters Italy through the Carnic Alps (therefore from southern Austria or western Slovenia). If he had chosen to cross the Julian Alps (the southernmost segment of the Eastern Alps, continuing toward the south of the Carnic Alps), coming from western Slovenia through the Preval pass, bypassing the Nanos massif to the north and descending the Vipava valley, on the way, he would have encountered, well before Aquileia, the obstacle represented by Forum Iulii. Forum Iulii (Cividale del Friuli), we recall, is a well-equipped fortress on the banks of the Natisone, at the flat outlet of this river, between the last foothills of the Julian Prealps, in a defensive position between the Natisone and Isonzo valleys.

We don't mention the Claustra Alpium Iulianorum, because this defense line is unattended in 452 (more generally, no pass of the Eastern Alps is defended). Aquileia is the main stronghold to protect the northeast border of Italy.

Attila would not have encountered resistance, neither in the passes of the Carnic Alps, nor in the Upper and Central Friuli. This is incredible, but Aetius' strategy will be understood later. Apparently, Aetius is caught off guard by Attila's move. However, he certainly doesn't panic. Perhaps he is thinking of escaping and rescuing the emperor and the court, and what is certain is that he chooses to stay and resist. Indeed, he asks for and obtains the help of Marcianus, who is in Constantinople.

Attila heads straight for Aquileia. The Huns know that city quite well because they passed through there as mercenaries under Stilicho in 405 and then under Aetius in 425, as well as because of the subsequent fight between Aetius, a supporter of the usurper Joannes, and Aspar, champion of Galla Placidia, which resolved with no winners or losers. Therefore, they know that Aquileia is a rich prey, and they know the roads, fortifications, and the surrounding areas where they can camp.

"Aquileia fracta est"

Marcianus is a Thracian, or an Illyrian, and a former military commander who became a tribune and senator. After marrying Augusta Pulcheria, sister of the late Theodosius II, he denounced the pact that the latter had made with Attila, which forced the Eastern

Empire to pay tribute to the Huns in order not to be attacked, and he is waiting for the emperor of the West, Valentinian III, to recognize him as emperor of the East. He is probably convinced to intervene on the basis of the promise of that recognition made to him by Aetius, in agreement with Valentinian III. Marcianus recalls a fleet from Sicily and makes it available to Aetius, and he sets out at the head of an army toward Pannonia.

But the timely arrival of reinforcements is not enough to stop Attila's fury. The Huns are now encamped under the walls of Aquileia and devastate the fertile and well-kept countryside. The tents have banners fluttering in the wind on top. The city's defenses are tight. The defenders are all combatants, because the women, the old, the children, and the many others that could not have collaborated effectively in the defense were evacuated and, under the guidance of Bishop Secondus, took refuge in the lagoon of Grado, where the barbarians, inexperienced in naval navigation, cannot reach them.

The present-day lagoon of Grado extends for about 90 km², at the mouth of the Aussa and Corno rivers, and belongs to a wider lagoon, called Laguna di Grado and Marano. In those waters ends also the Natissa, the river crossing Aquileia. In the 5th century, the mainland prevails in all that area, but there are some islands, as for example Grado. Grado is about 10 km south of Aquileia. There is a port, which developed after AD 350 as the first port for ships entering the Natissa River, headed upstream to Aquileia. In 452, that port is the only port of Aquileia, given that the river port of Aquileia is no longer in operation. A Roman road connects Aquileia with its maritime port. Between the 4th and 5th centuries, a castrum 100 m long and 70 m wide was built on the long sandy dune that forms the island of Grado to guard the port militarily. On the occasion of the descent of the Huns that Roman fort allows the population of Aquileia to take refuge there, safe from the danger due to barbarian raids. With the definitive transfer of the Senate of Aquileia and many Aquileians to Grado, it will be enlarged (360 × 90 m) and equipped with towers with access doors.

The defenders of Aquileia reject the intimation of surrender, so assaults on the walls begin. The defenders resist with furious desperation. After three months, the siege is still ongoing. The besiegers make only trivial progress, and they cannot "skip" Aquileia and proceed further in the conquest of northern Italy because this would mean leaving behind a powerful military force and giving up a very rich prey. In practice, they are blocked, tiring themselves out and wasting time. Furthermore, they lack food, which they cannot find by raiding the countryside (the whole of northern Italy is in the grip of famine due to two recent unfavorable harvest years), and many of them have fallen ill, probably with malaria, due to the proximity of the marshes, or typhus, due to the disastrous hygienic conditions.

On 29 June 452 Valentinian III is in Rabenna, to which he returned ultimately (on 15 April 452, when Attila hadn't passed the Alps yet, he was in Rome), and from where he monitors the situation of Aquileia, hoping that the fleet sent by Marcianus will arrive in time and that this will prevent the fall of the city. In those days, the

Huns resign themselves to having to lift the siege and returning to Pannonia, but Attila, who wants to hold on, convinces them to stay, noting that a flock of storks has taken off from the city and interpreting the episode as an omen of victory (since the birds "feel" that the fate of Aquileia is sealed, they have abandoned the city and its defenders to their fate). This is a typical case of reality being distorted. A flock of storks may indeed have taken off from the besieged city, but the reason was quite different: they would have been starting their migration to their African and Asian winter quarters, which these birds begin in summer everywhere in Europe, usually between August and September, to return to the same places that they left in the following March, taking the same routes in the opposite direction.

The Huns then renew their assaults on the walls. In this second phase of the siege, some siege engines that imitate the Roman ones are used. This demonstrates the acquisition by the besiegers of armaments and techniques of the Romans, but also the tenacity of the resistance opposed by the defenders of the city, which confirms the reputation of the latter as an impregnable fortress, which was strengthened on the occasion of the siege of Maximin the Thrace and then of that of Iovinus, a general of Julian the Apostate. Therefore, the conquest of the city confirms to be a difficult undertaking. The attackers are hit by clouds of arrows, and those who manage to get under the walls and try to climb them, using long ladders, are hit by jets of pitch or boiling oil. Furthermore, the besieged sometimes make sorties to repel those who are undermining the walls or go to the enemy camp at night, set fire to siege engines, steal horses, poison wells, and kidnap people to be exchanged with other prisoners.

On 18 July 452, the collapse of part of the walls—precisely where a stork made its nest—causes the opening of a breach through which the Huns can break into the city (Proc. *De Bellis* 3.4). It is easy to imagine what happens in the first hours following the conquest on the basis of the precedents that the Huns have set, in which they have been both the architects and protagonists, in similar situations and circumstances. The Huns sack the city and slaughter all the defenders, dismember the fallen with ferocious cruelty, carry around their heads severed from their torsos on pikes as macabre trophies, flay prisoners alive or torture them to death, rape the women who refused to be evacuated until they bleed to death (a noblewoman named Digna, who lives in a tower of the city walls overlooking the river, throws herself into the void to avoid this tragic end),[1] and set everything on fire. An imposing column of black smoke rises above the houses, obscuring the sky, which can be seen from Grado. The city is not razed to the ground, but is made unrecognizable, both from the point of view of population and from the architectural and monumental point of view, as can be seen, for example, by the damage caused to the Christian basilicas.[2]

The Attilan devastation of Aquileia is seen in the contemporary world as a rift with a violent psychological impact, so much so that, in the beginnings of 6th century, it will be included in the *Consularia Ravennatia* as follows: *His consulibus [Fl. Bassus Heraclianus et Sporacius] Aquileia fracta est XV kal, Aug.* ("Under the consuls Flavius Bassus Heraclianus and Sporacius, Aquileia was annihilated on 18 July"). In this regard, it is important to draw attention to use in the translated sense of the verb *frango*, "to break", which evokes the idea of a crash, of a radical destruction, and gives a measure of the gravity of the news.[3]

Aquileia is repaired to some extent by the survivors, headed by bishop Niceta, the successor of Secundus in Aquileia and Grado. However, it is no longer the same. Its northern part remains abandoned, given that the resettlement affects only the southern part around the episcopal nucleus. In 543, the Aquileia Church is still alive and vital, so much to be able to quarrel with the Byzantine emperor Giustinian regards the Monophysite question (Three-Chapter Controversy). When the Lombards come to Italy in 568, they destroy the city completely. In 590, the Lombards destroy Aquileia again. The vital trajectory of the Roman city of Aquileia ends now. The incipient Middle Age will see the repopulation and reconstruction of the city in a minor form. The greatness of the Roman city, fourth in Italy and ninth in the Empire by extension and population, is now lost.

Attila devastates northern Italy

The taking of Aquileia makes the Huns more daring and bold, and they are pushing toward the west, not the south. Attila does not want to try his hand at the conquest of Rome because it is said, he is advised against it by soothsayers and shamans, who admonish him, reminding him that Alaric died shortly after having sacked and profaned the sacred city; nor does he think of taking Rabenna, impregnable against any army, above all because it is defended by swamps and marshes and because it can be supplied by the sea.

The Huns, therefore, spread across the Po-Venetian plain, most of them following the Via Gemina and Via Annia, which lead from Aquileia to Verona, and the so-called Via Gallica, which leads from Verona to Mediolanum, the former imperial capital, still the main city in the northwest of Italy. They leave behind a trail of unburied corpses and smoldering ruins in a territory already plagued by famine and pestilence. Wherever the conquest takes place, it happens in a bloody and brutal way, with no respect for anyone, much less for churches, clergy, and ecclesiastical properties. Everywhere, with the approach of the barbarians, the Roman provincials, already weakened by war and their tax burden, tormented by the plague and famine, and terrified by the ferocity of the barbarians, seek escape, most of them flocking to the lagoon areas.

Attila's advance to the Pianura Padana takes place through the Veneto plain, along the Via Annia, without difficulty as no city tries to resist; instead, all open their doors to the invader out of fear. After Aquileia, the Huns reach Concordia Sagittaria and Ad Quartum (Paulus Diaconus 15.2), then Patavium, Vicentia, and Verona.

Concordia Sagittaria is a city located at the intersection of Via Annia with Via Postumia. It was founded as a Roman colony in 42 BC by Julius Caesar, from whose family it derived its name. Its territory extends from the Livenza to the Tagliamento rivers and extends northward to the Prealps. It was parceled and distributed to veterans of civil wars. In its southern part, between the urban center and the coast, it has been reclaimed and populated with farms and rustic villas. Portus Reatinum (Caorle) is located there. Born as Iulia Concordia, this city grew and developed in the first two centuries of the Empire. In the 3rd century, it became a military outpost to reinforce the eastern border and the home of an arrow factory, which was so important that, between the end of the 4th and the beginning of the 5th century, it was known as Concordia Sagittaria. In 389, it became a bishopric and the seat of a large basilica. In the 5th century, it underwent a profound urban transformation. It is possible that it was affected by the invasion of the Huns, but, in any case, it does not seem to have suffered serious damage.

Ad Quartum (Quanto d'Altino) is a walled city and a river port, with city gates with two towers and an atrium, and piers, mooring docks, and warehouses, born from the transformation of an early Venetic center into an urban one, which took place between 89 and 49 BC. It rises in a swampy environment, where, however, the water renewal is guaranteed. Between 49 and 42 BC it became a *municipium*, and therefore it obtained Roman citizenship, like many other towns in Venetia. Later it grew and developed as a maritime emporium, thanks to the fact that it is located north of the Venetian lagoon and is at the center of a dense series of connections with a vast hinterland crossed by many roads, specifically, Via Annia, Via Augusta, a third road that connects it to Opitergium (Oderzo), and a fourth that connects it to Tarvisium (Treviso). It flourished in the 1st century AD, especially during the reign of Tiberius (AD 14–37), who gave it temples, arcades, and guardhouses when it became known as a center for the production of fine wools and for the breeding of mollusks (*canestrelli*) and dairy cows. The coast of Ad Quartum is populated by luxury villas, able to be compared to those of Baiae in Campania. The city fell into crisis in the 2nd century, but in the mid-4th century, it was still a noteworthy city and was a bishopric, with a cathedral church, basilicas, and martyrs' chapels. Altinum too will survive the invasion of the Huns.

Patavium (Padova), in the 5th century, is another of the most flourishing cities of the Empire,[4] with well-constructed buildings and internal cobbled streets, a theater, an amphitheater, aqueducts, sewers, and bridges. It is the seat of the *correctores Venetiae et Histriae*. The city is savagely captured and sacked by the Huns, and however many of its inhabitants are captured have to follow the Huns and are taken to Pannonia as slaves. Before the arrival of the Huns, however, many inhabitants of the city had found refuge in the lagoon, where they would later found Venice.

Late antique Vicentia is a modest town with a rectangular plan divided into almost square blocks and crossed by the Via Postumia, which constitutes its *decumanus*. There are internal cobbled streets, private homes, and basilicas decorated with marble columns and polychrome mosaics.

Verona is one of the main centers of the Po Valley. It lies on a bend in the Adige River, at the mouth of the Adige Valley, which descends from the Eastern

Alps, and at the intersection of several roads, connecting this valley—where the city of Tridentum (Trento) is—to the rest of Gallia Cisalpina—Emilia, Liguria, and the Western Po Valley. Not far from the city a stone wall bridge spans the Adige River. The Roman settlement was born as a military, given the strategic importance of the site for the defense of the Po Valley from the invasions through the Passo del Brennero in the Eastern Alps. In 89 BC, it became a Roman colonia; in 49 BC, a municipium. In the 3rd century, Emperor Gallienus doubled its walls and made it a solid fortress. Verona has developed from the half of the 1st century BC, around the Via Postumia, which crosses the city. The struggle between Constantine and Maxentius for control of northern Italy had its fulcrum in Verona in 312. In 334, some groups of Sarmatians were settled in the territory of Verona, as in other parts of northern Italy, to contribute to its defense. Stilicho defeated Alaric and his Visigoths here in 403. In the Late Roman Empire, Verona is one of the most important centers in northern Italy, such as Mediolanum and Aquileia; a big market, and a road junction of primary importance. Verona has replaced Aquileia in the role of a stronghold to protect the northeast of Italy. This explains the presence in the city of a weapons factory. Verona has a Forum and a theatre, built in the 1st century BC; and an amphitheater, completed around AD 30. The latter is the third-largest structure of its type in Italy after Rome's Colosseum and the arena at Capua: measures 139 m long and 110 m wide, and can seat some 25,000 spectators in its 44 tiers of marble seats. The shows and gladiator games performed within its walls are so famous that they attract spectators from far beyond the city. An arch, built in the 1st century AD, straddles the main road into the city, which follows the Via Postumia, coming from Patavium. An archway is the facade of a 3rd-century gate in the city walls. An inscription carved in it is dated AD 245 and gives the city name Colonia Verona Augusta. Another gate, opened in the 1st century BC, contains a small court guarded by towers. Here, carriages and travelers are inspected before entering or leaving the city. A church dedicated to the first Christian martyr was erected in Verona in the first centuries AD. It houses the burials of the first bishops of the city and encompasses a cruciform crypt with its forest of columns, arches, and cross vaults. The diocese of Verona is the most ancient of the Veneto. His bishop Lucilius, in fact, participated in the Council of Serdica in 343.

Close to Verona, the Via Gallica originates from the Via Postumia. It connects Verona to other major municipalities of the Po Valley: Brixia (Brescia), and Mediolanum (Milan), passing near Lake Garda. Attila's advance continues along that road, with the usual outfit of violence, robbery, and destruction.

Originally, Brixia was an important center of the Gauls Cenomani, who, in 196 BC, allied with the Romans. It became a municipium in 89 BC, thus obtaining the Latin law, for having helped the Romans, together with Veneti, Gauls, and Ligurians, to defeat enemies in the Social War. Later, Brixia became part of the Roman territory and its inhabitants were given Roman citizenship, ceasing to be Cenomani and becoming Brixiani. In 27 BC, Brixia became a Roman colony with the name of Colonia Civica Augusta Brixia. It also became an important religious center, administratively inserted in the *Regio X Venetia et Histria*. During the Imperial Period, Brixia enjoys strong economic development, and the zone of origin of many legionnaires enrolled in the Legio VI Ferrata. Emperors Augustus and Tiberius endowed it with a couple of aqueducts, mighty walls, an orthogonal road system around the two major axes (cardo maximus and decumanus maximus), and a first series of imposing public buildings, among which is a basilica. The city developed mainly during the Flavian dynasty (AD 69–96), was remodeled during the principality of Septimius Severus, in the 3rd century, and acquired the definitive urban layout in the late Empire. The Flavian dynasty encompassed the reigns of Vespasian (69–79), and his two sons Titus (79–81) and Domitian (81–96). In this period, a large temple, a theater, the Capitolium, and public baths have been erected. The Capitolium is a temple located in the northern part of the Forum, together with the nearby theater, which is connected by a portico. It is the most important city complex built in the 1st century AD. It was erected on a large terrace, which also previously had been the religious seat of the city. Before the Capitolium, a sanctuary had been built there in the 2nd century to seal the alliance between the Romans and the Cenomani, demolished when Brixia had become a municipium under Latin law in 89 BC, rebuilt in the Sillan period, finally destroyed by order of Vespasian between 73 and 74 to make room for the Capitolium. In the Flavian period, also, the basilica has been rebuilt. Located along the southern side of the Forum, it is of considerable size (47 m long by 19 m wide). Brixia is one of the two terminals of the via Mediolanum-Brixia, which connected it to Mediolanum also passing through Cassianum (Cassano d'Adda), and of the via Brixiana, a Roman consular road that connects Cremona, a Roman city located along the river Po, with Brixia, from which several Roman roads passed that branched off towards the whole of northern Italy.

Verona and Brixia (as Aquileia, Concordia, Ad Quartum, and Patavium) are in turn gradually looted and destroyed by the Huns. Roman citizens who fall into the hands of the Huns alive are killed on the spot or enslaved. For Mediolanum and Ticinum, things are different; they are neither destroyed, nor completely looted, and the inhabitants are largely spared.[5]

Ticinum (Pavia) got its name from the fact that it is located on the banks of the Ticino and is an important stronghold between this river and the Po. It has the typical plan of Roman military camps. It is connected to Mediolanum by an important Roman road and, thanks to its river port, it is a fundamental hub in river communications between the Upper Adriatic and Lake Maggiore.

Entering the *palatium* of Mediolanum, Attila is struck by a painting that portrays the Caesars seated on their thrones and the Scythian princes at their feet. To assert his superiority, he has it modified. The Caesars will be depicted in the act of emptying suppliant bags of gold before the throne of Attila himself.

Pope Leo I (450–461) meets Attila

Aetius, meanwhile, has decided to try the path of peace and manages to involve the head of the Catholic Church, who has long been in close contact with the imperial court, in this desperate enterprise. It is a result of this that, having reached the River Mincio,[6] Attila sees an embassy headed by Pope Leo I (450–461), which also includes the prefect Trygetius and Gennadius Avienus. The Mincio is the main outlet of Lake Garda. It starts from the southeastern tip of the latter at Peschiera del Garda, between Brixia and Verona; flows for about 65 km, passing through Mantua, and ends in the Po west of Hostilia (Ostiglia). Nobody knows what the Pope and the Hun said to each other on that occasion, but the fact is that Attila agrees to retire and leave Italy without demanding anything in return, neither taxes nor anything else. It is possible that he was induced to review his plans because his raid in Italy had lasted longer than expected, taking him very far from his starting point; his army had weakened due to food shortages and disease; he could be blocked in Italy by the imminent arrival of reinforcements sent to Aetius by Marcianus (which Attila knows are traveling by sea, perhaps because he was informed by the Pope himself, at Aetius' suggestion); and Marcianus' army could prevent him from retreating to the Danube. Perhaps his spoils of war have been replenished by gifts offered by the Pope. Or perhaps Attila is superstitious and fears that he will die, as happened to Alaric after the Sack of Rome.

The death of Attila

Attila, in retreating to Pannonia, leaves behind a devastated territory, reddened by the blood of countless victims, killed without reason. The following year he warns Marcianus that he will wage war on him over the issue of unpaid taxes, threatens anyone who resists him with slaughter and slavery and prepares for war. But first, he wants to marry Ildico, a young Germanic princess, who joins the already countless wives of Attila. But on his wedding night, he is suffocated by his own blood (he suffers from nosebleeds) while lying in his bed, dead drunk, after an evening of revelry. The next morning the servants find him dead, lying in his bed. Ildico is beside him, covered with a veil and crying. Attila's body is enclosed in three coffins, one of which is made of iron, one of silver, and the third of gold. After an impressive funeral, during which the Huns express their pain by cutting their hair and shredding their cheeks, the triple coffin is placed under a silk tent, and the best knights of the Hun people circle around it, in the manner of circus competitions. The coffin is then buried under a large mound. The people who made the coffin are killed and buried alongside Attila, along with the weapons and precious objects that belonged to the deceased ruler.

Notes

1   The invasion of the Huns in Aquileia, including the incident involving Digna, is narrated in Paulus Diaconus 14.9–10.
2   Archaeologists have found signs of the fire in the *horrea* (grain warehouses) area, now around the Basilica of Poppo, and the Domus and Episcopal Palace. The destruction of the Civil Basilica

is also attributable to that event. According to a legend, a treasure was buried in Aquileia to prevent it from being plundered.

3   This short text is one of the oldest sources of the destruction of Aquileia by the Huns. It comes from the so-called *Consularia Ravennatia*—a consular list with brief information of a chronological nature composed in the Palatine area in Ravenna at the latest in the 6th century—whose surviving fragments are preserved in a manuscript sheet in the chapter library of Merseburg in Germany (Dombibliothek ms. 202), datable to the middle of the 11th century. On this topic: Roberto 2016: 367–377.

4   This is how Pomponius Mela and Strabo speak of it.

5   For the cities affected by Attila's raid: Jord. 42; Paulus Diaconus 14.11. The latter reports that the raid by the Huns only affected Aquileia, Pavia, and Mediolanum.

6   The exact place of the meeting—referred to in Jord. 42—is unknown. Perhaps the current centers of Governolo and Quingentole, or, more likely, Peschiera.

Appendix

The Roman expansion in northern Italy

The pre-Roman peoples of northern Italy

Northern Italy is a wide region delimited in the north by the Alps and in the south by the Ligurian Sea, the Apennines, and the Upper Adriatic Sea. It is largely occupied by a plain that extends in the shape of a triangle, constantly remaining at about 100 m above sea level. That plain is called Padana, after the Po, the most important river in Italy, which originates on the Monviso (Western Alps) and crosses all of northern Italy up to the delta in the Adriatic Sea, receiving the waters of numerous tributaries. Some of the tributaries descend from the Alps, and others from the Tuscan-Emilian Apennines.[1] With its 47,000 square km of surface, the Pianura Padana is one of the largest lowlands in Europe.

The region considered is naturally rich in men, farm animals, pastures, woods, surface waters, minerals, and fertile soils, and is also known for the warrior virtues of its inhabitants and for their quick, subtle, and lively language. Among its agricultural production, its millet is worthy of note. Vast forests of oaks allow the breeding of pigs, from which a lot of meat is obtained, capable of satisfying the needs of populations and armies.

The Po divides that wide region into two parts: Cispadana and Transpadana (*cis*, in Latin, the language of the Romans, means "on this side", while *trans* means "beyond", from the perspective of an observer in Rome). The former extends south of the Po; the latter, north of the river. Gallia Cispadana is therefore that part of northern Italy that lies south of the Po, up to Liguria and the Tuscan-Emilian Apennines. Gallia Transpadana is located between the Po and the Alps.

Gallia Transpadana, in turn, is made up of two parts, one western and one eastern, divided by the Adige, a river that descends from the Central-Eastern Alps and flows into the Po at the height of the city of Verona. The western part extends from the Adige to the Western Alps. The eastern part goes from the Adige to the Eastern Alps—with particular reference to the Carnic and Julian Alps—and to the Adriatic Sea. Let us dwell on Gallia Transpadana.

The west of Gallia Transpadana corresponds to all the future regions of the Aosta Valley, Piedmont, Lombardy, Veneto (up to the Adige), and Emilia-Romagna. The east, on the other hand, corresponds to all the modern regions of Veneto (from the Adige onward), Trentino-Alto Adige, and Friuli Venezia Giulia.

In the Iron Age (from the 9th to the 4th century BC), Gallia Transpadana is inhabited by numerous peoples and ethnic groups—Camuni, Proto-Celts, Etruscans from the Po Valley, Reti, Veneti—who engage in contacts and exchanges between themselves and with Reti living beyond the Alps.

The Camuni live in Val Camonica, therefore in the Central Alps (the future province of Brescia). According to some, they are Leponti, and therefore Proto-Celts; according to others, they are Euganei (the predecessors of the Veneti), such as the Triumplini of Val Trompia and the Stoni. More likely, they are Reti, as their customs are common to those of the inhabitants of Rezia, the region that stretches from the Italian Alps to the Upper Rhine.

The Proto-Celts came to Gallia Transpadana from Gallia Transalpina (in particular, from the south of France) between the 3rd millennium BC and the Bronze Age. They settled permanently in the central-western part of this area, finding a _modus vivendi_ with the Camuni, who had already lived there since approximately 8000 BC, and with the Leponti, who, for the most part, live in Ossola, while the remainder live in the Canton of Ticino (Switzerland) and in Liguria. The Transalpine Gauls who emigrated to Liguria mixed there with the Ligurians, giving rise to the Celtic-Ligurians.[2]

The lands of the Proto-Celts—including the Celtic-Ligurians—the Camuni, and the Leponti extend, specifically, from the Alpine watershed to the Adda and Oglio rivers and to the Emilian Apennines; they are also crossed by many tributaries of the Po and are dotted with lakes. The region is divided into three bands: alpine, with peaks of 4,000 m; mountainous and hilly; and flat or undulating at most.

The Proto-Celts are an ethnic group formed by the Insubri, the Orobi, the Levi, and the Marici. The Insubri live mainly in the area south of Lake Maggiore, the Varese area, and a part of the Novara area. The Orobi live in the areas of Como and Bergamo. The Levi and the Marici live in Lomellina.

The Reti of Italy live in a mountainous area of Lombardy called Valtellina, on the shores of Lake Garda, in the Isarco Valley, in the Adige Valley, and in the Paduan area. Outside Italy, there are Reti in Bavaria, Engadine, the Canton of Grisons, and the Austrian Tyrol. They control the Brenner pass, the most important passage between South Tyrol and Germany through Lower Austria, a strategic area for communications between the Mediterranean world and Central Europe. Divided into various groups, though all belonging to the same culture, they are distinguished by their craftsmanship, way of living, and cultural practices. They have contacts and exchanges with other Alpine populations, the Veneti, and some groups of Celts, who live south and north of the Alps. Having had contact with the Etruscans has influenced their culture as regards writing, the symposium, and their way of representing the gods. The Reti, unlike the Veneti and the Etruscans, who inhabit cities, instead form village communities.

The Etruscans are a people who occupy a geographical area called Etruria, which embraces parts of central Italy (Tuscany, western Umbria, northern and central Lazio), parts of Cisalpine Italy (Emilia-Romagna, southeastern Lombardy, southern Veneto), parts of southern Italy (Campania), and Corsica. The Etruscan civilization evolved from the Villanovan culture, attested from the 9th century BC, which in turn derived from the Proto-Villanovian culture (12th–10th century BC). The Etruscans are organized in a confederation of large city-states and small states,[3] have peculiar economic, social, and political systems, and have a flourishing trade, which they practice within and abroad. Their political order, over time, has passed from monarchy to aristocracy (from the 5th century BC) and subsequently to democracy. An important moment in their national history was the Battle of the Sardinian Sea, fought between an Etruscan-Carthaginian coalition and the Greeks of Alalia (Aleria in Corsica) for the primacy of merchant traffic in the Western Mediterranean. The clash took place in around 535 BC, probably in the waters between Sardinia and Corsica, and ended with the victory of the Greeks. The Greeks we are talking about were Phocians, that is, refugees from an Eastern Greek city called Phocaea.[4] Their commercial leadership was linked to the foundation of emporiums and populous colonies. As part of that policy, the Phocians of the west, in around 600 BC, founded Massalia (Marseille) on the coast of the Gulf of Lion. The price of their success in the Battle of the Sardinian Sea was so high as to induce them to emigrate. They stopped in Rhegion (Rhegium, Reggio Calabria), then they founded a city on the coast of Campania: Elea (Velia, Ascea). The Etruscans took advantage of the Phocian retreat to expand into Corsica (this happened after they had taken control of Rome). Another naval battle was fought in 474 BC between an Etruscan fleet and a Syracusan fleet in the waters of Cuma and was won by the latter. This marked the end of the territorial expansion process of the Etruscans in central and southern Italy.

In particular: the people of the northeastern corner

The Veneti, or Eneti, live between the Po river, the Adige river, the Cadore mountains, the Livenza river, and the mouth of the Timavo (Bocche del Timavo), where they settled permanently between the 2nd and the 1st millennium BC, expelling the Euganei. They are a people born from the mixing of groups of immigrants who came from Central Europe and local populations of the Proto-Villanovan culture.

Several ancient authors speak of the Eneti (Greek ethnic), or Veneti (Latin ethnic). Homer (*Iliad* 2.851–852) reports that they came from the Asian shores of the Black Sea, under the leadership of Pylaemenes. In particular, Homer mentions Paphlagonia, a region of Anatolia, squeezed between Bithynia and Pontus, as their place of origin. Titus Livius (*Historiae* 1.1) tells another story. A large number of Paphlagonians, driven out of their country by a revolution, fled to Troy, but lost their leader in the fighting under the walls of the besieged city and turned to Antenor, wise adviser to the Trojans, to guide them in their search for a new homeland. They left Troy together with a group of Trojans and arrived in the Upper Adriatic. They would have landed on the west coast and settled between the Alps and the sea, having driven out the Euganeans. Virgil (*Aeneid* 1.242–249) describes the sea voyage of Antenor and his group of Paphlagonians and Trojans across the Adriatic Sea, beyond the mouth of the Timavo. Another Latin author, Servius, in his commentary on the *Aeneid*, specifies that Antenor landed in Venice. All the ancient authors are therefore in agreement in believing that the Eneti came from northwestern Anatolia and that they arrived in Italy shortly after the Trojan War, between the 13th and 12th centuries BC. The archaeological findings document the evolution of the civilization of the Veneti from its most ancient phase, datable to the passage from the Bronze Age to the Iron Age between the 11th and 9th centuries BC.

The Veneti know the urban lifestyle. Their main settlements are Atheste (Este) and Patavium (Padua). The former is located on the banks of the Adige; the latter, on the banks of the Brenta.[5] The Veneti clearly differ from other pre-Roman peoples of northern Italy. See, for example, the aspects related to religion and worship and to political institutions, documented by funerary and votive inscriptions. They speak Venetian, an Indo-European language that shows strong similarities with Latin, and they know its script, which they learned from the Etruscans (the Venetian script recalls the Etruscan one, from which it derives). They are primarily farmers and ranchers, but also hunters and gatherers. Both Homer and other Greek authors—Alcman, Euripides—report that they are famous for breeding horses. Their artisans work with clay, bone, horn, glass, and amber. They spin, weave, melt bronze, and work iron, obtaining fabrics, work tools, and weapons of war. Among their artisanal products, those that are in excess of internal needs fuel trade. Goods are often transported along rivers. Their fighters are armed with large swords and equipped with ovoid shields and Gallic helmets. In the past, they were equipped with round shields, helmets of other shapes, and spears.

Among the deities of the Veneti, the most revered is Pora Reitia, healer, lady of Nature, dispenser of fertility, and protector of births. Pora Reitia is depicted in effigy wearing a knee-length tunic, a pointed hat, a belt with embossed bronze plates, a pair of leather boots with rolled edges, personal ornaments, and a key in her hand, which she uses to open and close the doors to the afterlife. The places of worship of the Veneti are clearings in the woods, near the waterways, perhaps fenced. Among other things, processions take place there, with songs and dances. Votive offerings consist of cups, bronze ladles, bronzes, and plates.

The Veneti trade with the Greeks, the Etruscans, the Gauls, and the Romans, mainly in Baltic amber, iron, gold, and salt from Noricum, copper from the Balkans, skins, furs, marble, wine, coral, Attic ceramics, and slaves.

Amber is a fossil resin of conifers from the tertiary sector, which fascinates for many reasons: its transparency, warm color, and properties, to which magical, therapeutic, and analgesic virtues are attributed. In fact, if rubbed, amber produces electricity; if heated in your hands, it gives off a pleasant scent. It is commonly believed that it brings good luck and helps to ward off nightmares, delirium, and other diseases, including sore throats; it is also used to detect the presence of poisons in food. This substance is collected from the waves of the sea and after storms on the beaches of the Baltic Sea and the North Sea (mainly along the coasts of the Samland peninsula, near Kaliningrad in Russia, but also in Lithuania, Latvia, Estonia, and Poland), as well as in Sicily (the Sicilian variety of amber, red-orange, red-purplish, or red-brown in color, can be found on the banks of the Simeto River, where it has been harvested since the end of the 4th millennium BC). It is exported because it is considered a precious commodity and a symbol of prestige and wealth. The Baltic amber trade originated in the 2nd millennium BC, mainly in the area between the Elbe, Vltava, and Danube rivers; it reached the Brenner pass or the Resia pass, then Lake Garda, and—across the Mincio river—the Po. In the early stages of the Bronze Age, buyers did not buy pendants so much but primarily vague necklaces of various shapes (spheroidal, discoid, cylindrical) and conical buttons with V-shaped perforations. At the end of the Bronze Age (12th–10th century BC), the main route of amber seems to have moved toward the Morava and the Oder. Following the course of the rivers, the raw product reached the Adriatic through the Soča Valley, and from here continued toward Istria and the Kvarner Bay (Orsini 2010: 21–36, esp. 31–33 with bibliography; Negroni Catacchi 1979: 42). The Proto-Villanovan center of Frattesina di Fratta Polesine (Rovigo), which grew and developed between the 11th and 10th centuries BC on a northern branch of the Po, was an important sorting center for Baltic amber. From there, the processed amber reached Emilia-Romagna, Tuscany, Lazio, the Lipari Islands, Sardinia, and Dalmatia (Croatia), while the raw material reached the island of Cephalonia, Boeotia, the islands of the Saronic Gulf, Crete, Rhodes, and even Ugarit (Syrian coast), carried by Mycenaean merchants, who had come to Frattesina from the Aegean Sea, using coastal navigation to go up the Adriatic. After being processed in Greece, amber returned to the centers of the Upper Adriatic as a finished product. In the Iron Age, the amber trade intensified. In the 8th century BC, the first ambers sculpted with human or animal figures in the context of orientalizing art appeared in Tuscany and Lazio, mainly imported by the Etruscans. A greater increase in the traffic of amber occurred between the 7th and 6th centuries BC, thanks to the activity of Greek artisans who had an orientalizing cultural background. The territory of Adria and Spina, in the second quarter of the 6th century BC and in the 5th and 4th centuries BC, respectively, was the site for the processing and sale of amber. The material was also modeled in the form of small animals, beetles, monkeys, and human figures and exported to the Bocche del Timavo, Istria, and the Kvarner Bay. Between the end of the 4th and the 1st century BC, the trade in amber in the Po valley seems to have decreased due to the invasion of the Gauls. However, Adria continued to be a large market, where, in addition to amber, tin, silver, ceramics, and worked glass were exchanged, also coming from the Danubian-Carpathian area, through the Eastern Alps, or from the coasts of the Black Sea, going up the Danube and the Drava. The name Adria was used by the Greeks to define the Upper Adriatic—Adrias Kolpos (Gulf of Adria)—and, by extension, the entire Adriatic Sea. An artificial canal—the Filistina—connected Adria to a series of lagoons along the entire western coast of the Upper Adriatic (Caput Adriae), from the Po delta to Grado and the Bocche del Timavo.

The Timavo is a very particular river: it originates in the area of Monte Nevoso in Croatia, crosses the Slovenian Karst,[6] sinks into the chasm of San Canzian d'Isonzo, flows underground for 40 km, erupts from the subsoil 2 km from the sea, divides into three branches, and finally flows into the Gulf of Trieste. Its delta is called the Bocche del Timavo and is an area rich in brackish, sweet, and healthy springs, which allow a supply of drinking water. There, the short course of the river and the nearby basin form a peaceful natural harbor, the northernmost landing place in the Adriatic Sea. The Bocche del Timavo, in Protohistory, marked the border between the lands of the Venetian Adriatic, those of the Istri, and those of the Taurisci and were a melting pot of commercial and cultural experiences.[7] There was also a sanctuary of an aquatic deity called Timavo (visitors to the site recognized the presence of the sacred in the unusual phenomenon of water that gushed from the subsoil not as a spring, but as an already-formed river), under whose reassuring gaze trade was practiced, in a general context characterized also and above all by pilgrimages and religious ceremonies.

The memory of two legendary characters is linked to the Bocche del Timavo: Diomedes and Antenor. Diomedes is a character from Greek mythology, a legendary hero, an immortal figure. It is said that he was born and raised in Argos in Argolis (Peloponnese) and that he was one of the main Achaean heroes in the Trojan War and in the War of the Epigones (the sons of the seven leaders who fought against Thebes). Under the protection of Athena, Diomedes wounded the god Ares and the goddess Aphrodite, participated in embassies together with Odysseus (Ulysses), and stole the Palladium. After the Trojan War, he returned to Argos, but he left soon after to escape the plots of his wife, the treacherous Aegialia. He went to Africa, Spain, and Italy. In the 7th–6th century BC, the Greeks made the cult of Diomedes a propaganda tool to establish diplomatic and commercial relations with the indigenous peoples of the Adriatic. Therefore, Diomedes is credited as the one who spread civilization to the islands and continental coasts of the Adriatic Sea. His memory is linked to the foundation of a number of cities of Daunia: Arpi (Arpinova), Canusium (Canosa), Brundisium (Brindisi). The Trojan Antenor is commonly known as the mythical founder of Patavium (Padua) and as the progenitor of the Veneti. Leaving Troy in flames,[8] as part of the group of refugees led by Aeneas in search of a new homeland, he disassociated himself from Aeneas during the journey, together with Aquilius, Clodius, and other refugees, and guided his companions toward the Venetian lagoon, where they founded Patavium, Aquileia, and Clodia (Chioggia).

The Veneti are now divided into the Veneti in the strict sense and the Veneti of the Adriatic. The former are widespread in the Veneto plain, in the Adige valley, and as far as Lake Garda. The others, in the extreme northeast of Italy, north of the Livenza river (nowadays, the Friuli Venezia Giulia).

That part of Italy has always been a sparsely populated area due to the harsh winter climate, the frequent flooding of the numerous waterways that cross it, the presence of wetlands, and the dense forest cover, present not only in the mountains but also in the flatlands. Despite this, some parts of it—in particular, the Middle Friuli, the

Lower Friuli, and the Isonzo area—soon became a meeting place, a welcoming place, and a place for different civilizations to mix. As early as the 2nd millennium BC, two commercial itineraries were intertwined: the Via Ambra, or Via degli Iperborei, along which Baltic amber circulated, and the Via del Ferro, or Via Argonautica, which was traveled by merchants of tin, silver, and raw metallurgical products from Central and Eastern Europe.

In the 4th century BC, the Veneti occupied the entire Friulian plain up to the Tagliamento river. In addition, they have expanded territorially into the Isonzo valley, the Triestine Karst, and the coast of the Gulf of Trieste, beyond the Bocche del Timavo. On the shores of the Gulf of Trieste, they came into contact with a rich substratum of local cultures, accentuating the intercultural characterization of the territory.

Continuing southeast, they reached San Rocco (Muggia), a town located between Val Rosandra and the Ospo. The latter is a modest river, which flows into the sea in the Muggia valley and separates Venezia Giulia (Italy) from Istria (Slovenia and Croatia). There, in a relatively fertile and water-rich area, at the foot of the Karst plateau and on the shores of the Gulf, where the Veneti of the Adriatic, Galli Carni, Istri, other Illyrians, and Pannonians had intertwined relationships since time immemorial, they formed a settlement whose emporium function was reflected in its name, Tergeste, given to it by the Veneti (on Tergeste: Càssola Guida & Càssola 2002; Fraschetti 1975: 319–335; Rossi 1992: 161–167; 2001: 119–139). Tergeste, in fact, is a Venetian word, which derives from the root *terg*, "market", combined with the suffix *-este*.[9]

At the end of the 4th century BC, or at the latest at the beginning of the 3rd century, the Veneti of the Adriatic had to retreat to Lower Friuli due to the expansion of the Galli Carni into Middle Friuli.

Friuli is the majority of present-day Friuli Venezia Giulia, the extreme northeast of Italy; Venezia Giulia is the remainder. Friuli is in turn divided into Lower, Middle and Upper, in order of succession, starting from its sea coast.

It is noteworthy that *Galli* (the singular, *Gallus*; in English: Gauls) is the ethnic name with which the Romans called those peoples who were instead called *keltoi*, "Celts", by the Greeks, with the caveat that the Greeks of Attica, the region of Athens, were calling collectively βαρβάρους (varvárous), "stammerers", the peoples who didn't speak the Attic dialect, and half-varvárous those who spoke the other Greek dialects, that is the Ionic and the Doric. The Romans instead, were calling collectively *barbari*, all the peoples whom they had the historical mission of ruling, protecting, and civilizing, in order to assure peace and justice, and make of the entire mankind a unique *gens*, "only one nation", and of Rome the capital of the world, and the homeland common to all the peoples of the Earth.

The Galli Carni, together with the Veneti, were the pre-Roman peoples of the northeastern corner of Italy (present-day Friuli Venezia Giulia), separated from the rest of Europe by the Carnic Alps and the Julian Alps (beyond which there are today Austria and Slovenia respectively). In order to provide a general framework in this regard, it is necessary to say as follows.

In the high Iron Age (7th–6th centuries BC), the Gauls who lived in the plain of Bavaria had to abandon their fertile lands to escape the pressure of the Germans and came to Italy through the Eastern Alps, settling in the geographic spaces that today correspond to the mountainous areas of Veneto, Trentino, and Upper Adige/South Tyrol, all in Italy, more disadvantaged than those from which they came, but safer.

The other Gauls of Bavaria instead withdrew for the same reason to Switzerland (Canton of Grisons, Engadine), Austria (Salzburg Tyrol, Styria, Carinthia, Carniola), Slovenia, and northeastern Croatia.

In the 4th century BC, or at the latest at the beginning of the 3rd century BC, a tribe of Gaulish migrants, coming from the present-day Carinthia and named Galli Carni, passed over the Carnic Alps and settled in the mountainous areas which separate the extreme northeast of Itay (Friuli Venezia Giulia) from Austria (we refer to the present-day Carnia, Val Canale, and Canale del Ferro). These areas, all together, form the Upper Friuli. Therefore, the Galli Carni came (or expanded) from Carinthia (southern Austria) to Upper Friuli (northeastern Italy). These Gauls gave the name to the current Carnia, where they lived.

Carnia encloses the upper basin of the Tagliamento river and the valleys of the But and Fella rivers, tributaries of the Tagliamento. There are high peaks, dense woods, deep green lakes, bubbling waterfalls, meadows with aromatic and medicinal herbs, and a series of valleys, wide or narrow and recessed, which intertwine with each other. The rich local wildlife also includes deer, chamois, and golden eagles.

It is necessary to specify that the Gauls from Austria settled in Carnia as well as in the rest of Upper Friuli. The Gauls living in Carnia dedicated themselves to mixed agriculture and mountain and craft activities and maintained relationships both with the Veneti and with other Gauls living beyond the Eastern Alps, through whom they imported amber and iron. In the beginning, they either were not attracted by the foothills of Friuli or the Friulian plain or did not have the military skill to occupy them. Later (at the end of the 4th century BC, or at the latest at the beginning of the 3rd century BC), they expanded toward the south—in particular, the Middle Friuli —reaching as far as the Livenza river.

Subsequently, in about 221/220 BC, they also expanded in the Triestine Karts, up to the edge of the lands of the Istri (today the phisical border between Venetia Giulia and Istria is the course of the Ospo river, flowing between Trieste and Muggia, nearer to Muggia).

It seems probable that, on the occasion of the expeditio *ad Alpes* of the consuls Publius Cornelius Scipio Asina and Marcus Minucius Rufus (in 221 BC), and the subsequent consuls Lucius Veturius Filo ad Caius Lutatiius Catulus (in 220 BC), the Romans made a pact with the Galli Carni, which involved the payment of tribute to Rome (Zonar. 20.10; Bandelli 1999: 285–301). This could explain why the Galli Carni, as they were not hostile to the Veneti, their neighbors and allies of the Romans, were not hostile to the Romans in 186 BC.

They maintained this attitude for a long time, cooperating with the Romans and the Veneti on several occasions. A proof of this is that a chieftain named Catmelus led 3,000 Carnic auxiliaries in the Third Istrian War (178–177 BC) in support of the four legions of the proconsul Aulus Manlius Vulso and Marcus Junius Brutus in a march toward Istria.

The good relations between the Galli Carni and the Romans ceased before 115 BC, the year in which the consul Marcus Aemilius Scaurus waged a *blitzkrieg* against the first, subduing them definitively and thus moving the sovereignty of Rome to the watershed of the Carnic Alps.

The Hannibalic War: operations on the Cisalpine front

Cisalpine Gaul was the scene of battles between the Romans, the Carthaginian invaders, and the Cisalpine Gauls allied with the Carthaginians. This happened in the context of the Second Punic War (218–202 BC), also called the Hannibalic War after Hannibal Barca, the Carthaginian general who led the war operations in Europe. The conflict broke out after the capture of Saguntum (Sagunto)—a city on the Spanish coast of the Levant, allied with the Romans—which was the site of an immense massacre after a siege. But the underlying cause of the conflict lay elsewhere. The Romans had taken advantage of the Revolt of the Mercenaries (240–238 BC), which forced Carthage to fight a particularly bitter and bloody war, to snatch Sardinia and Corsica from it and force it to pay 1,200 talents more than the war indemnity that had been imposed on it by the Treaty of Lutatius, which put an end to the First Punic War (264–241 BC). This fueled the desire of the Carthaginians to take revenge, who found in Hannibal Barca the champion who could satisfy this desire.

The Ligurians of the West, living in the Apuan Alps and the Apennines, provide troops to Hannibal, as they hope that he will free them from the oppression of the Romans. The Ligurian Genuati, the Ligurians of the Levant, and the Galli Taurini, on the other hand, maintain their support for the Romans. Even the Galli Cenomani, in 218 BC, fight alongside the Romans against Hannibal. The same year, Hannibal attacks the Taurini and, after a brief siege, takes Taurinia, or Taurasia, the main garrison of the Taurini, or their only "city", probably located at the junction between the Po river and the Dora Riparia (Conchiglietta in Turin).[10] The Genuati participate at the Battle of the Trebbia (18 December 218).

The history of Hannibal's alliance with the Sardinians can be summarized as follows. In 218, therefore immediately after the Roman conquest of Cisalpine Gaul, the Romans founded two colonies in Val Padana—Cremona (Cremona) and Placentia (Piacenza)—with the settlement of 6,000 Roman citizens on each side. These are the first Roman colonies in northern Italy. Both are placed on the Po, on the border of a flat, low plain, in territory confiscated from the Gauls, who in turn had snatched it from the Etruscans, who either had settled there instead of the Ligurians or were strongly influenced by the Ligurians, but were in any case a population of the

Terramare culture.[11] Cremona is on the northern bank and Placentia on the southern one, not far from the point where the Trebbia flows into the Po. Their function is essentially to watch over a ford, and thus to protect the Po from being crossed by the Gauls. Therefore, they are both firmly armed. Cremona was born as an elliptical city, surrounded by ramparts. The local economy is linked to the production and exchange of products from the rich surrounding countryside, especially processed dairy products. Over time, it will diversify its economy. It will resist the assaults of the Gauls and Hannibal. Placentia is characterized by the square layout typical of the castrum. Powerfully fortified, it will be an impregnable bulwark, including at the Battle of the Trebbia, resisting Hannibal.

As for Medhelan (future Mediolanum, today Milan), it falls into the hands of the Romans when they victoriously clash with the Insubri and the Taurini. Meanwhile, the acts of genocide carried out by the Romans against the Ligurians have caused a massive reduction in the indigenous presence in northwestern Italy.

In August 216, Hannibal scores a further victory over the Roman army at the Battle of Cannae in Apulia (Puglia, southeastern Italy). Hannibal has 28,500 heavily armed infantry, 11,500 lightly armed infantry, and 10,000 cavalry, including Phoenician-Punic, Numidian, and Iberian allies and Gallic mercenaries. The Romans have two armies, commanded by the consuls Lucius Aemilius Paullus and Caius Terentius Varro: in all, 16 legions—eight of Roman citizens and eight allied—for a total of 86,000 men, of which 75,000–80,000 are infantrymen, 2,400 are Roman horsemen, and 3,600 are allied horsemen. The fight, unspeakably bitter and bloody, is decided by a pincer maneuver by the Carthaginians. Caught in a vice, the Romans are overwhelmed, with the loss of 86,000 men (70,000 infantry, 6,000 horsemen, and 10,000 prisoners), or, according to another estimate, 67,500 (45,500 infantry, 2,700 cavalry, and 19,300 prisoners). After the battle, some of the Roman fallen are found with their heads stuck in a hole, dug to suffocate for fear of the enemy. The consul Paullus, the quaestors Lucius Atilius and Lucius Furius Bibaculus, 29 military tribunes, some ex-magistrates, including ex-consuls, ex-praetors and ex-builders, and 80–90 senators and eligible magistrates also fell in combat after having signed up as volunteers.

After the Battle of Cannae, the Ligurians and the Galli Boii defeat the army of the consul designate Lucius Postumius Albinus, whom they ambushed (Battle of Silva Litana, 216). The column of Roman soldiers had entered the depths of a forest when the Ligurians and the Boii drop the trees they had previously sawed through, precariously balanced to remain standing. As in a game of dominoes, the trees collapse one after the other from the right and left of the path, burying the soldiers. A situation of unspeakable confusion is created, in which those Romans who have not been crushed by the trees fight to the limit not to be captured and are killed. Some, including Albinus, try to escape by fleeing but are caught near a bridge (Liv. 23.10–11). The Gauls capture the equipment, armaments, and all the various materials of the army left under the trees, and, according to Celtic use, they cut off the heads of the dead enemies to make trophies. Albinus' skull is stripped and becomes a cup encrusted with gold, to be used in the rites of the Celtic religion.

Also in 216, the Sardinians rise up against the Romans under the leadership of Hampsicora and win a battle at Su Campu 'e corra, near the city of Cornus (near modern Cuglieri). However, they are later defeated by Titus Manlius Torquatus, who came from Rome to replace the praetor Quintus Mucius Scaevola, who had fallen ill, probably with malaria. In that clash, 3,000 Sardinians lose their lives and almost 800 are taken prisoner. The surviving Sardinians take refuge in Cornus. In 215, a Carthaginian expeditionary force—15,000 soldiers, commanded by Hasdrubal the Bald—land in Sardinia and, together with the Sardinians of Hampsicora, wage battle with Torquatus north of Caralis (Cagliari), in the southern part of the Campidano plain (between Decimomannu and Sestu). The Battle of Decimomannu ends with the victory of the Romans. Twelve thousand Sardinians and Carthaginians are killed, including the son of Hampsicora, Hiostus, while another 3,700 are taken prisoner. Hasdrubal is also captured, together with the noble Hanno, a Punic from Tharros, who had led the revolt with Hampsicora. The same can be said for a member of the Barca family named Mago. Hampsicora manages to save himself with some knights but, upon hearing of the death of his son, taken by desperation, he commits suicide. The survivors find protection and refuge in Cornus. But Cornus' resistance only lasts a few days. Shortly after, the other cities that supported the revolt also surrender, with the delivery of hostages. Torquatus demands the Sardinians pay tribute in money and grain to Rome and returns to Caralis, from where he will sail to Rome. The remains of the Carthaginian expeditionary force embark in a hurry to return to North Africa but are intercepted at sea by a Roman fleet, which attacks and routs them. Subsequently, the Senate of Rome sends two legions to Sardinia to complete the repression of the revolt and ensure that there are no others that could bring the island back to the side of the Carthaginians.

Meanwhile, the Romans are also advancing in the northeast. They have the Veneti as allies. The Veneti are always on the side of the Romans and help them whenever they can, both because they have understood their strength and because they are in some ways similar to them. In fact, they pride themselves on having in common with the Romans the fact that they are descended from a Trojan refugee: Antenor. In turn, the Romans trace their ancestry to the Trojan Aeneas, prince of the Dardans and hero of the Trojan War. Aeneas is the focal point of the intertwining of the Trojan myth and the legend of the origins of Rome.[12] The same can be said for his son Ascanius, or Iulus, founder and first ruler of the city of Alba Longa and founder of the dynasty of Alban kings. A few centuries after the founding of Alba Longa, a member of the royal family of that city named Romulus founded Rome and became its first king.

The First Macedonian War (215–205 BC)

In 217 BC, after Hannibal Barca had defeated the Roman army at the Battle of Lake Trasimene, Philip V, on the advice of Demetrius of Pharos, makes peace with the Aetolian League (Peace of Naupactus), allies himself with Hannibal, and arms a fleet to conduct operations in the Adriatic Sea against Rome. At the moment, Rome is busy on other fronts. It has just achieved a definitive victory over the Ligurians and is trying to regain control of the situation in Sardinia and Corsica, where a rebellion had broken out, reflecting the Ligurian War.

Aetolia is a region of the northwestern part of the Peloponnese (Greece), bordering Acarnania, Dolopia, and Locris. Its cities, in the 4th century, federated to defend themselves from the expansionist aims of the Kingdom of Macedon. Thus was born the Aetolian League, which still persists today. The political institutions of the Aetolian League are an assembly made up of all citizens aged over 30 and of free-standing and a *strategos*. The assembly meets in the spring and fall, makes the laws, and annually elects the *strategos*, who presides over the League and commands the army. The *strategos* is assisted by a council of 30 members and by some minor magistrates. In 279 BC, the Aetolian League, after having helped to repel the Great Expedition of the Celts in Greece, became part of the Delphic Amphictyony[13] and acquired very considerable power and political weight, which allowed it to get bigger. It thus ended up embracing Acarnania, Phocis, Locris, Boeotia, Elis, Messenia, and the city of Megalopolis in Arcadia.

The Aetolian League is the enemy of the Achaean League, an alliance of Greek cities that was formed in the 5th century in Achaea (a region of the north-central Peloponnese), refounded in 281/280, and then extended to other cities, such as Sicyon (251), Corinth (243), Megalopolis (235), and Argos (229). In 241, it supports Antigonus II Gonatas in his war against the Achaean League, when Aratus of Sicyon is the *strategos*, but is defeated in Pellene in Achaea. In 229, the Cleomenean War broke out. In 222, the Aetolian League is forced to ask the Macedonian king Antigonus III Doson for help to fight the Spartans at Sellasia. The Spartans are defeated, and their king Cleomenes III is forced to flee. The Macedonians, through the Achaean League, re-establish their control over the Peloponnese. In 220, Philip V convenes a Panhellenic conference in Corinth, in which he condemns the Aetolian aggression. In 219, the Aetolian League clashes with Philip V and the Achaean League in the Social War.

In 215, Marcus Valerius Laevinus (who was consul in 220) is a pilgrim praetor, and therefore he deals with the disputes between foreigners present in Rome and between Roman citizens and foreigners. But the demands of the Hannibalic War require that all civic magistrates also exercise military command. Therefore, Laevinus receives both the command of the legions just returned from Sicily and the command of 25 ships with the task of controlling Puglia and the coast between Brundisium (Brindisi) and Tarentum (Taranto), as well as the movements of the Macedonians in view of a possible war against their king Philip V, the strongest monarch in the Hellenistic world. Philip watches the expansion of Rome into Illyria with dismay, as this hinders his plan to take over the Greek cities of central Dalmatia and give Macedon an outlet on the Adriatic Sea.

The defeat at Cannae changes the perception of Roman power that exists beyond the Adriatic, with the effect of tarnishing its image. Philip takes advantage of this by stipulating a treaty of alliance and mutual aid with Hannibal. The agreement suits

Hannibal because it opens a second front in Illyria, and it suits Philip because it aims to expel the Romans from any place east of the Adriatic and give him command over the Greek cities of Central Dalmatia. In 215, a war breaks out between the Kingdom of Macedon and the Achaean League on one side and Rome on the other. Philip goes on the offensive in Epirus (First Macedonian War, 214–205 BC), conquering the city of Oricum and besieging Apollonia. Without hesitation, Laevinus crosses the Adriatic, recaptures Oricum, breaks the siege of Apollonia, and takes over the camp of the besiegers. Philip is forced to retire to Macedonia. Meanwhile, the Achaean League is fighting in the Peloponnese due to border disputes, mainly between Megalopolis and Messene, Sparta's attempts to regain the influence and territories it lost with the defeat of Cleomenes III at Sellasia, and its conflicts with the cities and the confederations that challenge its hegemonic position, especially Sparta, Elis, and Messene. In 214, Demetrius of Pharos attempts to take Messene, a well-fortified Doric city-state located in Laconia (Peloponnese), but he meets his death in the attempt.[14]

Laevinus' command is confirmed three times in a row. In 214, he remains quartered in Oricum. In 213, 212, and 211, he controls the movements of Philip in Aetolia and Achaea with 50 ships and a legion. In the fall of 212, he makes an agreement with the Aetolian League against Philip; in the meantime, the latter has taken the important port of Lissus (Lesh), thus gaining access to the Adriatic and control of the adjacent territories. The agreement attributes all the conquered areas north of Aetolia to the Aetolians and all the prisoners and spoils of war, respectively, to the Romans; the cities that surrender will become part of the Aetolian state, maintaining their autonomy. The treaty expressly excludes that either party may conclude a separate peace and provides that other states may also be part of the alliance. In fact, shortly after, Attalus I (241–197 BC), King of Pergamon, joins Rome and the Aetolian League; he will fight against Prusias I (228–182 BC), King of Bithynia.

In 211, Laevinus expels the Macedonians from the island of Zakynthos and from Aenias and Nasus in Acarnania and is elected to the consulate for the second time (for 210). In 210, he takes Anticyra in Phocis (today Boeotia), which he will leave to the Aetolians, keeping the spoils of war he has won from his sack. However, he then falls ill. He will be replaced by Publius Sulpicius Galba Maximus and will return to Rome, where, once recovered, he will be appointed governor of Sicily.

In 209, the Achaean League finds a strong and decisive leader in Philopoemen (Aratus of Sicyon died in 214, perhaps poisoned by order of Philip V). Philopoemen reorganizes the League's army. Meanwhile, Machanidas, a man of obscure origins, deposes the child-king Pelops from the throne of Sparta, becomes regent, and sacks the Peloponnese as far as Olympia. Philopoemen confronts Machanidas in battle at Mantinea and kills him (207 BC). Machanidas' successor is Nabis, another adventurer of dark origins, who continues his predecessor's expansionist policy until he is defeated by Philopoemen at the Battle of Tegea in 201 and leaves the scene.

In 207, Placentia resists Hasdrubal, and Hannibal's brother, Mago, besieges Placentia, but the city resists, and he will not be able to conquer it.

Meanwhile, Scerdilaidas, Agron's brother and Pinnes's uncle, has succeeded the latter on the throne of *regnum Illyricum* (212). Faithful ally of the Romans against Philip V, he has associated his son Pleuratus with the throne. It is included in the treaty between Rome and Aetolia (212). He dies in 205 before the Peace of Phoenice puts an end to the First Macedonian War. That treaty is signed in 205 after the Aetolian League had signed a separate peace with Philip (206), forced by the latter, in violation of the treaty with Rome. On the one hand, it confirms the Roman protectorate over the Greek communities of the coast of the eastern Adriatic and the Partini and, on the other, it cedes the territory of the Atintani to Philip. The result of the war is, therefore, the restoration of the status quo ante. In practice, Philip failed to expel the Romans from the Illyrian coast.

In 205 BC, Mago Barca, Hannibal's brother, leads the Carthaginian fleet against Genua (Genova), seizes it, and plunders and destroys it.[15] He will bring the spoils of war to Savo (Savona), the management center of the Ligurian Sabazi, after which he will sail to Carthage, which is under threat from the army of Publius Cornelius Scipio, the future Africanus.

The first years following the Peace of Phoenice are characterized by a climate of good relations between the Istri and the Illyrians and between the Istri and the Romans. Relations between the Romans and the Macedonians, however, remain very bad. Philip V did not put aside his resentment toward them, nor did he renounce control of Illyria forever. No longer having to defend himself from the Romans and the Aetolians, he can, however, turn his attention elsewhere. In 204, he authorizes the Aetolian Dicearcus to wage a private war against the communities of the Greek islands and to support Crete in its war against Rhodes. This is followed by the deception of Heraclides of Tarentum, an adventurer in the service of Philip, at the expense of the Republic of Rhodes, which costs the latter the loss of its arsenals and damage to the fleet (Polyb. 13.13.4–5; 18.54.7–12). In 202, Philip moves his fleet toward Thrace and the region of the Straits. He sacks several city-states, all allies of the Aetolian League: Lysimachia and Perinthus, both located in Thrace, one on the Gallipoli Peninsula, the other on the European coast of the Sea of Marmara; and Chalcedon (Kadıköy, now a district of Istanbul) and Kyos (Gemlik), both located on the Asian coast of the Sea of Marmara, the former opposite Byzantion (Istanbul), the latter on the shores of the Gulf of Gemlik. He destroys Kyos, after which he delivers it, together with the city of Myrlea, to Prusias I, King of Bithynia, who has been an ally of Macedon since the time of Demetrius II Aetolicus, whose daughter he married (Polyb. 15.22.5–23, 9). This causes the Aetolians to resume hating him (Polyb. 15.22.5–23.9). Later, Philip V rages against the island of Thasos (northern Aegean Sea) (Polyb. 15.24) and, later on, the Cyclades. Finally, he seizes the Ptolemaic fleet in Samos. The Republic of Rhodes and the Kingdom of Pergamon react: Philip V defeats the Republic of Rhodes at the Battle of Lade (201 BC) and clashes with the Kingdom of Pergamon in the Battle of Chios (201 BC), which has an uncertain outcome. Then he invades the Kingdom of Pergamon and takes possession of some cities in Perea Rhodia and Caria, and although he is blocked by the Rhodian and Pergamene fleets in the Gulf of Bargylia, he manages to get out, thanks to the help of Zeuxis, a Seleucid satrap in Asia Minor (Polyb. 16.1.8–9, 24).

The Second Macedonian War (200–197 BC)

In 200 BC, the Second Macedonian War breaks out between Rome and its allies—Attalus I, King of Pergamon, the Republic of Rhodes, and the Aetolian League (which in the meantime has returned to the side of the Romans)—on one side, and Philip V of Macedon and his ally Prusias I, King of Bithynia, on the other. In the agitated moments that preceded the outbreak of the conflict, diplomats of Athens and Rhodes were involved in negotiations that aimed at averting it.

In 197, Pleuratus II (205–180 BC), son and successor of Scerdilaidas, gave the Romans a hand in helping the offensive in Macedonia. The war ends in the same year with the evacuation by Philip of every Greek city still in his possession, both in Europe and in Asia. In the summer of 196, in Corinth, during the inauguration ceremony of the Isthmian Games, in the presence of thousands of people coming from all parts of Greece, the consul Titus Quintius Flamininus solemnly and unexpectedly announces the liberation and political independence of the whole of Greece, arousing scenes of indescribable joy and enthusiasm, as well as disappointment among the ranks of the Aetolian League, which had expansionist aims in Thessaly.

The Gallic War (200–191 BC)

After the Second Punic War (218–202 BC), the Insubri and the Boii, with the addition of the Cenomani, who broke away from the Romans, rise up against the latter, and the Ligurians are also involved.[16] The first sign of the revolt occurs in 200 BC, when 40,000 Gauls, between Insubri, Ligurians, Cenomani, and Boii, led by a Carthaginian named Hamilcar, attack Placentia and take it with a huge massacre (only 2,000 inhabitants remain alive, and they will be taken prisoner). The city is sacked and burned and suffers serious damage. Then the Gauls go to Cremona, but the city resists and asks the praetor Lucius Furius Purpureo, who is in Ariminum (Rimini), for help. The latter has only 5,000 men, so the request for help is forwarded to the Senate of Rome, which will send the requested reinforcements. At the same time, the Senate of Rome sends a protest note to Carthage. It asks for the delivery of Hamilcar. The Carthage government says it cannot comply with the request but will be able to condemn Hamilcar to exile and the confiscation of his assets. A battle takes place between the Gauls and the Romans near Cremona. The Romans win, inflicting a loss of 35,000 men on the Gauls. Hamilcar and three other commanders, taken prisoner, are killed. Placentine prisoners are released.

In 199 BC, the Insubri, the Boii, and the Cenomani take revenge on the Romans, defeating the new praetor, Cnaeus Bebius Tamfilus, in the lands of the Insubri.[17] In 198, Gallia Cisalpina is calm again, and the former Placentine prisoners are convinced to return to their city to repopulate and rebuild it. In 197, the consul Quintus Minucius Rufus devastates the lands of the Boii, south of the Po, incinerating crops, villages, highlands, and farms. The Boii, who have recently given support to the Insubri, ask the Insubri and Cenomani to help them defend their lands, but they do not move. The episode undermines the "national solidarity" of the Gauls, who, therefore, split up. The Boii return to their lands, while the Insubri and Cenomani camp on the banks of the Mincio river. The consul Caius Cornelius Cethegus, the colleague of Rufus, arrives and convinces the Cenomani to return to the embrace of Rome, having discovered that the Cenomani youth have taken up their weapons against the will of the elders.[18] Therefore the Cenomani detach themselves from the Insubri. This leads to the Battle of the Mincio River, which is fought between the Insubri, commanded by Corolamus, and the Romans, and ends with the victory of the latter and a toll of thousands of dead and thousands of prisoners. Many Gallic village communities surrender to the Romans. Thus ends the revolt of the Gauls, which began in 200 BC. Cethegus celebrates a triumph in Rome, parading the spoils of war, including the prisoners and the Placentines who had been enslaved by the Gauls and had been freed by him. Meanwhile, his co-consul Rufus has tried in vain to induce the Boii to confront his legions in the open field, though without succeeding, because each community of Boii villagers prefers to stand apart on its own, separately from the others, and so he continues to plunder their lands.

In 196, the army of consul Marcus Claudius Marcellus is setting up camp in the territory of the Boii when it is attacked by the Boii. Three thousand men lose their lives in the fight. Shortly after, Marcellus leaves the lands of the Boii, crosses the Po, and invades the lands of the Insubri, heading for Como, their main center. The Insubri attack him while he is on the march but are repelled. Como and the 28 highland settlements that surround it surrender to the Romans (Marcellus accumulates important spoils of war, which he will dedicate in part to the Temple of Jupiter Capitolinus in Rome). Marcellus and his colleague, Lucius Furius Purpureo, then return to the lands of the Boii, which they will devastate as far as Bononia (Bologna). Most of the Boii give up. Then Marcellus and Purpureo attack the Ligurians, but the Boii secretly follow them, set up ambushes, and carry out sudden attacks. This puts the Romans in difficulty, as their military organization is suitable for fighting in the open field, not for opposing guerrillas. The Boii go to the lands of the Levi and the Libui, north of the Po, in search of booty, then they return to attack the Romans, but they are massacred. In 195, the Boii are again defeated near the Silva Litana.

In 194, the Boii, under the guidance of Dorulatus, cross the Po and manage to bring the Insubri back to their side, together with whom, under the guidance of Boiorix, the successor of Dorulatus, they wage battle near Medhlan. However, they are defeated by Lucius Valerius Flaccus, who was consul in 195. The Insubri lay down their arms and become allies of the Romans again, while the Boii continue the fight.

In 193, the Ligurians devastate the territory but are disastrously defeated under the walls of Medhlan (Mediolanum, Milan) by the consuls Lucius Cornelius Merula and Quintus Minucius Thermus (Liv. 35.4–6). After that, the consuls turn against the Boii again. When, finally, the Boii agree to clash with the Romans in a pitched battle, they are massacred (Battle of Modena). In 192, the Romans return to devastate the lands of the Boii, and the latter surrender in part (namely, the council of elders, the knights, and other personalities; the young people take up arms for the purpose of looting and retreat to inaccessible forests, where they will resist) (Liv. 35.22.4–35.40.3). The Boii are definitively defeated in 191 by the consul Publius Cornelius Scipio Nasica, who, in exchange for peace, obtains hostages. Scipio Nasica confiscates half of the lands of the vanquished and then celebrates a triumph in Rome. The Romans carry out unprecedented massacres in the lands of the Boii, leaving only the elderly and children alive. Some of the survivors are relegated to peripheral areas of Emilia, others are expelled from Italy and emigrate to Bohemia, where they will live in contact with the Taurisci (for the emigration of the Boii to Bohemia: Strab. 5.1.213).

The Romanization of Gallia Transpadana[19]

The Romans treated the Insubri and the Cenomani completely differently. They do not carry out any military or political-social intervention against them, nor confiscations of any kind; they do not modify their social order (the order of the communities remains unchanged, the hierarchies remain the same), nor the territorial structures (no Roman road will cross their lands), and they will respect their choices. All this is done in order to protect their territorial and social assets. The *foedera* stipulated between the Romans and the Insubri and the Cenomani only provide that the latter pay the *tributum* to Rome and provide it with support troops. They expressly exclude the granting of Roman citizenship to individuals and groups, even to support troops who particularly distinguished themselves in battle.

In 190 BC, the Senate of Rome sends reinforcement to Placentia and Cremona. The operation has the meaning and value of a new foundation. The main beneficiary is Cremona. This colony will become an obligatory point of reference for the Transpadan economy, which is also in contact with the ports of the Upper Adriatic, through which it imports Mediterranean products, wine, and especially oils from Puglia, from other production centers of the Adriatic, and from Rhodes. Its market, specialized in the trade of livestock, will attract merchants from all over Italy (but especially from Insubria, home to large pig farms), as only that of Campi Macri, near Mutina (Modena), is otherwise able to do. Cremona will also become a large artisan production center, specialized in the production of architectural terracotta bricks and fine Italian traditional tableware (see, for example, its black glazed pottery, used both to form funerary kits and in daily life). Its finished products and related technologies will spread throughout Cisalpine Gaul through the Po valley's waterways, which are the "infrastructure" through which the bulk of the valley's trade takes place. Due to the Romanizing effect on local traditions of the peaceful diffusion of objects, ideas, and ways of life, Cremona will become the center of radiation of the Romanization of the Transpadana area. One aspect of this process will be the spread of the monetary economy.

With the final victory of Scipio Nasica over the Boii, Felsina, as well as the other surrounding fortresses and almost all the Boii, submit to the Romans who had roamed the lands of the Boii, sacking them.[20] On 30 December 189, the Senate of Rome decides to refound Felsina as a colony of Latin law called Bononia (Bologna). The aim of the enterprise is to defend the new northern border of Roman Italy. It will be completed by the triumvirs Lucius Valerius Flaccus, Marcus Atilius Serranus, and Lucius Valerius Tappo, with 3,000 settlers. Among the participants, the *equites* (knights) will receive 70 *iugera* of land, the others 50.[21] With the founding of the colony, the city will be significantly enlarged and equipped with public facilities, such as a theater, a basilica, and a temple complex.

In 187, the consuls Marcus Aemilius Lepidus and Caius Flaminius employ the army in the construction of two extra-urban roads: the Via Aemilia and the Via Flaminia Minor (also called the Via Flaminia Secunda, or Altera, or Militaris). The former will connect Ariminum and Placentia and will coincide with the new northern border of Roman Italy. The latter will unite Bononia and Arretium. Both serve to enhance the newly acquired territories but also to make them safe and stable, as well as to control the stretch of the Apennines occupied by the Ligurians.

Colonies are the most effective tool that Rome uses to consolidate its control over the territory in its newly acquired lands. But what are they? What does it mean?

The colonies of the Romans

A city-state is a community of citizens who exercise sovereignty over a city and its territory. The Romans, first under the monarchy and then under the res publica, founded various political organizations of this type in the lands confiscated from the vanquished that were then classified as *ager publicus populi romanorum* ("state property"). They call them *coloniae*. In theory, the *coloniae* are politically independent organizations. In practice, they are closely linked to Rome by one or more international treaties (Latin *foedus*, pl. *foedera*), which regulate trade, defense, and external relations and both impose the obligation to provide Rome with military aid in the event of war and play a strategic-defensive, economic and political role, compatible with its general interest. Therefore, the *coloniae* have their own political institutions, but they depend on the motherland for external projection and its foreign policy.

The institutions we are talking about may differ from each other, but more often than not, they mirror their correspondents in Rome to varying degrees. In fact, they consist of civic magistracies, one popular assembly, and a Senate. The civic magistrates of a colony exercise administrative functions and administer justice. There are two of them, and they are called duumvirs, or *duoviri*. The popular assembly makes the laws. The Senate—a college of former and current magistrates—deals with foreign policy and state administration.

The foundation of a colony is the happy outcome of an enterprise promoted and organized by the Roman state, in the execution of a law approved by the Roman people gathered in an assembly, on the proposal of the Senate of Rome. The enterprise aims to repopulate a territory that has been confiscated from a conquered people and become the collective property of the Roman people; to control it and defend it from external threats; to enhance its resources in an economic key; and to establish a military stronghold or a commercial center in the territory of friendly and allied people, in agreement with the latter. The law identifies the portion of the territory to be attributed to the new foundation and the size of the colonial contingent. Usually, the latter is made up of Roman citizens, other Latins, and Italics in numbers between 2,000 and 6,000. Mostly, these are people from low social backgrounds, enticed to participate in the business by the possibility of acquiring an economic autonomy that they know they could not acquire otherwise. Once the enterprise has been completed, they will receive a plot of arable land in the colony's territory. The Senate of Rome entrusts the management and responsibility of the colonial contingent to the *triumviri deducendae coloniae*, that is, to three magistrates whose sphere of competence embraces the material preparation of the enterprise, the actual transfer of the colonists, the establishment in the strict sense of the colony, the drafting of the laws and general rules for the administration of the city, and the operations connected with the election of decurions.

Usually, the foundation of the colony is preceded by the execution of deforestation and reclamation works, which are all the more necessary and indispensable when the territory to be colonized is covered by a dense forest with some clearings, rich in streams and ponds, marshes, and swamps. This is followed by the planning of the territory to be attributed to the colony for the purpose of the subsequent assignment of the lots to the settlers, the arrangement of the same lots, and the calculation of any taxes to be levied. The most common territorial planning model consists of tracing a network in the territory formed by systems of parallel and orthogonal roads, which separate square modules of 710 m on each side. The roads with a north–south orientation are called *cardines*; those that are oriented east–west, *decumani*. The model distinguishes between the territory to be attributed to the city, the agriculture to be cultivated, the agriculture to be kept for community use, the part of the territory to be reserved for indigenous people, the border area, the portions of land to be allocated to the infrastructural system, and improvement work necessary for the implementation of the soil management program. These technical operations are carried out by surveyors and require considerable expertise.

The urban center of the colony develops according to a unitary project, usually in the typical quadrilateral shape of a military camp, with the *cardo maximus* oriented in a north–south direction and the *decumanus maximus* oriented in an east–west direction. The intersection of the main and secondary streets creates a network in which each square or rectangle is a block (*insula*) and in which the dwellings, the shops of the traders, the workshops of the craftsmen, and all the public buildings of the city are located: temples, institutional headquarters, buildings intended for public performances (theater, amphitheater), headquarters of corporations, other buildings and monuments, barracks, prisons, baths, public latrines, and gyms for physical education of youths.[22] Often the internal streets are paved and/or flanked by arcades. Under the street level, the sewers run in brick tunnels with a vaulted roof; they are accessible through manholes for cleaning operations.[23] The center of the city is the area of the Forum. This is located at the intersection of the *decumanus maximus* and the *cardo maximus* and consists of a paved square surrounded by arcades, temples, office buildings, thermopolia (places where anyone can eat and drink for a fee), inns, and shops and is crowded with tombstones, statues, and reliefs, which have the function of preserving the collective memory of the inhabitants, the memory of past glories. Among the facades of buildings overlooking the square, there are those of the Temple of Jupiter Capitolinus, the building of the *duoviri iure dicundo*, the building of the aediles, the Curia, the market, the office of weights and measures, etc. The Forum is the beating heart of the civil and religious life of every Roman city. It is a meeting place for ordinary citizens, entrepreneurs, and merchants. Electoral rallies, trials, ceremonies take place there, and laws and decrees are declared in it.[24]

In particular: the colonies of Latin law

Roman law distinguishes between Roman colonies and colonies of Latin law. The difference is in the type of citizenship attributed to the single colony by its founding law.

In the event that the colonial enterprise aims at the foundation of a Roman colony, then those colonists who do not already possess full Roman citizenship (*civitas*) acquire it automatically as participants in the enterprise. If, on the other hand, it is aimed at the foundation of a colony under Latin law, the colonists will keep, or will automatically acquire, a different type of citizenship, so-called *latinitas*.

Latinitas is partial citizenship, *i.e.* reduced citizenship (compared to *civitas*), but it is a privileged condition with respect to non-citizens, as it recognizes the right to marry a Roman man or woman (within certain limits), the right to trade with Roman citizens, and the right to vote (exercisable in a tribe drawn by lots if the Latin colonist is in Rome on election day); moreover, if the Latin colonist moves to Rome or to a Roman colony, he will be able to acquire *civitas*.

Depending on whether it has been given *civitas* or *latinitas*, a city founded *ex novo* in the *ager publicus* will be a colony of Roman law or a colony of Latin law, and its citizens will enjoy full citizenship or partial citizenship. Furthermore, by virtue of the possession of *latinitas*, the single colony of Latin law will enjoy, within certain limits, the right to self-government. Participants in a company aimed at the foundation of a colony governed by Latin law automatically acquire *latinitas*; if they are in possession of *civitas* upon departure, they will lose it and will have to settle for *latinitas*. *Civitas* and *latinitas* can also be acquired after the foundation of the colony by an interested party who did not participate in the foundation under certain conditions. Both *civitas* and *latinitas* are transmitted from father to son, unless one passes from one to the other or the holder has been deprived of it because he has been found guilty of a crime punishable by deprivation of citizenship, understood as an accessory penalty.

The colony of Latin law is an institution that Rome inherited from the Latin League, dissolved in 338 BC. It is still in use in 181–180 BC. After 180 BC, all the new foundations of Rome will be Roman colonies.

Notes

1   Polyb. 2.16.8: "rich in a volume of water no less than that of any river in Italy, because all the watercourses that descend to the plain flow into it from all over the Alps and the Apennines."

2   The Ligurians were the oldest people in Europe, just as the Scythians were the oldest people in the East and the Ethiopians were the oldest people in Africa. Their origins, therefore, are lost in the mists of time. They appear in the mythology of the Greeks. Jason and the Argonauts, during their pilgrimage across the rivers of Europe (Danube, Po, Reno, Rhone), cross the territories of the Ligurians (and the territory of the Celts), hiding from the enemy thanks to a god who sends fog. The Ligurians also appear in a legend of the origins of Rome. Together with a few other populations, they join the Latin king and the group of Trojan refugees led by Aeneas in the war against the Rutuli. A group of Trojan refugees founds Genua (Genoa) when the leaders of the Ligurians are Cunarus and the young Cupavo, son and successor of Cycnus. The Ligurian king Cycnus also appears in the mythology of the Romans. He is a good friend, or lover, of Phaeton, son of the solar divinity Helios and of an Oceanid, and he cries for him when he falls from the sky near the Eridano (Po) river. Having driven the flaming chariot of the sun for a day, he is struck by a lightning bolt from Zeus, who was shocked by the destruction caused by Phaeton for getting too close to Earth. Cycnus is a talented musician and, after his own death, he is transformed into a swan by Apollo. The Ligurians are originally from the Italian region that took the name Liguria from them, as did the sea that bathes it (Ligurian Sea), located between the Tyrrhenian Sea and the Gulf of Lion. In around 2000 BC, they expanded territorially both to the south, up to the Apuan area, and to the north, up to Piedmont, remaining however south of the Po, as well as in the Western Alps, Provence, and the Languedoc. In Provence, they met the Celts and mingled with them, giving life to the Celtic-Ligurians. The Ligurians also expanded into the Iberian Peninsula, driving out the Sicans from their lands near the Sicanus River. In the beginning, therefore, the lands of the Ligurians extended from Tuscany to southern Spain. However, it seems that some of the Ligurians lived in Germany. Subsequently, new migratory waves—of Italics, Veneti and Celts—forced the Ligurians to retreat to their area of origin, but the Celtic-Ligurians remained where they were. This explains why, since protohistory, a relatively homogeneous and continuous environmental, social and cultural system has extended between the Rhone and the Adige.

3   The political organization of the Etruscans was a confederation and linked the following cities to each other: Caisra (Caere, Cerveteri), Tarchna (Tarquinia), Velch (Vulci), Veii (Veio), Velzna (Volsinii, Bolsena), Clevsi (Clusium, Chiusi), Aritim (Arretium, Arezzo), Perusna (Perusia, Perugia), Rusel (Rusellae, Roselle), Vetl (Vetluna, Vetulonia), Velathri (Volaterrae, Volterra), and Velzna (Volsinii, Bolsena).

4   The city of Alalia was founded in the 6th century by a group of refugees from Phokaya, a Greek city in Asia Minor, who had left it to escape the military pressure of Cyrus the Great, King of Persia.

5   Originally, Este was located on the banks of the Adige. In 589, however, a great flood of the river changed its course, moving it further south. Padua developed on a bend in the Brenta, which is now filled by the Bacchiglione.

6   The Karst is a rocky, limestone plateau that extends between Italy (Friuli Venezia Giulia, the provinces of Trieste and Gorizia), western Slovenia, and Croatia, starting from the foot of the Julian Prealps to the Adriatic Sea and then continuing into western Slovenia and northern Istria, up to the Velebit massif (extreme northwest of Croatia). The Trieste Karst is also called the Classical Karst. It is full of various sized caves, among which the most famous are the Grotta Gigante, the Grotta delle Torri di Slivia, and the Grotte di San Canziano, all in Italy, and the Postojna caves in Slovenia.

7   A quantity of material belonging to an advanced phase of the later Iron Age (7th or 6th century), the Roman Age and the Middle Ages emerged during the dredging of the Locavaz Canal (where the numerous finds were sedimented in the layers of slime), in the III Ramo del Timavo, the easternmost (where a stratified deposit has been brought to light), and in the nearby site of Moschenizze. The findings document a non-homogeneous cultural picture, which takes us back to the Veneti of the Adriatic, to the Istri, the southeastern Galli Carni, and the Taurisci.

8   Troy was a city-state in Asia Minor. It was located on the Asian coast of the Dardanelles, in a place now called Truva.

9   It is uncertain whether Tergeste was an emporium founded and managed by the Veneti of the Adriatic or a market frequented by the Veneti. The fact that Tergeste is a Venetian toponym, however, supports the former hypothesis.

10   Later, with the displacement of the front of the Hannibalic War in Central Italy and with the defeat of its Gallic allied troops (the Ligurians of the West), the central area of Piedmont was slowly integrated into the Roman empire. In Val di Susa and Val Chisone, the Kingdom of the Cozii (named after one of their sovereigns), an ally of Rome, was formed, and it formally retained its independence until the end of the 1st century.

11   A technology complex mainly of the central Po valley, in Emilia-Romagna, northern Italy, dating to the Middle and Late Bronze Age (c. 1700–1150 BC).

12   The myth of Aeneas, in the Augustan Age (27 BC–14 AD), became the subject of the *Aeneid*, an epic poem by Virgil, though it had already existed for many centuries before, during which it underwent numerous changes and additions, which had in common the fact that, uniquely among the great heroes of the Trojan War, Aeneas had had a future. Therefore, the *Aeneid* is only a variant of that myth, albeit the most authoritative. The fundamental difference between the Virgilian variant and the others is that Aeneas is not seen as the one who founds a new city of Troy on the ruins of the old one but as the descendant of Dardanus, son of Coritus, king of the homonymous city-state of maritime Etruria, and as the origin of the process that will lead to the foundation of a city in the area of origin of the Troadic lineage, that is, central Tyrrhenia, destined to be the fulcrum of a millenary empire. See Publio Virgilio Marone 2012; Bettini and Lentano 2013 (with its extensive bibliography).

13   In ancient Greece, an amphictyony is a league of states having in common the cult of a particular divinity, whose feast they celebrate together.

14   The walls of Messene were strengthened by towers with slits and were accessible through four doors, including the monumental Arcadian Gate. Built in the 4th century, they were one of the most significant examples of Greek military construction.

15   Genua was rebuilt by the Romans.

16   This is discussed in detail in books 31 to 36 of the *Histories* of Livy.

17   The Cenomani continued to waver in their relations with the Romans after 197. Their insurrection of 116 was bloodily suppressed by Quintus Marcius Rex.

18   Liv. 42.30.6: *non ex auctoritate seniorum inventutem in armis esse.*

19   Romanization is defined as the set of processes of assimilation, acculturation, and integration that were imposed by the Romans on the enemies they had subdued in order to transform them into friends and allies. Their integration into the imperium—in Latin, *societas*, "alliance"—took

place through the stipulation of a bilateral contract, called *foedus* (pl. *foedera*). The *foedus* obliged Rome to help the *socius* in the event of an enemy attack and the *socius* to provide food and support troops to Rome to contribute to its military expenses, including expenses for the safety of the members. One aspect of Romanization was the granting of Roman citizenship. This happened gradually. Initially, with the exclusion of the right to vote. Later, with the recognition of that right as well. Usually, the community in the process of Romanization that had obtained Roman citizenship without suffrage became a prefecture; that is, it was administered by a prefect, who acted on behalf of a praetor. When, later, it obtained full Roman citizenship, it became a *municipium*.

20 Liv. 33.37.4: *Inde iunctis exercitibus primum Boiorum agrum usque ad Felsinam oppidum populante peragraverunt. Ea urbs ceteraque circa castella et Boi fere omnes praeter iuventutem, quae praedandi causa in armis erat - tunc in devias silvas recesserat - in deditionem venerunt.*

21 Liv. 37.57.7: *Eodem anno ante tertium Kal. Ianuarias Bononiam Latinam coloniam ex senatus consulto L. Valerius Flaccus M. Atilius Seranus L. Valerius Tappo triumviri deduxerunt. Tria milia hominum sunt deducta; equitibus septuagena iugera, ceteris colonis quinquagena sunt data. Ager captus de Gallis Bois fuerat, Galli Tuscos expulerant.*

22 In Aquileia, the *cardo maximus* is still traced today by the Via Giulia Augusta, which goes toward Grado, while the *decumanus maximus* correlates with the Canal Anfora.

23 A section of Aquileia's sewer network came to light under the decumanus that leads to the Forum and the river port.

24 The Republican Forum of Aquileia has not yet been found. The architectural remains that we find today at a certain point of the *decumanus maximus* belong to a Forum of a later period, built at the end of the 2nd century or the beginning of the 3rd, in a place most likely different from the older Forum

Chronology

c. 1600–1200 BC	Bronze Age settlements
c. 1000–800 BC	Iron Age settlements
c. 500–181 BC	Emporium of the Veneti of the Adriatic
191–181 BC	Second Istrian War
186 BC	The *transgressio in Venetiam*
181 BC	The foundation of the colony of Latin law of Aquileia
178–177 BC	The Third Istrian War
171–168 BC	The Third Macedonian War
169 BC	Strengthening of the colony
169 BC	The Third Illyrian War
157–156 BC	The First Dalmatian War
141 BC	An expedition against the Scordisci
138–161 BC	Origins of the church of Aquileia
135 BC	The Second Dalmatian War
129 BC	The Third Dalmatian War
115 BC	M. Aemilius Scaurus' blitzkrieg
78 BC	A rebellion in Dalmatia
58 BC	The massacre of the Helvetians
58 BC	J. Caesar's confrontation with Ariovistus
58–57 BC	Caesar winters in Aquileia
52 BC	The Iapodes attack Tergeste
52 BC onward	The strengthening of the northeastern border
44 BC	Octavianus opens the way to Central-Eastern Europe
AD 7	Institution of the *Venetia et Histria*
AD 14	The separation of Pannonia from Illyricum
AD 98–117	The expansion of Aquileia and Tergeste
AD 166	Smallpox arrives in Italy via Aquileia
AD 166–167	The Quadi and the Marcomanni besiege Aquileia
AD 167	M. Aurelius concentrates troops in Aquileia
AD 238	Aquileia's war
AD 337–350	The Great Constantinian Aquileia
AD 351–352	Aquileia becomes the residence of the usurper Magnentius
AD 361–362	The siege of Aquileia by Julian
AD 371–374	Saint Jerome lives in Aquileia
AD 375	The stays of Valentinian I in Aquileia

AD 380s	Aquileia is the ninth city of the Empire; the Church of Aquileia plays a leading role in the evangelization of the Goths
AD 380	The Council of Aquileia
AD 385	The division of the Roman Empire
AD 388/389–408	Cromatius is bishop of Aquileia
AD 394	The Battle of the Frigidus, near Aquileia
AD 401	The siege of Aquileia by Alaric
AD 424/425	Valentinian II winters in Aquileia
AD 452	Aquileia's fall

Bibliography

Alfoldy, A. 1966. "Les cognomina des magistrats de la République romaine." In *Mélanges d'archéologie et d'histoire offerts à A. Piganiol*, edited by R. Chevalier, 709–722. Paris: S.E.V.P.E.N.

Alfoldy, G. 1984. *Romische Statuen in Venetia et Histria. Epigraphische Quellen*. Heidelbergher altistrische Beitrage und epigraphische Studien 4. Heidelberg: Franz Steiner Verlag.

Auriemma, R. 2000. "Le anfore del relitto di Grado e il loro contenuto." *Mélanges de l'école française de Rome* 112, no. 1: 27–51.

Bakker, L. 1993–1994. "Der Siegesaltar zur Juthungen Sschlacht von 260 n. Chr. Ein spektakulärer Neufund aus Augusta Vindelicum/Augsburg." *Antike Welt* 4: 274–277.

Bandelli, G. 1981. "La guerra istrica del 221 a.C. e la spedizione alpina del 220 a.C." *Athenaeum* 69: 3–28.

Bandelli, G. 1984. "Le iscrizioni repubblicane." *Antichità Alto Adriatiche* 24: 169–226.

Bandelli, G. 1989. "Contributo all'interpretazione del cosiddetto elogium di C. Sempronio Tuditano." *Antichità Alto Adriatiche* 35: 111–131.

Bandelli, G. 1999. "Roma e la Venetia orientale dalla Guerra Gallica (225–222) alla Guerra Sociale, 91–87." In *Vigilia di romanizzazione. Altino e il Veneto orientale tra il II e il I sec., Proceedings of the Conference (Venezia, 2-3 dicembre 1997), Studi e ricerche sulla Gallia Cisalpina 11*, edited by G. Cresci Marrione & M. Torelli, 285–301.

Bandelli, G. 2003. "Aquileia colonia latina. Dal senatus consultum del 183 a.C. al supplementum del 169 a.C." *Antichità Altoadriatiche* 54: 51–52.

Bastien, P. 1964. *Le monnayage de Magnence*. Wetteren: Editions Cultura.

Bettini, M. & M. Lentano. 2013. *The Myth of Aeneas: Images and Stories from Greece to Today*. Torino: Einaudi.

Biasutti, G. 2005. *La chiesa di Aquileia dalle origini alle fine dello scisma dei tre Capitoli (secc. I-VI)*. Udine: Gaspari Editore.

Bonetto, J. 2003. "Difendere Aquileia, città di frontiera." *Antichità Altoadriatiche* 59: 151–196.

Bonetto, J. 2009. "Le mura della città." In *Moenibus et portu celeberrima. Aquileia: storia di una città*, edited by F. Ghedini, M. Bueno & M. Novello, 83–92. Rome: Istituto Poligrafico dello Stato.

Bonfioli, M. 1973. "Soggiorni imperiali a Milano e ad Aquileia da Diocleziano a Valentiniano III." *Antichità Altoadriatiche* IV: 125–149.

Bouras, Ch. 2012. "Alaric in Athens." ΔΧΑΕ — Δελτίον της Χριστιανικής Αρχαιολογικής Εταιρίας 33: 1–6.

Braccesi, L. 1972. *La leggenda di Antenore*. Venezia: Marsilio.

Brizzi, G. 1992. "La presenza militare romana nell'area alpina orientale." In *Castelraimondo. Scavi 1998-1990*, vol. 1 (Cataloghi e monografie dei Civici musei di Udine 2), 111–123. Udine: L'Erma di Bretschneider.

Broughton, T.R.S. 1951. *The Magistrates of the Roman Republic*, vol. 1. New York: American Philological Association.

Brusin, G. 1968. "Un tempio del Timavo ad Aquileia." *Aquileia Nostra* 39: 15–28.

Buhrens, F. 1884. *Fragmenta poetarum Romanorum*. London: Forgotten Books.

Buora, M. 2008. "Militari in Aquileia e nell'arco alpino orientale." In *Cromazio di Aquileia. Al crocevia di genti e religioni, Catalogo della mostra (Udine, 2009)*, edited by S. Piussi, 155–161. Milan: Silvana.

Burgess, R.W., ed. and trans. 1993. *The Chronicle of Hydatius and the Consularia Constantinopolitana*. Oxford: Clarendon Press.

Callegher, B. 2007. "Circolazione monetaria ad Aquileia: ricerche e nuove prospettive." *Antichità Altoadriatiche* 65: 327–362.

Cameron, A. 2011. *The Last Pagans of Rome.* New York: Oxford University Press.

Canfora, L. 2008. "*Cesare scrittore*". In *Giulio Cesare. Man, business, the myth ", Catalog of the exhibition, Rome, Bramante cloister, 23 October 2008-3 May 2009*, edited by G. Gentili, 33. Milan: Silvana Editore, Cinisello Balsamo.

Casari, P. 2004 (2005). *Iuppiter Ammon e Medusa nell'Adriatico nordorientale: simbologia imperiale nella decorazione architettonica forense.* Studi e ricerche sulla Gallia Cisalpina (Antichità Altoadriatiche Monografie 1). Rome: Edizioni Quasar.

Càssola Guida, P. 1972. "Storia di Aquileia in età romana." *Antichità Altoadriatiche* 1: 23–42.

Càssola Guida, P. 1989. *I bronzetti friulani a figura umana. Tre protostoria ed età della romanizzazione* (Cataloghi e monografie archeologiche dei Civici Musei di Udine 1). Rome: Edizioni Quasar.

Càssola Guida, P. & F. Càssola. 2002. "Tergeste preromana e romana: nuove considerazioni." In *La necropoli di San Servolo. Veneti, Istri, Celti e Romani nel territorio di Trieste*, 7–16. Trieste: Civici Musei di Storia ed Arte di Trieste.

Cecovini, R. 2013. "Galli Transalpini transgressi in Venetiam: summary of previous studies and new interpretative hypothesis." *Arheoloski vestnik* 64: 187.

Chiabà, M. 2013. "Lo strano caso dell'iscrizione frammentaria di Gaio Sempronio Tuditano, cos. 129 a.C., da Duino (agro di Aquileia)." *Epigraphica* 75, no. 1–2: 107–125.

Colombo, M. 2008. "Constantinus rerum novator: dal comitatus dioclezianeo ai palatini di Valentiniano I." *Klio* 90: 124–161.

Conti, S. 2002. "The siege of Aquileia of 361–362,: new investigation perspectives." *Bulletin of the Aquileian Archaeological Group* 12: 16.

Cuscito, G. 2013. "Teodoro vescovo di Aquileia." In *Costantino e Teodoro. Aquileia nel IV secolo*, 25–27. Milan: Electa: Fondazione Aquileia.

Dobesch, G. 1993. *Die Kelten in Osterreich nach den altesten Berichten der Antike. Das norische Konigreich und seine Beziehungen zu Rom im 2. Jr. v. Chr.* Wien, Koln, Weimar: Böhlau.

Egger, R. 1954–1957. "Ricerche di storia sul Friuli pre-romano e romano." *Atti Accademia di Scienze, Lettere e Arti di Udine* XIII: 386–387.

Fontana, F. 1997. *I culti di Aquileia repubblicana. Aspetti della politica religiosa in Gallia Cisalpina tra il III e il II sec. a.C.* Studi e Ricerche sulla Gallia Cisalpina 9. Rome: Edizioni Quasar.

Fozzati, L. 2013. *Costantino e Teodoro. Aquileia nel IV secolo.* Milan: Electa.

Fraschetti, A. 1975. "Per le origini della colonia di Tergeste e del municipium di Agida." *Siculorum Gymnasium* 28: 319–335.

Fundling, J. 2009. *Marco Aurelio.* Roma: Salerno Editrice

Goldsworthy, A. 2011. *La caduta di Roma.* Milan: Elliot.

Guerra, N. & P. Ventura. 2010. *Via Annia. Un lungo viaggio nel tempo verso Aquileia.* Aquileia: Comune di Aquileia, Soprintendenza per i Bebi Archeologici del Friuli Venezia Giulia.

Iacumin, R. n.d. *Radici e sviluppo del Cristianesimo.* Available at: http://www.comune.aquileia.ud.it/fileadmin/_migrated/content_uploads/Radici_e_sviluppo_del_Cristianesimo.pdf.

Jones, A.H.M., J.R. Martindale & J. Morris. 1980. *"Rufinus 8", Prosopography of the Later Roman Empire*, Vol. 2. Cambridge: Cambridge University Press.

Lançon, B. 2021. *La caduta dell'Impero romano. Una storia infinita.* Palermo: 21Editore.

Lettich, G. 2003. "Itinerari epigrafici aquileiesi. Guida alle iscrizioni esposte nel Museo Archeologico Nazionale di Aquileia." *Antichità Alto Adriatiche* 50: 40.

Mainardis, F. 2008. *Iulium Carnicum. Storia ed epigrafia.* Trieste: Editreg.

Maniacco, T. 1985. *Storia del Friuli.* Roma: Newton Compton.

Maniacco, T. 1996. *Breve storia del Friuli. Dalle origini ai giorni nostri.* Roma: Newton Compton.

Marchetti, G. 1958. "L'origine di Aquileia nella narrazione di Tito Livio." *Memorie Storiche Forogiuliesi, Deputazione sopra gli studi di Storia Patria per il Friuli, Cividale* XLIII: 1–17.

Maselli-Scotti, F. 1999. "Foro romano. Indagini e restauri 1999." *Aquileia nostra* LXX: 360–367.

McNab, Ch. 2011. *The Army of Rome.* Gorizia: LEG.

Negroni Catacchi, N. 1979. "Le vie dell'ambra." *Antichità Alto Adriatiche* XV, no. 1: 42.

Orlandi, S. 1999. "Due note di epigrafia tardoantica." In *Rendiconti della Accademia Nazionale dei Lincei. Classe di Scienze Morali, Storiche e Fililogiche* 9, 10, 575–594. Rome: Accademia Nazionale dei Lincei.

Orsini, B., ed. 2010. *Le lacrime delle Ninfe. Tesori d'ambra nei musei dell'Emilia-Romagna.* Bologna: Compositori.

Paschini, P. 1909. *La Chiesa aquileiese e il periodo delle origini.* Udine: Tip del Patronato

Pastorino, A., ed. 1971. *Ausonio, Opere.* Torino: Utet.

Pietri, Ch. 1982. "Une aristocratie provinciale et la mission chretienne: lexemple de la Venetie." *Antichità Altoadriatiche* 22: 89–137.

Piganiol, A. 1972. *L'Empire Chrétien (325–395).* Paris: Presses Universitaires de France.

Piovene, G. 1888. "Chronicle of earthquakes in Vicenza." *Annals of the Italian Central Meteorological and Geodynamic Office* II, vol. 8, part 4: 45–57.

Potter, D.S. 2004. *The Roman Empire at Bay, AD 180-395.* London: Routledge.

Publio Virgilio Marone. 2012. *Eneide,* edited by M. Geymonat, translated by A. Fo. Torino: Einaudi.

Ralf-Peter, M. 2018. *Le Alpi nel mondo antico. Da Otzi al Medioevo.* Milan: Bollati Boringhieri 64.

Roberto, U. 2016. "Aquileia Fracta Est XV Kal. Aug.: la distruzione dell'' Emporio d'Italia' nel 452 d.C. e il valore politico e culturale del sincronismo. In *Antichità Altoadriatiche.* Trieste: EUT Edizioni Università di Trieste.

Rossi, R.F. 1973. "La romanizzazione della Cisalpin." In *Antichità Altoadriatiche IV (1973). Aquileia e Milano,* 35-55. Trieste: EUT Edizioni Università di Trieste.

Rossi, R.F. 2001. "Romani, Preromani, non Romani nel territorio di Tergeste." In *Celti nell'alto Adriatico,* edited by G. Cuscito, 119–139. Trieste: Editreg.

Rossi, R.F., ed. 1992. "Insediamenti e popolazioni del territorio di Tergeste e delle aree limitrofe." In *Tipologia di insediamento e distribuzione antropica nell'area veneto-istriana dalla protostoria all'alto medioevo, Proceedings of the Conference, Asolo, 3-5 novembre 1989,* 161–167. Monfalcone: Edizioni della laguna.

Rubinich, M. 2013. *Costantino e Teodoro. Aquileia nel IV secolo.* Milan: Electa.

Runkel, F. 1903. *Die Schlacht bei Adranopel.* Berlin: University of California Libraries.

Sartori, F. 1960. "Galli transalpini transgressi in Venetiam." *Aquileia Nostra* 31: 12–16.

Šašel Kos, M. 1997. "The End of the Norican Kingdom and the Formation of the Provinces of Noricum and Pannonia." In *Akten des IV. Internationalen Kolloquiums uber Probleme des provinzialromischen Kunstschaffems/Alti IV. mednarodnega kolokvija o problemih rimske provincialne umetnosti, Celje 8.-12. Mai/maj 1995 (Situla 36),* edited by B. Djuric & I. Lazar, 23–25. Ljubljana: Lazar (Situla 36).

Scrinari, V. 1975. *Sculture romane di Aquileia.* Roma: La Libreria dello Stato.

Smith, W. 1867. *Dictionary of Greek and Roman Biography and Mythology,* vol. I. Boston: Little, Brown & Company.

Sotinel, C. 2005. *Identité civique et christianisme. Aquilée du IIIe au VIIe siècle.* Rome: Écoles française de Rome.

Spinelli G. 1982. "Ascetismo, monachesimo e cenobitismo ad Aquileia nel sec. IV." In *Antichità Altoadriatiche, 22 - Antichità Altoadriatiche XXII, Vol. 1.* Trieste: EUT Edizioni Università di Trieste.

Strazzulla, M.J. 1990. "L'edilizia templare ed i programmi decorativi in età repubblicana." In *La città nell'Italia settentrionale in età romana. Morfologie, strutture e funzionamento dei centri urbani delle Regiones X e XI (Proceedings of the Conference, Trieste, 13-15 marzo 1987)* (Collection de l'École Française de Rome 130), 279–304. Trieste-Rome, Ecole française de Rome.

Strazzulla, M. J. 1987. "Le terrecotte architettoniche della Venetia romana. Contributo allo studio della produzione fittile nella Cisalpina (II a.C. - II d. C.)." *Aquileia Nostra, Associazione Nazionale per Aquileia*: 232–243.

Tantillo, I. 2001. *L'imperatore Giuliano*. Roma-Bari: Laterza.

Tantillo, I. 2014. "Gli uomini e le risorse." In *Roma Antica*, edited by A. Giardina, 85–111. Rome-Bari: Laterza.

Tiussi, C. 2009. "L'impianto urbano." In *Moenibus et portu celeberrima. Aquileia: storia di una città*, edited by F. Ghedini, M. Bueno & M. Novello, 61–81. Rome: Istituto Poligrafico dello Stato.

von Gebhart, O., ed. 1896. *Hieronymus, De viris inlustribus in griechischer übersetzung* (Texte und Untersuchungen zur Geschichte der altchristlichen Literatur 14, 1). Leipzig: J. C. Hinrichs.

Weichert, A. 1830. *Poetarum Latinorum reliquiae*.

Williams, S. & G. Friell. 1994. *Theodosius: the Empire at Bay*. London: Routledge.

Zaccaria, C. 1992. "L'arco alpino orientale nell'età romana." In *Castelraimondo. Scavi 1998–1990*, vol. 1, *Cataloghi e monografie archeologiche dei Civici musei di Udine 2*, 75–98. Rome: L'Erma di Bretschneider.

Zaccaria, C. 2000. "Permanenza dell'ideale civile in epoca tardo antica." *Antichità Altoadriatiche* 47: 91–113.

Zaccaria, C. 2001a. "La 'trasformazione' del messaggio epigrafico tra II e IV secolo. A proposito di un palinsesto rinvenuto nel foro di Aquileia." In *Varia Epigraphica. Atti del Colloquio Internazionale di Epigrafia. Bertinoro, 8-10 giugno 2000*, edited by M.G. Bertinelli & A. Donati, 475–494. Faenza: Stabilimento grafico Lega.

Zaccaria, C. 2001b. "Tergeste e il suo territorio alle soglie della romanità." In *I Celti nell'Alto Adriatico. Le ragioni di un convegno di studio*, edited by G. Cuscito, 95–118. Trieste: Editreg.

Zaccaria, C. 2005. "Diocleziano e Massimiano ad Aquileia e nelle regioni limitrofe." In *I Santi Canziani nel XVII centenario del loro martirio, Proceedings of the Conference internazionale di studi (Pieris, 2003; San Canzian d'Isonzo, 2004)* (Fonti e Studi per la Storia della Venezia Giulia), edited by G. Toplicar, S. Tavano, M. Sterle, M. Gomboc, *et al.*, 91–125. Gorizia: Consorzio culturale del Monfalconese, Ronchi dei Legionari.

Further reading

Alfoldy, G. 1999. *Städte, Eliten und Gesellschaft in der Gallia Cisalpina. Epigraphisch-historische Untersuchungen*. Stuttgart: Franz Steiner Verlag.

Bandelli, G. 1983. "Per una storia della classe dirigente di Aquileia repubblicana." In *Les bourgeoisies municipales italiennes aux IIe et Ier siècles av. j.-c., Actes du Colloque International du CNRS n. 609 (Naples 1981)*, Publications du Centre Jean Bérard, Editions du CNRS, Collection du Centre Jean Bérard, 6, edited by M. Cébeillac-Gervasoni, 175–203. Naples: Centre Jean Bérard.

Bandelli, G. 1987. "Per una storia della classe dirigente di Aquileia repubblicana: le iscrizioni di un edificio di spettacolo." *Antichità Altoadriatiche* 29, no. 1: 97–127.

Bandelli, G. 1988. *Ricerche sulla colonizzazione romana della Gallia Cisalpina. Le fasi iniziali e il caso aquileiese*. Studi e Ricerche sulla Gallia Cisalpina 1. Trieste-Roma: Edizioni Quasar.

Barfield, L. 1970. *Northern Italy*. London: Thames and Hudson.

Basso, P. 2018. *L'anfiteatro di Aquileia. Ricerche di archivio e nuove immagini di scavo*. Mantova: Quingentole.

Basso, P. 2019. "L'anfiteatro di Aquileia." *Quaderni Friulani di archeologia* 1: 133–142.

Bauchhenns, G. 1984. "Apollo Belenus." *LIMC* 2, no. 1: 462–463.

Beatrice, P.F. & A. Peršič, eds. 2011. *Chromatius of Aquileia and His Age*. Instrumenta Patristica et Mediaevalia (IPM) 57. Turnhout: Brepols.

Bertacchi, L. 1972. "Topografia di Aquileia." *Antichità Altoadriatiche* 1: 43–57.

Bertacchi, L. 1979. "Presenze archeologiche romane nell'area meridionale del territorio di Aquileia." *Antichità Altoadriatiche* 15, no. 1: 259–289.

Bertacchi, L. 1981. "Contributo alla conoscenza delle Grandi Terme di Aquileia." *Aquileia Nostra* 52: 37–64.

Bertacchi, L. 1994. "Aquileia: teatro, anfiteatro e circo." *Antichità Altoadriatiche* 41: 163–181.

Blason, S., ed. 1995. *Gli Unni dal IV al V secolo, in Attila e gli Unni, Catalogo della mostra itinerante*. Rome: L'Erma di Bretschneider.

Bonetto, J. & M. Salvadori. 2012, *L'architettura privata ad Aquileia in età romana, Proceedings of the Conference di Studio (Padova, 21-22 febbraio 2011)*. Antenor Quaderni, 24, Padova. Rome: Edizioni Quasar.

Bratoz, R. 2003. "Aquileia tra Teodosio e i Longobardi." *Antichità Altoadriatiche* 54: 477–527.

Brusin, G. 1939. "Beleno, il nume tutelare di Aquileia." *Aquileia Nostra* 10: 1–26.

Brusin, G. 1972. "Aspetti della vita economica e sociale di Aquileia." *Antichità Altoadriatiche* 1: 15–22.

Buora, M. 1996. *Lungo la via dell'ambra. Apporti altoadriatici alla romanizzazione dei territori del Medio Danubio (I sec. a.C. - I sec. d.C.), Proceedings of the Conference, Udine-Aquileia, 16-17 settembre 1994*. Udine: Arti Grafiche Friulane.

Buora, M. & Jobst, W. eds. 2002. *Roma sul Danubio. Da Aquileia a Carnuntum lungo la via dell'Ambra*, Cataloghi e monografie archeologiche dei Civici Musei di Udine. Rome: L'Erma di Bretschneider.

Calderini, A. 1930. *Aquileia romana*. Milan: Vita e Pensiero.

Casari, P. 2005. "Ritratti imperiali ad Aquileia tra I e II secolo d.C.: qualche osservazione." *Antichità Altoadriatiche* 61: 193–226

Càssola, F. 1991. "La colonizzazione romana della Transpadana." In *Die Stadt in Oberitalien und in den nordwestlichen Provinzen des Römischen Reiches: Deutsch-Italienisches Kolloquium im Italienischen Kulturinstitut Köln (Kölner Forschungen)*, edited by W. Eck & H. Galsterer, 17–44. Mainz am Rhein.

Cecconi, G.A. 2003. "Aquileia come centro amministrativo in età imperiale." *Antichità Altoadriatiche* 54: 405–423.

Coppola, A. 1993. *Demetrius of Pharos: un protagonista dimenticato, L'Erma di Bretschneider.* Rome: L'Ermadi Bretschneider.

Cracco Ruggini, L. 1987. "Aquileia e Concordia: il duplice volto di una società urbana del IV secolo d.C." *Antichità Altoadriatiche* 29: 57–95.

Cuscito, G. 2009. "Lo spazio cristiano." In *Moenibus et portu celeberrima. Aquileia: storia di una città*, edited by F. Ghedini, M. Bueno & M. Novello, 83–92. Rome: Istituto Poligrafico dello Stato.

Duval, N. 1973. "Les palais impériaux de Milan et d'Aquilée. Realité et mythe." *Antichità Altoadriatiche* 4: 151–158.

Grilli, A. 1989. "Ennio, Aquileia e la guerra istriana." *Aquileia*: 31–41.

Groh, S. 2011. "Ricerche sull'urbanistica e le fortificazioni tardoantiche e bizantine di Aquileia." *Aquileia Nostra* 82: 153–204.

Groh, S. 2012. Research on the Urban and Suburban Topography of Aquileia, in Proceedings of the second Workshop on The New Technologies for Aquileia (NTA2012). Available online: http://ceur-ws.org/Vol-948/paper4.pdf.

Humphreys, J. 1986. *Roman Circuses: Arenas for Chariot Racing.* London: Batsford.

Jaggi, C. 1990. "Aspekte der stddtbaulichen Entwicklung Aquileias in fruhchristlicher Zeit." *Jahrbuch für Antike und Christentum* 33: 158–196.

Laffi, U. 1987. "L'amministrazione di Aquileia in età romana." *Antichità Altoadriatiche* 30: 39–62.

Lettich, G. 1982. "Concordia e Aquileia: note sull'organizzazione difensiva del confine orientale d'Italia nel IV secolo." *Antichità Altoadriatiche* 22: 67–87.

Lopreato, P. 1987. "La villa imperiale delle Marignane in Aquileia." *Antichità Altoadriatiche* 30: 137–149.

Lopreato, P. 2004. "Le Grandi Terme di Aquileia: i sectilia e i mosaici del Frigidarium." *Antichità Altoadriatiche* 59: 339–377.

Maraspin, F. 1967–1968. "Il culto di Beleno-Apollo ad Aquileia." *Atti del Centro studi e documentazione sull' Italia romana* I: 145–161.

Marcone, A. 2002. "Tra Adriatico e Danubio nel IV secolo." In *Roma sul Danubio. Da Aquileia a Carnuntum lungo la via dell'ambra*, Cataloghi e monografie archeologiche dei Civici Musei di Udine 6, edited by M. Buora & W. Jobst, 173–178. Rome: L'Erma di Bretschneider.

Mian, G. 2004. "I programmi decorativi dell'edilizia pubblica aquileiese. Alcuni esempi." *Antichità Altoadriatiche* 59: 470–496.

Mian, G. 2006. "Riflessioni sulla residenza imperiale tardoantica." *Antichità Altoadriatiche* 62: 423–442.

Panciera, S. 1957. *Vita economica di Aquileia in età romana.* Rome: Istituto Tipografico Editoriale.

Panciera, S. 1978. "Aquileia romana e la flotta militare." *Antichità Altoadriatiche* 13: 107–134.

Pavan, M. 1979. "Presenze militari nel territorio di Aquileia." *Antichità Altoadriatiche* 15, no. 2: 461–513.

Pellizzari, A. 2014. "Tra adventus imperiali e bella civilia. L'Italia settentrionale e Aquileia nei Panegyrici Latini di età tetrarchico-costantiniana." *Antichità Altoadriatiche* 78: 145–160.

Rebaudo, L. 2006. "Il frigidarium delle Thermae Felices: caratteri strutturali e osservazioni sulla decorazione pavimentale." *Antichità Altoadriatiche* 62: 446–476.

Rebaudo, L. 2012. "La Villa delle Marignane ad Aquileia. La documentazione fotografica di scavo (1914-1970) con Appendici di A. Savioli e E. Braidotti." In *L'architettura privata ad Aquileia in età romana, Proceedings of the Conference di Studio (Padova, 21-22 febbraio 2011)*, Antenor Quaderni 24, edited by J. Bonetto & M. Salvadori, 443–473. Rome: Edizioni Quasar.

Rees, R. 2002. *Layers of Loyalty in Latin Panegyric, AD 289-307.* Oxford: Oxford University Press.

Riess, W. 2001. "Konstantin und seine Sohne in Aquileia." *Zeitschrift für Papyrologie und Epigraphik* 135: 267–283.

Rossi, R.F. 1996. "La via dell'ambra e il Caput Adriae nell'età della romanizzazione." In *Lungo la via dell'ambra. Apporti altoadriatici alla romanizzazione dei territori del Medio Danubio (I sec. a.C. - I sec. d.C.), Proceedings of the Conference, Udine-Aquileia, 16-17 settembre 1994*, edited by M. Buora, 307–312. Udine: Arti Grafiche Friulane.

Rubinich, M. 2012. "Dalle 'Grandi Terme' alla 'Braida Murada': storie di una trasformazione." In *L'architettura privata ad Aquileia in età romana, Proceedings of the Conference di Studio (Padova, 21-22 febbraio 2011)*, Antenor Quaderni 24, edited by J. Bonetto & M. Salvadori, 619–637. Rome: Edizioni Quasar.

Sartori, A., ed. 2008. *Dedicanti e cultores nelle religioni celtiche, VIII Workshop F.R.C.AN. (Gargnano del Garda, 9-12 maggio 2007)* (Quaderni di Acme 104). Milan: Monduzzi Editoriale.

Šašel Kos, M. 2001. "Divinità celtiche nelle regioni alpine orientali." *Antichità Altoadriatiche* 48: 309–315.

Sotinel, C. 2003. "Aquilée de Dioclétien à Théodose." *Antichità Altoadriatiche* 54: 375–392.

Sperti, L. 2003. "Aquileia: scavi dell'edificio detto 'delle Grandi Terme', Campagne 2002–2003." *Aquileia Nostra* 74: 181–286.

Sperti, L. 2004. "Scultura microasiatica nella Cisalpina tardoantica: i tondi aquileiesi con busti di divinità." *Eidola* l: 151–193.

Stucchi, S. 1950. "The Celtic hypogeum of Cividale known as Carceri Longobarde." *Studi Goriziani* XII: 147 ff.

Vannesse, M. 2007. "I Claustra Alpium Iuliarum: un riesame della questione circa la difesa del confine nord-orientale dell'Italia in epoca tardoromana." *Aquileia Nostra* LXXVIII: 314–339.

Vedaldi Iasbez, V. 1989. "Magistrati romani ad Aquileia in età repubblicana." In *Aquileia romana e imperiale*, 83–110. Udine: Arti grafiche Friulane.

Vedaldi Iasbez, V. 2002. "Aquileia: dalla seconda guerra istrica all'età postsillana." In *Aquileia dalle origini alla costituzione del ducato longobardo: storia, amministrazione, società*, 119–154. Trieste: Editreg.

Verzar, M. & G. Mian. 2001. "Le domus di Aquileia." *Antichità Altoadriatiche* 49: 599–628.

Vetters, H. 1961–1963. "Zur Altesten Geschichte der Ostalpenlander." *Jahreshefte des Österreichischen Archäologischen Institutes* XLVI: 201 ff.

Villa, L. 2004. "Aquileia tra Goti, Bizantini e Longobardi. Spunti per un'analisi delle trasformazioni urbane nella transizione tra Tarda Antichità e Alto Medioevo." *Antichità Altoadriatiche* 59: 561–632.

Williams, S. & G. Friell. 1999. *Teodosio: l'ultima sfida*. Genova: ECIG.

Zaccaria, C. 2014. "Costantino ad Aquileia: tra epigrafia e retorica." *Antichità Altoadriatiche* 78: 179–192.